Revised Edition

FLORIDA

Gardener's Guide

Published by Cool Springs Press, 101 Forrest Crossing Boulevard, Suite 100, Franklin, Tennessee 37064.

MacCubbin, Tom, 1944-
    Florida gardener's guide / by Tom MacCubbin and Georgia B. Tasker.-- Rev. ed.
      p. cm.
    Includes bibliographical references (p.   ).
    ISBN: 1-930604-78-5 (pbk. : alk. paper)
    1. Landscape plants--Florida. 2. Landscape gardening--Florida.
    I. Tasker, Georgia. II. Title.
  SB407 .M238 2002
  635.9'09759--dc21
                                                    2001006792

First printing 2002
Printed in the United States of America
10 9

Editor: Angela Reiner Downing
Horticulture Editor: Dr. Derek Burch
Copyeditor: Sara Goodrum
Horticultural Copyeditor: Diana Maranhao
Designer: Sheri Ferguson
Production Artist: S.E. Anderson

On the cover: Orchid, photographed by Dency Kane

Visit the Cool Springs Press website at www.coolspringspress.net

Revised Edition

FLORIDA
Gardener's Guide

Tom MacCubbin
Georgia B. Tasker

COOL
SPRINGS
PRESS

Franklin, Tennessee

Acknowledgments

This author would like to acknowledge the information provided on plant growth and care by Tom Wichman and Celeste White, horticulturists at the University of Florida's Orange County Extension Service. Their vast experience in plant culture helped add detailed information to the listings. I would also like to express appreciation to the many University of Florida Extension specialists who have contributed information over the years that increased my knowledge of the plants contained in this book.

—Tom MacCubbin

Gardeners are a generous group by nature, readily offering cuttings or seeds or plants to those who share their interests. From this wellspring of generosity I have received a great deal of kindly help. I particularly want to thank Don Evans, Don Gann, and Peter Strelkow, who answered harried calls; Debra DeMarco, David Bar-Zvi, Doris Rosebraugh, Dolores Fugina, Bob Fuchs, Jesse Durko, Amy Donovan, Tim Anderson, Monroe Birdsey, and Alan Meerow, all of whom fielded questions or tracked down answers as this project proceeded. They, and a long list of others, have been unstinting tutors over the years, though any mistakes or omissions are my own.

—*Georgia B. Tasker*

The publisher wishes to thank Robert Bowden, Executive Director of the Harry P. Leu Botanical Gardens, Orlando, for serving as horticultural editor of the first edition of *The Florida Gardener's Guide*.

Table of Contents

Gardening
in Florida

Welcome to gardening in Florida, a state of remarkable contrasts. Our state is not all beaches, nor is it all Orange groves. It is not all Rhododendrons, nor is it all Palm trees.

It is an exciting and sometimes unexpected mix of all these things. We have regular frosts and occasional hurricanes, beautiful clear days and lots of sweltering ones. We have freshwater marshes, 7000 lakes, sandy ridges, mucky swamps, and more miles of coastal area than just about any other state. To garden here is to experience firsthand the stuff we're made of, from the high pines of the Panhandle to the 25-million-year-old central sandy ridge to the relatively new geology of the southern peninsula.

The Natural Terrain in Florida

The rock beneath our impertinent finger of land is limestone. The peninsula is some 400 miles long and about 100 miles wide (not counting the Panhandle). It is warmed on the southeast by the Gulf Stream and chilled in the northwest by regular arctic fronts.

Gardeners in the northwestern part of the state, north of Tallahassee, know of remnants of Appalachian plants that were pushed south in the last Ice Age meltwater. Imagine coming across Mountain Laurel and Yew Trees in ravines and on bluffs around the Apalachicola River—and all this so near white sand and Saw Palmetto.

Around Gainesville, gardeners are familiar with Live Oaks hung with Spanish Moss, Pine trees in the flatwoods, Bear Grass, Deer Tongue (Wild Vanilla), Wax Myrtle, Scrub Oak, and Sweet Bay Magnolias that bloom in the summer. The climate is subtropical in this area, where Marjorie Kinnan Rawlings wrote and immortalized Cross Creek and its plants, animals, seasons, and two-footed critters.

When traveling south through the Pine landscapes of the Ocala National Forest, you'll come upon one of our rarest landscapes, the scrub, where the Sand Pine and Rosemary, the Myrtle Oaks, and Wire Grass have staked out their spot on high dunes millions of years old. The scrub is arid, desertlike, and populated by many of our most interesting plants and animals, including the endangered scrub jay and the gopher tortoise.

From the chain of lakes that feeds the Kissimmee River, which empties into Lake Okeechobee, the land begins to flatten out, to gradually sink toward the sea. Vast Pond Apple forests once grew south of the lake, before it was diked. At that time water ran from the lake through the Sawgrass into the Cypress strands and around the tree islands until it reached the Gulf of Mexico on the west coast, or it drained into the Atlantic Ocean on the east through rivers and finger glades.

Live Oak

By the time you reach the southern end of the peninsula, you'll be gardening where temperate and tropical mix in a rich blend, where Gumbo Limbo, Fiddlewood, Strongbark, and Blolly romance the Oak and flirt with the Mastic, where a particular kind of Slash Pine and its companions grow in highly endangered, scattered shards of Pine rockland, and where Wild Coffee snuggles up to the Pigeon Plum and Paradise Tree.

On the upper Florida Keys, where West Indian plants make a fragile forest, you'll have to dig into fossilized coral or build a raised bed. The rock here was a reef once, and only a thin layer of leaf litter disguises these stony skeletons. By the time you reach the middle and lower Keys, limestone has resurfaced. Slash Pines and Silver Palms eke out a meager existence, and Mangroves surround it all.

This is how we look in our more natural gardens, those we have left and are trying to hang on to.

Planted Gardens in Florida

Our planted gardens are very different from the natural areas, although there has been a trend toward native gardens in the past decade.

Gardening has tended to be more relaxed and leisurely in North Florida than in the southern part of the state. The feverish rush to create instant gardens and overnight jungles that often characterizes garden-making in South Florida is not found here. In northern Florida, gardens are influenced by the Southern states: Dogwoods, Redbuds, Azaleas, Camellias, and Rhododendrons are prized garden plants, making spring a glorious season. Alfred B. Maclay State Gardens in Tallahassee features Azaleas and

Camellias, and there are displays of these shrubs at Eden State Gardens. Antebellum homes, rolling hills, lakes, and pinelands suffuse many gardens with a sense of history and a connection to the North.

Central Florida has been feeling the ripple effects of Walt Disney World for more than 25 years. The lavish use of color, which is Disney's specialty, is not as intense in home landscapes, but the color impulse is quickened here. In newer neighborhoods, where sunlight is more abundant than in older residential areas, the changing of annual color marks the change of season. In Winter Park, older sections of Orlando, and neighboring small towns, Azaleas, Laurel Oaks, Cabbage Palms, and Sago Palms (Cycads) are garden mainstays. Bulbs such as Day Lilies, Society Garlic, and Amaryllis are sources of perennial color, as are Roses and Crape Myrtles. The Harry P. Leu Gardens in downtown Orlando has a huge collection of Camellias, Roses, Palms, Cycads, Bamboo, and a wonderfully tranquil lakefront walk. Lakes are everywhere—we even have a county named Lake.

Lake Wales, a tiny town south of Orlando, has one of the state's most elegant gardens. This is Bok Tower Gardens, designed by the Frederick Law Olmsted firm, which is famous for having designed New York City's Central Park. Bok's carillon, majestically rising atop Iron Mountain (a high point at 295 feet), overlooks reflecting pools and is surrounded by gentle, classic garden walks around huge old Azaleas and beneath Live Oaks. Next door is Pinewood, a home built in 1929 by a Bethlehem Steel executive, Charles Austin Buck. It is on the National Register of Historic Places. William Lyman Phillips designed the garden (Phillips was with the Olmsted firm and designed other gardens in Florida, including Fairchild Tropical Garden in Miami).

Tourist attractions and winter homes of the wealthy have influenced the home gardens on both southern coasts, from McKee Jungle Gardens (now McKee Botanical Gardens), another Phillips design, in Vero Beach; to Jungle Larry's Caribbean Gardens near Naples (which was pioneer botanist Henry Nehrling's old garden in the 1920s); to Henry Flagler's White Hall in Palm Beach; to Henry Ford's winter home in Fort Myers next door to Thomas Edison's; to John Ringling's estate in Sarasota.

On the west coast, the former home of Marie Selby in Sarasota is now a botanical garden specializing in epiphytes, or air plants. The two-story white Selby home is a book and gift shop. The grounds are on a small peninsula that juts into Sarasota Bay, surrounded by Mangroves and native plants. You will find huge Ficus—as well as in other areas of the coast, such as the Thomas Edison home in nearby Fort Myers—along with a Hibiscus collection, water garden, and Bamboo stands.

Thomas Edison, like other early South Florida garden and plant lovers, collected plants from around the world. His home looks onto the Caloosahatchee River; behind it is his large collection of tropical fruit trees. Edison loved Palms, and he lined his street in Fort Myers with Royal Palms, a legacy that still stretches all the way to Fort Myers Beach.

The Deering brothers, among the founders of the giant farm machinery company International Harvester, spent winters in Miami. James built the Italianate palace and formal gardens called Vizcaya; Charles settled farther south and kept his surroundings more naturalistic, though he had a Mango grove, a lawn sweeping down to Biscayne Bay, and Royal Palms brought in from the Everglades.

Gardens of contemporary wealthy snowbirds in the town of Palm Beach are kept screened from hoi polloi by enormous hedges of *Ficus benjamina* or Weeping Fig. Graceful Jamaica Coconut Palms still exist in this gem-like town, kept alive on antibiotics in order to evade lethal yellowing disease. And there are many famous historic trees documented in a visionary manner at the behest of the Garden Club of Palm Beach. If you manage a glimpse of an estate, expect to see Hibiscus, Palms, white Birds-of-Paradise, Bougainvillea, broad lawns, sparkling pools, and many relaxed and perfectly groomed gardens. The Society of the Four Arts Garden, a treasure bequeathed to the town of Palm Beach by the garden club back in 1938, is enchanting. It was started to show people how to grow various plants on the island, and today its Japanese garden, water garden, and small formal fountains are all to be cherished.

Fairchild Tropical Garden in Miami (officially in Coral Gables) was begun in the 1930s by Palm enthusiast Robert Montgomery and named for David Fairchild, one of this country's most esteemed plant explorers. It has one of the world's best Palm collections. The 83-acre garden features long vistas over man-made lakes built by the Civilian Conservation Corps, collections of tropical flowering trees, vines, and shrubs, a conservatory, and a museum of plant exploration. The garden is considered to be Phillips's masterpiece. In southeastern Florida, Palms, Cycads, and other plants distributed to Fairchild members have found their way into many home gardens.

Gardeners in Miami Beach, Coral Gables, and Coconut Grove have different garden styles, and they utilize an increasing number of tropical plants to express them. The popularity of Crotons, Ixoras, and fruit trees is a legacy of early gardeners. Long before Marjory Stoneman Douglas would write *The Everglades: River of Grass,* she and Mabel White Dorn wrote a garden book for South Florida gardeners called *The Book of Twelve,* published in 1928. They presented a dozen trees, shrubs, groundcovers, and vines, and mentioned a dozen more. Dorn was the founder of the South Florida Garden Club.

Today you will find intimate little gardens of exuberant tropical foliage and color in South Beach and more manicured gardens elsewhere. Coral Gables has the wealth to keep gardeners busy clipping and shearing, while Coconut Grove is far more lush, if not overgrown, with many different plants used more playfully.

The look of the Florida Keys, with their vacation mindset, aquamarine waters, and love of Bougainvilleas, is tropical-island-pretty, with Palms, flowering trees and shrubs, white picket fences, and Poinciana trees.

The Latin American influence in South Florida has meant much more use of color and gardens with an abundance of plants. Nurseries have become better sources of plants, so the desire to add Gingers, Heliconias, unusual Palms, and flowering plants can be satisfied with an increasing diversity of species.

Gardening with Native Plants

Few can resist flowering plants from the tropics or the big, glorious tropical leaves of the Aroids and Banana families. Yet native plants are on the rise as more gardeners understand the need for habitat restoration and natural gardens for birds, butterflies, and wildlife. In Florida's public areas, native plants often are mandated by law as more and more of the native vegetation disappears to development, particularly in congested South Florida. Many people are planting native trees and shrubs as a hedge against cold, drought, and hurricanes. And there is an increasing awareness of the dangers of too many pesticides, which has made the insect and disease resistance of many natives more appealing.

Often the cover of large native trees can be used to create the right microclimate for tropical plants, and gardeners are increasingly sophisticated about using these trees.

Create Your Own Garden

To create your garden, first think about what you want your garden to do, how you want to use it, how it might fit into your life, and how much of your life you want to fit into it. Consider the appropriateness of the plants you select to reach those goals. Consider the care they might take, the size they might reach, the resources they might require. Anything is possible, but is it practical? Will it require a constant battle against pests and diseases? Constant watering and fertilizing to baby it along? Will your garden be ruined if a freeze hits, or a drought?

A solid framework of native plants appropriate to your area can be an invaluable support for more delicate, sensitive plants, protecting, sheltering, cooling, and warming them by turns. If you have a patio, a balcony, or an estate in which to garden, the gardening opportunities are always more powerful than the limitations.

Climate

Soil, climate, and microclimate are the parameters within which you will work. Begin by finding your location on the United States Department of Agriculture's hardiness zone map (page 16). The most recent map divides the state into areas with the same annual minimum temperatures, from Zones 8 through 11. Zones 8, 9, and 10 are subdivided into Zone 8A, Zone 8B, Zone 9A, Zone 9B, Zone 10A, and Zone 10B.

A small wedge of North Florida, in Zone 8A, has minimum winter temperatures of 10 to 15 degrees Fahrenheit, while Zone 11 in the Florida Keys has minimum winter temperatures above 40 degrees. This is quite a difference. Most of the state is considered subtropical, while North Florida is similar to Texas, Louisiana, and Georgia. Extreme southern Florida is tropical, particularly the Zone 10B areas in southern Broward, most of Dade, and the eastern corners of Monroe and Collier counties. Central Florida is often hotter in the summer and cooler in the winter than South Florida, which is favored by southeastern breezes in the summer and far from the impact of most cold fronts in winter.

Bromeliad

Florida's winter is December through February; spring is March and April; summer is May through September; autumn is October and November. The widest variation in seasons occurs in the north, the least in the south.

Superimposed on the temperate seasons are the two tropical ones: wet and dry. The rainy season spans May through October, with the beginning and the end of the season having the most rainfall. Thunderstorms and lightning strikes occur more often in Florida than in any other state.

North Florida has more rain in March than Central and South Florida. The dry season of Central and South Florida often ends in drought in April and May before the rains return. The Florida Keys, unlikely as it seems, have considerably less rainfall (about 20 inches less) than South Florida.

A booming population has put a severe strain on the state's freshwater supply, which is rainfed and obtained from underground aquifers. It serves not only Florida's millions of people, but also its agriculture and natural resources. No gardener can afford the luxury of using limitless supplies. While common sense would tell us to group plants by their water needs, we must go a step farther and design gardens that reduce water (and fertilizer) use. Many of the plant entries in this guide suggest fertilizing plants two or three times a year. Once you become adept at reading plants, you may learn to fertilize only when the plants tell you they require it. Leaves that are generally paler, or yellow between the veins, and plants that produce fewer blooms are three signs of fertilizer need.

Soil

Soils in the northern and western part of the Florida Panhandle tend to be poorly draining clay, while the southern Panhandle and highlands are sloping, sandy-loamy soils, particularly around the Tallahassee hills. The central ridge is sandy with some underlying limestone to the west of the ridge. Most of Central Florida (with the exception of the ridge) is flat, with poorly drained sandy soils; the area is commonly called Pine flatwoods.

In South Florida, the central Everglades marshes and swamps are flanked by marl and sand over limestone or outcroppings of limestone. On the West Coast, shells of countless sea creatures have been crushed and washed ashore, making a coarse, calcareous substrate.

The Pine flatwoods are characterized by acid sand that doesn't contain many nutrients and doesn't long contain water. Where limestone is near or at the surface, the soil is neutral to alkaline. (Cabbage Palms in Pine flatwoods, which occur on both coasts, are an indication of lime below acid sands, according to *Ecosystems of Florida*, University of Central Florida Press.) Generally, South Florida has alkaline soils, which limit the availability of certain micronutrients to plants.

Most plants prosper in slightly acid to neutral soils, though there is a long list of plants, both native and exotic, that will tolerate high-pH (alkaline) soils. The alkalinity may cause leaf yellowing from magnesium, manganese, or iron deficiency, and foliar sprays of micronutrients are recommended in these areas three or four times a year. Use iron drenches annually to help plants in such soils.

In both sands and rocky soils, certain mineral elements will leach away in heavy rains. (Sandy and rocky soils both require irrigation, but limestone will hold water longer in little niches and crevices.)

A good many of the newer developments in Coastal and South Florida are built on fill, or land that has been sheared of its organic top layer, and dredged for raising the houses above standing water. The fill material tends to be highly alkaline with extremely poor drainage because of compaction. You may have to build up mounds of good soil to plant in these conditions. Eventually, the roots of trees and shrubs will penetrate the compacted rocky soil and loosen it.

Soil testing is available through the University of Florida's Cooperative Extension Service. Every county has an Extension office, and the listing is under the individual county listings in the telephone directory. Botanical gardens often have pamphlets that tell how to grow certain plants, and they offer classes in gardening. Plant societies are wonderful sources of in-depth information on particular types of plants. Garden clubs can offer newcomers a helping hand with more general horticulture. These are some of the resources you may want to explore when learning to garden in our state.

Light Requirements

For best growing results, plants need to be placed where they will receive the proper amount of light. The amount of light suitable for each plant's growing requirements is indicated.

Philodendron

Gardening Across the State

Because of the broad range of plants that can be grown in Florida, from temperate in the north to tropical in the south, the *Florida Gardener's Guide* was written by two authors: Tom MacCubbin, urban horticulturist in Orlando, has written about the more northern and central Florida plants, and Georgia Tasker, Garden Writer for *The Miami Herald* in Miami, has covered the more southern ones. Regional information is provided for plants that may be grown differently in different areas. Some tropical plants may be grown in Central and North Florida as annuals or container plants, while some northern flowers may be used as annuals in winter in South Florida.

Planting times may differ as well. In South Florida, vegetables and flowers are planted in the winter, while trees and shrubs are usually planted at the beginning of summer. Summer is the start of the rainy season, a season which helps in conserving water in an area that has a burgeoning population, large agricultural industry, and needy natural resources (Everglades National Park, for example).

Wherever you garden, remember that all our gardens are connected, that our natural areas are affected by what goes on in our planted yards, and our planted yards benefit from a knowledge of what grows in our natural areas. So garden carefully, and may you have all the sun and all the rain you require.

—G.B.T.

How to Use This Book

Each entry in this guide provides you with information about a plant's particular characteristics, habits and basic requirements for active growth as well as our personal experiences and knowledge of the plant. We have included the information you need to help you realize each plant's potential. Only when a plant performs at its best can one appreciate it fully. You will find such pertinent information as mature height and spread, bloom period and seasonal colors (if any), sun and soil preferences, water requirements, fertilizing needs, pruning and care, and pest information. Each section is clearly marked for easy reference.

Sun Preferences

Symbols represent the range of sunlight suitable for each plant. The icon representing "Full Sun" means the plant needs to be sited in a full sun (8-10 hours of sun daily) location. "Part Sun" means the plant likes full sun, but will appreciate a few hours of protection from harsh, late afternoon sun. "Part Shade" means the plant can be situated where it receives partial sun all day, or morning sun, or dappled shade. "Full Shade" means the plant needs a shady location protected from direct sunlight. Some plants can be grown in more than one range of sun, so you will sometimes see more than one sun symbol.

Full Sun   **Part Sun**   **Part Shade**   **Full Shade**

Additional Benefits

Many plants offer benefits that further enhance their appeal. The following symbols indicate some of the more important additional benefits:

 Attracts Butterflies

 Attracts Hummingbirds

 Produces Edible Fruit

 Has Fragrance

 Produces Food for Birds and Wildlife

 Drought Resistant

 Suitable for Cut Flowers or Arrangements

 Long Bloom Period

 Native Plant

 Supports Bees

 Provides Shelter for Birds

 Good Fall Color

Companion Planting and Design

Landscape design ideas are provided as well as suggestions for companion plants to help you achieve striking and personal results from your garden. This is where we find the most enjoyment from gardening.

My Personal Favorite

"My Personal Favorite" sections describe those specific cultivars or varieties that we have found particularly noteworthy. Give them a try....or, perhaps you'll find your own personal favorite.

USDA Cold Hardiness Zone Map

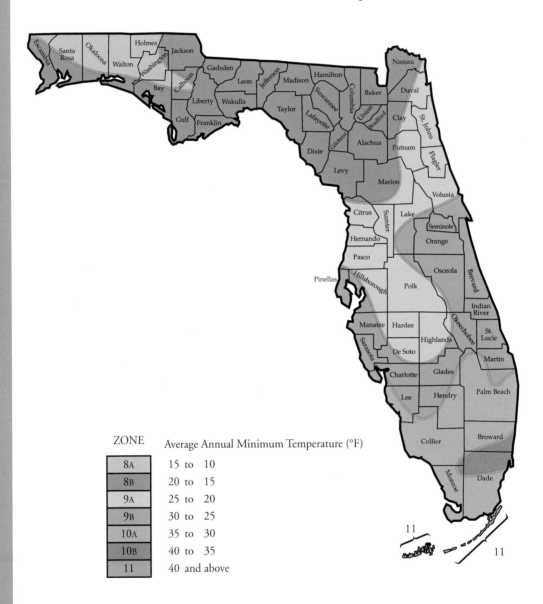

ZONE	Average Annual Minimum Temperature (°F)
8A	15 to 10
8B	20 to 15
9A	25 to 20
9B	30 to 25
10A	35 to 30
10B	40 to 35
11	40 and above

Hardiness Zones

Cold-hardiness zone designations were developed by the United States Department of Agriculture (USDA) to indicate the minimum average temperature for an area. A zone assigned to an individual plant indicates the lowest temperature at which the plant can be expected to survive over the winter. Florida has zones ranging from 8A to 11. Though a plant may grow (and grow well) in zones other than its recommended cold-hardiness zone, it is a good indication of which plants to consider for your landscape. Unless otherwise noted, the plants in this book are suitable for all of Florida.

Annuals *for Florida*

Florida gardeners have learned that a quick way to add color to the landscape is to use annual flowers. Most can be purchased with blooms at local garden centers to bring home and create an instant garden. And the selection of annuals for the landscape is almost endless. As the name annual implies, the plants last only a season or two, but offer plenty of color for six to eight weeks. A few, including Geraniums, Impatiens, and Coleus, continue growing until seasonal changes in temperature cause the plantings to decline.

Considerations Before Planting

In Florida you have to learn when to plant certain annuals. There are two main types: the warm-season and the cool-season flowers. Warm-season annuals usually grow well between March and November.

Then as the days shorten and temperatures dip into the 40s or lower at night, it's time to add the cool-season types. They are usually planted November through February in most areas of Florida. Some cool-season annuals, including Pansies, Johnny Jump-ups, Calendula, Dianthus, and Snapdragons, can withstand a light freeze. Obtain a list of annuals for the proper time of the year from your Cooperative Extension Service office to make sure you are staying on schedule.

Most annuals prefer the bright locations with at least six to eight hours of sun. Impatiens are an exception and must have shade to filtered sun during the hotter months. Others, including Torenias, Coleus, and Begonias, can take light shade and still provide good flowers. When picking a location for the flower bed, remember the shifting pattern of the sun throughout the year. During the winter, the sun dips down in the southern horizon to create more shade in many locations.

Torenia

Give annual flowers some of your best soil. It pays to enrich sandy sites with lots of organic matter. Work in liberal quantities of compost, peat moss, and manure. Till the ground to a depth of 6 to 8 inches before planting. Also test the soil acidity. All annuals prefer a pH around 6.5. Make adjustments as needed, following test recommendations. (For rocky alkaline soils, build raised beds.)

Starting Your Annuals

Some gardeners like to start annuals from seed. It's difficult to pass the seed racks at garden centers and not purchase several packs of flowers to plant. Remember the proper growing season must be followed, and starting flowers from seed takes a little time. Very few seeds can be just tossed in the garden to grow. Most must be sown in pots or cell-packs and take six to eight weeks to be ready for the garden. If you decide to start your own transplants, choose an easy-to-grow annual such as Marigold, Salvia, Impatiens, or Calendula for first attempts. These seeds are large and can be easily seen and handled at planting time. They are also some of the more vigorous varieties.

Use a germinating mix for the sowings, and cover the seed lightly. Keep the seeded containers moist. Most seeds germinate within a week. Then give the seeds the suggested light level noted on the seed packet label. Most need full sun immediately. Feed the seedlings with a 20-20-20 or similar fertilizer solution and you should have plants for the garden shortly.

Gardeners wishing to skip seedling culture can find a large selection of transplants at local garden centers. They are usually available at the proper time for planting in Florida. Sometimes garden centers also get unusual Northern flowers including Foxglove, Delphiniums, and Poppies that Florida gardeners can treat like annuals. For years flowers were marketed in cell-packs, but recently, the 4-inch pot has become the standard size for the garden. The plants in these larger pots are usually well rooted and in bloom, ready to create the instant garden. Buy those with fewest flowers open to make sure plants haven't bloomed themselves out while still small.

Check the label of each type of annual selected for the garden to note the spacing needed. Small types like Pansies may need only a 6- to 8-inch spacing, but Geraniums can be set one foot or more apart. Many of the large growing annuals need some extra room to expand and produce numerous flowering shoots. Check the rootballs of the plants you are purchasing. If the roots have formed a tight web in the ball shape, it may be an old plant and near the end of its life cycle. Plants with tight balls of roots seldom grow out into the surrounding soil. If these are the only plants available, try fluffing the roots apart a little at planting time to encourage growth out into the planting site.

Growing Tips

Plant annuals at the same depth that they were growing in the pots or a little higher. If planted too deep, some rot rather quickly. After planting, give the soil a good soaking. Many gardeners also like to add mulch. If you do, keep the mulch back from the stems, and use only a 1- to 2-inch-thick layer. The new plants need everyday watering for the first week or two. Then gradually taper off the waterings to "as needed." When the surface inch of soil starts to feel dry to the touch, it's usually time to water.

Annual flowers also need frequent feedings. Many gardeners like to use a liquid fertilizer solution such as a 20-20-20 or similar product. This should be applied every two to three weeks throughout the growing season. Dry fertilizers of a 6-6-6 or similar analysis can be applied monthly. Gardeners can also use slow-release fertilizers or aged manure.

Enjoy your annual plantings, and take frequent walks in the gardens to cut bouquets. Check for pests that may be affecting the plantings. The flowers usually have few pests, but some that may affect annuals include caterpillars, mites, and leaf spots. Where needed, hand pick the pests or affected portions from the plants, or use a University of Florida recommended control.

After several months of growth and flowering, most annual flowers decline. It's the culmination of a natural process of flowering and setting seeds. Sometimes you can delay the decline by keeping the old flowers cut off. When most of the plants turn yellow to brown, it's time to replant. Till the soil, work in more organic matter, and select something appropriate for the season to put the color back in the flower beds and container gardens.

Plant annual flowers where you need bursts of color. Some gardeners like to add large beds to the landscape; others just want a cluster of a few plants or a pot of flowers. Annuals growing in containers can be added to the balcony, patio, or entrances. Don't forget the tradition of using annuals in windowboxes and hanging baskets.

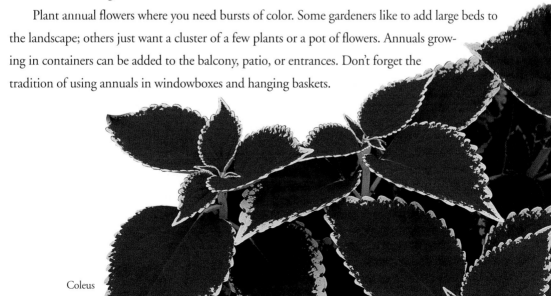

Coleus

Ageratum
Ageratum houstonianum

The low-growing Ageratum is ideal as a compact plant along a walkway or as a carpet of blossoms leading up to shrub plantings. The small flowers are borne in tight clusters that are held well above the plant, creating a blanket of color. Ageratum varieties provide the sometimes all too elusive blue colorations as well as pure whites. The most popular hybrids grow from just 8 inches to more than 2 feet tall, making many selections also suitable for container plantings and windowboxes. Ageratum can be planted in beds, container gardens, planter boxes, and hanging baskets. Some popular varieties include 'Adriatic', 'Blue Horizon', 'Blue Lagoon', 'Blue Mink', and 'Hawaii' hybrids for plants that grow from just 8 inches to more than 2 feet tall. (TM)

Other Name
Floss Flower

Bloom Period and Color
Spring to summer blooms in white, blue

Mature Height
8 inches to 2 feet

When, Where, and How to Plant
Ageratum is a tender annual that is grown during the warm seasons. Just a little frost or any freezing weather can cause major damage to the plants. Transplant to the garden whenever temperatures are consistently above 32°F, or be ready to protect the plants from cold weather. Plantings can extend into the summer season, but high temperatures and damp, rainy weather often cause the plants to decline. Locate the plantings in full sun where they can be seen and enjoyed. Add plenty of organic matter to sandy soil, and till the ground to a depth of 6 to 8 inches. Thoroughly moisten dry soils, then add the transplants. Give Ageratum a 12- to 18-inch spacing because most sprawl out over the garden soil. To prevent root rot problems, be sure not to plant too deeply. Immediately after planting, thoroughly moisten the soil.

Growing Tips
Add a light mulch layer. Keep the mulch several inches back from the stems of the plants. Ageratum need frequent watering for the first few weeks. In sandy soils daily watering may be needed. Ageratum growing in containers may need more frequent watering. Check these plants daily, and water when the surface soil feels dry to the touch.

Regional Advice and Care
Gardeners in South Florida can plant Ageratum from October through April to take advantage of the long warm season. Central Florida residents may also plant during these months but most likely will lose the plants due to cold during the winter months. North Florida residents should delay plantings until March. Ageratum may have caterpillars, mites, and garden flea hoppers as pests. Hand pick pests from the plantings, or treat them with a pesticide recommended by the University of Florida.

Companion Planting and Design
A great border plant to stage with taller fall through spring plantings of Bush Daisy, Dusty Miller, Marigolds, Salvia, Snapdragons, and Petunias as a backdrop.

My Personal Favorite
Blue is a hard color to find in flowers. But you won't be disappointed with variety 'Blue Blazer' because it's a really deep blue color.

When, Where, and How to Plant

Grow Calendula during the cooler months. The plants are resistant to frost but can be damaged by freezing weather. Add plenty of organic matter to sandy soil, and till the ground to a depth of 6 to 8 inches. Thoroughly moisten dry soils. Transplant Calendula to full sun with a 12- to 18-inch spacing. To prevent root rot problems, be sure not to plant too deeply. Immediately after planting, thoroughly moisten the soil. Some of the beauty of Calendula plants is marred by declining blossoms. When possible, these should be removed to make the plants more attractive and keep the color coming.

Growing Tips

Add a light mulch layer. Keep the mulch several inches back from the stems of the plants. Calendula need frequent watering for the first few weeks. In sandy soils daily watering may be needed until the roots grow out into the surrounding soil. Gradually reduce watering to times when the surface inch of soil feels dry to the touch, then give the plantings a good soaking. Calendula growing in containers may need frequent watering. Check these plants daily, and water when the surface soil feels dry.

Regional Advice and Care

South and Central Florida gardeners can plant Calendula throughout most of the winter. North Florida gardeners may want to wait until late winter when the weather is consistently warm to make the first plantings. In all areas of the state as the days consistently reach 80°F, Calendula rapidly decline. Planting the flowers at the proper time of the year and in well-drained soil can prevent most problems. Calendula may have caterpillars as a pest. Hand pick pests from the plantings, or treat them with a pesticide recommended by the University of Florida.

Companion Planting and Design

Mix with cool season flowers of Pansies, Snapdragons, or Petunias. Or just plant them with greenery from Coleus, silvery leaf Dusty Miller, and low growing shrubs.

My Personal Favorite

When I plant Calendula, I want a good selection of color to form an eye-catching bed. The variety 'Prince' will provide all the color your garden needs.

Calendula are bright-flowering plants that, to many gardeners, bear strong resemblance to Marigolds. Floridians are able to enjoy the sunshine yellow to bright orange of Calendula outside in fall and winter gardens. Calendula provide wonderful masses of color grown in a flower bed but are equally suited in container plantings or in windowboxes. Calendula can be planted in ground beds, container gardens, planter boxes, and hanging baskets. The colorful flowers are usually more than 2 inches in diameter, which makes them quite suitable as cut flowers in floral arrangements. One older variety that seems to grow well in local landscape is 'Pacific Beauty'. It appears to have some resistance to rot problems. Others that should be tried include 'Bon Bon' and 'Prince'. (TM)

Other Name
Pot Marigold

Bloom Period and Color
Fall to winter blooms in yellow, orange

Mature Height
8 inches to 2 feet

Celosia
Celosia cristata

Few plants offer bright colors in as unique a way as Celosia. The plumed Celosia sends flower spikes high above the foliage. Feature the unusual plant by itself for warm-season color in a flower bed, mix it with other plantings, use as a central focal point as a backdrop for other lower growing annuals, or in container gardens. Many gardeners like to cut the flower spikes for use in fresh bouquets. Celosia also dries well, making it suitable for use in dried floral arrangements. Good varieties include 'Apricot Brandy', 'Castle', 'Century', and 'Kimono' mix. The Celosia group also contains Cockscomb-type selections of Celosia cristata. Good varieties are found in the 'Chief' mix, 'Fireglow', 'Prestige Scarlet', 'Jewel Box', and 'Treasure Chest' selections. (TM)

Other Name
Cockscomb

Bloom Period and Color
Fall to late spring blooms in yellow, orange, red, and pink

Mature Height
10 inches to 18 inches

When, Where, and How to Plant
Celosia is a warm-season annual that's affected by frosts and freezes. It's also affected by rainy, damp weather, which causes the flower clusters to rot. In warmer locations plantings can begin during the fall and continue into spring. Celosia can be planted in full sun in ground beds, container gardens, or planter boxes. Add plenty of organic matter to sandy soil, and till the ground to a depth of 6 to 8 inches. Thoroughly moisten dry soils, then add the transplants. Give Celosia a 10- to 12-inch spacing. To prevent root rot problems, be sure not to plant too deeply. Immediately after planting, thoroughly moisten the soil. Where possible, remove the declining blooms to allow new shoots to develop. Celosia gives about six to eight weeks of good color before needing replacement.

Growing Tips
Many gardeners like to add a light mulch layer. Keep the mulch several inches back from the stems of the plants. Celosia need frequent watering for the first few weeks. In sandy soils daily watering may be needed until the roots grow out into the surrounding soil. Gradually reduce watering to times when the surface inch of soil feels dry to the touch, then give the plantings a good soaking. Celosia growing in containers may need more frequent watering.

Regional Advice and Care
North Florida gardeners should delay plantings until March or April. Central and South Florida gardeners can plant September through May but must be ready to give winter protection during the colder weather. Celosia may have caterpillars as pests. Hand pick the pests from the plants, or apply a control recommended by the University of Florida.

Companion Planting and Design
Plant a bed of mixed colors or cluster with Zinnias, Marigolds, Salvia, or green shrubs. Make them an accent feature in dish gardens with an herbal border.

My Personal Favorite
Bright spikes of color are sure to catch your attention and that of visitors. The selection 'Castle' mix appears to be brighter than others and comes in a good variety of colors.

Coleus
Coleus × hybridus

When, Where, and How to Plant

Coleus are available at garden centers for year-round planting. Most plantings are made March through October. Coleus can be planted in full sun or part shade in ground beds, container gardens, and planter boxes. Add plenty of organic matter to sandy soil, and till the ground to a depth of 6 to 8 inches. Thoroughly moisten dry soils, then add the transplants, spacing plants 12 to 18 inches apart. Be sure not to plant too deeply. Immediately after planting, thoroughly moisten the soil. With the long Florida growing season, Coleus may grow too tall for the planting site. When this happens, cut the plants back to the desirable height.

Growing Tips

Many gardeners add a light mulch layer. Keep the mulch several inches back from the stems of the plants. Coleus need frequent watering for the first few weeks. In sandy soils daily watering may be needed until the roots grow out into the surrounding soil. Gradually reduce watering to times when the surface inch of soil feels dry to the touch, then give the plantings a good soaking. Coleus growing in containers may need more frequent watering. Check these plants daily and water when the surface soil feels dry.

Regional Advice and Care

North Florida gardeners can expect to replant the Coleus after each winter. Unless the plants are given extra winter protection, they are usually lost during the heavy freezes. Central and South Florida gardeners may keep the plants growing for several years. Coleus may have caterpillars and slugs as pests. Hand pick the pests from the plants, use slug bait, or apply another control recommended by the University of Florida.

Companion Planting and Design

Mix many foliage colors together or pick flowering plants with blooms to match the leaves. Also great plantings to mix with low growing Gingers, Ivy, and Liriope.

My Personal Favorite

Perhaps it's the crinkled edges of the leaves, but more likely what I like the best is the wide selection of color combinations that form the 'Wizard' mix, which is easy to grow from seed.

Ranging from lance type to broad, rounded leaves, the foliage of Coleus is the focal point of the plant. Coleus offers a feast of colorful foliage with mixes that have every color of the rainbow or varieties with pink, green, bronze, or red foliage. The variously shaped leaves are interestingly edged with a slightly toothed shape to a ruffled border. Coleus provides good, reliable eye-catching color whether filling a flower bed or serving as a backdrop for other plantings. The most useful varieties for the landscape are those that grow from 1 to 2 feet tall. You will find Coleus with the most sun tolerance among the newer varieties. Good selections can be found among the 'Carefree', 'Fiji', 'Rainbow', 'Saber', 'Wizard', 'Brilliant', and 'Fairway' varieties. (TM)

Bloom Period and Color
Year-round foliage in pink, green, bronze, or red mixes

Mature Height
1 to 2 feet

Dianthus
Dianthus × hybrida

Modern Dianthus are known to most gardeners as "Pinks," partially because so many selections come in a range of pink hues and partially because the fringed edge of each flower petal appears as if it has been trimmed with pinking shears. A perennial plant that is treated as an annual in Florida, the Dianthus grown in Florida are cool-season flowers that can withstand a light frost. Often with just a little protection, the plants can also survive a light freeze. The plants can be used as a large mass of color in flower beds or just as a small splash along the walkway. Some good performers for the Florida garden include selections from the 'Baby Doll', 'Carpet', 'Charms', 'Flash', 'Floral Lace', 'Ideal', and 'Telstar' varieties. (TM)

Other Name
Pinks

Bloom Period and Color
Fall through spring blooms in pink, white, or red

Mature Height
8 to 18 inches

When, Where, and How to Plant
Start new plantings during the fall months, and continue through spring. Dianthus can be planted in a sunny location in ground beds, container gardens, and planter boxes. Some gardeners get a few plants through the summer by keeping them in planters that can be moved to a cooler location for the hotter months. Add plenty of organic matter to sandy soil, and till the ground to a depth of 6 to 8 inches. Thoroughly moisten dry soils, then add the transplants spacing 10 to 12 inches apart. To prevent root rot problems, be sure not to plant too deeply. Immediately after planting, thoroughly moisten the soil.

Growing Tips
Many gardeners like to add a light mulch layer. Keep the mulch several inches back from the stems of the plants. Dianthus need frequent watering for the first few weeks. In sandy soils daily watering may be needed until the roots grow out into the surrounding soil. Gradually reduce watering to times when the surface inch of soil feels dry to the touch. Dianthus growing in containers may need more frequent watering.

Regional Advice and Care
Dianthus are given similar culture throughout the state. Northern plantings may freeze during the winter months. Southern plants are often shorter lived due to the hotter spring and summer seasons. Dianthus may have caterpillars as pests. Hand pick the pests from the plants, or apply a control recommended by the University of Florida. Some varieties produce dead flowers all at once while the new blossoms begin to emerge. Deadheading at this time keeps the bed attractive. Dianthus can live for more than one growing season, especially during the cooler months.

Companion Planting and Design
Plant in container gardens with borders of Ageratum, Pansies, or herbs. Add clusters to garden with Dusty Miller, Salvia, Snapdragons, and Petunias.

My Personal Favorite
I like the low growing types with many colors. One that has performed well for me is the 'Magic Charm' mix that is easy to grow from seed.

Dusty Miller
Senecio cineraria

When, Where, and How to Plant
Plant Dusty Miller after the rainy season ends and cool weather begins. You can expect a fall planting to last until the hot summer season arrives. Give Dusty Miller a sunny location for best growth. Add plenty of organic matter to sandy soil and till the ground to a depth of 6 to 8 inches. Thoroughly moisten dry soils, then add the transplants, spacing 10 to 12 inches apart. To prevent root rot problems, be sure not to plant too deeply. Immediately after planting, thoroughly moisten the soil.

Growing Tips
Many gardeners like to add a light mulch layer. Keep the mulch several inches back from the stems of the plants. Dusty Miller needs frequent watering for the first few weeks. In sandy soils daily watering may be needed until the roots grow out into the surrounding soil. Gradually reduce watering to times when the surface inch of soil feels dry, then give the plantings a good soaking. Dusty Miller growing in containers may need more frequent watering. Check these plants daily, and water when the surface soil feels dry.

Regional Advice and Care
For most of Florida the months for planting are October through April. South Florida residents may delay Dusty Miller planting until late fall, when the cooler temperatures favor best growth. In North and Central Florida Dusty Miller often survives into the early summer months. As the hot, damp weather arrives for the summer, most plantings rapidly decline and should be replaced. Dusty Miller may have caterpillars as pests. Hand picking the pests from the plants is best.

Companion Planting and Design
Add plants with contrasting colors to this garden. Some great combinations would include Dusty Miller with red Salvia, pink Celosia, purple Petunias, and red Begonias.

My Personal Favorite
The more silvery, the better and it has fancy leaves, too. You will love the foliage of 'Silver Dust' with its deeply cut leaves.

The foliage of Dusty Miller makes a perfect foil for brightly colored annuals in the flower bed. The fuzzy, gray-green leaves give the garden a silvery look. When planted with bright red Salvia or purple Petunias, Dusty Miller provides a tranquil resting spot for the eyes. The shape of the leaves varies, from coarsely toothed to lacelike in appearance, and adds textural interest to the garden. For best performance, plant during the cooler months. Dusty Miller proves freezeproof throughout Florida but deteriorates rapidly during summer's rainy days. Dusty Miller can be planted in ground beds, container gardens, and planter boxes. Fancy-leaved types can also be used as border plants for flower beds. Good varieties for the landscape include 'Cirrus', 'Silver Dust', and 'Silver Queen'. (TM)

Bloom Period and Color
Though rarely seen, late May and June blooms are orange or creamy yellow

Mature Height
12 to 18 inches

Geranium

Pelargonium × hortorum

A beloved bedding plant, the Geranium produces colorful flowers on plants that are bright green with rounded leaves. The foliage can have zonal marking, which provides added interest. Geranium flowers are produced in clusters at the end of long stems and are held well above the foliage. Some members of the genus are perennials, but Geraniums in Florida are treated as cool-season annuals. While a few gardeners sneak the plant through the summer with special protection, most Geraniums will need to be replaced with warm-season annuals at the start of the summer rainy season. Geraniums can be planted in ground beds, container gardens, and planter boxes. Good selections for the Florida garden include the 'Elite', 'Multibloom', 'Orbit', 'Freckles', 'Maverick Star', and 'Pinto' varieties. (TM)

Other Name
Common Geranium

Bloom Period and Color
Fall through spring blooms in pink, red, and lavender plus white and blends

Mature Height
18 to 24 inches

When, Where, and How to Plant
If you are willing to give Geraniums winter protection, planting can begin in October. Delay forming large beds until March. Give Geraniums a sunny location for best flowering. The plants tolerate some shade, but don't expect a single blossom until they are moved out into the sun. Add plenty of organic matter to sandy soils, and till the ground to a depth of 6 to 8 inches. Thoroughly moisten dry soils, then add the transplants spacing 12 to 18 inches apart. To prevent root rot problems, be sure not to plant too deeply. Immediately after planting, thoroughly moisten the soil.

Growing Tips
Many gardeners like to add a light mulch layer. Keep the mulch several inches back from the stems of the plants. Geraniums need frequent watering for the first few weeks. In sandy soils daily watering may be needed until the roots grow out into the surrounding soil. Gradually reduce watering to times when the surface inch of soil feels dry, then give the plantings a good soaking. Geraniums growing in containers may need more frequent watering. Check these plants daily, and water when the soil feels dry to the touch.

Regional Advice and Care
Geraniums grow well throughout the state. Northern gardeners should plant only in containers until March, when beds can be created. These Geraniums may last a little longer into the summer season. In South and Central Florida it's worth taking the risk of planting during the fall months and tossing a cover over the beds on colder nights. Geraniums may have caterpillars as pests. Hand picking the pests from the plants is best.

Companion Planting and Design
Use in gardens or planters with cool season annuals and perennials. Pick colors of Ageratum, Dianthus, Salvia, Snapdragons, and Begonias that contrast with the Geranium blossoms.

My Personal Favorite
You want plenty of blooms from Geraniums to provide a constant display of color. The 'Multibloom' hybrids are ones that are overachievers.

When, Where, and How to Plant

Impatiens are added to Florida gardens throughout most of the year. The major planting time for North and Central Florida is March through October; winter is the time for Impatiens in South Florida. Add plenty of organic matter to sandy soil, and till the ground to a depth of 6 to 8 inches. Thoroughly moisten dry soils, then add the transplants spacing 12 to 14 inches apart. To prevent root rot problems, do not plant too deeply. Immediately after planting, thoroughly moisten the soil. After months of growth, Impatiens usually become tall and lanky. Renew the more desirable growth by pruning the plants back to within 1 foot of the ground.

Growing Tips

Many gardeners like to add a light mulch layer. Keep the mulch several inches back from the stems of the plants. Impatiens need frequent watering for the first few weeks. In sandy soils daily watering may be needed until the roots grow out. Gradually reduce watering to times when the surface inch of soil feels dry, then give the plantings a good soaking. Impatiens growing in containers may need more frequent watering. Check these plants daily, and water when the soil feels dry.

Regional Advice and Care

North and Central Florida gardeners must be ready to give Impatiens protection during the winter months. Replace Impatiens in summer in South Florida. Impatiens may have caterpillars, slugs, and mites. Hand pick the pests from the plants, or treat them with a pesticide recommended by the University of Florida. Nematodes can also be a pest for which there is no easy control. Presently, the best recommendations are to replace the soil in infested beds or grow the plants in containers.

Companion Planting and Design

Plant with annuals and perennials in the shady spots. Some good flowers include Begonias, Bromeliads, Crossandra, and Gingers. Plant with Ivy and Vinca in beds and containers.

My Personal Favorite

If you want lots of vigor and color choose the 'Accent' hybrids. These are well-tested selections that have given good garden performance.

Gardeners should not dismiss Impatiens as too common for their purposes before considering the usefulness of this shade-loving plant. Impatiens provide color in areas where other flowering plants refuse to bloom. One Impatiens plant creates a mound of blossoms normally 1 foot or more in diameter, thus making it an economical way to fill a large area with color. In warmer locations, Impatiens can also grow almost indefinitely. Where the planting is affected by cold, it often grows back either from stems surviving near the ground line or from seeds. Impatiens can be planted in ground beds, container gardens, planter boxes, and hanging baskets. Some garden favorites include selections from the 'Dazzler', 'Accent', 'Super Elfin', 'Swirl', 'Shady Lady', and 'Tempo' hybrids. (TM)

Other Name
Busy Lizzie

Bloom Period and Color
Year-round blooms in all colors

Mature Height
10 to 24 inches

Marigold

Tagetes patula

What is often referred to as the American Marigold is actually the African Marigold, Tagetes erecta. Both the African Marigold and the French Marigolds, Tagetes patula, originated in the Americas. Early explorers took the plants to Europe and Africa where they were thereafter considered natives. For Florida gardeners, the best time to grow either type is during the warm seasons. Normally seen blooming in yellows or oranges, the adventuresome gardener might seek out a white Marigold for a more exotic look. With their compact size, Marigolds are suitable for use in flower beds, along walkways, or in containers. French Marigold for the garden include the 'Aurora', 'Bonanza', 'Hero', 'Boy', Janie, and 'Little Devil'. Good African varieties to try include 'Antigua', 'Crush', 'Excel Jubilee', and 'Inca'. (TM)

Other Name
French Marigold

Bloom Period and Color
Spring through fall blooms in yellow, orange, red, maroon, white

Mature Height
8 inches to over 1 foot

When, Where, and How to Plant
In the warmer locations, Marigolds may be planted year-round, but for most areas of the state, this is a warm-season annual that can be added to gardens and planters in March through September. Just wait until the cooler weather is over, or be prepared to protect the plants with a cover during periods of frost or freezing weather. Marigolds can be planted in full sun in ground beds, container gardens, and planter boxes. Add plenty of organic matter to sandy soils and till the ground to a depth of 6 to 8 inches. Thoroughly moisten dry soils, then add the transplants spacing 10 to 18 inches apart. To prevent root rot problems, be sure not to plant too deeply. Immediately after planting, thoroughly moisten the soil.

Growing Tips
Many gardeners like to add a light mulch layer. Keep the mulch several inches back from the stems of the plants. Marigolds need frequent waterings for the first few weeks. In sandy soils, daily waterings may be needed until the roots grow out into the surrounding soil. Gradually reduce watering frequency—when the surface inch of soil feels dry, give the plantings a good soaking. Marigolds growing in containers may need more frequent waterings. Check these plants daily and water when the surface soil feels dry to the touch.

Regional Advice and Care
Northern and Central Florida gardeners must give up Marigolds when the weather turns cold. Frost and freezes kill the plants. Marigolds may have caterpillars, garden flea hoppers, mites, and leaf miners as pests. Hand pick the pest from the plants, or apply a control recommended by the University of Florida.

Companion Planting and Design
Use in ground or in containers with warm season annuals and perennials. Good combinations include Marigolds with Ageratum, Salvia, Torenia, and Zinnias. Also mix with herbs and vegetables.

My Personal Favorite
I like Marigolds with plenty of color on a compact plant. The bronze and gold colored 'Queen Sophia' selection has been a great performer for small gardens.

Nicotiana

Nicotiana alata

When, Where, and How to Plant

This is definitely a warm-season annual best planted during the spring season and possibly again for fall. The hot, rainy season destroys the flowers. Nicotiana does not grow well during the cooler winter months. Give Nicotiana a sunny location for best growth. Add plenty of organic matter to sandy soil, and till the ground to a depth of 6 to 8 inches. Thoroughly moisten dry soils, then add the transplants, spacing 12 to 18 inches apart. To prevent root rot problems, be sure not to plant too deeply. Immediately after planting, thoroughly moisten the soil. The flowering season can be extended by keeping the plants from going to seed. As the flowering stalks finish blooming, cut them back to encourage new shoots to form.

Growing Tips

Many gardeners like to add a light mulch layer. Keep the mulch several inches back from the stems of the plants. Nicotiana needs frequent watering for the first few weeks. In sandy soils daily watering may be needed until the roots grow out into the surrounding soil. Gradually reduce watering to times when the surface inch of soil feels dry, then give the plantings a good soaking. Nicotiana growing in containers may need more frequent watering. Check these plants daily, and water when the surface soil feels dry.

Regional Advice and Care

North and Central Florida gardeners normally limit the Nicotiana plantings to spring gardens. Southern gardeners often plant both spring and early fall. Nicotiana may have caterpillars as pests. Hand picking the pests from the plants is best. Gardeners can also apply the *Bacillus thuringiensis* caterpillar control or another control recommended by the University of Florida.

Companion Planting and Design

Mix with warm season flowers including Celosia, Marigolds, Salvia, Torenia, and Zinnias. Use as an accent feature in planters with vining Verbena or herbs down the sides.

My Personal Favorite

If you like a compact plant with plenty of color the 'Domino' hybrids would be ideal for your garden. They come in a good assortment of reds, pinks, and pure white.

Many gardeners are returning to the nostalgic plants that they remember blooming in the gardens of their mothers or grandmothers. Nicotiana is one of those plants that is enjoying renewed attention in modern gardens. The plant's newly enjoyed popularity is due in part to breeders' efforts to introduce new varieties, which feature better flowering on shorter plants. Most varieties grow to a height from 18 to 24 inches, making them suitable as a bedding plant alone or as a backdrop for other plants. Nicotiana is striking as an accent when placed in the center of a container planting. Nicotiana can be planted in ground beds, container gardens, and planter boxes. Good selections for the garden come from the 'Domino', 'Nicki', and 'Starship' selections. (TM)

Other Name
Flowering Tobacco

Bloom Period and Color
Spring and fall blooms in red, pink, or white

Mature Height
18 inches to 2 feet

Pansy
Viola × wittrockiana

Gardeners love their Pansies. This is the first cool-season annual they look for during the fall months. Pansies need really cool weather and grow best when night temperatures are in the 50s. They are very hardy and won't mind a frost or freezing weather. After some of Florida's coldest weather, Pansies may be the only flowers in the garden still in bloom. Some appear like little faces looking up from the ground. Others are solid color. Pansies can be planted in ground beds, container gardens, planter boxes, and hanging baskets. As cut flowers, they are perfect for use in a bouquet. Some good varieties for the garden include 'Happy Face', 'Imperial', 'Accord', 'Swiss Giant', 'Majestic Giants', 'Crystal Bowl', and 'Universal' selections. (TM)

Bloom Period and Color
Fall and winter blooms in all colors

Mature Height
10 inches to 12 inches

When, Where, and How to Plant
Wait until there is a consistent chill in the air before planting Pansies. It's best to wait until at least late October or November to guarantee good growth. Your Pansies should then last well into March. The last time to plant Pansies is usually during February. Add plenty of organic matter to sandy soil, and till the ground to a depth of 6 to 8 inches. Thoroughly moisten dry soils, then add the transplants, spacing 6 to 8 inches apart. The plants do not fill in rapidly. The closest spacing gives the best looking garden. To prevent root rot problems, don't plant too deeply. Immediately after planting, thoroughly moisten the soil. Gardeners should remove old blossoms to keep new flowers forming on the plants.

Growing Tips
Many gardeners like to add a light mulch layer. Keep the mulch several inches back from the stems of the plants. Pansies need frequent watering for the first few weeks. In sandy soils daily watering may be needed until the roots grow out. Gradually reduce watering to times when the surface inch of soil feels dry, then give the plantings a soaking. Pansies growing in containers may need more frequent watering. Check these plants daily, and water when the surface soil feels dry to the touch.

Regional Advice and Care
North Florida gardeners can get a slight jump on most Pansy growers by adding Pansies to the garden a month or two ahead of schedule. The plants also last longer into the spring season. Pansies may have aphids and slugs as pests. Hand pick the pests from the plants, or treat them with a pesticide recommended by the University of Florida.

Companion Planting and Design
Edge borders or fill entire gardens with a mix of Pansy colors. Or use just one selection to contrast with other cool season Dianthus, Dusty Miller, Petunia, and Snapdragons.

My Personal Favorite
Plenty of little faces will appear to be peeking out from among dark green foliage when you plant the 'Accord' hybrids. They give plenty of color over many months.

Petunia
Petunia × hybrida

When, Where, and How to Plant

When the weather starts to cool during October or November, it's the best time to plant Petunias. Add plenty of organic matter to sandy soil, and till the ground to a depth of 6 to 8 inches. Thoroughly moisten dry soils, then add the transplants. Give Petunias a 10- to 12-inch spacing. To prevent root rot problems, be sure not to plant too deeply. Immediately after planting, thoroughly moisten the soil. Most plantings tend to grow lanky and full of old blossoms and seedpods. Periodically encourage new growth and extend the life of the plantings with a rejuvenation pruning to remove the old and declining portions.

Growing Tips

Many gardeners like to add a light mulch layer. Keep the mulch several inches back from the stems of the plants. Petunias need frequent watering for the first few weeks. In sandy soils daily watering may be needed until the roots grow out into the surrounding soil. Gradually reduce watering to times when the surface inch of soil feels dry to the touch, then give the plantings a good soaking. Petunias growing in containers may need more frequent watering. Check these plants daily, and water when the surface soil feels dry.

Regional Advice and Care

North Florida gardeners can often get a head start on more southern growers by planting Petunias up to a month ahead of schedule. Plantings in the cooler portions of the state may grow into late spring and early summer. Plantings in North Florida are likely to need protection from the sometimes severe freezing weather. Petunias may have caterpillars and aphids as pests. Hand pick pests from the plantings or treat them with a pesticide recommended by the University of Florida.

Companion Planting and Design

Mix with greenery or other cool season plantings in beds, planters, and hanging baskets. Good companions include Calendula, Dianthus, Nicotiana, Salvias, and Snapdragons. Also cluster among shrub and bulb plantings.

My Personal Favorite

Get the most from your Petunias with the `Wave' hybrids. They can last into the warmer months and there is also a good selection of colors.

With flowers that range from just over 1 inch to those that are 4 inches in diameter, the Petunia offers a wide variety of bedding choices for the cool season. Gardeners growing Petunias can count on good coverage from any of the varieties they choose. The new milliflora tend to be the most compact, giving an 8- to 10-inch diameter mound of color. Its ability to take light frosts and its extended bloom period from the fall season right through the spring guarantee color at a time when many gardens need it most. Petunias can be planted in ground beds, container gardens, planter boxes, and hanging baskets. Petunia varieties for the garden include 'Prime Time', 'Ultra', 'Frost', 'Celebrity', 'Picotee', 'Cloud', 'Madness', 'Aladdin', 'Carpet', and 'Fantasy' selections. (TM)

Bloom Period and Color

Fall through Spring in all colors and blends

Mature Height

12 to 18 inches

Portulaca
Portulaca grandiflora

Portulaca provides color in the most sun-drenched areas of the summer garden—even when many other plants wither beneath Florida's hot strong sun. The plump flower buds and spreading growth habit make it a natural for the rock garden or other dry land plantings where a desert look is desired. Breeding efforts have resulted in varieties that provide a full day of color any time the sun shines. Portulaca grow best during the warm months of spring through summer. The plants open flowers for six to eight weeks before gradually declining. Portulaca can be planted in ground beds, container gardens, planter boxes, and hanging baskets. Some good Florida varieties include 'Afternoon Delight', 'Sundance', 'Sundial', and 'Calypso'. (TM)

Other Name
Mexican Rose

Bloom Period and Color
Spring through summer blooms in brilliant reds, pinks, oranges, yellows, creams, and white

Mature Height
3 to 6 inches

When, Where, and How to Plant
This is definitely a warm-season flower. The plantings seem to feed on Florida's hottest days. Start plantings by April, and continue through the summer months into early fall. Cool weather and short days appear to signal the decline for Portulaca plantings. Portulaca should be planted in a well-prepared garden site. Add plenty of organic matter to sandy soil, and till the ground to a depth of 6 to 8 inches. Thoroughly moisten dry soils, then add the transplants, spacing 8 to 10 inches apart. To prevent root rot problems, be sure not to plant too deeply. Immediately after planting, thoroughly moisten the soil.

Growing Tips
Many gardeners like to add a light mulch layer. Just be sure to keep the mulch several inches back from the stems of the plants. Portulaca needs frequent watering for the first few weeks. In sandy soils daily watering may be needed until the roots grow out into the surrounding soil. Gradually reduce watering to times when the surface inch of soil feels dry to the touch, then give the plantings a good soaking. Portulaca growing in containers may need more frequent watering. Check these plants daily, and water when the surface soil feels dry to the touch. Don't worry if you skip a watering or two; Portulaca is quite drought tolerant.

Regional Advice and Care
South Florida gardeners start planting Portulaca a few weeks to a month earlier than Central or North Florida gardeners. Portulaca may also last longer into the fall in the South. Portulaca may have mites as pests. When present, apply a soap spray or a control recommended by the University of Florida.

Companion Planting and Design
Best used as a border or in hanging baskets with taller plants. Plant with Marigolds, Salvia, Vinca, and Zinnias. Also used to highlight beds of greenery.

My Personal Favorite
Get a wide selection of color from the 'Sundial' hybrids that brighten beds or hanging baskets. The flowers remain open for a long time during the day, which is important.

Salvia

Salvia splendens

When, Where, and How to Plant

The best time to plant a Salvia bed is during the spring months. Plantings often continue through the summer and early fall months. Give Salvia a full-sun location. Be careful when purchasing pot-grown plants that they are not overly potbound and incapable of growing out into the surrounding soil. Add plenty of organic matter to sandy soil, and till the ground to a depth of 6 to 8 inches. Thoroughly moisten dry soil, then add the transplants, spacing 10 to 16 inches apart. To prevent root rot problems, do not plant too deeply. Thoroughly moisten the soil immediately after planting. Keep the plants attractive and encourage new shoots by periodically removing the old flower heads and extra-long stems.

Growing Tips

Many gardeners like to add a light mulch layer. Keep the mulch several inches back from the stems of the plants. Salvias need frequent watering for the first few weeks. In sandy soils daily watering may be needed until the roots grow out into the surrounding soil. Gradually reduce watering to times when the surface inch of soil feels dry, then give the plantings a good soaking. Salvias growing in containers may need more frequent watering. Check these plants daily, and water when the surface soil feels dry to the touch.

Regional Advice and Care

North Florida gardeners can expect Salvias to be damaged by winter frosts and freezes. Central Florida gardeners can help most Salvia plants survive the winter with just a covering during the cold weather. In South Florida, Salvia can be grown as a perennial. Salvia may have caterpillars, mites, and slugs as pests. Hand picking the pests from the plants is best.

Companion Planting and Design

A bed of Salvia of many types and colors makes a garden. They are ideal additions to Dusty Miller, Marigold, Petunia, Snapdragon, and Wax Begonia plantings.

My Personal Favorite

If you want a sure-to-grow annual, the 'Lady in Red' selection is must. The plants are vigorous and fill beds easily. They also reseed freely.

A warm-season mainstay of the garden, Salvia provides some of the brightest color in the landscape. With lots of rocketlike spikes, Salvia can be counted on for almost year-round color. For years this plant was known as Scarlet Sage for its bright red coloration. Red still continues to be the most popular and reliable color, but breeders have now developed some excellent pinks, whites, and violets for added variety. The flowering plant can grow from 8 to 18 inches tall. Salvia gives the best display when planted in clusters for an impressive burst of color. Salvia can be planted in ground beds, container gardens, and planter boxes. Varieties for the Florida garden include 'Hotline', 'St. John's Fire', 'Bonfire', 'Red Hot Sally', 'Sizzler', 'Carabiniere', and 'Top' selections. (TM)

Other Name
Scarlet Sage

Bloom Period and Color
Year-round blooms in red, salmon, pink, white, purple

Mature Height
8 to 18 inches

Snapdragon
Antirrhinum majus

The Snapdragon is another old-fashioned flower that has been rejuvenated for use in the modern garden. Now there are lower-growing and more colorful Snapdragons. Many of these new varieties still have the dragonlike heads of old, but breeders have developed a butterfly series of flower forms. These appear to give a lot more color from the open blooms. New varieties are much more compact, growing from only 8 to 20 inches tall. One thing hasn't changed about Snapdragons—they are still perfect in a bouquet. Snapdragons can be planted in ground beds, container gardens, and planter boxes. Some good varieties for the garden include 'Bells', 'Chimes', 'Floral Carpet', 'Tahiti', 'Liberty', and 'Sonnet' selections. Gardeners who still want the tall garden types should plant 'Rocket' hybrids. (TM)

Bloom Period and Color
Fall through spring blooms in all colors

Mature Height
8 inches to 3 feet

When, Where, and How to Plant
Snapdragons are available for fall through early spring plantings. The plants are tolerant of frost and light freezes. Give Snapdragons a sunny location for best growth. Add plenty of organic matter to sandy soil, and till the ground to a depth of 6 to 8 inches. Thoroughly moisten dry soils, then add the transplants, spacing 10 to 14 inches apart. To prevent root rot problems, be sure not to plant too deeply. Immediately after planting, thoroughly moisten the soil. Taller varieties often need staking to support the flower spikes. Use a garden wire or individual stakes to prevent wind damage to the plants. Removal of the flowers and seed heads encourages new shoots and prevents the rapid decline of plantings.

Growing Tips
Many gardeners like to add a light mulch layer. Keep the mulch several inches back from the stems of the plants. Snapdragons need frequent watering for the first few weeks. In sandy soils daily watering may be needed until the roots grow out into the surrounding soil. Gradually reduce watering to times when the surface inch of soil feels dry, then give the plantings a good soaking. Snapdragons growing in containers may need more frequent watering. Check these plants daily, and water when the surface soil feels dry to the touch.

Regional Advice and Care
North and Central Florida gardeners should give plantings winter protection to avoid major damage. South Florida gardeners should delay plantings until the cooler weather arrives. In the warmer areas the plantings may not last through spring. Snapdragons may have caterpillars as pests. Hand picking the pests from the plants is best.

Companion Planting and Design
Create a bed of a single color or use a mixture of various types. A good combination is Snaps in the middle and Ageratum, Pansies, and Petunias around the sides.

My Personal Favorite
I like tall Snaps that you can cut for bouquets. There is a wide color selection and tall-growing plants among the 'Rocket' hybrids.

When, Where, and How to Plant

Start adding Torenia to the garden as soon as the cold weather is over. Most gardeners can make the plantings from March through August. Give Torenia a full sun to lightly shaded location for best growth. Locate the plantings where they can be seen and enjoyed. In the landscape fill a bed with only Torenia or use them as a groundcover. Torenia should be planted in a well-prepared garden site. Add plenty of organic matter to sandy soil, and till the ground to a depth of 6 to 8 inches. Thoroughly moisten dry soils, then add the transplants, spacing 8 to 12 inches apart. To prevent root rot problems, be sure not to plant too deeply. Immediately after planting, thoroughly moisten the soil.

Growing Tips

Many gardeners like to add a light mulch layer. Keep the mulch several inches back from the stems of the plants. Torenia need frequent watering for the first few weeks. In sandy soils daily watering may be needed until the roots grow out into the surrounding soil. Gradually reduce watering to times when the surface inch of soil feels dry to the touch, then give the plantings a good soaking. Torenia growing in containers may need more frequent watering. Check these plants daily, and water when the surface soil feels dry.

Regional Advice and Care

Torenia need similar care throughout the state. Northern gardens should delay plantings until consistently warm weather arrives. Torenia may have caterpillars and slugs as pests. Hand picking the pests from the plants is best. Gardeners can also apply a *Bacillus thuringiensis* caterpillar control, use slug bait, or apply another control recommended by the University of Florida.

Companion Planting and Design

Plant in a hanging basket, or create a bed of color with the various selections. They also look great as edging with Celosia, Marigolds, Nicotiana, and Vinca in the middle.

My Personal Favorite

I like the vigor of Torenia and the 'Clown' hybrids seem to have plenty of it. There is also a great color assortment among the flowers, produced on compact plants.

A warm-season plant that covers the ground in a blanket of foliage and flowers, Torenia is a plant of many names. Often called the Summer Pansy because the flowers grow best during warm weather when Pansies are long gone, Torenia serves the same landscape needs as its namesake. This plant is a must for the garden due to its tolerance of heat, rain, and light shade. All of the flowers are accented with a spot of yellow in the throat of the blossom. Expect the sprawling plants to last for the entire warm season, producing one flush of blooms after another. Torenia can be planted in ground beds, container gardens, planter boxes, and hanging baskets. Some good varieties include 'Clown', 'Happy Faces', and 'Panda' selections. (TM)

Other Name
Wishbone Flower

Bloom Period and Color
Spring through fall blooms in lavender, white, blue, and pink combinations

Mature Height
6 to 12 inches

Verbena

Verbena × hybrida

Verbena provides some of the best garden blues and purples for the landscape while also sporting attractive foliage. With most Verbena varieties growing only 10 to 12 inches tall, the wide-spreading plants are ideal for use as a colorful groundcover to fill flower beds. Verbena leaves are deep green and usually have an attractive scalloped edge, which adds to the beauty of the plantings. Verbena is particularly lovely when filling containers with its vinelike stems of foliage during warm-weather months. The plant is mainly a warm-season annual that tends to trail off in the early winter months. Verbena can be planted in ground beds, container gardens, planter boxes, and hanging baskets. Some good varieties include 'Romance', 'Peaches and Cream', 'Amour', 'Trinidad', and 'Novalis' selections. (TM)

Other Name
Garden Verbena

Bloom Period and Color
Spring through early winter blooms in blue, purple, red, white, and cream

Mature Height
10 to 12 inches

When, Where, and How to Plant
Begin plantings during March and continue through October. Most selections give 6 to 8 weeks of good flowering before needing to be replaced. Give Verbena a sunny location for best growth. Add plenty of organic matter to sandy soil, and till the ground to a depth of 6 to 8 inches. Thoroughly moisten dry soils, then add the transplants. Give Verbena a 10- to 14- inch spacing. To prevent root rot problems, be sure not to plant too deeply. Immediately after planting, thoroughly moisten the soil.

Growing Tips
Many gardeners like to add a light mulch layer. Just be sure to keep the mulch several inches back from the stems of the plants. Verbena plantings need frequent watering for the first few weeks. In sandy soils daily watering may be needed until the roots grow out into the surrounding soil. Gradually reduce watering to times when the surface inch of soil feels dry to the touch, then give the plantings a good soaking. Verbena plantings growing in containers may need more frequent watering. Check these plants daily, and water when the surface soil feels dry to the touch.

Regional Advice and Care
Verbena plantings are cold sensitive and may be damaged by frost and freezes in North and Central Florida gardens. Early plantings should be protected from winter injury with covers when cold weather is expected. Southern gardeners may start planting a month or more ahead of schedule due to warmer growing conditions. Verbena may have caterpillars, mites, and garden flea hoppers as pests. Hand pick the pests from the plants, or apply a control recommended by the University of Florida, following label suggestions.

Companion Planting and Design
Fill a hanging basket with color or use them as edging over the sides. Plant in beds with Begonias, Celosia, Dusty Miller, Geraniums, Marigolds, and Snapdragons.

My Personal Favorite
It's nice to find plants to use in borders and in hanging baskets. It's equally nice to find a selection of color as you find with the 'Obsession' mix.

Wax Begonia
Begonia × semperflorens-cultorum

When, Where, and How to Plant
Begonias establish best if planted before days become consistently hot. Where possible, plant beds March through May to have the plants well rooted in the ground by summer. Add plenty of organic matter to sandy soil, and till the ground to a depth of 6 to 8 inches. Thoroughly moisten dry soils, then add the transplants, spacing 10 to 12 inches apart. To prevent root rot, do not plant too deeply. Immediately after planting, thoroughly moisten the soil. Begonias may grow for several seasons to a year or more before declining. Often the plants become lanky and can be pruned back to renew the compact attractive growth habit.

Growing Tips
Many gardeners like to add a light mulch layer. Keep the mulch several inches back from the stems of the plants. Wax Begonias need frequent watering for the first few weeks. In sandy soils daily watering may be needed until the roots grow out into the surrounding soil. Gradually reduce watering to times when the surface inch of soil feels dry, then give the plantings a good soaking. Wax Begonias growing in containers may need more frequent watering. Check these plants daily, and water when the surface soil feels dry to the touch.

Regional Advice and Care
North and Central Florida gardeners usually lose their Begonias to frost and freezing weather. Avoid making plantings too late in the year, or provide cold protection. In South Florida Begonias can be planted year-round. Wax Begonias may have caterpillars and slugs as pests. Gardeners can apply a *Bacillus thuringiensis* caterpillar control or use a slug bait, a soap spray, or a product recommended by the University of Florida.

Companion Planting and Design
Grow with sunny or shady plantings in beds or containers. Create a bed of single to mixed colors, or combine with Ageratum, Dianthus, Dusty Miller, Torenia, Verbena, and Zinnias.

My Personal Favorite
Be sure to plant the varieties recommended by your garden center. The 'Cocktail' mix has a good assortment of leaf and flower colors for sun or shade.

Begonia is a dependable, minimal–care plant that thrives in a variety of garden situations. Attractive almost the entire year, Begonias thrive in the shady spots of the garden along with those receiving full sun. The tidy, mounding plants are available with flowers in a variety of colors. The plants flower continuously to create spots of color. Most also have the familiar little spot of yellow stamens in the center of the blossoms. Begonia foliage is very attractive, varying from bright green to bronze in color. All plants are compact and well rounded in shape. Wax Begonias can be planted in ground beds, container gardens, planter boxes, and hanging baskets. Some good varieties include the 'Encore', 'Varsity', 'Olympia', 'Prelude', 'Victory', 'Cocktail', 'Senator', 'Pizzazz', and 'Ambassador' selections. (TM)

Bloom Period and Color
Year-round blooms in all shades of pinks and reds plus some very pure whites.

Mature Height
12 to 18 inches

Zinnia

Zinnia elegans

The Zinnia is a bright, carefree flowering plant with big, long-lasting blossoms. Most Zinnias grow a little larger than other garden flowers. Lots of gardeners remember the older varieties, such as 'Giants of California', that grew more than 3 feet tall. Now there are Zinnias for every spot. Some grow just 8 inches tall, and others grow in the 12- to 24-inch range. The flowers are big and beautiful, ranging from 2 to 5 inches in diameter. There is an excellent assortment of colors—Zinnias are great to enjoy in the garden or cut to bring indoors. Zinnias can be planted in ground beds, container gardens, and planter boxes. Good varieties include 'Dasher', 'Dreamland', 'Peter Pan', 'Pulcino', 'Small World', 'Thumbelina', 'Short Stuff', 'Profusion', and 'Ruffles' selections. (TM)

Bloom Period and Color
Spring blooms in pinks, reds, oranges, and plums plus white.

Mature Height
8 inches to 3 feet

When, Where, and How to Plant
Get plantings in the ground during early spring before the weather gets too hot and humid. Best plantings are made during March and April to avoid pest problems. Add plenty of organic matter to sandy soil, and till the ground to a depth of 6 to 8 inches. Thoroughly moisten dry soils, then add the transplants, spacing 10 to 20 inches apart, depending on the ultimate size of the variety. To prevent root rot problems, do not plant too deeply. Immediately after planting, thoroughly moisten the soil. Extend the flowering period by removing the declining blossoms.

Growing Tips
Many gardeners like to add a light mulch layer. Keep the mulch several inches back from the stems of the plants. Zinnias need frequent watering for the first few weeks. In sandy soils daily watering may be needed until the roots grow out. Gradually reduce watering to times when the surface inch of soil feels dry, then give the plantings a good soaking. Zinnias growing in containers may need more frequent watering. Check these plants daily, and water when the surface soil feels dry.

Regional Advice and Care
North Florida gardeners can enjoy a little longer planting season due to the often cooler spring and early summer weather. Central and South Florida gardeners must plant Zinnias early to enjoy the 6 to 8 weeks of good flowering. Zinnias may have caterpillars, leaf spot, and powdery mildew as pests. Caterpillars can be hand picked or treated with a *Bacillus thuringiensis* control recommended by the University of Florida. Zinnia diseases are best controlled by plantings made during the spring or application of a copper fungicide or another University-recommended fungicide.

Companion Planting and Design
Plant smaller varieties as an edging and use taller types as a central feature of beds and container gardens. Attractive when mixed with Marigolds, Nicotiana, Salvia, Torenia, and Verbena.

My Personal Favorite
The 'Profusion' series has caught the attention of home gardeners due to its vigor and disease resistance. This selection seems to do well in the summer when other Zinnias have problems.

Bulbs *for Florida*

Could it be their ephemeral quality that makes us love them? Bulbs are plants that have found a niche in time and work quickly to take advantage of it. The temperate bulbs of the northern woods appear in late winter before the snow has melted, rising, flowering, and setting seed before the leaves return to intercept the light. Crocus, then Iris, and Squill, by turns, accompany the earth to the spring equinox.

Tropical bulbs must work between wet and dry seasons, finding sustenance in the rainy months, storing within the bulbs the means to get through the dry, often resting during drought, sending up flowers as or before the rains return.

Bulb Options

Amaryllis have become such popular Christmas plants that we forget they are forced to bloom at that time, and normally bloom in spring. These are the Dutch Amaryllis, which are classified botanically as *Hippeastrum*; the true Amaryllis is *Amaryllis belladonna,* which has smaller, fragrant pink flowers that appear in the fall.

Caladiums are the summer bulbs in Florida, providing some of the most beautiful leaves anywhere. They are from Central America and northern South America. Early this century, Henry Nehrling, a botanist and plantsman living in Gotha, near Orlando, and then in Naples, created about 1500 Caladium hybrids, some of which are still grown today. 'Freida Hemple' may be one of his best-known hybrids.

Clivia

39

Voodoo Lily

Rain Lilies, both *Zephyranthes* and *Hebranthes*, are delightful little bulbs to have around because their rain-sparked flowers seem to appear so suddenly. The foliage is like Liriope or Lilyturf, and you might try using Rain Lilies instead of Liriope in a nice shaded area. Debra DeMarco, a landscape designer in South Miami, often uses Society Garlic, another bulb, in place of Liriope.

One of the most spectacular of all bulbs is the Voodoo Lily, *Amorphophallus*. This largest of all flowers from Sumatra, *Amorphophallus titanum,* can stand 5 to 6 feet tall. The first reports of the plant seemed so exaggerated that no one believed it. Smaller species are grown in South Florida from time to time, and they never fail to attract attention when blooming.

Several bulbs of this incredible plant were collected in the 1990s and distributed to botanical gardens around the country. One enormous bulb weighs about 70 pounds, and has flowered twice at Fairchild Tropical Garden in Miami. When it opens and is ready for pollination, the flower sends out waves of stench to attract pollinating carrion beetles. After pollination, the flower swells slightly, then collapses. The whole flowering episode lasts about three days. A single leaf appears next, and may achieve a height of 20 feet. Smaller species are grown in South Florida from time to time, and they never fail to attract attention when blooming.

Preparing for Bulbs

Most bulbs are in garden centers (and catalogs) in the fall. If you live in South Florida, you can buy temperate bulbs and store them in the refrigerator's vegetable bin until midwinter. Then plant them for spring flowers, and expect them to last only a season. *The Reader's Digest Illustrated Guide to Gardening*

offers this advice for refrigerating bulbs: never put them in the same refrigerator bin as fruit, for the ethylene gas from the fruit will kill the bulbs.

Tropical bulbs may be left in the ground year-round in South Florida. The winter's dry season will give them the rest they need, and you should water sparingly until they begin to put up new leaves, then fertilize and keep the area moist.

Bulbs like a rich soil that drains well, and peat moss, compost, or aged manure can be added to the soil to help it drain and to keep it somewhat moist.

As border plants or bedding plants, as accents, as just the right plant for a special place, bulbs bring a charm of their own to the garden. They can make lovely tabletop flowers when forced. As cuts, they can be spectacular in clear crystal with nothing but themselves for company.

Day Lily

African Iris
Dietes bicolor

Sometimes called Fortnight Lily, The African Iris is considered a hardy (for a tropical plant) and drought-tolerant bulb. Its 3 outer petals are marked with yellow and are longer than the 3 inner ones. Flowers of the World and other references classify it as Moraea. The Moraea is from the name of (a) an 18th-century English botanist, Robert More, or (b) the father-in-law of Linnaeus, J. Moraeus. (We do wish these references would get their references straight.) No matter. They bloom off and on throughout the season at roughly 2-week intervals, which is why one common name includes the word "fortnight." Dietes vegeta (or Moraea iridioides) has large white flowers with orange/brown and blue markings; 'Lemon Drops' and 'Orange Drops' have yellow or orange markings. (GBT)

Other Name
Fortnight Lily

Bloom Period and Color
Spring and summer blooms in white, cream, yellow

Mature Height
2 feet

Zones
9 – 10B

When, Where, and How to Plant
Plant any time during the year, spacing 18 inches to 24 inches. Plant in full sun. Enrich the planting hole of the rhizome with organic matter, such as compost, peat moss, and pine-bark mulch. Sand will help increase drainage. Put a little bone meal in the bottom of the planting hole, which should be 2 to 3 inches deep. Cover the hole, and fertilize with 1 to 2 teaspoons of a slow-release fertilizer, and then mulch. Water. If drainage is a problem, grow *Dietes bicolor* in raised beds using a mix of peat moss or compost and sand, plus slow-release fertilizer and potting mix.

Growing Tips
If using a granular fertilizer, 2 to 3 pounds per 100 square feet of bulb bed is sufficient. Bulbs already contain enough stored food to go through their first flowering. Rhizomes also store water as well as food, which is one reason these are said to be drought tolerant. But they will profit in their flowering capacity if you water them regularly: two to three times a week if it does not rain. Reduce watering after flowering.

Regional Advice and Care
Where cold is a problem, grow tropical bulbs in pots to bring inside in winter. Grasshoppers and snails love *Dietes*. The newest product for use to fight grasshoppers is *Nosema locustae*, a protozoa which has various commercially packaged names such as Semaspore or Nolo Bait or Grasshopper Attack. It causes grasshoppers to produce fewer eggs. For snails or garden slugs, protect African Iris with copper screen barriers or, in dry seasons, with diatomaceous earth.

Companion Planting and Design
The African Iris is a versatile perennial that is useful as a border plant along woodsy paths or at the edges of planting beds, even in rock gardens.

My Personal Favorite
The yellow flowers of the Fortnight Lily are quite lovely.

African Lily
Agapanthus africanus

When, Where, and How to Plant

Rhizomes of African Lilies are best planted from October through March in the Florida landscape. Container plants in bloom are available from garden centers for planting throughout the year. They can be added to the landscape at any time. They grow best in areas with 6 to 8 hours of sun and bright light for the remaining portions of the day. Select areas that do not flood during the rainy season. All bulbs should be planted in well-drained soil. When planting in containers, use a loose potting mix and large containers. African Lilies grow well in sandy soils as long as they are given plenty of water and all the nutrients needed for growth. Work liberal quantities of compost or peat moss and manure into the planting site. African Lilies should be set in the soil with the tops of the rhizomes just below the surface of the ground. Space the rhizomes 12 inches apart, and then provide adequate water to thoroughly moisten the soil.

Growing Tips

A light mulch can be added to maintain soil moisture and supply some nutrients. The African Lily needs a light feeding once in March, May, and September. Use a 6-6-6 or similar garden fertilizer, following label instructions for bulbs or perennial plantings. African Lilies may be affected by caterpillars and grasshoppers. Hand pick pests from the plants, or treat them with a pest-control product recommended by the University of Florida, following label instructions.

Regional Advice and Care

African Lilies grow best in North and Central Florida gardens. In the colder portions of the state, protect them from the more severe freezes. Plantings in South Florida are usually short-lived.

Companion Planting and Design

African Lily is a workhorse of the bulbs, planted in clusters as a ground cover among perennials and shrubs. Grow as a backdrop for flowerbeds of annuals, tropicals, and other bulbs.

My Personal Favorite

Only the species is available in Florida.

Gardeners who want spring color in a great accent plant will love the durable African Lilies. The plants give an eye-catching flower display, shooting up an inflorescence that's topped with a ball-like cluster of blue or white flowers. Each blossom is 1 to 2 inches long. When not in bloom, the plants provide dark-green straplike foliage from year-round greenery. After the plants have flowered, cut the old stalks back to near the ground to allow the plant's energy to go into bulb production or allow the plant to continue seed development. Add African Lilies to the perennial flower bed, or spot them among shrub plantings throughout the landscape. Some gardeners also like to grow the plants in containers for the patio or entrance area. (TM)

Other Name
Lily-of-the-Nile

Bloom Period and Color
Spring blooms in white or blue

Mature Height
3 feet

Zones
8 – 10

Amaryllis
Hippeastrum hybrids

A favorite Christmas present for Florida gardeners, the Amaryllis today has become a true knockout. 'Apple Blossom' and 'Red Lion' are old-time hybrids that are recommended by Amaryllis expert Alan Meerow with the USDA Subtropical Research Station in Miami. Individual flowers don't last terribly long, but they are so beautiful one forgives them for their lack of staying power. Amaryllis also comes in doubles. One of these is a double salmon/light orange flowering Amaryllis, Hippeastrum 'Smoked Salmon'. Butterfly Amaryllis, H. papilio, can be found in mail-order catalogs and at plant sales. It is a light greenish white overlain with crimson/maroon markings. Another red cousin is the Jacobean Lily, Amaryllis formosissima, which looks like a cross between an Orchid and an Amaryllis. (GBT)

Other Name
Barbados Lily

Bloom Period and Color
Winter and spring blooms in red, pink, orange, salmon, white

Mature Height
2 feet

Zones
8 – 10B

When, Where, and How to Plant
Plant in September, October, or November, or again in late winter to early spring. Plant in an enriched soil, blending 2 parts peat moss with 1 part sand and 1 part pine-bark mulch or chips, either in the soil or in pots. Meerow recommends digging the whole bed and replacing soil with this mix. Add bone meal to the bottom of the individual planting holes, placing the bulbs just at the soil level or slightly above, spaced a foot or a little more apart. Add a couple of teaspoons of 6-6-6 or slow-release fertilizer for each bulb after backfilling and then mulch to help keep the soil evenly moist. Remove spent flower stalks before the plants form seeds (this occurs quickly). This will direct energy back into bulb formation.

Growing Tips
Fertilize three times a year, at the least. When flowers begin to form, spray with a 20-20-20. A foliar micronutrient spray also is helpful, particularly if you see leaves beginning to turn yellow before flowering. After flowering, keep watering the plants until the leaves turn yellow and then allow them to rest. Some may not die back. But when plants seem to go into a slow-down or resting stage, withhold water for a while, or dig and refresh the planting bed.

Regional Advice and Care
Plant bulbs in pots to bring indoors when freezing is predicted. Grasshoppers and snails can demolish Amaryllis leaves quickly. The protozoa product containing *Nosema locustae*, mentioned for African Iris (Nolo Bait, etc.) can be useful for Amaryllis. Also, check in pots and under mulch for snails at night and hand pick.

Companion Planting and Design
After the holiday season is over, you can plant Amaryllis in the garden as border plants or in beds of their own. Amaryllis are useful at the feet of leggy shrubs, or in pots on the pool deck.

My Personal Favorites
My favorite is 'Apple Blossom', which is white with pink edges and piping, although 'Red Lion' has a stunning velvet 'finish' and is the color of Merlot wine.

Amazon Lily
Eucharis grandiflora

When, Where, and How to Plant

Amazon Lilies can be planted at any time of the year. Division of clumps is best done during the fall through early spring months. They grow best in areas with filtered sun but have produced good foliage and flowers in shady areas under trees. Foliage exposed to full sun usually burns. Work liberal quantities of compost or peat moss and manure into the planting site. Plant the Amazon Lily with the tip of the bulb at the surface of the soil. Space bulbs 3 to 4 inches apart. In a container, add 3 to 4 bulbs to an 8-inch pot. After planting, provide adequate water to thoroughly moisten the soil. Flowering can usually be encouraged by alternating moist and dry periods for about a month. After the treatment, feed the plants to start growth and flowers. After the plants have flowered, cut the old stalks back to near the ground.

Growing Tips

A light mulch can be added to maintain soil moisture and supply some nutrients with in-ground plantings. Keep planting sites moist. Amazon Lilies need a light feeding once in March, May, and September. Gardeners can use a 6-6-6 or similar garden fertilizer, following label instructions for bulbs or perennial plantings. Plants in containers can be fed monthly with a 20-20-20 or similar product at label rates.

Regional Advice and Care

Amazon Lilies are quite cold sensitive. North Florida and some colder areas of Central Florida should restrict plantings to container gardens. Amazon Lilies may be affected by caterpillars and slugs. Hand pick pests from the plants, or treat with a pest-control product recommended by the University of Florida.

Companion Planting and Design

A ground cover and flowering plant for the shade. Can be used in beds or pots as a substitute for Hostas. Plant with Caladiums, Gingers, Impatiens, and Begonias.

My Personal Favorite

Only the species is available in Florida.

The snow-white blossoms of the Amazon Lily held high above the plant resemble those of a large Narcissus. Flowering is sporadic but usually occurs during the winter and early spring months. The plant could bloom at almost any time of the year, however. The large, rounded deep-green foliage may reach 6 inches in diameter. This plant works well in the shady gardens of Central and South Florida. Grow it with other perennials, or use it as a ground cover in front of other greenery. Many gardeners prefer to grow the Amazon Lily in containers where they can control the water and fertilizer to encourage more reliable flowering. Potted Amazon Lilies can be grown on the porch or patio or at an entrance. (TM)

Other Name
Eucharis Lily

Bloom Period and Color
Winter and early spring blooms in white

Mature Height
1 foot

Zones
9 – 11

Blood Lily
Scadoxus multiflorus

Perhaps the name really tells the story about the Blood Lily flowers. These bright-red attention getters pop up along with the spring foliage to form a 6-inches or larger ball of color. One of Florida's most exotic bulbs, the Blood Lily can be grown with perennials or added to plantings in front of shrubs. Or it can be grown in containers on a porch or patio or near an entrance. Many gardeners like to add the plants to rest areas where visitors can stop and study the inflorescence made up of many individual blooms. The bright-green foliage sprouts each spring; the long, ovate leaves remain attractive until fall when the plants go dormant. Only one species of Blood Lily is commonly marketed in Florida. (TM)

Bloom Period and Color
Spring and summer blooms in red

Mature Height
18 inches to 2 feet

Zones
8 – 11

When, Where, and How to Plant
Most Blood Lilies are planted from January through March in the Florida garden. Container plants are often available year-round and can be added to the landscape at any time. Make divisions from fall through early winter when the plants are dormant. They grow best in an area with filtered sun for most of the day but can also be grown under the more intense shade of trees. Blood Lilies tolerate sandy soil but are easier to maintain if the soil is improved with organic matter before planting. Work liberal quantities of compost or peat moss and manure into the planting site. Blood Lily bulbs should be planted with the tips just below the surface of the soil. Space the bulbs 6 to 8 inches apart. In a 6- or 8-inch pot, several bulbs may be grown. After the plants have flowered, most gardeners cut the old stalks back to near the ground to allow the plant's energy to go into bulb production.

Growing Tips
After planting, provide adequate water to thoroughly moisten the soil. A light mulch can be added to maintain soil moisture and supply some nutrients for in-ground plantings. Keep planting sites moist. Blood Lilies need a light feeding once in March, May, and August. Use a 6-6-6 or similar garden fertilizer. For container-grown plants, use a 20-20-20.

Regional Advice and Care
Blood Lilies grow well in all areas of Florida. In northern regions, add some extra mulch to the soil for cold protection. Blood Lilies may be affected by caterpillars and slugs. Hand pick pests from the plants, or treat them with a pest-control product recommended by the University of Florida.

Companion Planting and Design
Add to the perennial or bulb garden or mix among shrubs in the full sun to light shade. Blood Lily combines well with Amaryllis, Crinum, Impatiens, Gingers, and African Iris.

My Personal Favorite
Only the species is available in Florida.

Blue Flag Iris
Iris virginica

When, Where, and How to Plant
Plant in the late summer or fall, spacing rhizomes 8 inches apart. Plant in low-lying swales, in pots submerged in ponds, or in bog conditions. (Bogs can be created by removing soil to a depth of several inches, lining the area with plastic, then a layer of rocks, then a highly organic mix of peat moss and muck and sand.) Muck in Florida is really a decomposed peat of sawgrass and other aquatics. On the edges of freshwater marshes and swamps, muck has some rocky and sandy components mixed in with it. When dry, it tends to blow away, particle by particle, and so a lawn or yard built on a 50-50 mix of sand and muck will eventually become just sand, with no nutrient-holding capacity at all. Keep the rhizome within 2 inches of the surface, using a regular garden potting soil. Cover the surface with rocks before submerging so the soil won't float off and fish won't dig up the plants. Mix 6-6-6 or 10-10-10 into the soil when planting.

Growing Tips
To fertilize later, wrap an appropriate amount of fertilizer in newspaper and wedge it into the pot to get it close to the roots. Fertilizer plugs are available for aquatic use. Dig the rhizomes yearly, in fall or late winter. Separate the rhizomes, clean, and repot. Use plugs or fertilizer pellets if planting in containers to be submerged, or scatter fertilizer on top of the bog as you would for any other landscape plant. Propagate by cutting the rhizome into sections, each containing a bud.

Regional Advice and Care
Blue Flag Iris grows well throughout Florida, except in the Keys.

Companion Planting and Design
For ponds, the upright Iris looks elegant when seen against the flat, round leaves of Water Lilies and the superlative Lotus in Central Florida. Keep it visually removed from other upright plants.

My Personal Favorite
The blue-purple Iris, when planted strategically around a pond edge, is quite lovely.

Among the prettiest plants of the wetlands or margins of the wetlands are the Blue Flags. These ephemeral flowers appear in the spring, and if you're lucky, you'll venture into a park at just the right time. The flowers are a light lavender-purple with long, yellow-and-white-marked sepals and three narrow upright petals. The Flags are rhizomatous plants, not true bulbs, yet they are capable of growing in wet soil, in pots barely submerged beneath the surface of ponds. Accustomed to growing in muck, these plants are acid lovers. Iris virginica is basically an aquatic plant. Another warm-growing Iris is Louisiana Iris which grows to 3 feet and comes in a range of colors, from blue through yellow, according to Jacqueline Walker in The Subtropical Garden. (GBT)

Other Name
Southern Blue Flag

Bloom Period and Color
Spring blooms in lavender to purple

Mature Height
To 3 feet

Zones
8 – 10B

Caladium

Caladium × hortulanum

Rosy-pink with dark-pink spots; white with wine-colored spots; green veins on white; rosy-red outlined in white, separating into little islands of red against a sea of green . . . these are the Caladiums. Aroids by birthright, charmers by God, these plants are far more durable than they look, taking the heat and humidity of summer as if to the station born. In South and Central Florida, they are magical sources of summer color, planted in beds beneath trees, which provide protection from the midday sun. For flower arrangers, the leaves offer a good source of color and will last a long time. Some old favorites include 'Candidum', 'Candidum Jr.', 'Freida Hemple', 'Gypsy Rose', 'Pink Beauty', 'Pink Gem', 'Red Frill', 'White Christmas', and 'White Wing'. (GBT)

Other Name
Fancy Leafed Caladium

Bloom Period and Color
Summer foliage in red, rose, pink, white, silver, bronze, green

Mature Height
18 inches to 2 feet

Zones
9 – 11

When, Where, and How to Plant
Plant in the late winter or spring. Plant in enriched soil, in the shade, among Ferns, Alocasias, or around the base of potted plants. Set tubers 1 to 2 inches below the soil surface and 12 to 18 inches apart. Use a peat or another type of soil amendment if you wish, and mulch bulbs with pine bark. Water sparingly until the leaves emerge. In a pot, use a regular sterile potting soil or soilless mix, and add a small amount of slow-release fertilizer, following the directions below.

Growing Tips
Water two or three times a week. Fertilize them once a month with a balanced fertilizer, such as 6-6-6, or use a slow-release fertilizer. You may want to add more slow-release fertilizer at least once during the warm growing season to keep them performing well. While their soil should drain well, it also should remain moist. Notice that Caladiums look quite wonderful after two or three days of rain. Beginning about November, Caladiums will die back, shed their leaves, and disappear. Reduce water and allow them to stay in the ground, or dig them up, clean them, and separate the bulbs. Dust the cleaned bulbs with a fungicide and put them in a paper bag in a cool place. You can replant in April in place of winter annuals. After about three years, you may wish to replace the tubers, which tend to get smaller.

Regional Advice and Care
In the fall, the leaves die back naturally, and the bulbs can be dug, dried, and saved in a dry place (never the refrigerator because they're tropical) for the following year. See instructions above.

Companion Planting and Design
Their marvelously complex color forms mean most Caladiums look best when seen in masses. Several can be used at the ends of beds, or around the base of trees to replace Impatiens or Wax Begonias.

My Personal Favorite
'White Christmas' is a standout because it can be seen at night.

Calla
Zantedeschia spp.

When, Where, and How to Plant

Callas are best planted from September through January. Some gardeners prefer to dig the rhizomes after the flowers and foliage decline. They will grow best in areas with 6 to 8 hours of sun and bright light for the remaining portions of the day. The plantings like a moist soil with good drainage. Select areas that do not flood during the rainy seasons. Callas grow well in sandy soils as long as they are given plenty of water and all the nutrients needed for growth. Plants are easier to maintain if the soil is improved with organic matter before planting. Work liberal quantities of compost or peat moss and manure into the planting site. Calla rhizomes should be planted 1 to 2 inches deep and 12 to 24 inches apart. After planting, provide adequate water to thoroughly moisten the soil. When planting in containers, use large containers and a loose potting mix.

Growing Tips

A light mulch can be added to maintain the soil moisture and supply some nutrients. Keep planting sites moist by watering whenever the surface soil feels dry to the touch. Pay attention to water needs during the hotter, drier months of spring. Callas should be given a light feeding once in March, May, and August. Gardeners can use a 6-6-6 or similar garden fertilizer, following label instructions. After the plants have flowered, cut the old stalks back to near the ground.

Regional Advice and Care

Callas grow best in North and Central Florida. Container culture is best in South Florida. Callas may be affected by spider mites and thrips. Treat plants with a pest-control product recommended by the University of Florida.

Companion Planting and Design

Help create the tropical look with clusters of Calla Lilies among plantings that like the warmer climate. Some good companions include Philodendrons, Caladiums, Anthuriums, Gingers, Canna, and Bananas.

My Personal Favorite

The new Calla hybrids appear to have more vigor and flower quicker than the older selections. One good performer is the new hybrid Calla 'Dwarf Pink'.

Most Florida gardeners can enjoy the springtime blooms of Callas for years without transplanting. Callas call attention to themselves with their large 4- to 6-inch blooms. The white, pink, or yellow blossoms are borne on tall stems that can be left in the garden or cut as bouquets. Add the plantings to a perennial garden, or spot them throughout the landscape in front of other greenery. After flowering, the foliage gradually declines, and the plants go dormant for the fall and winter months. A number of Calla species and varieties may be planted in Florida. The large, white flowering selections appear to grow best. Every year, check for new introductions that might be suitable for planting in your landscape. (TM)

Other Names
Common Calla, Calla Lily

Bloom Period and Color
Spring blooms in white, pink, yellow, cream, lavender, and purple

Mature Height
To 2 feet

Zones
8 – 10

Canna
Canna hybrids

In 1846, according to Flowers of the World, *a French consular agent in Chile, one M. Annee, collected Cannas from South America and took them home to Paris to hybridize them. According to* Gardening in the Tropics *by R. E. Holttum and Ivan Enoch, the plants were then further hybridized in Italy, where the first to become a "modern" Canna appeared in 1890. C. flaccida, the aquatic, yellow-flowering species, is a Florida native. Hybridization among species has given us bold Cannas, but it has also made them difficult to maintain. They require a good deal of attention and are subject to such leaf mutilation by the canna leaf roller, a moth larva, that they are not widely grown in South Florida. (GBT)*

Bloom Period and Color
Spring and summer blooms in red, orange, yellow, pink, cream, white, bicolors

Mature Height
2 feet to 4 feet

Zones
9 – 11; *C. flaccida* to Zone 8

When, Where, and How to Plant
Plant in the late winter to spring. Plant the rhizomes in an area that can be irrigated regularly. Cannas like a rich soil, so a single planting hole can have organic material (peat moss, compost, aged manure) added to it, or a whole bed can be dug and soil replaced with those ingredients. Plant about 1 to 2 feet apart and 2 inches deep. Dig and divide, then replant every year to keep Cannas flowering well.

Growing Tips
Given their marshy origins and even aquatic components, Cannas love moist soil and, to be vigorous, require frequent fertilizing. The Parrot Jungle gardeners, who must keep their signature red Cannas beautiful for tourists, use a low-nitrogen granular, such as 4-7-5, a small amount monthly, and they supplement that with a weekly spray of 20-20-20. Water two or three times weekly, early in the morning, so any wet foliage will dry by nightfall to avoid fungal diseases. Cannas like moist soil and are heavy feeders, so they are not candidates for water-saving gardens unless used in an area around the house where other water-thirsty plants grow. Thin the rhizomes periodically to give plants a rejuvenating boost.

Regional Advice and Care
In South and Central Florida, the plants can be grown in the ground all year. As far south as Palm Beach, they will die down in winter. Use as an annual in North Florida and as a perennial in Central Florida, except for *C. flaccida,* the aquatic. Regularly inspect for leaf rollers and fungus. Spider mites can be a problem in the dry season. Like the Frangipani, the Canna is subject to rust, a fungus that looks like its name. This can be controlled by sulfur spray or a copper fungicide. Contact your local Extension Service office for a recommendation.

Companion Planting and Design
Tropical leaves that are broad and sometimes striped mean this tropical bulb may best be seen by itself or with other broad-leafed tropicals, such as Bananas or Gingers.

My Personal Favorite
Canna 'Tropicana', with wine and orange-striped leaves, is wildly tropical and eye-catching when used with discrimination.

Day Lily
Hemerocallis hybrids

When, Where, and How to Plant
Day Lilies can be added to the landscape at any time of the year as bareroot transplants or container-grown plants. They grow best in an area with 6 to 8 hours of sun and bright light for the remaining portions of the day. The plantings like an enriched soil with good drainage. Select areas that do not flood during the rainy seasons. All bulbs should be planted in well-drained soil. Day Lilies grow well in sandy soils as long as they are given plenty of water and all the nutrients needed for growth. Plants are easier to maintain if the soil is improved with organic matter before planting. Work liberal quantities of compost or peat moss and manure into the planting site. Day Lilies should be set with the base of the foliage at soil level. It's better to plant a little above the ground than too deep.

Growing Tips
After planting, provide adequate water to thoroughly moisten the soil. A light mulch can be added to maintain soil moisture and supply some nutrients. Keep planting sites moist, watering whenever the surface soil feels dry to the touch. Day Lilies need a light feeding once in March, May, and September. Gardeners can use a 6-6-6 or similar garden fertilizer, following label instructions for bulbs or perennial plantings.

Regional Advice and Care
South Florida growers should check with local garden centers for the best adapted selections. Not all grow well in the hotter sections of the state. They may be affected by caterpillars, aphids, thrips, and grasshoppers. Hand pick pests from the plants, or treat them with a pest-control product recommended by the University of Florida.

Companion Planting and Design
Gardeners often like to create entire beds of Day Lilies but they also mix well with annuals, perennials, and shrubs. They are especially attractive with African Iris, Crinums, and Cannas.

My Personal Favorite
Some flowers just catch your eye with their great color. There are many Day Lilies to pick from but the one called 'Futuristic Art' gets my vote.

Florida boasts of some of the most popular breeders, growers, and varieties of Day Lilies in the nation. Day Lilies sold at plant stores represent just a small portion of selections available from Day Lily nurseries. As the name implies, most Day Lily blossoms last only a day, but the buds along the stems are numerous and each stalk can continue to open blossoms for weeks. Some may bloom sporadically throughout the year. Use Day Lilies in large beds, rock gardens, perennial borders, and pots. These versatile plants can fit into just about any landscape situation. The best Day Lilies for Florida are the evergreen and semievergreen types. Deciduous varieties that lose their leaves during the winter have been poorer performers in most Florida landscapes. (TM)

Bloom Period and Color
Spring to summer blooms in yellow, orange, pink, red, lavender, and blends

Mature Height
To 2 feet

Zones
8 – 10

Gladiolus
Gladiolus hybrids

Gardeners love their Gladiolus for the tall spikes of color. The flowers come in most colors of the rainbow in addition to some blends. The trumpetlike blooms open from the base of the flower stalk and continue up the stem to the very tip. The flowering process often lasts a week or more. Often the stalks are never allowed to mature in the garden but are cut for bouquets. The lancelike foliage grows straight up. Plant Gladiolus in perennial beds and rock gardens, or use them among shrub plantings. After a few months of growth and flowering, the plants gradually decline for a rest period before starting new growth. Many varieties, in addition to short and tall forms, of Gladiolus are available from garden centers and mail-order nurseries. (TM)

Bloom Period and Color
Spring thru summer blooms in all colors and blends

Mature Height
To 2 feet

Zones
8 – 11

When, Where, and How to Plant
Gladiolus can be planted at any time of the year. The bulblike corms are available from January through May for home planting. They grow best in an area with 6 to 8 hours of sun and bright light for the remaining portions of the day. The plantings like an enriched soil with good drainage. Gladiolus grow well in sandy soils as long as they are given plenty of water and all the nutrients needed for growth. Work liberal quantities of compost or peat moss and manure into the planting site. Gladiolus corms should be set 2 to 3 inches deep and spaced 4 to 6 inches apart in the ground. After planting, provide adequate water to thoroughly moisten the soil. Glads may need staking when the stalks are produced to prevent wind damage. After the plants have flowered, most gardeners cut the old stalks back to near the ground to allow the plant's energy to go into corm production.

Growing Tips
A light mulch can be added to maintain soil moisture and supply some nutrients. Keep planting sites moist, watering whenever the surface inch of soil feels dry to the touch. Gladiolus need light feedings monthly during the growing period. Gardeners can use a 6-6-6 or similar fertilizer, following label instructions for bulb plantings.

Regional Advice and Care
Gladiolus grow well in all areas of Florida but may be affected by cold weather. North and Central Florida plantings are usually restricted to the spring through summer months. Gladiolus may be affected by caterpillars, grasshoppers, and thrips. Hand pick pests from the plants, or treat them with a pest-control product recommended by the University of Florida.

Companion Planting and Design
Often planted in a row, Gladiolus are equally attractive in clusters with other bulbs and perennials. The can be mixed with Canna, Crinum, Society Garlic, and Zephyr Lilies.

My Personal Favorite
Call me sentimental, but my dad liked 'Dusty Miller'. It's still my favorite with the dusty look that catches the eye.

Gloriosa Lily
Gloriosa spp.

When, Where, and How to Plant

Gloriosa Lilies are best planted from January through April in Florida landscapes. Tubers can be dug and separated from established plantings at any time of the year. They grow best in an area with 6 to 8 hours of sun and bright light for the remaining portions of the day. The plantings like an enriched soil with good drainage. Gloriosa Lilies grow well in sandy soils as long as they are given plenty of water and all the nutrients needed for growth. They can withstand periods of drought but die back and then resume growth when damper weather returns. Work liberal quantities of compost or peat moss and manure into the planting site. Gloriosa Lilies should be planted 2 to 4 inches deep in the ground and spaced 12 to 18 inches apart. After planting, provide adequate water to thoroughly moisten the soil. Gloriosa Lilies may grow out of bounds and need some trimming of the vining portions to prevent them from growing among other plantings.

Growing Tips

A light mulch can be added to maintain soil moisture and supply some nutrients. Keep planting sites moist, watering whenever the surface inch of soil feels dry. Gardeners can use a 6-6-6 or similar garden fertilizer, following label instructions for bulbs or perennial plantings.

Regional Advice and Care

Gloriosa Lilies grow well in all areas of Florida. Plants go dormant in North and Central Florida when affected by cold. Trim off dead vine portions, and wait for new growth to begin. Gloriosa Lilies may be affected by caterpillars. Hand pick pests from the plants, or treat them with a pest-control product recommended by the University of Florida.

Companion Planting and Design

Plant as a backdrop for a garden or part of a perennial planting that declines during the winter. Use with lower growing African Iris, Crinum, Gingers, and Society Garlic.

My Personal Favorite

Other than the species, there is not much from which to choose. *G. rothschildiana* appears to have the vigor I like and it has good crimson and yellow color combinations in the blooms.

For a spectacular, colorful flowering plant, add a Gloriosa Lily near the patio or entrance to the home. The large blooms, which open in an inverted position, are a blend of crimson and yellow colors. The plants start to grow shortly after planting the V-shaped tubers. You can plant Gloriosa Lilies individually, or you can train several along a wall or fence, since it is one of the few vining bulbous plants. After months of flowering, the plants die back or, in cooler regions, are killed back to the ground by cold weather. There are two species of Gloriosa Lilies usually planted in Florida: Gloriosa rothschildiana and Gloriosa superba. The species are similar, varying in the amount of crimson and yellow color in the blooms. (TM)

Other Name

Climbing Lily

Bloom Period and Color

Spring thru summer blooms in red banded with yellow

Mature Height

To 6 feet

Zones

8 – 11

Kaffir Lily
Clivia miniata

Only a few gardeners plant the Kaffir Lily. Perhaps one reason is that the plants are relatively expensive. But the plants multiply rather rapidly, and you can increase the collection in just a few years. The shade-tolerant Kaffir Lily can be planted in lower light areas where the selection of flowering plants is limited. The bulbs are best clustered together to form a spot of color during the spring. Use them in perennial beds, among shrub plantings, and in containers to display the plants in bloom on porches, patios, and balconies; they can also be brought indoors. Container culture is best in North Florida and portions of Central Florida where the plants may be affected by cold. Plant breeders have produced a yellow-flowering Kaffir Lily. (TM)

Other Name
Clivia

Bloom Period and Color
Spring blooms in bright orange

Mature Height
18 inches to 2 feet

Zones
9 – 11

When, Where, and How to Plant
Give Kaffir Lilies a partial-shade to shady location. They grow best in an area with filtered sun under tall trees. Kaffir Lilies grow in sandy soils as long as they are given plenty of water and the nutrients needed for growth. Work liberal quantities of compost or peat moss and manure into the planting site. Kaffir Lily bulbs should be planted with the tips of the bulbs just below the surface of the soil. Space plants 18 to 24 inches apart. For containers, grow 1 bulb in a 6- or 8-inch pot with a loose potting mix. After planting, provide adequate water to thoroughly moisten the soil. After the plants have flowered, cut the old stalks back to near the ground or allow the plant to continue seed development. New plants take three years to flower.

Growing Tips
A light mulch can be added to maintain soil moisture and supply some nutrients for in-ground plantings. Keep planting sites moist, watering whenever the surface soil feels dry. Kaffir Lilies need a light feeding once in March, May, and September. Gardeners can use a 6-6-6 or similar garden fertilizer, following label instructions for bulbs or perennial plantings. Feed container plantings monthly with a 20-20-20 or similar fertilizer.

Regional Advice and Care
Kaffir Lilies are cold sensitive and best grown in containers in North Florida and the cooler portions of Central Florida. Protect all plantings from freezing temperatures. Keep the plants on the dry side during the winter months. Kaffir Lilies may be affected by caterpillars and grasshoppers. Hand pick pests from the plants, or treat them with a pest-control product recommended by the University of Florida.

Companion Planting and Design
Spot these bulbs in clusters among other greenery and perennial plantings or display in decorative planters. Combine with shade lovers of Alstroemeria, Begonias, Caladium, Eucharis Lily, Impatiens, and Peacock Ginger.

My Personal Favorite
If you like something a little different in Kaffir Lilies then the yellow selection, 'Sahin's Yellow' is sure to be a pleaser. Expect to pay a little more for this special plant.

Pride of Burma
Curcuma roscoeana

When, Where, and How to Plant
Plant the rhizomes in late winter to early spring. Plant in a partially shady location with good drainage; morning sun is ideal. The relatively small rhizomes can be fairly snug in a pot or several inches apart. They should be within 2 or 3 inches of the soil surface. Enrich the soil with aged manure, compost, or peat moss, with the addition of perlite or sand for drainage if necessary. Loose, leafy mulch is best. Water in after planting and when the leaves emerge.

Growing Tips
Keep soil evenly moist. Fertilize with slow-release fertilizer or a fertilizer formulated for palms with slow-release nitrogen and potassium. You might occasionally spray them with a micronutrient spray or the same water-soluble fertilizer you use on Orchids, such as 8-8-8. When applying a foliar spray, add a commercially prepared spreader-sticker, or a teaspoon of liquid Ivory (1 teaspoon per gallon of water). It only takes a few minutes for nutrients on leaves to be absorbed. One secret of using nutritional spray is to apply it early on a sunny morning when the plants are photosynthesizing at a good clip. Dig and separate the rhizomes in the fall as the plants begin to go dormant. You can keep the rhizomes in sawdust until early spring, planting seasonal color in their spot; or if you don't dig the plants to separate the rhizomes, simply remember where the dormant plants are, or put a marker on the spot.

Regional Advice and Care
Curcumas can be kept in pots in areas where freezing occurs. Some hybrids will do well in cooler climates.

Companion Planting and Design
Curcumas make good understory plantings for a palm, or as a soft foil for shade-loving Bromeliads. Or, keep them in a pot so they can be moved inside during winter dormancy.

My Personal Favorite
The species, *C. roscoeana*, has bright orange flowers easily seen among the leaves.

When the Curcuma leaves appear, you know spring is in the air. The beautiful understated leaves—simple, with raised veins like ribs—are nice enough to let appear seasonally in the garden by themselves. The cone of bracts resemble miniature wall sconces back-to-back on a stem, with flowers blooming out of each bract one or two at a time. In the winter, some Curcumas go dormant and die back. Because of the seasonality, I keep my Curcuma hybrids in a container. The Curcuma most readily available is 'Pride of Burma', but other cultivars are finding their way to collectors' gardens and can be found through mail order or at plant shows. Curcuma indora has an inflorescence topped with pink bracts. The lower bracts remain green. Flowers are yellow. (GBT)

Bloom Period and Color
Spring blooms in pink to lavender

Mature Height
To 3 feet

Zones
9 – 11

Shell Ginger
Alpinia zerumbet

Gardeners in Central and South Florida can enjoy summer color from the Shell Ginger. As the name implies, individual flowers resemble small seashells about 1 inch long, mainly white with yellow, brown, and red markings. The blossoms are borne in large clusters that remain attractive for weeks. Summer is the major flowering period, but sporadic flowering may occur year-round. The plants are good landscape specimens, producing long, broad, bright-green leaves. Better give this plant plenty of room to grow because the rhizomes increase rapidly. They are best used as a backdrop for other plantings, as space dividers, or as specimen plants. A Shell Ginger with green-and-yellow foliage of the variety 'Variegata' makes an attractive accent. The plant is a reluctant bloomer in most gardens. (TM)

Other Name
Shell Flower

Bloom Period and Color
Summer blooms are white with yellow, brown, and red markings

Mature Height
To 8 feet

Zones
9 – 11

When, Where, and How to Plant
Shell Ginger can be added to the landscape at any time of the year. Garden centers make the plants available as rhizomes from late winter through summer. It's a great plant for the partially shaded garden. Shell Ginger grows best in an area with 6 to 8 hours of sun and bright light for the remaining portions of the day. The plantings like an enriched soil with good drainage. Plants can tolerate areas that may be dry for short periods of time. Shell Gingers grow well in sandy soils as long as they are given plenty of water and the nutrients needed for growth. Work liberal quantities of compost or peat moss and manure into the planting site. Plant rhizomes just below the surface of the soil, spaced 12 to 24 inches apart. After the plants have flowered, cut the old stalks back to near the ground.

Growing Tips
A light mulch can be added to maintain soil moisture and supply some nutrients. Keep planting sites moist, watering whenever the surface soil feels dry. Shell Ginger needs a light feeding once in March, May, and September. Gardeners can use a 6-6-6 or similar garden fertilizer, following label instructions.

Regional Advice and Care
Shell Ginger grows best in Central Florida and southward. North Florida gardeners may grow the plants in containers to bring indoors during freezing weather. Even in Central Florida, plants may be affected by cold and need a spring trimming before growth begins. Shell Ginger may be affected by caterpillars and grasshoppers. Hand pick pests from the plants, or treat them with a pest-control product recommended by the University of Florida.

Companion Planting and Design
Combine with sun or light shade lovers as an accent feature or create a backdrop for gardens. Mix with African Lily, Coleus, Crinums, Jacobinia, or Split Leaf Philodendron.

My Personal Favorite
You might miss the Shell Ginger in the landscape if you don't plant some of the cultivar called 'Variegata' which has green and yellow foliage.

Swamp Lily
Crinum americanum

When, Where, and How to Plant

Plant any time, but winter is best for spring flowers. Plants tend to look just a little nicer in high shade. A low-lying area that has occasionally wet conditions (or a homemade bog) will serve well. A basic rule of thumb for wetland plants: a wetland plant can be grown in dry conditions, but an upland plant cannot be grown in wet conditions. Enrich the planting hole with 2 parts peat moss, 1 part each sand and pine bark mulch (not large nuggets). Add some bone meal to the bottom, and plant the bulb at the same depth at which it grew in the container, making sure that the neck of the bulb is above the soil line. If planting several, dig a bed at least 6 to 8 inches deep, enrich the entire bed, and space 1 to 1¹/₂ feet apart.

Growing Tips

Irrigate regularly to keep the area evenly moist, and fertilize in spring, summer, and fall. Be sure to mulch.

Regional Advice and Care

These lilies can grow into Zone 9 and even into Georgia. Allow them to rest after flowering. *C. americanum* has a fungus that requires some work: every few weeks it needs a spray of fungicide. Beginning in March, lubber grasshoppers hatch and emerge from underground nests, and start eating their way through the landscape. Until, that is, they happen on a Lily. They can take it to the mat in record time. Use a protozoa with the trade name Nolo Bait, Grasshopper Killer, or Semaspore. Better yet, step on them when they're tiny and all in one area. The bigger they get, the messier the task.

Companion Planting and Design

Since these Lilies grow in wetland conditions or on the edges of wetlands, they look most at home in a garden bog or with such plants as Ferns, in a crescent design or a group of three or five.

My Personal Favorite

Swamp Lily has starlike flowers and a sweet fragrance.

Crinum americanum *and* Crinum asiaticum, *sisters beneath the skin, are spring-blooming tropical Lilies with big showy flowers.* Crinum americanum, *the Swamp Lily, is a bulb native to Florida and Georgia. These Lilies stand out against the swampy margins of freshwater marshes like stars in the night. In such vastness, they seem smaller than they are. At home in your garden, you will find they are substantial. The flowers are starbursts of white petals with showy stigmas and stamens on long stalks in the center. The Swamp Lily is a perfect candidate for low-lying swales or where water stands occasionally.* Crinum asiaticum, *the Tree Lily, rears itself up on a trunk, with leaves several feet long and stalks of flowers equally large. (GBT)*

Other Name
Southern Swamp Crinum

Bloom Period and Color
Spring blooms are white

Mature Height
To 2 feet

Zones
8 – 11

57

Voodoo Lily
Amorphophallus spp.

The name "Voodoo Lily" suggests there might be a little magic in the plant, and there is. It grows from nothing in early spring to a tall plant in just weeks. The leaves are deeply cut and up to several feet long and wide. It has an interesting trunk with green streaks and splotches. Mature plants have spectacular reddish-brown spring flowers. A. titanum is among the world's largest flowers, and can reach 8-plus feet high. A not-so-pleasant surprise is that flowers may have a very foul odor, which is emitted in waves, to attract pollinating flies. Some grow only a few feet tall, and others grow large enough for a child to stand under. (TM)

Other Name
Snake Lily

Bloom Period and Color
Spring blooms in reddish-brown

Mature Height
Leaf 6 feet; some flowers to 8 feet or more

Zones
8 – 11

When, Where, and How to Plant
Voodoo Lilies are best planted in late winter through spring when the corms are just beginning to grow. Container-grown plants are available from garden centers year-round. They grow best in areas with 6 to 8 hours of sun and bright light for the remainder of the day. The plantings like an enriched soil with good drainage. Select areas that do not flood during the rainy seasons. Voodoo Lilies grow well in sandy soils as long as they are given plenty of water and all the nutrients needed for growth. Work in liberal quantities of compost or peat moss and manure. Voodoo Lily corms should be planted 3 to 4 inches deep and spaced 1 foot or more apart. After planting, provide adequate water to thoroughly moisten the soil. After the plant has flowered, the shriveled blossoms can be removed.

Growing Tips
A light mulch will maintain soil moisture and supply some nutrients. Keep planting sites moist, watering when the surface soil feels dry. Voodoo Lilies need a light feeding in March, May, and August. Use a 6-6-6 or similar fertilizer, following label instructions.

Regional Advice and Care
Voodoo Lilies vary as to their hardiness. Most can be grown throughout the state if the soil is mulched after they die back during the fall. All can be grown in containers and brought indoors during freezing weather. Voodoo Lilies may be affected by caterpillars and grasshoppers. Hand pick pests from the plants, or treat them with a pest-control product recommended by the University of Florida.

Companion Planting and Design
Best use as an accent in container gardens, featured with perennials, or mixed with shrub plantings for summer interest. Surround with African Iris, Bird-of-Paradise, Crinums, Heliconias, and Philodendrons.

My Personal Favorite
There are a number of selections but the one called 'Konjac' is the most popular. It also has spotted stems.

Walking Iris
Neomarica spp.

When, Where, and How to Plant

Plant any time of the year in partial shade, in a foundation planter, a shrub bed, or in a Japanese garden-like setting. Enrich the planting hole with peat, pine bark mulch, and sand so it retains moisture but drains well. Make the planting hole slightly larger than the rootball in the container, and slide off the container, carefully placing the Walking Iris in the hole. Water in and mulch. From divisions or plantlets, plant just below the surface of the soil. To hasten and direct the rooting of small plantlets from the stolons, you can bend the stolon and use wire cut in the shape of hairpins to push them down and keep them in place.

Growing Tips

Walking Iris has a low tolerance for droughty conditions, so irrigate twice a week in winter, two to three times in summer if there is not enough rain. Fertilize with slow-release fertilizer in spring, mid-summer, and fall. Slow-release fertilizer can last up to two or three months in South Florida, in spite of longer claims made by manufacturers, due to high heat and rain. However, allow the plant to indicate when it needs more fertilizer. Pale yellow leaves and fewer flowers can indicate lack of nutrients. Occasionally clean out the old stolons and leaves from beds of Walking Iris. Brown, dead material can build up like thatch in turfgrass and not only disguise weeds but also prevent plantlets from rooting.

Regional Advice and Care

A tender plant, this will die to the ground in Central Florida in winter but grows back from the rhizome. Walking Iris can be replaced with Bearded Iris, or grown in pots in North Florida.

Companion Planting and Design

Use this as a tallish groundcover around the Mango tree or the Areca Palms. Or, in a Japanese garden, in a rocky area where the fan shape of the flat leaves can be highlighted against an inorganic substrate.

My Personal Favorite

The yellow flowers of *Neomarica longifolia* seem like dots of golden light.

The Walking Iris is so-named because the flower stalk gradually sinks to the ground and little plants form and root where it falls, allowing the clump to expand or "walk." These Iris are good for a vertical effect in a bed. They can also be used alone, where they are tall enough to hold their flowers up for inspection. Like other bulbs, they like a moist and rich bed, although I've seen them thrive in low-lying, untended swales where weedy plants muck about in agreeable company. According to Betrock's Reference Guide to Landscape Plants by Timothy Broschat and Alan Meerow, Neomarica caerulea has blue flowers; N. gracilis has white flowers with blue markings; N. longifolia is the commonly seen yellow flowering Iris. (GBT)

Bloom Period and Color
Year-round blooms in white, yellow, blue, and brown

Mature Height
To 3 feet

Zones
10B – 11

Zephyr Lily
Zephyranthes spp.

Most Zephyr Lilies are referred to as Rain Lilies because the flowering season begins at the return of the rainy season. They grow well throughout the state, and the blossoms might remind relocated gardeners of Crocus. Zephyr Lilies are best planted in clusters as if naturalized in flower beds and perennial gardens. They can also be used along walkways, as a groundcover, and in containers. The bright-green thin foliage is present year-round but may die back during drought if not supplied with adequate water. All Zephyr Lilies are very drought tolerant but grow best in moist soils. Three main species are grown in Florida: Zephyranthes rosea, a pink; Z. candida, a white; and Z. citrina, a yellow. The pink is most common. (TM)

Other Name
Fairy Lily

Bloom Period and Color
Spring through early fall blooms in white, yellow, pink

Mature Height
To 8 inches

Zones
8 – 11

When, Where, and How to Plant
Zephyr Lilies can be added to the landscape at any time of the year. They grow and flower best in an area with 6 to 8 hours of sun and bright light for the remaining portions of the day. Select areas that do not flood during the rainy seasons. Zephyr Lilies grow well in sandy soils as long as they are given plenty of water and all the nutrients needed for growth. Work liberal quantities of compost or peat moss and manure into the planting site. Zephyr Lilies should be planted 1 to 2 inches deep in the ground and spaced 3 to 4 inches apart. After planting, provide adequate water to thoroughly moisten the soil. After the plants have flowered, cut the old stalks back to near the ground or allow the plant to continue seed development. Mature seeds germinate quickly when sown in a loose potting mix. Zephyr Lilies are best divided during the fall through spring months.

Growing Tips
A light mulch can be added to maintain soil moisture and supply some nutrients. Keep planting sites moist, watering whenever the surface soil feels dry. Less water will be needed during the winter months than during the hotter, drier months of the year. Zephyr Lilies need a light feeding once in March, May, and September. Gardeners can use a 6-6-6 or similar garden fertilizer.

Regional Advice and Care
Zephyr Lilies grow well in all areas of the state with similar care. Zephyr Lilies may be affected by caterpillars and grasshoppers. Hand pick pests from the plants, or treat them with a pest-control product recommended by the University of Florida.

Companion Planting and Design
Plant as a seasonal accent with perennials or a border along walkways. Use as a ground cover with a backdrop of Indian Hawthorn or Dwarf Yaupon Holly.

My Personal Favorite
They are all favorites, but I like the profusion of color from the pink species *Z. rosea*. It survives periods of drought to pop up with the first rains of summer.

Alstroemeria (*Alstroemeria* spp.)

Other Name Peruvian Lily; **Bloom Period and Color** Spring and early summer blooms in green/red, pink, yellow, white, lavender; **Mature Height** 18 inches to 2 feet; **Zones** 8–10

When, Where, and How to Plant Alstroemeria is best planted from late winter through spring in Florida gardens. Consider these plants more for lower light or filtered light areas. They grow well in areas with 4 to 6 hours of sun and bright light for the remaining portions of the day. Select areas that do not flood during the rainy seasons. Alstroemeria grows well in sandy soil as long as it is given plenty of water and all the nutrients needed for growth. Work liberal quantities of compost or peat moss and manure into the planting site. The tuberous roots of Alstroemeria should be set 6 to 9 inches deep and 1 foot apart in the ground.

Growing Tips After planting, provide adequate water to thoroughly moisten the soil. A light mulch can be added to maintain soil moisture and supply some nutrients. Keep planting sites moist, watering whenever the surface soil feels dry to the touch. Less water will be needed during the winter months. Alstroemeria needs a light feeding once in March and May. Gardeners can use a 6-6-6 or similar garden fertilizer, following label instructions for bulbs or perennial plantings. After the plants have flowered, cut the old stalks back to near the ground to allow the plant's energy to go into tuberous root production or allow the plant to continue seed development.

Regional Advice and Care Alstroemeria appears to grow best in North and Central Florida. Select varieties from local landscapes or growers to get the hardiest types for South Florida. Alstroemeria may be affected by slugs and cutworms. Hand pick pests from the plants, or treat them with a pest-control product recommended by the University of Florida.

Louisiana Iris (*Iris* hybrids)

Bloom Period and Color Spring blooms in yellow, blue, red, white, and purple; **Mature Height** To 18 inches; **Zones** 8–9

When, Where, and How to Plant Louisiana Iris are best planted from spring through summer. They are available as container-grown specimens and as rhizomes from aquatic gardens and mail-order nurseries for year-round planting. They grow best in an area with 6 to 8 hours of sun and bright light for the remaining portions of the day. Plantings can grow in or near standing water, but the rhizomes must be above the water. The Louisiana Iris is one of the few bulbs that must have a damp to wet soil. To have success with the new plants, bog conditions must be created or already exist. They grow in sandy soils, but most gardeners like to improve the soil with organic matter. Work liberal quantities of compost or peat moss and manure into the planting site. Plant the rhizomes 8 to 12 inches apart at the soil surface with the roots in the ground. After planting, provide adequate water to keep the soil moist.

Growing Tips A light mulch can be added to maintain soil moisture and supply some nutrients. Keep planting sites moist, watering whenever the surface soil starts to feel dry. Louisiana Iris need a light feeding once in March, May, and September. Use a 6-6-6 or similar fertilizer, following label instructions. After the plants have flowered, cut the old stalks back to near the ground.

Regional Advice and Care Louisiana Iris are best grown in North and Central Florida. South Florida gardens cannot provide the cool weather needed for good growth. They may be affected by caterpillars and grasshoppers. Hand pick pests from the plants, or treat them with a pest-control product recommended by the University of Florida.

Cycads *for Florida*

Even before that matriarchal land mass called Pangaea broke into continents, Cycads were here. Perhaps as long as 150 million years ago they spread over most of the earth. Today, in areas such as Florida and southern California, they are prized garden plants, and in their remnant home territories they are highly endangered species.

They look like curious Palms; the name Cycad comes from a Greek word meaning "palm." Their stems often form trunks, and spiky stiff leaves comprise the crowns. There are about 185 species of Cycads around the world, primarily found where summers are hot and wet and winters are cool and dry. Australia, South Africa, Central and South America, parts of China and Japan, and some Pacific islands have scattered groups of these plants. Florida has one native Cycad, the Coontie (*Zamia pumila*).

How Cycads Grow

Some Cycads produce one new set of leaves every year, though some slow growers don't get around to leaf production except every two or three years. We think of these plants as prehistoric, belonging to the Jurassic Age or the Age of Dinosaurs (any dinosaur exhibit worth its salt includes Cycads). While they may not be nimble in the evolutionary sense, they are still evolving. In the last twenty years, a new

Cycad

Cycad

genus has been named, Chigua from South America, and a new species of Bowenia has been identified: *B. serrulata* from Australia.

Like conifers, Cycads have seed-bearing cones, and plants are either male or female. The cones produce aromas, from sweet-fruity to wintergreen, and the male cones, which are longer and thinner than the female cones, produce heat, sometimes becoming up to 20 degrees hotter than the surrounding air temperature. (A few female cones do the same thing.) In the genus Zamia, the temperature change occurs near sundown, before pollen is shed. Male cones of the *Dioon* and *Encephalartos* genera produce heat just after sundown. Scientists believe this quality may be tied to pollen release and the need to attract pollinators.

The roots of most Cycads, called *coralloid* because they grow up in coral-like shapes, are infested with blue-green algae. These roots fix atmospheric nitrogen at the surface, which is used as a nutrient by the plants.

Kings and Queens

Cycas circinalis, Queen Sago, and *C. rumphii,* King Sago, are the Cycads most often seen in Florida in older landscapes. The Queen Sago is the larger, both in stature and in leaf size. Many 50- or 60-year-old Queen Sagos stand 12 to 15 or more feet tall and develop multiple heads on spreading stems that cluster around the original. King Sago is compact, with upright, stiffly held, and sharp leaves. These species have been attacked in recent years by scale. Many have been killed. Dioon species are good substitutes.

Dioon species of Cycads are native to the New World, or the Americas, and can be found from sea level to 9000 feet. *Dioon edule* has 4- to 5-foot leaves, pinnately compound, and holds them elegantly up as if in a fountainlike spray. Females of the Dioon species have relatively grand cones that are soft and furry, covered with a down, and may last two years on the plant. *Dioon edule* may be the slowest growing, and Cycad specialists believe it may reach ages approaching 2000 years.

Encephalartos horridus from Africa has wickedly spiny leaflets that are blue-gray once they mature, pinkish when they first flush out. *E. ferox* females add color to the landscape with brilliant-red cones. In nature the seeds are dispersed by mammals, such as monkeys and hornbills.

The name *Encephalartos* is Greek and was assembled this way: en, or "in"; cephale, meaning "head"; and artos, meaning "bread." The inner part of the upper trunk is edible.

The plants in South Africa are fire tolerant and have thick trunks, suckering from the base. Gardeners in South Florida have found it may take fifteen to twenty years for one of these to produce a cone, so patience is a must.

Zamia is a West Indies and Latin American group of Cycads in the same tribe as Dioon. Zamia cones are upright, and those of *Z. furfuraceae* break open to release brilliant red seeds. *Z. furfuraceae* is called the cardboard palm by landscapers because of the texture of its flat, roundish leaves. Its stems are armed with short nodules that make pruning tricky. Florida's only native Cycad, *Zamia pumila,* was endangered by overcollecting in the 19th and early 20th centuries, when it was made into starch. (GBT)

Mature Height

18 inches to 20 feet

Zones

10 – 11

When, Where, and How to Plant

Plant in late spring or early summer before the annual flush of new leaves. Leaves form a rosette at the top of the stem. Before new leaves flush, cataphylls, or protective scale-leaves, will appear. When you see these thorny growths, you know it is time to plant or transplant. The most important condition for Cycads is excellent drainage. The plants can grow in sun to partial shade, but they will rot in wet soil. A rule of thumb on light is this: blue leaves tolerate sun; blue-green leaves need some shade; green leaves prefer more shade. Treat a Cycad like a Palm, and provide a wide hole as deep as the rootball. Backfill without enriching with compost or peat moss. If your soil does not drain especially fast, you may want to build up a mound, incorporating sand into a good potting soil to ensure good drainage.

Growing Tips

A fertilizer formulated for Palms can be used on Cycads—try a 8-4-12-4 that has slow-release nitrogen and potassium in addition to micronutrients. When new leaves are still soft, apply a foliar micronutrient spray.

Regional Advice and Care

Yellowing old leaves signal magnesium deficiency; yellowing new leaves are a sign of manganese deficiency and possibly iron deficiency. Scale and mealybugs can be problems on Cycads. Combat pests with insecticidal soap or systemic insecticide sprayed alternately with light horticultural oil. Do not spray with oil in summer; oil can damage leaves in heat above 85 degrees Fahrenheit.

Coontie

Cycas circinalis and *C. rumphii,* the Queen and King Sagos, experienced a fungal problem in the early 1990s after the 1989 freeze in South Florida. They have recently been under attack from a deadly scale infestation new to Dade County, particularly in the Coral Gables and Pinecrest areas. The scale is from China and Thailand, and it is extremely difficult to control. It is distinguished by many more male scales, which are long, than female, which are round. Both are white, and the leaves quickly start to look covered with snow. Control scale with consistent use of a light horticultural oil, used alternately with insecticidal soap, systemic insecticide, and Orthene™. The scale is much less active in winter than summer. Unfortunately, many old specimens of these plants have been lost to scale.

Companion Planting and Design

Gardens benefit from Cycads because these plants are so architectural. They can be used as specimens, as regal guardians of the entryway, and as accents. Two are small enough to be ground covers—notably *Zamia pumila* and *Z. fischeri.* Cycads go with Palms like ham with cheese. They can be striking when given a ground cover of rock or mulch or a low-growing flowering cover. They can be stunning when collected in a bed or artfully set on a mound or around a pine. They grow well with Aloes. Cycads are also exquisite when planted in open beds by themselves and mulched with rock. The rosette form of the plants and their usually stiff leaves make them living sculptures.

My Personal Favorite

Encephalartos horridus is a lovely blue-gray color. It has unusually shaped, and horridly armed, leaves.

Ground Covers *for Florida*

Could there be lawn chairs or lawn bowling without a lawn? Croquet without grass? Chinch bugs without St. Augustine? No. Could there be happier gardeners without mowing, raking, edging, sweeping, irrigating, and fixing the sprinkler heads? Assuredly.

Give yourself this challenge: enlarge your planting beds 5 to 10 percent each year for the next 5 years and see if you don't love your garden more. This is where ground covers come in: Ferns instead of Zoysia, Bromeliads instead of chinch bugs, Kalanchoe instead of dollar spot. Serendipity instead of a national obsession. Furthermore, and this is not breaking news, ground covers can reduce the amount of fuel we waste on lawn mowers and fertilizers, the amount of noise we must suffer with leaf blowers, and the hours and hours we spend every Saturday harvesting the crop only to let it decompose, or worse, to throw it away.

Kalanchoe

We are not completely pro-ground cover, anti-grass. We have dogs that need a place to run. We have parts of the yard we like to visit, and that require walking across a lawn to get there. We even like the nice contrast grass provides against the ground covers. But we also like our lives to be our own.

Considering Ground Covers

The concept of ground cover may be the most variable in landscaping. A garden with small Agaves as accents may have pea rock as a ground cover, while another garden may feature the Agaves themselves as the ground cover.

In the name of creativity, small shrubs can be roped into service. Mexican Heather, which is a dwarf shrub, is often used as a ground cover, though it likes attention to look its best. Coontie, the small native Cycad, serves well, too. Beargrass, a kind of Yucca, is another relatively small plant that might be useful in small areas.

Where is the best place to put ground covers? Around and beneath trees where grass won't grow; around shrub beds and Palms; around the edges of the garden in curving beds to soften the geometry; at the base of shrubs so the plants can serve as a visual link between the flat, floorlike grass and the elevated shrub level; on slopes or grading to keep soil from eroding; on lake fronts; in swales; next to hard surfaces such as patios or decks, again to soften the hard lines of nonliving elements and connect them with living elements.

Creeping Fig

First Things First

To successfully prepare an area for ground covers, first get rid of the grass. There are a couple of ways to do this. One involves covering the area with clear plastic, weighting it down, and allowing the heat to kill the grass. You may not want to wait that long. In that case, you can use Roundup, a herbicide that breaks down quickly. Wait then for the grass to die, remove it, and till the soil, adding compost or peat moss to enrich it. You can add a light application of a slow-release fertilizer at this time, plant the ground covers and add mulch, then water well.

The goal is to have the edges of the ground cover plants overlap to shade out any weeds. It may take a full growing season or two. In the interim, you'll have to weed and fertilize at appropriate times, keep the soil irrigated, and be patient.

Thinking Ahead

As the water supply becomes critical, ground covers will become more important elements in Florida gardens. Plants, animals and people grow just fine with an ample supply of water. Yet, without it, nothing grows.

In many scenarios of climate change, rain patterns are going to change and rising seas are going to change the topography. Rain "events" will replace the rainy season and droughts will increase as well, as South Florida already has experienced.

Even without dramatic change, the water picture is critical. Drinking water, water for agriculture and water for natural areas must all be obtained from the same source: the aquifers.

Ground covers are the gardener's best friend and the sponge that is the lawn may be not only a liability but a misdemeanor in the future.

Artillery Plant
Pilea microphylla

Two of the many characteristics that make this West Indies plant useful are its color, which is that of Granny Smith apples, and its texture, which is rather like foam. It also is durable, taking the rainy season in stride with the dry season, bearing up under heat and not even noticing cold. Artillery Plant gets its name from the way the stamens shoot out pollen, in a little cloud, as if the tiniest canon had been fired. A related Pilea, Aluminum Plant (Pilea cadierei), is dark green with silver markings. It likes more water and shade, but it spreads quickly. Pilea 'Stop Light' has slightly larger round leaves and is a darker color. The little flowers are red, which accounts for the name. (GBT)

Other Name
Artillery Fern

Bloom Period and Color
Good foliage color

Mature Height × Spread
6 to 10 inches × 12 inches

Zones
10 – 11

When, Where, and How to Plant
Plant at the beginning of the rainy season, to help your little transplants take off. Artillery Plant can be used in many situations, either sunny or somewhat shady. Provide good drainage by mixing some sand into the planting bed. Then trowel out a planting hole a little larger than the rootball in the container, and slide the plant from the container into the hole. Fill the planting hole and water. Water well for a few weeks to get this established, if it doesn't rain. For ground covers, plant about 12 inches apart in staggered rows. After three or four years, a mat of dead stems forms beneath the new tops, and eventually these have to be cleaned out. It is easier to take out a whole bed and replant. That can be done from cuttings by cutting the top 4 or 5 inches off old plants and replanting them in a clump. If growing in moist mulch, the cuttings never wilt.

Growing Tips
Water in the dry season about once a week. I use Artillery Plants beneath Palms. The whole area gets mulched twice a year, and the Palms are fertilized two to three times a year, so the Artillery Plants get nutrition by virtue of their location. Periodically, remove old woody stems and replace.

Regional Advice and Care
Artillery Plant needs protection in winter in Central and North Florida. Artillery Plant may get a *Rhizoctonia* blight, a fungal disease. When plants are given too much water, they rot out. Snails often hide in the Artillery Plants, eating them while they're at it. If plants are growing well, they will not show minor damage.

Companion Planting and Design
Use at the feet of Palms, or near tall flowering herbaceous perennials such as Ornamental Bananas, in full sun; in partial shade, use against Persian Shield with metallic purple and silver leaves.

My Personal Favorite
The cultivar 'Spotlight' has large and darker green leaves that makes an attractive cover.

When, Where, and How to Plant

Plant any time in South Florida. Plant in full sun. Blue Daze is salt-tolerant, so it could serve well in seaside gardens or oceanfront condo balconies. Space plants about 1 to 1^1/$_2$ feet apart. If mulching, try to keep the mulch away from plant stalks to reduce the threat of fungus. Blue Daze is a moderately fast grower, and can cover an area with silver-green foliage in a matter of weeks.

Growing Tips

Use a slow-release fertilizer, following package directions. A site that drains well is best to avoid the too-wet conditions that result in disease. Water faithfully after planting in order to help the small Morning Glories become established.

Regional Advice and Care

Prof. Ed Gilman, writing a fact sheet for the University of Florida, says Blue Daze survives "on almost any soil in full sun to partial shade, with light fertilizations . . . . This is almost a no-maintenance plant." When too wet, however, *Rhizoctonia* fungus may set in. This is the fungus that's the cause of damping-off and other diseases of roots and stems. Check with the University of Florida Extension Service for an appropriate fungicide. Cut back the foliage in spring for a fresh start. Protect from cold, or use as an annual in areas where frost regularly occurs. Gilman, in *Betrock's Florida Plant Guide* and Broschart and Meerow in *Betrock's Reference Guide to Florida Landscape Plants* concur that Blue Daze is moderately drought tolerant. For Central and North Florida, Blue Daze may best be kept in containers, using a soilless potting mix. For assurance that the pots drain well, put a layer of terra cotta shards in the bottom and add extra perlite to the mix.

Companion Planting and Design

This tiny Morning Glory (called 'Blue Haze' by Logee's) is wonderful in a pot that accents a shady corner of the patio, or as a ground cover for Yellow Allamanda, Carolina Jasmine, or Yellow Shrimp Plant.

My Personal Favorite

'Hawaiian Blue Eyes' is a nice plant whether in the ground or in a container.

There was a good deal of excitement a few years ago when Blue Daze was new to the area, primarily because of the blue color. But Blue Daze folds up its flowers around midday, so you have to get excited about this first thing in the morning. It can be utilized in planters or containers (where its long branches may drape over the sides), in borders, in beds, and as a ground cover. Blue Daze gives its best color in full sun. The plant is in the Convolvulaceae family. The term convolvo means to "twine around," and the family is full of vines, such as Morning Glories. (Evolvulus is from the term evolvo, meaning "untwist or unravel.") Evolvulus purpureo-coeruleus has ultramarine flowers with white centers and purple lines. (GBT)

Other Name

Hawaiian Blue Eyes

Bloom Period and Color

Year-round blooms in cornflower blue

Mature Height × Spread

12 inches × 10 inches

Zones

10 – 11

Broad Sword Fern
Nephrolepis biserrata

Nephrolepis is an often-cultivated genus of epiphytic Ferns, made famous by Nephrolepis exaltata 'Bostoniensis', or Boston Fern. The fronds of these Ferns are similar: long and linear with varying sizes of pinnae or leaflets. This is a Fern for covering a large area. It is versatile enough to take moist to dry conditions, and dense shade to sun. A cultivar of this is the Fishtail Fern, Nephrolepis biserrata 'Furcans'. This big, billowy Fern has forked ends. It forms beautiful round mounds. Nephrolepis exaltata pinnae are widely spaced and form a sharp tip. There are any number of cultivars of this, including 'Fluffy Ruffles'. Nephrolepis cordifolia, the Tuber Sword Fern, is more controlled in the landscape, with shorter fronds and smaller, regular pinnae. (GBT)

Other Name
Giant Sword Fern

Bloom Period and Color
Year-round foliage

Mature Height × Spread
5 to 6 feet × 4 feet

Zones
10 – 11

When, Where, and How to Plant
Plant at the onset of the rainy season. Plant beneath tree canopies and Palms. These Ferns are wonderful beneath Oaks that drop a lot of leaves, because they absorb them and turn them to mulch. They take moist (not wet) conditions. Pull aside mulch, and make some chicken scratches in the soil, setting the clumps near the surface. Bring mulch back around the clumps. Large clumps are not for small yards. Smaller Ferns, such as the Tuber Sword Fern, can be planted on 12-inch centers; larger Ferns can be set 24 to 36 inches apart. They can cover space in your garden while you plant more permanent Palms or shrubs. And they are good neighbor plants: you can give them away readily; people are always on the lookout for Ferns. All of these Ferns are wanderers, sending out runners beneath mulch to colonize the garden.

Growing Tips
While these Ferns can take drying, they will look better if you irrigate them. With regular watering they will plump up, look lush and full, and spread quickly. In winter, once or twice weekly watering is best. Three or 4 times a year, spray with a fish emulsion or $1/4$ strength 20-20-20 to keep them green.

Regional Advice and Care
Ferns may turn brown over winter if hit by extreme cold or freezing weather, but they will come back. Trim off the brown fronds in the spring. *Nephrolepis multiflora,* and *Nephrolepis hirsuta* 'Superba', are on the invasive exotic plant lists compiled by the Exotic Pest Plant Council. All of these Ferns will travel and invade. Careful cultivation is required.

Companion Planting and Design
The Broad or Giant Sword Fern, which looks at home in a swamp, is an untidy thing that is best suited for a naturalistic garden, where it can roam among trees such as Pigeon Plum and Gumbo Limbo.

My Personal Favorite
Nephrolepis cordifolia, the Tuber Sword Fern, has a more cultivated, less ragged look as a ground cover, though it must be controlled.

When, Where, and How to Plant

Cast Iron Plants can be added at any time of the year. The most stress-free time to plant is the late fall through early spring. Plant in spring and early summer in South Florida. Outdoors it's impossible to find a light level that's too low for these plants. They like a well-drained soil. Work in several inches of compost or peat moss and manure with the existing soil. Space Cast Iron Plants 12 to 18 inches apart. After planting, water the entire planting site thoroughly. Plantings grow slowly but eventually fill in the bed with a dense stand of foliage. Control is needed to keep the shoots from invading nearby plantings. Add a 2- to 3-inch mulch layer to keep the soil moist and control weeds. Provide the first feeding four to six weeks after planting.

Growing Tips

Cast Iron Plants are drought tolerant but make the best growth with a moist soil. During periods of severe drought, provide weekly watering with $^1/_2$ to $^3/_4$ inch of water. Feed Cast Iron plantings once in spring, summer, and early fall. Use a 6-6-6, 12-4-8, or similar fertilizer.

Regional Advice and Care

Cast Iron Plants may be affected by caterpillars and slugs. Hand pick the pests from the plantings, or treat them with a pesticide recommended by the University of Florida Cooperative Extension Service. The Cast Iron Plant is cold sensitive and is frequently damaged in Central Florida by freezing weather. It cannot be grown as a ground cover in the more northern portions of the state but can be established in containers and given winter protection. When the plant is damaged by cold, prune off the brown leaves before spring growth begins.

Companion Planting and Design

Plant with other shade lovers of Jacobinia, Ivy, Asiatic Jasmine, Begonias, Eucharis Lily, and Peacock Gingers. Use as a back drop for smaller plants or as a ground cover.

My Personal Favorite

Plain green is fine but when you can add a little color, go for the more interesting selections. 'Variegata' adds this extra interest with its white-striped foliage.

Need a ground cover just for shade? Then you might like the Cast Iron Plant. The name probably says it all. It's durable, takes most soil conditions, and needs limited care. The Cast Iron Plant can beat out most weeds, so once it's established, you won't have to eliminate unwanted vegetation. Because it cannot take direct sun, it may be the ideal plant for gardeners asking for something for the shade. It produces dark-green foliage that has a tropical and exotic look. Each wide leaf grows to 2 feet long, and there are plenty of them. Use the Cast Iron Plant near the patio, along walkways, in containers, or wherever greenery is desired. One variety, 'Variegata', has green-and-white-striped foliage and grows well in local landscapes. (TM)

Bloom Period and Color
Year-round foliage

Mature Height
2 to 3 feet × 2 feet

Zones
9 – 11

Creeping Fig
Ficus pumila

Creeping Fig is a ground cover that hugs the soil. Its bright-green leaves vary with the stage of plant maturity. When the plants are young and said to be in a juvenile stage of growth, the leaves are small, oval, and 1 inch long. When the plants get older and mature, the leaves are oblong and 2 to 4 inches long. Creeping Fig does flower and produce a fig, but the fruit is inedible. Use Creeping Fig as a ground cover leading up to the turf and walkways, as a wall covering, in hanging baskets, or to cover stuffed topiaries. Numerous selections of Creeping Fig have been made for use in the landscape, including varieties 'Minima' with all-juvenile foliage, 'Quercifolia' with lobed leaves, and 'Variegata' with cream-and-green leaves. (TM)

Bloom Period and Color
Year-round foliage

Mature Height
6 to 8 inches × 3 feet

Zones
8 – 11

When, Where, and How to Plant
Creeping Fig can be planted at any time of the year. The most stress-free time to add Creeping Fig to the landscape is the late fall through early spring season. The plant likes a well-drained soil. Work in several inches of compost or peat moss and manure with the existing soil. Space plants 12 to 18 inches apart. Dig the hole wider than the root-ball but not deeper. Set the plant at the same planting depth as it was growing or a little higher out of the ground. Add soil and water to the hole to make good root-to-soil contact. After planting, water the entire planting site thoroughly. Add a 2- to 3-inch mulch layer to keep the soil moist and control weeds.

Growing Tips
Provide the first feeding four to six weeks after planting. Creeping Fig plantings are drought tolerant but make the best growth with a moist soil. During periods of severe drought, provide moisture weekly with $1/2$ to $3/4$ inch of water. Feed Creeping Fig once in spring, summer, and early fall. Use a 6-6-6, 12-4-8, or similar garden fertilizer at the recommended rates.

Regional Advice and Care
Creeping Fig grows well in all areas of the state. No special care is needed for the different regions. Plant during the rainy season in South Florida. Creeping Fig is an aggressive plant that can climb trees, shrubs, and nearby buildings. Periodic trimming is needed to keep the plantings in bounds. Pests are usually few, but Creeping Fig may be affected by caterpillars. Hand pick the pests from the plantings, or treat them with a pesticide recommended by the University of Florida Cooperative Extension Service.

Companion Planting and Design
Use to disguise a wall or use as a ground cover. It forms an excellent backdrop for sunny annuals of Marigolds and Salvia or shade loving perennials such as Jacobinia and Begonias.

My Personal Favorite
Put a little color in the landscape with a creeping ground cover with cream and green leaves. Select 'Variegata' where you want to attract some extra interest.

When, Where, and How to Plant

Plant Dwarf Carissa in spring, if you can provide irrigation, or at the beginning of the rainy season or throughout the warm months. Carissa is tolerant of many soil types. Plant in full sun. To use as a ground cover, plant on 2-foot centers in staggered rows. Enrich the soil with peat, compost, or well-aged manure so that no more than $^1/_3$ of the backfill is organic. Dig a hole as deep as the container and slightly wider; slip the container off the rootball, and position the shrub in the planting hole; water in the backfill. Mulch, keeping the mulch from direct contact with the shrub trunks to prevent disease.

Growing Tips

Water so that the plant's roots stay moderately moist. If in a windy location, Dwarf Carissa may require watering every other day because wind pulls moisture out of soil and leaves. Three times a year, fertilize with slow-release 14-14-14 containing micronutrients, or with a granular 6-6-6. Slow-release provides nutrients on a steady basis and helps keep a rush of fertilizer out of the water supply.

Regional Advice and Care

Carissa's white flowers are fragrant and produced throughout the warm season. Then, in the fall, small, edible fruit ripen to red, making a good addition to yards that aspire to areas of wildlife habitat. Spider mites, scale, and sucking pests such as mealybugs and thrips can infest Carissa. These can be controlled with a soap and water spray (1 tsp. of liquid Ivory per gallon of water), with alcohol on cotton or malathion. Because the shrub is thorny, use care when working with alcohol and cotton. Carissa may be grown in protected areas in Central Florida.

Companion Planting and Design

As a low-lying shrub, Dwarf Carissa, such as 'Bonsai', 'Horizontalis', 'Nana', and 'Prostrata', are for little niches in a patio or around a pool, especially in gardens near the ocean.

My Personal Favorite

'Boxwood Beauty' is a thornless dwarf form that is easy to handle.

The Atlantic Ocean and Gulf of Mexico are reasons many of us live in Florida. On the East Coast, we boast of summer's southeasterly breezes and remember those Midwest summers of still, hot air and impending tornadoes. The people who live next to the shore, however, often are at a loss for salt-tolerant plants in their gardens. Natal Plum, or Carissa, comes in two sizes: the shrub size, which can reach 10 feet but usually doesn't, and this dwarf form, which can be used as a ground cover. The plants, introduced by David Fairchild, thrive in sandy and alkaline soils, and their thick, waxy leaves won't be torn by wind. The little shrubs are also good for containers on balconies facing the sea, where wind rips and tosses Hibiscus, Weeping Figs, and other trees in large containers. (GBT)

Other Names

Cultivars include 'Horizontalis', 'Green Carpet', 'Emerald Beauty'

Bloom Period and Color

Year-round blooms in white

Mature Height × Spread

1 to 2 feet × 2 to 4 feet

Zones

10B – 11

English Ivy
Hedera helix

For many gardeners relocated to Florida, the English Ivy is the little bit of home they can bring with them. It can fill the problem spots in the landscapes where some quick-growing greenery is needed. Use it in low-light areas, dry spots, and poor soils. Many gardeners have replaced turf in shady areas with Ivy. It's also good on banks and areas along walkways too small for turf. English Ivy can be trained to walls and fences, and used in hanging baskets. Another species worth planting in most areas is Hedera canariensis; its leaves are usually three-lobed, and it grows larger than English Ivy. It is used as a ground cover but must be protected from cold in the more northern portions of the state. (TM)

Bloom Period and Color
Year-round foliage

Mature Height × **Spread**
10 to 12 inches × trailing

Zones
8 – 9

When, Where, and How to Plant
English Ivy can be planted at any time of the year. The most stress-free time to plant English Ivy is the late fall through early spring. It likes a well-drained soil. Work in several inches of compost or peat moss and manure with the existing soil. Space plants 18 to 24 inches apart. Set the plant at the same depth as it was growing or a little higher. After planting, water the entire planting site thoroughly. Add 2- to 3-inch mulch layer to keep the soil moist and control weeds.

Growing Tips
Provide first feeding 4 to 6 weeks after planting. Continue watering to keep the soil moist until the plants are established. Air circulation is required to prevent root and stem rot during the rainy season. English Ivy plantings are drought tolerant but make the best growth with a moist soil. During periods of severe drought, provide weekly waterings with $1/2$ to $3/4$ inches of water. Feed English Ivy once in spring, summer, and early fall. Use a 6-6-6, 12-4-8, or similar fertilizer.

Regional Advice and Care
English Ivy can grow rather rapidly to fill beds. It needs periodic pruning to keep it in bounds and off trees and buildings. English Ivy grows well in the northern and central areas of the state. In Central Florida it is best grown in partially shady to shady areas. English Ivy does not grow well in South Florida. English Ivy may be affected by scale insects and mites. Hand pick, or treat them with a pesticide recommended by the University of Florida Cooperative Extension Service. Leaf spots and rot problems affect plantings that stay too moist.

Companion Planting and Design
Plant in shady spots as a lawn substitute or in beds. Combine with a backdrop of shade loving perennials like Jacobinia, Cast Iron Plant, Begonias, Bromeliads, and Ferns.

My Personal Favorite
You are going to have to search out the better landscape varieties here. Ironically they are simply sold as Old English Ivy selections. Most growers have their favorites for the landscape.

Kalanchoe
Kalanchoe blossfeldiana

When, Where, and How to Plant
Plant any time in full sun to partial shade. Choose well-draining, sandy soil. The standard nursery topsoil, a 50-50 mix of sand and muck, can be used. Even a mix of 70 percent sand and 30 percent muck will do. Space 6 to 10 inches apart. At the time of planting, use 2 teaspoons of slow-release fertilizer with micronutrients either in the plant hole or on top of the root zones, and water in. Cut back the flower heads, called racemes, after the bloom period stops to remove seeds, make the plants neater, and to avoid fungus. Kalanchoes are easy to start from cuttings in the spring. Snip off 4 or 5 inches, remove the bottom leaves, and root in a peat moss-perlite mix that is kept moist and in the shade. Roots should form in 4 to 6 weeks. Or, remove plantlets that form along the stems.

Growing Tips
Use slow-release fertilizer, applying in spring and fall. While the somewhat succulent plants from Africa and Madagascar are wonderfully drought-tolerant when established, you will find that regular irrigation during the spring growing season, and even during the summer if rain is sparse, makes them much more attractive and robust. However, if you want a succulent or rock garden, then they are able to thrive there, too, along with water-thrifty Aloes, Agaves, Crown-of-Thorns, Portulaca, Stapelia (which bears those pointy, balloon-like flowers that open to attract flies), and certain Bromeliads. The important cultural requirements are drainage and protection from summer's intense midday sun.

Regional Advice and Care
Plant in part shade and protect from freezing. Kalanchoes are excellent indoor houseplants, and thrive in an east or west window.

Companion Planting and Design
An excellent ground cover for use around Palms, with Dusty Miller as a fine contrast, with taller and spikier plants, such as Agave or some Cycads, among Bromeliads.

My Personal Favorite
Red-flowering Kalanchoe appears around the winter holidays and adds to the seasonal color.

Kalanchoes are effective plants to add winter color to those far reaches of your garden where you either don't want to water or water infrequently. The leaves store water and are waxy to the touch. The plants are upright when young and somewhat sprawly when full grown. Their size and color make them good candidates for garden edges, where they look pretty against gravel or mulch as well as against greener and more upright plants behind them. Many cultivars of Kalanchoe are sold, and their flowers come in several colors. A related species called K. tomentosa, the Panda Plant, with silver-gray, fuzzy leaves makes a nice houseplant, patio plant, or rock garden specimen. K. pumila has silver leaves with stalks of pink flowers; use as a houseplant. (GBT)

Other Name
Flaming Katy

Bloom Period and Color
Winter and spring blooms in red, yellow, orange, white, and salmon

Mature Height × Spread
1 foot × 1 foot

Zones
10 – 11

Liriope

Liriope muscari

This may be one of the most popular ground covers of recent years. The dark color and slender leaves that spike up and arch over in a small clump make it a nice contrast to St. Augustine, mulch, shrubs, and trees. The drawback is that you cannot walk on it. But many ground covers share that characteristic, so most of us bipeds are well trained not to step on it. Lilyturf takes a wide range of conditions, from sun to shade, well watered to dry. A number of cultivars of Liriope are now sold, including those with silver or gold variegation, and pink, white, blue, or lavender flowers. 'Big Blue' and 'Evergreen Giant' are the tallest, but there also are 'Monroe White', 'Silvery Sunproof', 'Variegata', and 'Variegated Giant'. (GBT)

Other Name
Lilyturf

Bloom Period and Color
Summer and late-summer blooms in white, pink, blue, lavender, or violet

Mature Height × Spread
1 foot × 1 foot

Zones
8 – 10

When, Where, and How to Plant
Plant in the early summer. Liriope is slow growing, and early summer planting will give it a full growing season to take hold. Shade is preferable, although cultivars for sun are available. Be sure to specify where it will be used, and ask your nurseryman or garden center expert for sun-tolerant cultivars if your site is sunny. For covering or edging, plant these 8 to 10 inches apart. The dwarf types can be more closely spaced. Sometimes, if containers are quite full in the nursery, you can simply divide them when planting.

Growing Tips
Fertilize annually in spring. Keep moist for the first month or so to allow the plant to become established. Water in extremely dry weather. In shade, when given too much water from rain or overirrigation, the plants can succumb to fungus. A broad-spectrum fungicide can be used according to directions on the label.

Regional Advice and Care
In Central and North Florida, protect from freezes. The large, arching tufts of Liriope leaves are favorite hatching spots for lubber grasshoppers in South Florida. Lubbers hatch in the early spring, about March, and sometimes can be found by the dozens on just a couple of blades of Liriope. When newly hatched, they don't move for a few hours, and if you spot them, you can step on them—without hurting the Liriope. Once you find a group of the grasshoppers, it's best to check regularly for one or two more weeks. Morning is an ideal time to make grasshopper rounds. Lilyturf does get scale; insecticidal soaps and horticultural oils (in winter) can be used to combat them. 'Webster Wide Leaf' is susceptible to leaf spot, a fungal disease.

Companion Planting and Design
Liriope is one of the great all-purpose ground covers. It is useful when used as a border plant and when planted with shrubs such as Crotons, Brunfelsia, Brugmansia, or even planted with non-living elements in the garden such as decks, steps, or boulders.

My Personal Favorite
The 'Big Blue' cultivar is a sturdy plant where a swath of dark green is needed.

Mexican Bluebell

Ruellia brittoniana

When, Where, and How to Plant

Plant spring through fall. Plant in partial shade (the color will be deeper) to mostly sun. Select a sandy mix with a peat moss component that drains well but can retain some moisture. For ground covers, plant 12 inches apart in staggered rows. With compact types, plant closer to 6 inches on center. Water well to establish, and provide with a time-release fertilizer at the time of planting, either in the planting hole or scattered around the root zones. Cut them back a couple of times a year if you're using the tall variety.

Growing Tips

Water a couple of times weekly in winter, every 2 or 3 days in summer if rain is light. Reapply fertilizer in midsummer and in October. The plants will become light green if they are hungry.

Regional Advice and Care

Snails are fond of the foliage, and tend to collect on these ground covers. Inspect for them early in the morning after a rain, or on a cloudy day. Deadline™ is a snail bait that lasts several days in South Florida's rainy season, and can be used beneath the plants. Experienced growers in Central Florida say Bluebells are weedy, reseeding everywhere. Use care when planting, and pull unwanted seedlings, lest they escape. In North and Central Florida, Mexican Bluebells can be taken back to the ground in winter weather, but usually they resprout from basal buds.

Companion Planting and Design

Try them in beds, to accent yellow-flowering Hibiscus or Walking Iris, to use around yellow-flowering Shrimp Plant, around green and yellow *Schefflera arboricola* or beneath *Cordia lutea*, a small yellow-flowering tree. They also complement purple Verbena and Royal Blue Plumbago, with Golden Shrimp, beneath white Mussaenda for contrasting color, or low-growing Moss Rose.

My Personal Favorite

The dwarf varieties produce low-growing plants with comparatively large flowers. The cultivar *Ruellia brittoniana* (syn.- *Ruellia tweediana*) 'Katie' is blue, and a morning bloomer. (Don't use it near natural areas, as these are invasive.)

Blue flowers are an acquired taste, and some plants shouldn't be forced to produce them—Roses, for instance, or Daisies. The blue flowers of Mexican Bluebells are gloriously blue. This indeed is the blue of the West, a fierce blue, potent and capable, which, when it darkens on its way into the flower's throat, becomes the purple-blue of mesas. The delicately textured flowers open one or two at a time on stalks that develop in the axils of the terminal leaves. They last but one day, so that each morning flowers are fresh again—providing they have been watered and fed sufficiently. A compact line of Mexican Bluebells has been developed, and it is ideal for ground covers. The dark-green, linear leaves form little mounds. A mauve-colored cultivar is available; 'Chi-chi' is a good, tall pink. (GBT)

Bloom Period and Color

Throughout the warm season, blooms in blue, white, pink, lavender

Mature Height × Spread

2 feet × 1 1/2 feet

Zones

10 – 11

Mexican Heather
Cuphea hyssopifolia

Mexican Heather is such a little guy that it almost cries to be used as a ground cover or in a raised pot, close to the eye. As a ground cover, its power is lost if you fail to take care of it. The better care it receives, the larger the leaves and the more flowers it will produce. The size of this dwarf shrub, combined with the cooler color, should tell you that it must be positioned somewhere within a few feet of the viewer, or it won't be noticed. Several cultivars are carried by nurseries, including one called 'Georgia Scarlet', which has flowers shaped like Mickey Mouse. Cuphea ignea has tubular flowers that are red with a black ring, hence the common name, Cigar Plant. (GBT)

Other Name
False Heather

Bloom Period and Color
Spring and summer blooms in white, pink, purple

Mature Height × Spread
1 feet × 2^1/$_2$ feet

Zones
10 – 11

When, Where, and How to Plant
Plant in the spring in South Florida or year-round in Central Florida. Plant in full sun to light shade. To the planting soil add compost, peat moss, or aged manure so the ratio is about 1:3 amendment to original soil. Then, in this enriched soil, place plants about 18 inches apart.

Growing Tips
Keep Mexican Heather, from Guatemala as well as Mexico, well irrigated and fertilized. The plants don't like to dry out completely, or they'll die. Mulching can mediate soil moisture. Fertilize three times a year, or use a slow-release fertilizer, such as 13-13-13 or 14-14-14 with micronutrients.

Regional Advice and Care
Freezing weather will kill branchlets on these little shrubs, but you can prune them back in spring to remove the dead twigs and let them re-sprout. In Central and North Florida, use them in containers, either alone or as edging for a larger plant. Or, consider them as annuals, planting in the summer. The plants are susceptible to nematodes that attack their roots. Nematodes are microscopic worms that can reduce the vigor of plants and ultimately cause their demise by invading the roots, stems, or leaves. Root-knot nematodes interfere with the water and nutrient uptake of plants. Look for round nodules, almost like underground galls, on roots. Nematodes are kept somewhat at bay by keeping plants growing vigorously so root hairs form frequently, and by mulching.

Companion Planting and Design
Use this sturdy miniature shrub in 3-foot urns at the front door, or massed as a ground cover, toward the front of the planting bed, where readily visible.

My Personal Favorite
Purple-flowering Mexican Heather is a good container plant.

Mondo Grass

Ophiopogon japonicus

When, Where, and How to Plant

Mondo Grass can be planted at any time of the year. The most stress-free time to add Mondo Grass to the landscape in Central and North Florida is the late fall through early spring. At that time of the year it is possible to dig and divide clumps. It's hard to find an area in the landscape that has too low a light level for Mondo Grass. The plants like a well-drained soil. Work in several inches of compost or peat moss and manure with the existing soil. Space plants 8 to 10 inches apart. Set the plant at the same planting depth as it was growing in the container. After planting, water the entire planting site thoroughly. A 2- to 3-inch layer of mulch can be added to keep the soil moist and control weeds. Mondo Grass slowly fills in the bed sites. After several years of growth, it may invade nearby areas. Dig out the plants to fill in bare areas.

Growing Tips

Provide the first feeding 4 to 6 weeks after planting. Continue watering to keep the soil moist until the plants are established. Mondo Grass plantings are drought tolerant but make the best growth with a moist soil. During periods of severe drought, provide weekly waterings with $1/2$ to $3/4$ inch of water. Feed Mondo Grass once in spring, summer, and early fall. Use a 6-6-6, 12-4-8, or similar garden fertilizer.

Regional Advice and Care

Mondo Grass grows well throughout all but the most southern portions of Florida. Mondo Grass may be affected by scale insects. Apply an insecticide recommended by the University of Florida Cooperative Extension Service.

Companion Planting and Design

A filler for use along walkways, in large beds or where you need just a little greenery. It's often planted with shrubs of Pittosporum, Dwarf Yaupon Holly, and Indian Hawthorn.

My Personal Favorite

The more dwarf the form, the better I like it. There are a number of selections but 'Nana' is a good dwarf Mondo Grass that does well in our landscape.

Florida gardeners rely upon Mondo Grass as a ground cover for shady areas. It's not a true grass, but the leaves are linear and give a turflike look to landscapes. As with most ground covers, it cannot take foot traffic but can be used among steppingstones for a pathway through the planted areas. The dark-green leaves are about $1/4$ inch wide. Use Mondo Grass on hard-to-mow slopes and along walkways. It can fill in an area near the home, under trees, or in front of shrubs. Mondo Grass often appears in Oriental gardens. This durable ground cover grows where other plants cannot take the poorer, drier soils. Several selections of Mondo Grass have been made for Florida landscapes. One commonly available is 'Nana', a dwarf variety. (TM)

Bloom Period and Color
Year-round foliage

Mature Height × Spread
3 to 4 inches × same

Zones
8 – 10

Shore Juniper
Juniperus conferta

Shore Juniper grows in gardens in the cooler central parts of the peninsula and also on the shore, because this plant is tolerant of salt spray. It does not travel well into the hotter parts of the southern tip of the peninsula and the Florida Keys, but it will grow as far south as Zone 10A. The fresh Juniper smell and the blue-green of the foliage go a long way toward recommending it; the clincher is its toughness on the ocean front. Where wind is a factor, low, ground-hugging plants are among those most likely to succeed. Shore Juniper also is drought tolerant. The Shore Juniper bears cones in the spring. Two culti-vars are available: 'Blue Pacific', a trailing Juniper, and 'Compacta', a compact form. (GBT)

Bloom Period and Color
Year-round foliage

Mature Height × Spread
2 foot × 6 feet to 8 feet

Zones
8 – 10A

When, Where, and How to Plant
Shore Juniper can be planted at any time of the year in North or Central Florida. Place plants in full sun in sandy or well-draining soils. This plant is tolerant of infertile, sandy soils and will form a carpet in bedding areas. To allow the plants to succeed in forming a mat, the Junipers should be planted 18 inches apart. Utilize this ground-hugging conifer in seaside gardens, or on rocky outcrops or rock gardens. The fine texture and gray to blue-green color in these settings are quite striking.

Growing Tips
Don't overwater, or your shrubby ground cover will turn up with brown, fungus-infected patches.

Regional Advice and Care
Let this low-growing shrub have its way, and don't prune it. It will require little from you. Or try training it as a bonsai, wiring it to hang over rock faces or even rock boulders. The "windswept" look that is so desirable in bonsai containers can be acquired in real life if you live next to the ocean and let the wind ply its magic. Shore Juniper grows well all over the state, although in South Florida, spider mites can be a problem. Mites occur in dry weather; they are sucking insects, and usually infest the lowest branches first. You will notice brown foliage at the base of the plant. Miticides are avail-able, but a hard spray of water should be tried first.

Companion Planting and Design
On south-facing condo balconies, Shore Juniper can do well. Allow it to cascade over the sides of low containers. Plant so it will drape over the edges of stepped terraces. Or, use it simply as a full-sun and low-lying ground cover. Near the seashore, this low-lying plant will serve well, mixed with other salt-tolerant plants such as Agave, Indigo Berry, Necklace Pod, Seaside Goldenrod, and simi-lar natives naturally found there.

My Personal Favorite
'Blue Pacific' brings a blue-gray color to the garden as it trails over rocks or timber.

Small Leaf Confederate Jasmine
Trachelospermum asiaticum

When, Where, and How to Plant

Small Leaf Confederate Jasmine can be planted at any time of the year. The most stress-free time to add this Jasmine to the landscape is the late fall through early spring. Plant in the spring or summer in South Florida. It likes a well-drained soil. Work in several inches of compost or peat moss and manure with the existing soil. Space plants 24 to 36 inches apart. Set the plant at the same depth as it was growing or a little higher. After planting, water the entire planting site thoroughly. Add a 2- to 3-inch mulch layer to keep the soil moist and control weeds. The first feeding may be provided four to six weeks after planting. Continue watering to keep the soil moist until the plants are established and send roots out into the surrounding soil.

Growing Tips

Small Leaf Confederate Jasmine plantings are drought tolerant but make the best growth with a moist soil. Where extra growth is needed and during periods of severe drought, water weekly with $^1/_2$ to $^3/_4$ inch of water. Feed this Jasmine once in spring, summer, and early fall. Use a 6-6-6, 12-4-8, or similar garden fertilizer at the rates suggested on the label.

Regional Advice and Care

This plant is easy to grow, but its vining nature calls for periodic trimming to keep it in bounds. Small Leaf Confederate Jasmine grows well in all but the most southern region of Florida. It does not need special winter protection. Small Leaf Confederate Jasmine may be affected by scale insects and white flies. Where necessary, apply an insecticide recommended by the University of Florida Cooperative Extension Service.

Companion Planting and Design

A landscaper's dream for use in the more difficult areas as a lawn substitute and wall covering. Combine with shrubs and trees to fill beds and planters to complete the landscape.

My Personal Favorite

You can make this ground cover planting a bit zestier by using 'Variegatum'. The cream and green foliage is eye-catching.

Many landscape architects choose the Small Leaf Confederate Jasmine as their favorite ground cover due to its versatility. Only a few plants with their vining shoots are needed to fill in relatively large areas of the landscape; the plants are not particular about soil type. This species grows low and is not quite as rampant as the common Confederate Jasmine. Small Leaf Confederate Jasmine is best used in larger areas where you need a reliable dense mat of greenery, for example, under trees where other ornamentals fail to take root, on slopes, and in median strips. It can be used to hang over walls and to cascade from planters. Gardeners can select from 'Variegatum' with cream-and-green foliage, 'Bronze Beauty' with reddish foliage, and 'Minima', a dwarf variety. (TM)

Bloom Period and Color
Year-round foliage

Mature Height × Spread
1 foot × trailing

Zones
8 – 10

Wax Jasmine
Jasminum volubile

Once you know the fragrance of Jasmine, you'll always recognize it. Wax Jasmine is fragrant and sweetly pretty with its starry flowers against the green. It is a hardy plant that's able to endure without irrigation or with little supplemental irrigation. It takes full sun without turning yellow. As the state's population continues to climb, house lots are smaller. Water supplies are becoming more unreliable. Smaller landscape plants such as this can be doubly useful—as a ground cover, it can reduce the area of your garden devoted to thirsty St. Augustine; as a small shrub, it can serve well in small gardens. Jasminum sambac, *Arabian Jasmine, is recommended for Florida's Gulf Coast by David Bar-Zvi in* Tropical Gardening; J. grandiflorum *produces clusters of large flowers in the summer. (GBT)*

Bloom Period and Color
Spring and summer blooms

Mature Height × Spread
2 feet × 3 feet

Zones
10B – 11

When, Where, and How to Plant
Plant in the spring or at the beginning of the rainy season. Choose a location in full sun or partial shade. Prepare a large area with the addition of peat or compost. Once the bed components have been mixed to a depth of about 6 or 10 inches, you can place the plants (in their containers) 24 to 48 inches apart to determine how they look. Dig the hole, slip the container off the plant, and position the plant, backfilling and watering in as you do so. Mulch all the plants once you have finished planting. Mulch in ground cover beds will even out moisture and reduce weeds.

Growing Tips
Water daily for 1 or 2 weeks, reduce watering to every other day for another 2 weeks, then go to 2 times a week if rain is scarce, which sometimes happens in mid-summer. By summer's end, the plants should be growing well. Apply slow-release fertilizer at the time of planting and again in the fall, or a general-purpose 6-6-6 with micronutrients 2 to 3 times a year. Cut back the Jasmine quite hard once a year. Again, this is a springtime chore. Fertilize at this time. Or, if using this in a formal way, you can keep the plants clipped to a hedge. In this case, plant individuals on four-foot centers. By hedging or close clipping, sparse flowers will be even sparser, but it may be a desirable, low hedge for a property line barrier, a formal walk, or green edge around a patio area.

Regional Advice and Care
This is not a plant for cold regions.

Companion Planting and Design
A versatile plant that can serve well in a foundation planting or in a more formal setting because of its ability to be pruned. Use in an all white garden with Begonias, Gardenias, and Stephanotis.

My Personal Favorite
The species is a useful ground cover and suited to clipping for a more formal look.

TRINETTE VARIEGATED
SCHEFFIERA

SCHEFIERA
ARBORICOLA

Wedelia
Wedelia trilobata

When, Where, and How to Plant
Plant Wedelia at any time of the year. The most stress-free time to plant Wedelia is the late fall through early spring, or in the start of the rainy season in South Florida. Wedelia can be started by digging clumps or by removing offshoots from established beds in spring through summer. It likes a well-drained soil. Work in several inches of compost or peat moss and manure with the existing soil. Space plants 10 to 12 inches apart. Set the plant at the same depth as it was growing or a little higher. After planting, water the entire planting site thoroughly. Add a 2- to 3-inch mulch layer to keep the soil moist and control weeds. With proper care Wedelia quickly fills a bed. In time it can overgrow the area; it needs periodic trimming to stay in bounds.

Growing Tips
The first feeding may be provided 4 to 6 weeks after planting. Continue watering to keep the soil moist until the plants are established. Wedelia is drought tolerant but makes the best growth with a moist soil. During periods of severe drought, water weekly with $1/2$ to $3/4$ inch of water. Feed Wedelia once in spring, summer, and early fall. Use a 6-6-6, or 12-4-8, or similar fertilizer.

Regional Advice and Care
Wedelia is limited to the Central and South Florida landscapes. During some winters, it is burned back to the ground by freezing weather. Most landscapers and home gardeners mow or shear the damaged plantings down to near the ground to allow new spring growth. Wedelia may be affected by caterpillars, grasshoppers, and mites. Hand pick the pests, or treat them with a pesticide recommended by the University of Florida Cooperative Extension Service.

Companion Planting and Design
Planted for its greenery and pretty flowers or used in difficult situations as a turf substitute. Combine with bog plantings or flowers of Blue Salvias, Wild Petunia, and Pentas.

My Personal Favorite
Only the species is available in Florida.

In the search to find a colorful ground cover, you should be pleased with Wedelia. Its pretty yellow daisylike flowers open most of the year, and its foliage is bright green. It's suitable for most areas where you need to quickly cover the soil and the planting has to be durable. Use Wedelia under trees, on slopes, in hard-to-mow median strips, and in the areas between the street and the sidewalk. Wedelia is very drought tolerant but also survives in moist soils. Plantings in the deeper shade do not flower as well as those in the full sun, but they blossom occasionally. Some gardeners use Wedelia in planters and hanging baskets. (TM)

Bloom Period and Color
Year-round blooms in yellow

Mature Height × Spread
12 inches × 18 inches

Zones
9 – 11

More Ground Covers

Bugle Weed (*Ajuga reptans*)

Other Name Carpet Bugle; **Bloom Period and Color** Spring through summer blooms in white, pink, or purple; **Mature Height** × **Spread** 10 inches × runner spreading; **Zones** 8 – 10

When, Where, and How to Plant Bugle Weed can be planted at any time of the year. The most stress-free time to plant Bugle Weed is the late fall through early spring. Air movement around the plants is needed to prevent root rot, especially during the rainy season. The plants like a well-drained soil. Work in several inches of compost or peat moss and manure with the existing soil. Space the plants 10 to 12 inches apart. Dig the hole wider than the rootball but not deeper. Set the plant at the same planting depth it was growing in the container or a little higher. After planting, water the entire planting site thoroughly. Add a 2- to 3-inch layer of mulch to keep the soil moist and control weeds. Provide the first feeding four to six weeks after planting.

Growing Tips Bugle Weed is drought tolerant but grows best with a moist soil. During periods of severe drought, provide 1/2 to 3/4 inch of water weekly. Feed Bugle Weed in spring, summer, and early fall. Use a 6-6-6, 12-4-8, or similar fertilizer.

Regional Advice and Care Only partial-sun to shady planting sites are recommended when Bugle Weed is planted in the southern part of the state. The summer heat may limit its use in the extreme southern portions of the state. Bugle Weed may be affected by caterpillars and slugs. Hand pick the pests, or treat with a pesticide recommended by the University of Florida Cooperative Extension Service. Bugle Weed develops a dense foliage cover. It may slowly invade nearby plantings and may need to be removed. Rot problems are a major concern during the summer season.

Purple Queen (*Tradescantia pallida*)

Other Name Purple Heart; **Bloom Period and Color** Year-round foliage and blooms in pink; **Mature Height** × **Spread** 1 foot × 6 inches; **Zones** 9 – 11

When, Where, and How to Plant Plant anytime. Choose a location in full sun with good drainage. For an effective ground cover, space the plants 6 inches apart or weeds will creep in. Prepare the whole bed, adding some compost or peat to it and mixing in well. Set plants in holes dug as deep as the rootball but 2 or 3 times wider, fill in with soil, and mulch.

Growing Tips *Tradescantia* is tolerant of a wide range of soils, but likes to be watered a couple of times a week to look good. However, it has been used on highway medians in South Florida, proving that it can perform well under abusive conditions. Spiderwort, Wandering Jew, and plants in the Tradescantia Andersoniana Group are related to Purple Queen. Use a slow-release fertilizer in spring and fall. It may take a couple of years for the Purple Queen to cover; in the interim, replace mulch every few months. You can easily propagate this plant from tip cuttings by inserting tender stems a few inches long into moistened peat moss with 50 percent perlite. If the soil is kept moist, you may get these cuttings to root right in the beds rather than go through the intermediate stage of a rooting medium.

Regional Advice and Care Cover during freezing weather; prune out damaged parts in spring. Snails like the succulence and you may have to put a copper screening around the bed. Snail bait is toxic to pets, so be careful if you elect to use it. A bait called Deadline is quite effective.

Orchids *for Florida*

Cattleya

The splendor of Orchids is almost impossible to resist if you live in a climate where they can be grown easily. They are among the most romantic of flowers and comprise the largest plant family known, with more than 20,000 species and untold numbers of man-made hybrids.

The Many Faces of Orchids

There are Orchids that look like the back ends of female bees, Orchids that are moon-faced, Orchids that are spiderlike, and Orchids that seem to be playing dead. There are some that are leafless and some with minute flowers that develop right on the leaves. Some flowers are hairy, others are covered with warts, some have tails, and others hold up spiraling horns.

Orchids have become hugely popular in the last decade, with Phalaenopsis Orchids topping the charts. One reason is the long-lasting spray of flowers, which can remain pretty for two months. Commercial Orchid growers have developed highly colored Phalaenopsis blooms, with stripes, spots and splotches vying for attention in colors ranging from tangerine to deep mahogany. Cattleya flowers and plants have been hybridized as windowsill plants, shrinking in size but also becoming more colorful. And Vanda Orchids and relatives are able to produce flowers three or four times a year, rather than once, with smaller but more boldly colored flowers.

With the discovery of Chinese Lady Slippers and a Red Lady Slipper in South America called *Phragmipedium besseae*, the Slipper Orchids have experienced a resurgence in popularity and breeding.

Bulbophyllums, the largest genus of Orchids, are catching the eye of Orchid growers who want unusual flowers. While small (even minute) in size, the flowers of "bulbos" have an interesting lip that rocks back and forth. Some of these flowers can emit a carrion odor.

Enticing perfume is a characteristic of many Orchids. Cattleyas and Encyclicas, for example, may give off rich chocolate or vanilla aromas. Some Orchid growers sell Orchids advertised for their fragrance.

How Orchids Grow

Many Orchids, such as Cattleyas, are air plants, or epiphytes (epi means "upon"; phyte means "plant"). They grow on other plants, most often tree branches, expanding into clumps by means of a rhizome, or a stem from which roots grow downward and shoots grow up. They are not parasites—they take no nutrients away from the tree on which they grow.

To germinate in nature, Orchid seeds have to be infected with a fungus, a fact not known until the turn of the century. It would be years before Orchid scientist L. Knudson would discover how to create an artificial medium in agar on which to germinate seed. After that happened, these once priceless flowers began to soar in popularity. Today, Orchids are grown by people in every walk of life.

Some Orchids do grow in the ground. These "terrestrials" include *Phaius*, or the Nun's Orchid; *Haemaris*, the Jewel Orchids; *Spathoglottis* Orchids, now widely used for mass plantings and as ground covers in South Florida; the Lady Slippers; a few Florida natives such as *Bletia*; and Ladies Tresses, *Spiranthes*.

The epiphytic Orchids most easily grown in South Florida are the Cattleyas and relatives and hybrids, Vandas and several relatives and hybrids, Oncidiums, Phalaenopsis, Dendrobiums, and

Paphiopedilum

86

Paphiopedilums. Cattleyas are sympodial, meaning new growth arises at the base of a parent after the parent has flowered, forming a series of stems. Vandas, Phalaenopsis, and other Orchids are monopodial, meaning they grow on a single stem. Growing in trees, epiphytic Orchids have developed special roots that are photosynthetic, yet covered with a silver-gray coating of cells that absorbs water and protects against desiccation. These roots cling tightly to tree bark or clay pots. Pseudobulbs are water-storage organs. Orchids with pseudobulbs, such as Cattleyas and Oncidiums, require less water than do those without.

Examining Orchid Flowers

Orchid flowers, although wildly dissimilar, have several things in common: the pollen is found in two masses that look like round golden drops of resin, and these are attached to a stalk or column. Also in the column is the female stigma, or the reproductive surface. Insects—bees, flies, and moths—move the pollen mass (pollinia) of one Orchid to the reproductive surface of another, where the pollen germinates.

Seeds develop in pods and are produced by the millions. They have no endosperm, or the starchy tissue that normally feeds embryos; rather, they depend on fungi for food and germination.

Oncidium

Cattleya

Cattleya spp.

This is the queen of Orchids. Two pots of Cattleya 'Mary Felzer' are in my living room holding out the most dazzling golden-throated snow-white flowers you can imagine. Their fragrance swills around the room every morning with the dust motes and sunbeams. Throughout spring and summer, I watched the new shoot develop: the bulge of the "eye" at the base of the last mature stalk; the emergence of the leatherlike leaf; the thickening of the water-storing pseudobulb. Finally, when flower bulbs poked through the protective sheath, they seemed like newborn butterflies testing the air, pumping fluid into their wings, free at last from the confines of their fetal enclosure. I began growing Orchids with Cattleyas. They are extraordinarily tough and make good beginner plants. (GBT)

Bloom Period and Color
Fall blooms white, lavender, purple

Mature Height
20 to 40 inches

Zones
10B – 11 outdoors

When, Where, and How to Plant
"Planting" in the case of Cattleyas means potting or repotting, and that should be done in late February or early March. Soak a clean terra-cotta Orchid pot in water until air bubbles cease rising to the water's surface. Fill with an Orchid-growing mix that drains quickly to within 1 or 2 inches of the top. A Cattleya with 4 or 5 "back" bulbs should be positioned on a tall mound of mix. The new growth should be headed toward the center of the pot. Press the mix so the plant is solidly in place. Use a pot clip to anchor the rhizome; remember to remove it after roots develop to secure the Orchid. Water and place in a shady spot.

Growing Tips
Water every 2 or 3 days, allowing the medium to become almost dry. When growth resumes, put it on a water/fertilizer schedule appropriate to the conditions. Use a high-nitrogen (30-10-10) fertilizer if the medium is primarily bark. Use 20-20-20 every week or two weeks throughout the growing season in a medium-coarse Orchid mix containing charcoal, bark, fern, and perlite, or in straight Aliflor®. In October, switch to a 10-30-20 and use it once a month. Resume the 20-20-20 in March. Cattleyas like a relatively high humidity: 50 to 80 percent. A plant that doesn't bloom usually isn't getting enough light.

Regional Advice and Care
North and Central Florida gardeners can keep Orchids outdoors in trees or shade houses during the warmer months. Protection is necessary for Cattleya Orchids when temperatures approach freezing. To prevent fungus, don't overcrowd your plants. They can take a wide range of temperatures, from upper 90 to upper 30° Fahrenheit.

Companion Planting and Design
Attach Cattleyas to trees with rough bark in 50 percent light. Wire or tie your Cattleya to an Oak or Tabebuia trunk or limb. Or, plant in pots that can be brought inside when the flowers are glorious.

My Personal Favorite
Laelio cattleya Irene Finney 'Chicago' is a sentimental favorite because it was the first I bought as a bare-root plant and it required many years to flower. The big and beautiful lavender flowers were worth the wait.

Dendrobiums

Dendrobium spp.

When, Where, and How to Plant

Plant in the spring. Plant on pieces of cork, in pots in quick-draining medium, such as Aliflor® and charcoal, or on trees in 50 to 70 percent shade in shade houses. As with Cattleyas, when planting Dendrobiums in clay pots, put the oldest back canes against the sides of the pot so new growth heads toward the center. On cork or trees, use florist's tape (or the colored thin copper wires found inside telephone line) to attach the plant. Allow the tape or wire to remain on the plant until roots securely anchor it to the substrate.

Growing Tips

With deciduous plants, withhold most water in winter. There is a fine line between keeping the plant alive and allowing it to dehydrate to the point of death. However, water once a week, rather lightly, splashing a small amount of water its way. When a Dendrobium is overwatered, it may produce off-shoots on the cane. To remove those plants, use a straightedge to cut away a portion of the mother cane with the plantlet, and repot. With evergreen or persistent-leaved plants, reduce the amount of water and fertilizer in winter. When spring arrives, feed and water generously. You can use a 20-20-20 weekly or every two weeks. I use a few drops dish detergent, such as Ivory, to work as a spreader when applying water-soluble fertilizer. A commercial spreader-sticker allows fertilizer to adhere to leaves and roots for the few minutes it takes to be absorbed by the plant. Make sure the sun is shining when spraying liquid fertilizer so the plants can absorb it right away. A few slow-release pellets are fine, too.

Regional Advice and Care

North and Central Florida orchid growers can keep Dendrobiums outside in trees or shade houses during the warm months, but protection is needed when temperatures drop below 50° Fahrenheit.

Companion Planting and Design

Nobile types are wonderful species for attaching to tree limbs—especially to horizontal limbs where they can display their pendant growth, such as *Dendrobium anosmum.*

My Personal Favorite

Dendrobium spectabile produces flowers like curly fries, all twisted and kinked but wonderfully bizarre in their own right.

One of my favorite Dendrobium sights occurs in a tree in my yard. It's a white-flowering Dendrobium phalaenopsis *hybrid. Every fall, it sends out a long and lovely stalk of blossoms that poke their noses out from among tree branches and palm fronds. But what about* Dendrobium phalaenopsis? *Isn't Phalaenopsis a genus in and of itself? Well, yes, and that's what makes Dendrobiums such a challenge. There are many kinds of confusing Dendrobiums. The newest kids on the block are miniature Dendrobiums, which can flower (when pushed) when their canes are a year old. Select plants with moist potting medium, fresh flowers that have not faded or begun to droop, and canes that are nice and plump. After flowers drop, repot into a fast-draining medium. (GBT)*

Bloom Period and Color

Fall, spring, and summer blooms in white, yellow, lavender, rose, maroon

Mature Height

6 inches to 4 feet

Zones

10 – 11 outdoors

Epidendrum
Epidendrum spp.

In the Fakahatchee Strand of the Big Cypress National Preserve, Florida's Orchids still are growing—though in increasingly perilous situations as plant thieves periodically pillage them. The small Epidendrum rigidum is called the Rigid Orchid, grows among Bromeliads on Hammock Trees, and has small, greenish white flowers. Hikers still can see quite a lot of Epidendrum tampense (Encyclia tampensis), producing sprays of green petals and sepals and white lip spotted with magenta. There are Epidendrums still around, however, and it turns out that the Florida native called the Night-scented Orchid, Epidendrum nocturnum, is the model of the rest. Epidendrum nocturnum grows in clumps and has spidery, 2-inch flowers that open one at a time at night. They send a lovely fragrance into the darkness. (GBT)

Other Name
Encyclia

Bloom Period and Color
Spring, and summer blooms in greenish-white, red, yellow, lavender, pink

Mature Height
2 to 3 feet/2 to 6 inches

Zones
10B – 11 outdoors

When, Where, and How to Plant
Plant in the spring when new growth begins. Epidendrums are good candidates for growing on Oak trees since many grow that way naturally in South Florida. If using a terra-cotta pot, plant so that slender roots are embedded in a loose, fast-draining mix, such as charcoal and redwood chips. *Epidendrum radicans* (*ibaguense*) or Reed-stem Orchids, are excellent for using as ground covers in a mulched bed that drains well. They can take morning sun, and even some afternoon sun.

Growing Tips
Water as you would Cattleyas, allowing the plants to almost dry before watering again. Use a soluble 20-20-20 fertilizer every week or two weeks in the growing season. In winter, cut back on water and fertilizer. Use a bloom booster, 10-30-20, monthly in winter. For Epis in the ground, try mixing several colors in individual clumps. The soil must contain sand, perlite, or another material that allows for rapid run-off. A layer of mulch on the surface of the soil will keep in moisture and give the roots ample room for roaming. You may want to stake some of the larger cultivars. To get your Epidendrum garden started, water every day or every other. Fertilize "weakly weekly" at $1/4$ strength, using water-soluble fertilizer. The orange-flowering radicans will develop fairly quickly; others may take longer. Be sure to keep weeds out of the stems. New cultivars, with brighter and larger flowers, are now found at Orchid shows, nurseries, and on the Web.

Regional Advice and Care
Central and North Florida Orchid growers can keep Orchids outside beneath trees or in a shade house during warm months. However, these Orchids require some protection when temperatures drop below 50° Fahrenheit.

Companion Planting and Design
The "reed stem" types—*Epidendrum ibaguense* (*Epidendrum radicans*) and *Epidendrum cinnabarinum*—can be grown in the ground, and together they make an interesting garden of their own.

My Personal Favorite
Epidendrum pseudoepidendrum combines lime green with tangerine orange in a delicate flower that swoops into your field of vision and stays there.

Oncidium

Oncidium spp.

When, Where, and How to Plant

Plant Oncidiums after they flower and new growth begins. Plant on tree crotches, limbs, or the trunks of trees and palms. Use plastic-coated wire, florists' tape, or pantyhose to tie them in place. These Orchids like more light. Full-sized Oncidiums can be acclimated to tolerate sun, especially morning sun. Plant in a fast-draining mix, such as gravel developed for Orchids or Aliflor®, chunks of tree fern with horticultural charcoal, or a general Orchid mix over a layer of polystyrene peanuts. If using a general mix that contains wood chips, be alert to snow mold, a type of fungus, that can form when chips stay wet. This is true if you use tree fern as Orchid media.

Growing Tips

Oncidiums like to stay evenly moist, except for the miniature or Equitant Oncidiums (*Tolumnia*). Equitants like to dry between waterings. The large, soft-leaved types, such as *Oncidium* Sharry Baby, grow in medium to bright light and good air circulation. They like frequent fertilizing during the warm growing season: $1/4$ strength water-soluble fertilizer every week, or $1/2$ strength every two weeks. Consistency is the key. Some experts don't switch to bloom boosters at any time, but continue the same regimen year-round. A bloom booster, used three or four times in the fall, will encourage Orchids to harden the foliage they produced over summer in preparation for cooler and drier weather, and to initiate bud development.

Regional Advice and Care

North and Central Florida Orchid lovers can grow Oncidiums outside during warm months, but bring them in or provide protection when temperature drops below 50 ° Fahrenheit.

Companion Planting and Design

Oncidiums are star performers in trees in South Florida. Four or five bulbs of an Oncidium will multiply into a large clump in just a few years, and produce long, arching sprays of yellowish flowers.

My Personal Favorite

Oncidium sphacelatum 'Sweet Sugar' is a new version of an old favorite that produces flowers with large, bright yellow lips. The common name of *O. sphacelatum* is Golden Shower Orchid and it is a reliable and easy plant to grow.

Oncidiums have all the spots, stripes, and bright color you could possibly want to find in plants, but their flowers are produced in small doses. The plants have round pseudobulbs with long, narrow leaves. I have an often-divided clump of Oncidium sphacelatum *that flowers from its spot in my avocado tree. This ideal kind of Orchid performs consistently with little care. It tolerates all kinds of awful weather, except for freezes. And every spring, a cascade of yellow flowers pours out of the trees. Mule-ear Oncidiums have thick, stiff leaves that look just like their name suggests. They like to dry thoroughly between waterings. These plants are superior for growing outside in trees or pots. Equitant Oncidiums are miniatures that bloom several times a year. (GBT)*

Other Name
Dancing Ladies

Bloom Period and Color
Spring blooms in yellow with brown, maroon, or olive sepals

Mature Height
3 inches to 2 feet

Zones
10 – 11 outdoors

Paphiopedilum
Paphiopedilum spp.

If you love Paphiopedilum Orchids, you have to love them warts and all. Warts are part of the package—as are the balloonlike pouches that someone once believed resembled slippers. You cannot help being drawn to them, whether it's to look at the hairs, peer at the warts, admire the spiraling, ribbonlike sepals, or wonder at the splotched and waxy texture. Many of these Orchids are cool growers, found on high mountains. Be sure to discover the natural habitat and elevation of your choice. These Orchids are terrestrials (or, in some cases, grow on rocks). They like moisture and do not like their roots to dry. A good beginner's Paphiopedilum is P. concolor, now called Concoloria concolor, with mottled leaves and a little cream-colored flower with red dots. (GBT)

Other Name
Lady Slippers

Bloom Period and Color
Summer blooms in white, yellow, green, and combinations

Mature Height
8 inches to 30 inches

Zones
9 – 11

When, Where, and How to Plant
Plant before medium gets mushy, after plants have flowered. The mottled-leaved plants and those that produce flowers successively on one stalk are low-light growers, preferring the same place in the shade house as the *Phalaenopsis* Orchids, about 70 percent shade. The multifloral Paphiopedilum will flourish in brighter light, such as that given Cattleya Orchids, about 50 percent shade. Use a mix that retains moisture, but also drains well. Combine bark, perlite, horticultural charcoal, and chopped spaghnum moss. Or mix tree fern, charcoal, and perlite in equal parts as you might for orchid seedlings. Repot before the mixture turns to mush—these plants are prone to rot if that happens. Repot frequently, every 9 to 12 months—and into a pot the same size; if pot is too large, water will not drain fast enough for these plants and they can get fungus. Use sphagnum moss in your mix or a seedling mix in South Florida conditions. Should your plants develop crown rot, try hydrogen peroxide in the crowns.

Growing Tips
Paphs grow new shoots after flowering and form clumps in their pots. Each new shoot produces a flower. If you get no flowers, you are giving the plant too much nitrogen or too little light. Switch from a balanced 20-20-20 to a 10-30-20. Or increase the light. Or do both. Weak solutions of soluble fertilizer are okay, as is slow-release fertilizer—make sure that the plants don't get a huge dose at one time.

Regional Advice and Care
Paphiopedilum Orchids can be grown outside in North and Central Florida during the warm months, beneath trees, or in shade or lathe houses. When temperatures drop below 50° Fahrenheit, they should have some protection.

Companion Planting and Design
Both elegant and bizarre at once, these can only be grown in pots in South Florida. They should be grown together for company, just as it often is best to grow like with like in the garden.

My Personal Favorite
Paphiopedilum spicerianum has a white dorsal sepal or "lid" bisected by a maroon line, green petals, and a greenish pouch. This is an elegant Lady Slipper.

Phalaenopsis

Phalaenopsis spp.

When, Where, and How to Plant

Plant in the spring after the flowers have died. Keep in the shadowy parts of the shade house. They like more shade than Cattleyas or Vandas. Shadecloth that screens out 70 percent of the light is recommended, though you can grow them with 50 percent. Phals like to have their roots moist but not wet. They like to dry slowly, although never drying completely. Use a large-grade, loose-draining mix, containing perlite, redwood chips or bark, and tree fern, but add sphagnum to retain moisture.

Growing Tips

When watering Phalaenopsis, don't let water remain in the crown. Leaves develop from the center of the plant, pushing out and to the side. As new leaves form, a resulting cup in the crown can hold water; avoid leaving water in the cup. It can lead to crown rot. As plants enlarge, they tend to bend slightly, and this allows water to drain. Use a soluble 20-20-20 every one to two weeks during the growing season. As winter approaches, night-time temperatures drop into the 60s, and days grow shorter, the plants will begin to set buds. In the waning weeks of October, you may add 1 tablespoon of Epsom salts to a gallon of water and switch to a 10-30-20 bloom-booster fertilizer. The Epsom salts will strengthen the flower spike.

Regional Advice and Care

In North and Central Florida, grow Phals outside in shade structures during the warm months. The plants should be protected when the temperature drops below 55° Fahrenheit. Should crown rot occur, use Kocide 101, 1 tablespoon per gallon, to combat it. Physan 20 also combats fungal and bacterial infections.

Companion Planting and Design

Because Phals like a little more shade than many other orchids, these are grown in the same darker area of the shade house. Or attach to a tree limb so their bloom spike is suspended over the side.

My Personal Favorite

The light pink Phals are lovely plants, and there are many from which to choose. Hot pink and raspberry colors are often too harsh. It's hard not to be swayed by white Phals with sunset-colored lips, though.

For pure grace of line, these Orchids are the best. With beautifully shaped sepals and petals and intricately lobed and whiskered lips, Phals are the essence of sophistication and elegance. Their wide, dark-green, and succulent leaves can span 1 foot or more; their flowers can stay unblemished for weeks when kept inside. In addition, the number of flowers is increasing. More than 100 small flowers may hang from many-branched spikes like the daintiest of ornaments. The popularity of Phals has grown wildly in the last decade, and much of this excitement has come from French breeding, which introduced the spots; from German hybridizing, which added the pinks; and from California crossing, which contributed the stripes. The newest trend is flowers with blotches called Harlequin Phals. (GBT)

Other Name

Moth Orchid

Bloom Period and Color

Winter to spring blooms in white, yellow, pink, peach, bronze, orange, yellow with maroon, and spots

Mature Height

8 inches to 16 inches

Zones

10 – 11

Vanda

Vanda spp.

A wonderful thing has happened to the Vandas on the way to the Orchid show. They have taken on the color of the late summer sky just after sundown, the royal inclinations of amethyst, the sheen of golden Buddhas, and subtleties of milky jade. Some flowers are as big as jar lids; some are as small as quarters. Vandas are grouped by their leaf structure, which determines how much sun they require. 'Miss Joaquim' is a terete type, meaning her leaves are as round as soda straws, a reduction in leaf surface that allows teretes to survive in full sun. Semiterete Vandas have hard, V-shape leaves. They can stand full sun in South Florida's winters. Flat-leaved Vandas need shade. Vandas require daily watering (unless it's cool). (GBT)

Bloom Period and Color
Summer blooms in lavender

Mature Height
10 inches to 5 feet

Zones
10 – 11

When, Where, and How to Plant
Plant in March or April in wooden slatted baskets, with or without a medium. Horticultural charcoal or coarse gravel especially for Orchids is the usual medium, which retains some water, as does the wood of the basket. Many people grow them in baskets without any medium, or attached by wire to long S-hooks. You can put a small wooden basket into a larger one, soaking the plant's roots in water until they become pliable, then carefully winding them into the larger basket. Or, you can remove the smaller basket to prevent fungus forming between the wooden slats. To remove keikis (the small offshoots) snip the base of the keiki away from the mother plant when it has several small roots, and wire into a small basket to keep it steady as roots develop.

Growing Tips
Vandas like to be warm and well watered. Water only in the morning to allow water to dry on the leaves. Commercial growers use a very weak fertilizer solution whenever they water. You can get by with soluble 20-20-20 every two weeks in the warm months, once a month in winter.

Regional Advice and Care
Bring Vandaceous Orchids inside when temperatures reach 55 to 50° Fahrenheit. In Central and North Florida, they can be grown outside in warm months. Use Kocide® when you see fungal spots on the leaves. These are black spots surrounded by a yellow halo. Viral infections cause black spots and streaking on leaves and can affect flowers. Little can be done for viruses other than destroying the infected plant and using sterile tools. Never use secateurs (clippers) on more than one Orchid without sterilizing them between cuts. Dirty tools spread viruses.

Companion Planting and Design
Attached to the east side of a palm trunk, fastened to the slender stems of *Dracaena marginata,* or in wooden baskets or even on an S-hook with its roots hanging free in the air.

My Personal Favorite
There are many gorgeous hybrids in this group. The related *Rhyncostylis gigantea* is wonderfully citrus-scented and half a dozen cultivars have found their way into my collection.

Ornamental Grasses *for Florida*

Almost everyone has some turf but it's not the only grass that grows in the landscape. You can also use grasses as ornamental plants. Most are native types plus there are a few species from other countries. Like lawn grasses, the ornamental types are tough—but none makes a good lawn. For one thing, they grow too tall and they form clumps that spread out very slowly. Actually this makes them the ideal landscape plantings as they won't take over the garden with unwanted greenery. Most of the year they have attractive foliage and each offers some unique garden color.

Planning for Ornamental Grasses

Now the big question is: Where do you use ornamental grasses? Well, they simply double for other ornamental plantings. Taller types, including the Fountain Grasses, Pampas Grass and Sand Cordgrass, can act as view barriers that hide some of the things you would rather not have visitors see such as work areas and ugly fences. They also form good space dividers between areas of the landscape. Others, including Muhly Grass, Purple Lovegrass, and Wiregrass, serve as ground covers just a foot or two

in height. Ornamental grasses can be used as border plantings, along flower beds, or other shrub plantings. Many types also make a great backdrop for annual, perennial, and vegetable gardens.

Fountain Grass

Their Unique Features

Perhaps where ornamental grasses really shine is as accent features. The foliage alone is different than other ornamentals used in the landscape, being long and thin bladed, easily blown up by the winds to add some interest. Most stems of foliage grow upright with the ends of the leaf blades gracefully turning downward. Some have arching stems with leaves that reach out to touch one another. Most are in bloom when other plantings have stopped providing good seasonal color from midsummer through fall. And the inflorescence is unique, usually creating a feathery plume of color that can range from silver to pink, red, purple, and brown. Many of the flowers and seed heads yield feed and nesting materials for wildlife. And who hasn't collected the long plumes from Pampas Grass? Creative gardeners like to save these flower heads and others to use in dried arrangements.

You can plant clusters of ornamental grasses as barriers or just a few plants as an accent. Perhaps you would like a whole bed of grass to use as a ground cover. The grasses can create a prairie feeling for the landscape and become part of the natural Florida look. As you can guess most are very drought tolerant but do grow best with good care. They are great plants for the dry land setting used to conserve water in the landscape. However, they too tend to go dry during excessively dry periods. Good landscape combinations for grasses include the Palmettos, Scrub Oaks, native wildflowers, and dry land Hollies.

Planting Considerations

Ornamental grasses should be planted in well-drained areas of the landscape. Most are accustomed to the drier soils and may decline with wet feet. They also need sunny sites so find an open area with 6 to 8 hours of direct light. Plantings can be made in Florida's infertile sands, but care is often better if the soil is improved with organic matter. Give the grasses plenty of room to grow. It is a good rule to leave a distance equal to the expected height of the plants between neighboring grasses. Remember most are going to reach out and intertwine with each other. Some types with a more upright growth habit should get a little closer spacing. These include the Lopsided Indiangrass and Sand Cordgrass.

Plant ornamental grasses at the same depth as they were growing in their containers. Those already growing in the landscape can also be divided and set at the same level in the ground. Water the plants well to make good soil-to-root contact. Then keep the soil moist to help the roots grow out into the ground. Apply a 2- to 3-inch mulch to help prevent weeds. During early growth some weed control is normally needed to keep broadleaf weeds and other grasses from competing with the plantings. Most can be hand pulled from the beds, but a non-selective herbicide made for spot weed control among ornamental plantings can also be utilized.

A Little Care

Once the root system is established in the surrounding soil most ornamental grass can exist with minimal care. Native types are especially adapted to surviving with just moisture from rain. They also make needed growth using nutrients found in the rainwater plus decaying organic matter deposited on the soil surface. Growth is slow under these conditions and the grasses may not be as attractive as desired in the home landscape, but the native look is often sought in natural areas of the landscape. Most gardeners prefer to give the plantings a little better care: watering, especially during periods of drought, or as needed to encourage growth. For the best look most ornamental grasses should receive water from rainfall or irrigation once a week. Applications of lawn fertilizer can be made in February, June, or September. It's best to avoid using lawn fertilizers containing a weedkiller as the sensitivity of most ornamental grasses to herbicides is unknown.

The grasses make lots of growth spring through summer and by fall most are flowering and producing seeds. The plants also start to decline during fall and into the winter months. Maturing portions of many types turn brown, bronze,

Dwarf Pampas Grass

and reddish-colors often associated with the fall season. During the winter season many of the stems sag, and gardeners should make plans to remove the old shoots, foliage, and seed heads before spring growth begins.

Sometimes it's best to just trim the plants back close to the ground. Cut the lower growing types to within a few inches of the ground and taller selections to about a foot high. Many grasses have very sharp blades, so be sure to wear protective clothing. Heavy pruning encourages bright, new, green growth as spring begins.

Ornamental grasses are perennials, and after a period of time become crowded. Some types or varieties die out leaving an open center with shoots around the outer edges. Every three to five years the beds may need rejuvenation. At this time it's best to dig the clumps and divide them into new sections for plantings. Also improve the soil with organic matter and till the ground deeply before adding the grass. Ornamental grasses have few pest problems: caterpillars may feed on the foliage but are normally not numerous enough to need control.

Ornamental grasses add much to the landscape as accent features: their foliage serve as the perfect foils to other landscape plants, and with the wind's cooperation can add movement as another desirable dimension to the garden.

Florida Gamma Grass
Tripsacum floridana

If you need a low-growing, clumping grass for sun or light shade, consider Florida Gamma Grass. Plantings grow between 1 and 2 feet tall, and are as wide. The grass blades are bright green with a narrow white stripe along the midrib. In most areas of the state the grass remains evergreen until frosts and freezes arrive. The 1/2-inch-wide arching leaves add a light, airy feeling to landscapes. Flowering stems are produced above the foliage during the fall and provide golden-brown color. Use this grass as a groundcover. Its tolerance of most soil types makes it versatile in the landscape. This is a plant for difficult moist condition, when other ornamentals are not suitable. It can be clustered among shrub plantings as a small accent. (TM)

Other Name
Dwarf Fakahatchee Grass

Bloom Period and Color
Fall blooms in golden brown

Mature Height x Spread
1 to 2 feet x 2 feet

When, Where, and How to Plant
Florida Gamma Grass can be planted at any time of the year. The best planting time is between March and August when the grass is making good growth. Prepare a bed by working in liberal quantities of compost and peat moss plus manure. Space plants 24 to 36 inches apart. If the rootballs are tightly intertwined with roots, they should be lightly loosened to encourage new growth into the surrounding soil. Dig the holes wider but not deeper than the rootball, and set the plants in the ground at the original planting depth. After planting moisten the entire planting site and add a 2- to 3-inch mulch layer.

Growing Tips
Once established, they can exist with moisture from the rains and nutrients from decaying organic matter. Water weekly during the drier times of the year. Florida Gamma Grass can be fed with a general garden or lawn fertilizer once in February, June, and September. Follow lawn rates or just apply a light scattering of fertilizer.

Regional Advice and Care
Expect Florida Gamma Grass to turn brown in the colder areas of the state. In these areas, a late-winter pruning is needed to rejuvenate the plantings. Florida Gamma Grass is evergreen in the milder portions of the state. Where frost and freezes are common, it turns brown during the winter months. If needed, schedule a pruning to rejuvenate the planting during late winter. Florida Gamma Grass can be cut back to within 6 inches of the ground. After the pruning apply the winter feeding to encourage new growth. Caterpillars may feed on the foliage during the growing season but are seldom a serious problem.

Companion Planting and Design
Cluster plants together to create a fall accent or use them as a groundcover for native plant settings with Asters, Gaillardia, Liatris, Coreopsis, Iris, Bush Daisies, and other grasses.

My Personal Favorite
Only the species is available in Florida.

Fountain Grass

Pennisetum setaceum

When, Where, and How to Plant

Fountain Grass can be planted any time of the year. The best planting time is between March and August. Plantings should be made in sites that receive 6 to 8 hours of full sun and are bright throughout the remaining portions of the day. Prepare a bed for planting by working liberal quantities of compost or peat moss and manure into the soil. Space plants 24 to 30 inches apart. If the rootballs are tightly intertwined, loosen the roots a little to encourage new growth. Dig the holes wider but not deeper than the rootballs and set the plants in the ground at the original planting depth. After planting, moisten the entire planting site and add a 2- to 3-inch mulch layer. When the first real cold weather arrives, the grass begins to decline and finally turns totally brown.

Growing Tips

Grasses take minimal care. Once established, they can exist with moisture from rains and nutrients from decaying organic matter. Fountain Grass makes the best growth if watered during periods of drought. As a general rule, water weekly during the drier times of the year. Fountain Grass can be fed with a general garden or lawn fertilizer once in February, June, and September. Follow lawn rates or just apply a light scattering of fertilizer.

Regional Advice and Care

Throughout the warmer portions of the state, Fountain Grass may remain semievergreen for most of the winter. In Northern and Central Florida, it turns brown with the first frosts and freezes. It needs rejuvenation pruning by late winter. Caterpillars may feed on the foliage during the growing season but are seldom a serious problem.

Companion Planting and Design

Plant as a ground cover, or colorful accent for the landscape. Plants can also be used as stand alone view barriers or a backdrop for annual and perennial flowers or shrubs.

My Personal Favorite

Grasses can be just a mass of green but you can add lots of interest to this planting by growing 'Rubrum' which has a good reddish color.

Fountain Grass is one of the more popular ornamental landscape grasses for home landscapes. The foliage is bright green, about $1/4$ inch wide. Leaves are arching, often with the outermost rows touching the soil. Fountain Grass is added to perennial beds for an accent, and often used as a ground cover. Plantings remain green late into the fall but start to brown with the first hint of winter. Fountain Grass can be used in natural plant settings with a Florida look. A number of varieties of Fountain Grass are available, including dwarf forms that are ideal for containers and other types with colorful foliage. The most popular is Purple-leaf Fountain Grass, which grows to 5 feet tall. There are also reddish and copper-leaved forms available. (TM)

Bloom Period and Color
August to October blooms in pink to purple

Mature Height x Spread
3 feet x 3 feet

Lopsided Indiangrass

Sorghastrum secundum

Lopsided Indiangrass grows foliage to only 2 feet tall but can send up flower spikes that grow to 6 feet in height. This is a native clump-forming grass that ranchers refer to as "wild oats." It has a large seedhead with flowers and seeds borne on one side of the stalk, similar to oats. The leaves are light- to medium-green. They are about 1/2 inch wide and 24 inches long. During the fall the plant declines to a golden-brown color that matches the maturing seed stalks. Seed stalks may be used in dried flower arrangements. Gardeners may also want to plant a similar species known as Indiangrass, Sorghastrum nutans. Plantings turn a yellow to orange during fall and grow to about 5 feet tall. (TM)

Bloom Period and Color
Fall blooms in golden brown

Mature Height x Spread
2 feet (foliage) 6 feet (flowers) x 2 feet

When, Where, and How to Plant
Lopsided Indiangrass can be planted at any time of the year. The best planting time is between March and August. Lopsided Indiangrass is tolerant of light shade. Plantings are best made in landscapes that receive 6 to 8 hours of full sun and are bright throughout the remaining portions of the day. Lopsided Indiangrass is tolerant of varying growing conditions including damp soils. Prepare a bed by adding liberal quantities of compost or peat moss and manure. Space plants 18 to 24 inches apart. If the rootballs are tightly intertwined at planting, loosen them a little to encourage new growth out into the surrounding soil. Dig the holes wider but not deeper than the rootball, and set the plants in the ground at the original planting depth. After planting moisten the entire planting site and add a 2- to 3-inch mulch layer. During the fall the grass turns golden brown and begins to decline after producing flowers and seedheads.

Growing Tips
Grasses take minimal care. Once established they can exist with moisture from rains and nutrients from decaying organic matter. Lopsided Indiangrass makes the best growth if watered during periods of drought. Water weekly during the drier times of the year. Lopsided Indiangrass can be fed with a general garden or lawn fertilizer once in February, June, and September. Follow lawn rates or just apply a light scattering of fertilizer.

Regional Advice and Care
Northern and Central Florida plantings may mature earlier than Southern plantings. All need rejuvenation pruning by late winter. Caterpillars may feed on the foliage during the growing season but are seldom a serious problem.

Companion Planting and Design
Plants clusters to create a groundcover for a golden fall accent or mix with perennials including Gaillardia, Black-Eyed Susans, showy Primrose, Goldenrod, and Asters for a native Florida look.

My Personal Favorite
Only the species is available in Florida.

Muhly Grass

Muhlenbergia capillaris

When, Where, and How to Plant

Muhly Grass can be planted at any time of the year. The best planting time is between March and August. For best flowering, Muhly Grass plantings should be made in landscape sites that receive 6 to 8 hours of full sun and are bright throughout the remaining portions of the day. Gardeners can improve sandy soils with organic matter before planting. Space plants 12 to 18 inches apart. If the rootballs are intertwined at planting they can be loosened a little to encourage new growth. Dig the holes wider but not deeper than the rootball and set the plants in the ground at the original planting depth. After planting, moisten the entire planting site and add a 2- to 3-inch mulch layer. During the fall Muhly Grass begins to decline after producing colorful flowers and seedheads.

Growing Tips

Grasses take minimal care. Once established, they can exist with just moisture from rains and nutrients from decaying organic matter. Muhly Grass makes the best growth if watered during periods of drought. Water weekly during the drier times of the year. Muhly can be fed with a general garden or lawn fertilizer once in February, June, and September. Use one half the lawn rates or just apply a light scattering of fertilizer.

Regional Advice and Care

Northern and Central Florida plantings may brown earlier during the fall due to the arrival of cool weather. Muhly Grass growing in all areas of the state does need late winter rejuvenation to produce attractive spring growth. Caterpillars may feed on the foliage during the growing season but are seldom a serious problem.

Companion Planting and Design

Plant a large bed as a ground cover or just small patches among other natural plantings. Enjoy the fall color when mixed with other grasses, Asters, Goldenrod, and Daisies.

My Personal Favorite

Only the species is available in Florida.

It's easy to tell when fall arrives by the coloring up of the attractive Muhly Grass in Florida landscapes. Pink to purple flower clusters form high above the foliage to create an accent planting any gardener would love. The leaf blades are thin and bright green during the spring and summer months to create mounds of foliage. Use Muhly Grass in border plantings where some fine delicate foliage is needed. Add it to perennial gardens and natural settings. It's a great groundcover for drier areas. During late fall the plantings turn brown with the onset of colder weather. Muhly Grass is best planted where there is room to add clusters of plants to get the best effect from the fall color. (TM)

Other Name
Pink Muhly

Bloom Period and Color
Fall blooms in pink to purple

Mature Height x Spread
3 feet x 3 feet

Pampas Grass

Cortaderia selloana

One of the most sensational ornamentals for the Florida landscape is Pampas Grass, introduced from South America. It's a good grass to use in coastal areas due to its salt tolerance. The foliage is bright green, up to an inch in width, and quite sharp. Keep Pampas Grass away from pedestrian traffic to prevent injuries from brushing against the foliage. In warmer areas of the state it may remain evergreen throughout the cooler months, but it usually turns brown after the first periods of cold. It's a favorite to cut and add to dried arrangements. Some selections include 'Gold Band', 'Silver Stripe', and 'Sun Stripe' with variegated leaves. Gardeners can also add 'Rubra' with pink and 'Pumila', a dwarf for perennial beds and containers. (TM)

Bloom Period and Color
Late summer and fall blooms in white to pink

Mature Height x Spread
8 feet x 8 feet

When, Where, and How to Plant

Pampas Grass can be planted at any time of the year. The best time to plant is between March and August. For best flowers plant in landscape sites that receive 6 to 8 hours of full sun and are bright throughout the remaining portions of the day. Pampas Grass forms large clumps and needs plenty of room. It's not well suited to small landscapes. Prepare a bed by adding compost or peat moss and manure. Space plants 36 to 48 inches apart. If the rootballs are intertwined at planting, loosen the roots a little to encourage new growth. Dig the holes wider but not deeper than the rootballs and set the plants in the ground at the original planting depth. After planting moisten the entire planting site and add a 2- to 3-inch mulch layer. During the fall, Pampas Grass begins to decline after producing flowers and seedheads.

Growing Tips

Grasses take minimal care. Once established, they can exist with just moisture from rains and nutrients from decaying organic matter. Pampas Grass makes the best growth if watered during periods of drought. Water weekly during the drier times of the year. Pampas Grass can be fed with a general garden or lawn fertilizer once in February, June, and September. Follow lawn rates or just apply a light scattering of fertilizer.

Regional Advice and Care

Northern Florida growers can expect winter damage to their plantings. Keep the plants well mulched to prevent plant loss. All Pampas Grass needs pruning prior to spring growth. Caterpillars may feed on the foliage during the growing season but are seldom a serious problem.

Companion Planting and Design

Form an eye-catching accent, view barrier, or backdrop for gardens with groupings of Pampas Grass in the landscape. Add other grasses or contrasting native shrubs, perennials, and annual flowers for accents.

My Personal Favorite

Add a bit more interest to your Pampas Grass planting by selecting one with a little color. 'Rubra' has a pinkish cast which creates a stronger accent in gardens.

Purple Lovegrass
Eragrostis spectabilis

When, Where, and How to Plant

Purple Lovegrass can be planted at any time of the year. The best planting time is between March and August. Plantings of Purple Lovegrass should be made in landscape sites that receive at least 6 to 8 hours of full sun and are bright throughout the remaining portions of the day. Prepare a planting bed with compost or peat moss and manure. Space plants 12 to 18 inches apart. If the rootballs are tightly intertwined at planting, loosen the roots a little to encourage new growth out into the surrounding soil. Dig the holes wider but not deeper than the rootball and set the plants in the ground at the original planting depth. After planting moisten the entire planting site and add a 2- to 3-inch mulch layer. During the fall, Purple Lovegrass begins to decline after producing flowers and seedheads.

Growing Tips

Grasses take minimal care. Once established, they can exist with just moisture from rains and nutrients from decaying organic matter. Purple Lovegrass makes the best growth if watered during periods of drought. Water weekly during the drier times of the year. Purple Lovegrass can be fed with a general garden or lawn fertilizer once in February, June, and September. Follow lawn rates or just apply a light scattering of fertilizer.

Regional Advice and Care

Northern and Central Florida plantings may decline sooner than Southern Florida plantings due to early frosts and freezes. All do need trimming by late winter to renew the foliage during spring. Caterpillars may feed on the foliage during the growing season but are seldom a serious problem.

Companion Planting and Design

Use this pinkish flowered grass in clusters as a ground cover or late summer accent. Mix with native shrubs or wildflowers of Gaillardia, Asters, Daisies, Goldenrod, and Black-Eyed Susans.

My Personal Favorite

Only the species is available in Florida.

Catching the wind a foot or more above the foliage, the reddish purple flowers of Purple Lovegrass create a cloud of color and an excellent accent for the fall landscape. Plant large beds of this native clumping ornamental to enjoy what may be Florida's most attractive grass. Leaves of the grass are thin and offer good green growing compact mounds of foliage. During fall the foliage turns a reddish color that adds extra interest to the landscape. Use Purple Lovegrass as a replacement for one of your not-so-colorful ground covers, or add it to natural landscape areas for a real Florida look. Many gardeners also like to use the colorful inflorescence in dried arrangements. See 'Elliott' Lovegrass for another species to add to the landscape. (TM)

Bloom Period and Color

Fall blooms in reddish purple

Mature Height x Spread

2 feet x 2 feet

Sand Cordgrass
Spartina bakeri

Sand Cordgrass is one of Florida's wetland grasses for use lakeside and in marshlands. Plantings grow upright with a slight curve to the ends of the foliage. Leaf blades are about a quarter-inch wide, light green on the surface and dark green below. Florida ranchers refer to the clumps in the wetlands as Switchgrass, perhaps due to the long flexible stems. Flower heads arise above the foliage. Some gardeners cut the flower heads for use in dried arrangements. Plant Sand Cordgrass in wetland gardens and natural settings where the soil can be kept moist until the plants are established. Lake and canalside gardeners can consider Sand Cordgrass for use as a space divider, view barrier, and accent plantings. (TM)

Other Name
Switchgrass

Bloom Period and Color
May through June blooms in brown

Mature Height x Spread
5 feet x 5 feet

When, Where, and How to Plant
Plant at any time of the year. The best planting time is between March and August. Plantings should be made in landscape sites that receive 6 to 8 hours of full sun and are bright throughout the remaining portions of the day. Sand Cordgrass is a native bunch grass that prefers moist soil, but once established can tolerate dry conditions. It also needs plenty of room to grow and may not be suitable for small landscapes. Select only sites that can be kept moist. Prepare a bed by tilling in compost and peat moss plus manure. Space plants 48 to 60 inches apart. If the rootballs are tightly intertwined, loosen the roots a little to encourage new growth. Dig the holes wider but not deeper than the rootball, and set the plants in the ground at the original planting depth. After planting moisten the entire planting site and add a 2- to 3-inch mulch layer. During the fall, Sand Cordgrass begins to decline, turning a brownish color.

Growing Tips
Once established, Sand Cordgrass can exist with just moisture from the wetlands and nutrients from decaying organic matter. Water weekly during the drier times of the year. Sand Cordgrass can be fed with a general garden or lawn fertilizer once in February, June, and September. Use one half the lawn rates or just apply a light scattering.

Regional Advice and Care
Expect Sand Cordgrass to turn completely brown in the colder areas of the state. Some green may remain in the base of the plantings in warmer locations. Caterpillars may feed on the foliage during the growing season but are seldom a serious problem.

Companion Planting and Design
Create a view barrier or backdrop for a garden with seasonal flowers as accents. Also use as a ground cover grouped with Dwarf Yaupon Holly, Indian Hawthorn, and Junipers.

My Personal Favorite
Only the species is available in Florida.

Wiregrass
Aristida beyrichiana

When, Where, and How to Plant

The best planting time is between March and August. Wiregrass plantings should be made in landscape sites that receive 6 to 8 hours of full sun and are bright throughout the remaining portions of the day. Wiregrass grows well in the sandy landscape sites where it gets minimal maintenance. This actually helps prevent weeds of unwanted greenery from becoming established with the grass. Space plants 12 to 18 inches apart. When using transplants dig the holes wider but not deeper than the rootball and set the plants in the ground at the original planting depth. After planting moisten the entire planting site and add a 2- to 3-inch mulch layer. Wiregrass seed can also be sown in early winter. During the fall, Wiregrass begins to decline after producing flowers and seedheads.

Growing Tips

Once established, Wiregrass can exist with just moisture from rains and nutrients from decaying organic matter. It makes the best growth if watered during periods of drought. Water weekly during the drier times of the year. Fertilizer is not needed but can be used to speed growth with light feedings of a general garden or lawn fertilizer once in February, June, and September. Use one half the lawn rates or just apply a light scattering.

Regional Advice and Care

Culture of Wiregrass is similar throughout the state. It may start the winter decline earlier in Northern and Central Florida due to cool weather. It should be given a rejuvenation pruning each year in all areas of the state. Caterpillars may feed on the foliage during the growing season but are seldom a serious problem.

Companion Planting and Design

Create the Florida look with clusters or beds of Wiregrass as a ground cover among other native plantings of Wax Myrtle, local Hollies, Asters, Goldenrod, Pines, Palmettos, and Liatris.

My Personal Favorite

Only the species is available in Florida.

Wiregrass creates the natural Florida look many gardeners are trying to develop in large areas of the landscape. It needs the full sun to produce summer-through-fall fields of golden flower heads. This plant is a natural for wildflower plantings, seeming to give protection to the growing broadleaf plantings. This is a bunch-type grass that is best used in wide open spaces with other wildflowers or used alone as a groundcover. The leaves are wiry, quite thin, and upright to arching. With time plants grow to a mounded shape and to 1 and 1½ feet tall. Perhaps Wiregrass's greatest asset is its ability to grow in the poorer soils. It's ideal for use in site restoration plantings. (TM)

Bloom Period and Color
Summer through fall blooms in yellow

Mature Height × Spread
1½ feet × 1½ feet

Palms *for Florida*

Palm trunks, like those of trees, are individual, varying in their degree of lean, sway, and uprightness, in color and texture, in stoutness and thinness. Fronds or leaves of Palms can be blue-gray or olive-green, yellow-green or deep-green. The new leaves may emerge red or wine-colored. The fronds are either pinnate (feather-shaped) or palmate (shaped something like the palm of your hand). But within these two forms are variations on a theme: long and graceful pinnae (individual leaflets) or short, stubby ones; great, round, and stiff palmate fronds or deeply incised and graceful ones.

The flowers, which are tiny when seen alone, often are pretty sprays when seen as a whole on the branching flower stalk. Fruit is scarlet to deep-purple, blue-green or white, yellow or black, and can range from coconuts to dates to inedible little berries.

To Know Them Is to Love Them

Palms are like cats in many ways: you have to get to know them to see the gradations in character, from sober to puckish, from aloof to endearing. And one cat by itself will never do; cats must come in multiples. Unless it is a massive and handsome specimen, a Palm by itself is a lonely character indeed. It cries out for friends, for companionship of kind. Use them in groups. Make them taller and shorter within the group. Let them mingle like company at a cookout. To regiment them militarily is unnatural for them—they grow in groups and clusters, not in straight rows and long lines. (Royals, by virtue of their regal bearing, are used singly for property line markers or on either side of an entry. The caveat in doing so is their scale, which may be too large for small properties.)

Some Palm trunks are attractively marked, like those of Cabada Palms, which are green with distinct white rings rather like Bamboo. Some Palm trunks are clothed in fibers. The Lady Palms are wrapped

Pygmy Date Palm

in dark-brown to black fibers along their slim trunks. The Cabbage or Sabal Palms have a natural coating of old leaf stems called boots. *Coccothrinax miraguama*, a relative of the Florida Silver Palm, has matting that seems carefully handwoven on a loom.

In the wild, you find all kinds of things growing in this fiber or in the old leaf stems. I've seen a snake curled in the boot of a Cabbage Palm, dozing in contentment. Ferns love to germinate there, and Bromeliads and Orchids can lodge themselves into a boot as naturally as can be. If they don't do this on their own in your garden, you can help them along.

In rain forests, you find all manner of other plants growing on Palm fronds, though that seldom occurs in Florida. In your Florida garden, you can train Philodendrons up the trunk of a Palm for a tropical look.

Many Palms are cold tolerant and drought tolerant. In the wild, they can be found on the sides of mountains. Some species can also be flood tolerant.

One of my favorite sights is Palm fronds in moonlight. We are accustomed to our plants' shapes and colors in daylight, but at night they take on an ethereal quality. If there is the slightest breeze on a night of the full moon, the fronds (particularly the feathery or pinnate fronds) move magically and most beautifully.

My own garden is full of Palms, including the quick-growing Washingtonia Palm used to provide height in the background, and the Bailey Palm. I also have a Triangle Palm, which, like all other Palms, sends up one spear at a time, then somehow moves it into one of three trajectories so that the crown forms a perfect triangle. The Bottle Palms are flowering now after many years of growing fat bellies, and the upright, handsome Foxtails are beginning to produce bright-red seeds. I have four kinds of Licuala Palms because I love their orbicular, pleated fronds. The Hurricane Palm, *Dictyospermum album*, two species of *Aiphanes*, several species of *Coccothrinax* and *Thrinax*, *Cabada*, and different species of shade-loving, small Palms in the Chamaedorea genus also are included in my garden. These Palms are in groups, with beds of Bromeliads or Ferns at their feet. I've attached Orchids and Bromeliads to the trunks of some; others have been unwitting hosts to Ferns.

Growing Tips

You have to do some gardening things to grow Palms well, especially in alkaline soils or infertile sands. Palms in alkaline conditions often show micronutrient deficiencies, and a palm fertilizer has been formulated especially for them. It is 12-4-12-4, the last 4 being magnesium. The two 12s are nitrogen and potassium needed in equal amounts, and because they both leach from soil, they are in slow-release form in this particular fertilizer. The first 4 is phosphorus, which is especially plentiful in rocky soil of Dade and Broward Counties and the lower Keys. The abundance of phosphorus, which chemically ties up other micronutrients, means little more is needed.

Palms have the built-in ability to pull potassium from aging leaves, which is why pruning off old leaves interferes with the nutritional cycle of the plant. Wait until the entire frond has turned brown to prune it if it is not "self-cleaning"—meaning the fronds drop of their own accord.

Most Palms require water, fertilizer, and, in the event of a freeze, cold protection. But they are lovely creatures to have around, and like cats, once you have them, you'll wonder what you did without them.

Areca Palm
Dypsis lutescens

One of the most often used Palms in South Florida but still one of the most graceful. The arching fronds are feather-like (pinnate) and light green. The tips of the individual leaflets curve forward, adding to the arching effect. The crown shaft from which new spears emerge is golden with a powdery, waxy coating, and leaf bases are golden. The Palm forms thick clumps and, for that reason, it is widely used for screening or hedging. When kept pruned to allow light and air to flow through the clump, this is a beautiful specimen plant. Originally from Madagascar, the Areca's golden glow becomes a hungry yellow and unappealing if unfertilized. The Palm responds well to nutrients that include micronutrients. (GBT)

Other Name
Butterfly Palm

Bloom Period and Color
White flowers followed fairly quickly by fruit on many-branched inflorescences in the spring and early summer.

Mature Height × Spread
To about 20 feet, with 15-plus spread, depending on pruning.

Zones
10 – 11

When, Where, and How to Plant
It's best to plant Arecas in the early summer at the start of the rainy season in order to let summer rains keep the roots moist. Areca Palms are tolerant of many soil types and conditions. When buying Arecas, notice that some have been adapted to shade, making them appear darker green with longer fronds that those grown for sun. Ask about early growing conditions when purchasing your plant. In South Florida, avoid addition of compost, aged manure, or other soil additives when planting in rocky soil to avoid creating a container-like condition that discourages roots from penetrating poor surrounding soils. Add some organic matter in sandy soils to help retain moisture.

Growing Tips
Fertilize with 8-4-12 slow-release nitrogen and potassium fertilizer. Arecas are susceptible to potassium deficiency. Yellowing spots on older fronds may reflect potassium shortage, not age; older leaves also yellow due to magnesium deficiency. These two elements can be given together. Use magnesium and coated potassium sulfate 2 to 4 pounds per tree 4 times a year. Water the area around the root zone the day prior to applying the supplements, then water them in. Keep roots moist the first year, then irrigate once or twice a week, depending on rain.

Regional Advice and Care
Remove small suckers from the interior of the clump to keep air flowing through the stand. Open trunks are less vulnerable to fungus, scale, and mealybugs, as well as adventitious suckering. If palms in your garden have ganoderma, or butt rot, do not cut out individuals from overcrowded stands, as spores from the fungus can spread through the stumps. Conchs on the base of the trunks are symptomatic of the disease.

Companion Planting and Design
Arecas can be used as a large specimen clump, background planting, or screen. They are compatible with many tropical flowering shrubs, serving as a backdrop against which to display blooms.

My Personal Favorite
Areca or Butterfly Palms that have been pruned to expose and open up the clumping trunks are quite beautiful.

Bailey Palm

Copernicia baileyana

When, Where, and How to Plant

Similar to other Palms in planting requirements, plant so the crown is at the same level in the ground as it was in the container. Provide good drainage and plenty of room for the palm's ultimate size. Keep the root zone moist throughout the first growing season. Fertilize lightly every couple of months until December or cool weather. Resume fertilizing in late February. Because the Palms take a long time to emerge from the ground, fertilize three or four times a year once the young plant has enough frond to form a vase.

Growing Tips

Many Palms are drought-tolerant once established, which means you provide moisture frequently and regularly when the Palms are young, but allow rain to take over when they are established. Water weekly in the dry season. Also, fertilizer is a must for these robust palms as they produce giant leaves and trunks. Use palm-special fertilizer (formulated for Palms in alkaline soils) according to rates on the bag. The latest fertilizer recommendation is 8-4-12 with 4 percent magnesium and a full complement of micronutrients. A waxy coating on Copernicia leaves prevents absorption of foliar sprays.

Regional Advice and Care

The heavy fronds will collapse with their own weight. However, the old leaf stem bases, called boots, often are left attached to the gray-white trunk. Use a handsaw to remove the boots after palms are large enough to begin bringing their trunks out of the ground. Never tear these away and rip tissue. Palm leaf skeletonizers, the larvae of moths, can become pests. These caterpillars chew leaf tissue on the undersides of the fronds, build protective tunnels of frass or droppings, and disfigure the fronds. Use Sevin®.

Companion Planting and Design

Stately Bailey Palms on a lawn are without compare. When they are young, plant Bromeliads or other plants in the natural containers left by boots.

My Personal Favorite

There is only one Bailey, and it is a handsome and hunky Palm.

Cuba is home to many Copernicia Palms, including this most handsome one. Fronds are palmate, blue-gray, and the leaf stems are armed with recurving thorns. The genus is named for Copernicus, while the species remembers Liberty Hyde Bailey, botanist and horticulturist from Cornell University. The Palms are slow growing but monumental in stature and effect. A glade of Bailey Palms at Fairchild Tropical Garden was described by the late Brazilian landscape architect Roberto Burle Marx as orgasmic. Seedling Palms take many years to establish their roots, but they do, and once top growth is under way, these Palms seem to transform rapidly into big specimens. Leaf stems stay attached to the whitish trunks for years until you remove them. Fronds can be 5 feet across. (GBT)

Bloom Period and Color

Flowers are on long stalks that grow among the leaves; flowers are creamy white and appear from February to April; fruit from August to October.

Mature Height × Spread

Trunks can be two feet in diameter and Bailey Palms may reach 40 to 50 feet. Crowns are some 15 or more feet across.

Zones

10 – 11

Blue Latania Palm
Latania loddigesii

Blue-gray leaves have made this a popular Palm in recent years. The Palm's stately bearing gives it appeal as a specimen Palm or when used as a pair at the entrance to a driveway. The big leaves are "costapalmate," meaning palmate with a distinct midrib extending into the blade, which gives the frond a characteristic fold in the center. This Palm is from the Mascarene Islands, which have wet-dry seasons similar to South Florida's. The Latania is not nearly as big as the blue Bismarck Palms, with which it sometimes is confused. It only reaches 30 to 40 feet, compared to the Bismarck's 40-plus. Its leaves are less monumental as well. The Latania is slow-growing but speeds up its growth after the trunk has been established, like the Bailey Palm. Male and female flowers are on different plants. (GBT)

Other Name
Latan Palm

Bloom Period and Color
Summertime bloom stalks grow among the large leaves, and fruits are blue-gray, turning brown when mature from August to November.

Mature Height × Spread
30 feet tall, with crown width of 20-plus feet.

Zones
10 – 11

When, Where, and How to Plant
An adaptable Palm that does well in a range of soils, the Latania is suitable for yards where it has space to grow. Young Palms adapt readily to being transplanted at the start of the rainy season, and are more easily handled by homeowners than big specimens, which have to be root pruned over a period of time before transplanting. Placing the top of the rootball at the soil level is key. Palms planted too deep (as a method of stabilizing them) often die within several years. Mulch around the base, being careful to keep the mulch from crowding the trunk so you don't create conditions for disease.

Growing Tips
Broadcast 8-4-12 with 4 percent magnesium and micronutrients three times a year, beginning in late February/early March, June/July, and October. Follow the directions on the bag. Use 1/2 pound on newly planted specimens, gradually increasing. Latanias are highly drought tolerant; after keeping the roots moist during the first growing season, allow nature to take over. Only in times of drought will a Latania need supplemental water.

Regional Advice and Care
Avoid pruning this and other Palms until the leaf stalk is brown. Palms can translocate nutrients, especially potassium and magnesium, from old leaves to new. By pruning away old leaves, you are removing a source of nutrients. Palm leaf skeletonizers can take up residence on the undersides of the big leaves. These moth larvae rasp away leaf tissue, build protective tunnels of frass (their droppings molded with saliva), and remain protected from the elements. Use Sevin®, or a hard spray of water. For heavy infestation, remove the frond. Although aesthetically undesirable, skeletonizers seldom kill Palms.

Companion Planting and Design
The blue-green color of a Latania invites use of opposite or complementary colors nearby. Red Salvia, Geraniums, or Petunias in winter are successful; Plumbago, Ruellia, Purple Queen as perennials.

My Personal Favorite
Planted in twos or threes (but not within the same planting hole) these are statuesque and sophisticated.

Butia Palm

Butia capitata

When, Where, and How to Plant

University of Florida studies show that Palms make almost no root growth during the fall through early spring. For this reason Butia Palms dug from fields are best moved during the warmer spring through summer months. Well-established container specimens of the Butia Palm can be added to the landscape at any time of the year. They can be planted under most utility wires. The Butia Palm should be kept at least 10 feet from sidewalks, driveways, and buildings. Transplant the Butia Palm by digging a hole 2 to 3 times wider but not deeper than the rootball. Create a berm at the edge of the rootball to help thoroughly wet the rootball at each watering. After planting, add a 2- to 3-inch mulch layer over the root system. Periodically, Butia fronds decline and need removal. Prune them back as close to the trunk of the Palm as possible. The older bases gradually loosen and can be pulled from the plant.

Growing Tips

Newly planted Butia Palms should be kept moist until the roots begin to grow out. Make sure the soil does not thoroughly dry for several growing seasons. Once established, the Butia Palm is very drought tolerant and rarely needs special watering. The Butia Palm usually obtains needed nutrients from the feedings given to lawns and nearby ornamental plantings. To encourage growth and maintain the best color, apply a fertilizer once in March, June, and October. Use a 16-4-8, 8-4-12, or similar palm fertilizer.

Regional Advice and Care

Butia Palms grow throughout most of Florida, except for the most southern portion. They are susceptible to leaf spots and trunk rots that commonly affect palms.

Companion Planting and Design

There is plenty of room for ground cover plantings beneath this large palm. Some good ornamentals that repeat the needle-like look include Junipers, Liriope, Mondo Grass, and African Iris.

My Personal Favorite

Only the species is available in Florida.

Found naturally in South America, Butia Palms are not native to Florida, although they are certainly one of the state's finest landscape plants. Butias grow ever so slowly, and they need room to spread out because they grow about as wide as they are tall. Most gardeners know this Palm by a few other names, including Pindo and Jelly Palm. The latter comes from the fact that the fruits are edible and the sweeter selections make tasty jelly. Better selections have leaves in blue-green, and most twist a little toward the tip. They have an arching habit with the end curling toward the ground. Here is a very hardy and versatile Palm that is often planted as a focal point or to line the streets. (TM)

Other Name
Pindo Palm

Bloom Period and Color
Spring flowers yellow reddish; Fruit ripens July and August; color varies from yellow to red

Mature Height × Spread
15 feet × 15 feet

Zones
8 – 10

Cabbage Palm
Sabal palmetto

The Florida Cabbage Palm is the official state tree. The Palm is not a true tree but resembles one with its straight, tall growth and big thick trunk. This Palm has been more than a towering landscape addition, finding use in making hats, baskets, and roofs for early Native American homes. It has also been a source of food. As the older leaves mature and drop, the bases remain on the trunks for added interest. The Dwarf Palmetto Sabal minor is found throughout Florida growing mainly as an understory plant to 6 feet tall. Where possible, it should be left as a native plant in the landscape. Another relative, the Puerto Rico Hat Palm Sabal causiarum should be considered for larger home sites. (TM)

Bloom Period and Color
Summer; flowers are white and fruit black

Mature Height × Spread
40 feet × 10 feet

Zones
8 – 11

When, Where, and How to Plant
University of Florida studies show that palms make almost no root growth during the fall through early spring. For this reason Cabbage Palms are best moved during the warmer spring through midsummer months. Well-established container specimens can be added to the landscape at any time. This tall-growing Palm should be located where it has adequate overhead space and is away from electrical wires. It should be kept at least 5 feet away from sidewalks, driveways, and most buildings. The Cabbage Palm is very drought tolerant but also tolerates moist soils. It is dug and moved with very little root system at the base of the Palm. According to university studies, Cabbage Palms transplant best if all the fronds are removed after planting. All roots die back to the base of the Palm trunk after digging. Transplant the Cabbage Palm by digging a hole 2 to 3 times wider but not deeper than the rootball. Create a berm at the edge of the rootball to thoroughly wet the rootball at each watering. After planting, add a 2- to 3-inch mulch layer over the root system. Larger specimens of Cabbage Palms need bracing to prevent wind damage.

Growing Tips
Newly planted Cabbage Palms should be kept moist until the roots begin growing out. Make sure the soil does not dry for several growing seasons. Once established, the Cabbage Palm needs special watering only during extreme periods of drought. The Cabbage Palm can be fertilized once in March, June, and October. Use a 16-4-8, 8-4-12, or similar palm fertilizer, following label instructions.

Regional Advice and Care
Cabbage Palms grow well throughout the entire state.

Companion Planting and Design
Can be used as a single specimen but looks best in clusters of three or more. Use with plantings of Junipers, Indian Hawthorn, Dwarf Yaupon Hollies, and Liriope.

My Personal Favorite
Only the species is available in Florida.

Chinese Fan Palm

Livistona chinensis

When, Where, and How to Plant

Plant in late spring or early summer. Plant with plenty of room around the Palm because the crown is large. Dig a hole as deep as the rootball and 2 or 3 times as wide. Water in backfill, and mulch around the root zone. Water every day for 1 week, every other day for 2 weeks, and every third day for 2 weeks. To keep the rootball moist, keep on that schedule, throughout the first growing season if the rain is insufficient. By planting at the beginning of the rainy season, you reduce irrigation requirements.

Growing Tips

A Palm for the armchair gardener, the Chinese Fan Palm is not fussy and doesn't require babying. If fertilized a couple of times a year, it does quite nicely. You may be motivated to remove brown fronds when the Palms are small enough for these to be seen. The longer you can tolerate a brown frond, the better off the Palm will be, because these plants can pull back potassium from the old leaves as they age. Many Palm experts recommend trimming Palms only when the leaf stems are as brown as the fronds.

Regional Advice and Care

Grow these Palms in containers in areas of Central Florida where freezing temperatures are likely. This is not a Palm for North Florida. *Livistona chinensis* has some susceptibility to lethal yellowing disease (see information on the Coconut Palm for a full discussion of this). It may also get ganoderma or butt rot, a fungal disease found in older Palms. To prevent ganoderma, keep the area around the base of the Palm open so that air circulation is unhindered.

Companion Planting and Design

Older Chinese Fan Palms allow the use of large companions, such as the Bromeliads, *Aechmea mexicana, Aechmea mariae-reginae,* or a big *Hohenbergia.* Use these beneath or around them.

My Personal Favorite

Seeds of the Chinese Fan are deep blue-green and pretty, and add to the contributions this Palm makes to the landscape.

The faster one bolts through one's allotted hours, the more impatient one might be for others to keep up—this holds true even amongst slow-growing Palms. My group of four Chinese Fan Palms, planted in a tight circle more than twelve years ago, however, is like Baby Bear's porridge and seems just right. The tallest must be 20 feet, while the shortest is about 10. Their growth rate is not so important as the fact that I seldom water them, fertilize them twice a year, and have watched them survive three freezes and a hurricane. The ends of the fronds are divided, and they droop so the ends of each segment seem to be hung with a split ribbon. The trunks turn a corky brown-gray. The fruits are a beautiful blue-green. (GBT)

Bloom Period and Color

Warm season, late winter/spring; seeds ripen summer through fall.

Mature Height × Spread

20 to 30 feet × 15 feet; fronds 3 to 6 feet wide

Zones

9 – 11

Coconut Palm

Cocos nucifera

Palm Beach County and Palm Beach were named for Coconuts—but Palm Beach actually has a few of these lithe, Jamaica Tall Palms left. These are large Palms with gray trunks, gracefully held pinnate fronds, and edible fruit or seeds. One of the world's most used and useful plants, this bountiful tree has become a victim of an incurable disease, lethal yellowing. Today, Jamaican Tall Coconuts are all but a memory. In their place are somewhat less graceful, but reliable Coconuts, especially the Maypan. It resists the lethal yellowing disease. 'Red Spicata', 'Dwarf Green', and 'Golden Malayan' also are resistant to varying degrees. To avoid spreading the disease, never plant a seed from a neighbor's tree. Plant certified resistant seeds or plants only. (GBT)

Bloom Period and Color
Year-round, small and cream colored

Mature Height × Spread
50 (or more) feet × 30-foot crown

Zones
10B – 11

When, Where, and How to Plant
Plant in early summer. Use sprouted nuts obtained from disease-free nursery stock. Plant in an area where the large crown won't be crowded and where roots have good drainage. Lay the Coconut sideways in a thick and damp layer of mulch, with $2/3$ to $1/2$ of the husk buried. Keep the mulch moist, and perhaps add a light layer of leaves to soften the husk so the root and shoot can emerge.

Growing Tips
Fertilize every four months during the first year with a granular fertilizer formulated for Palms. Apply about 3 pounds of fertilizer around the base of your small Palm, and water it in. Apply a nutritional spray to the leaves every one to three months during the first year. Fertilize two to three times a year thereafter. If young Coconuts begin to turn brown or black and drop, and lower leaves of the crown start to yellow, suspect that your Coconut has begun the decline from lethal yellowing. Fronds at the bottom of the crown yellow first. Wilting and dying then proceeds toward the top of the crown, at last killing the emerging new spear. The disease has never left South Florida, and there are some Palms always infected. It is carried from Palm to Palm by a leaf hopper, a tiny insect that spends part of its life in St. Augustine Grass. Antibiotic injections can keep the Coconuts alive, but not rid them of the disease.

Regional Advice and Care
Coconuts don't like cold weather. Lower fronds can turn yellow and then brown when weather dips into the 30s; after a freeze, the Palm's lower fronds gradually die. They are quite oblivious to salt spray on the beach. This is not a Palm for Central and North Florida.

Companion Planting and Design
Along a beach, with background tropicals such as Hibiscus, Ixora, and Gingers.

My Personal Favorite
Red Spicata Coconut, which has resistance to lethal yellowing disease, has a nice copper-red color in the leaf stems and crown.

Florida Silver Palm
Coccothrinax argentata

When, Where, and How to Plant

Plant in late spring or early summer. Plant in full sun or light shade in an area with excellent drainage. Because it grows in such fast-draining, dry conditions, overwatering or wet feet can cause disease in this Palm. Hopefully, drainage will be excellent around your entryway, because this Palm can serve as a specimen plant to greet visitors. A crescent of them near the front door is an outstanding sight. Dig a hole large enough to accommodate the rootball. Water daily for a week; every other day for two weeks; every third day for two weeks; then just to keep the root zone moist during the first growing season. By planting at the beginning of the rainy season, you reduce irrigation requirements. Eventually, the Palm can withstand growing on its own, without any supplemental irrigation.

Growing Tips

Use a Palm fertilizer such as 8-4-12—with 4 percent magnesium and micronutrients three times a year—March, June, and October when the Palm is young. As it matures, you can allow it to get along on its own. However, if you notice the leaves becoming off-color, then apply nutrients again. If you wait long enough, the fronds on the *Coccothrinax* will fall, leaving the bottom stubs of leaf stems sticking up or out through the trunk fiber. Fiber does not stay attached to the trunk very long, however, as is the case with the Cuban native, the Old Man Palm, *Coccothrinax crinita*.

Regional Advice and Care

Grow the Florida Silver Palm in a container, and protect it from freezing in Central and North Florida.

Companion Planting and Design

This small, beautiful Palm grows so heroically on Big Pine Key that some of that other tough flora seems to beg to go with it: the Locustberry, Palmettos, and Dwarf Fakahatchee Grass.

My Personal Favorite

A group of three to five of these rugged yet beautiful small Palms can be highlighted by white rock mulch.

A single-trunked Palm with delicate, softly drooping fronds that are very silvery on the undersides, this Palm is slow growing and hardy. This graceful Florida native may reach 20 feet in your children's lifetime. The fragile-looking Florida Silver Palm is extraordinarily tough. Rainy-season fires, caused by lightning strikes, and blackened trunks of Palms are evidence that they can survive these, too. This Palm is good for seaside homes because it is highly salt tolerant. Its drought tolerance makes it an excellent candidate for Xeriscape and native gardens. Its size makes it suitable for patio and townhouse gardens where space is limited. The Florida Silver Palm should never be collected from the wild. Gardeners should buy only nursery-propagated or nursery-grown specimens. (GBT)

Other Name
Silver Palm

Bloom Period and Color
Spring to fall

Mature Height × Spread
20 feet × 5 feet

Zones
10B – 11

Hurricane Palm
Dictyosperma album

As much as the University of Miami Hurricanes would like to believe, this Palm was not named for them. Nor, alas, was it given its common name after the 1992 Hurricane Andrew. It garnered its name because of its ability to withstand tropical cyclones—hurricanes—generally. Its long fronds have a distinctively long-lasting "rein" of tissue that runs along the edge of the leaflets, holding individual leaflets perfectly in place. Trunks are light brown and more bark-like than many Palms. Originally from the Mascarene Islands in the Pacific, Dictyosperma is cut for its edible heart on Reunion, has disappeared in the wild from Mauritius, and is threatened by hybridization on Rodrigues. The World Conservation Union lists the Palm as endangered. (GBT)

Other Name
Princess Palm

Bloom Period and Color
Flowers and fruit occur at various times throughout the year.

Mature Height × Spread
The trunk is slender, often less than six inches in diameter, but may reach 30 ft. in height. The crown is twelve feet or so across.

Zones
10 – 11

When, Where, and How to Plant
As a solitary Palm, this strong and handsome specimen can be given star placement or used in groups of 3, 5, or 7, as is true of other single trunk Palms. The magical 3, 5, and 7 are more pleasing to the eye than trees planted in even numbers. Allow for excellent drainage. If in an area where fill has been dredged from grass prairies to get above the water table, create a mound that drains well and can keep the Palms' roots out of water. Plant at the start of the rainy season, keeping the root zone moist as you do with your other Palms. The crown of this Palm is quite handsome, and if you plant it where it will be seen against palmate Palms or big-leafed trees, the crown will be more distinguishable. There is a purple crownshaft form, which is rare; a red form, with reddish new leaves; a yellow form, with golden cast to the undersides of the leaves.

Growing Tips
Use 8-4-12 with 4 percent magnesium and a full complement of micronutrients to counter poor soils in South Florida that are often leached of nitrogen and potassium. Keep weeds away from the base of this and every Palm trunk for maximum growth. Grass and weeds compete with palm roots for nutrients and water. This Palm is moderately susceptible to lethal yellowing disease, which remains active in South Florida.

Regional Advice and Care
Keep your Hurricane Palm well fertilized and watered, and it can withstand full sun (as well as wind). It likes adequate water, but is drought tolerant when mature. A wonderfully hardy Palm.

Companion Planting and Design
Follow UM's lead, and use these Palms along the street, or as specimens in your yard, surrounded by tropical plants such as Bromeliads or Aroids.

My Personal Favorite
The variety with red leaf edges is an especially desirable landscape addition. It's called *Dictyosperma album* var. *rubrum*.

Lady Palm

Rhapis spp.

When, Where, and How to Plant

Plant at the beginning of the rainy season. If transplanting a large clump, root prune 4 to 6 weeks before the moving date; fill in the trench around the rootball, and keep moist until you transplant the palm. Then be diligent about watering so the rootball doesn't dry until the Palm puts out new growth. Once established, Lady Palms may be watered and allowed to become slightly dry before watering again. Plant as a hedge or a specimen in a well-draining area where the Palms can get partial shade. Dig a planting hole 3 times as wide, while just as deep, as the rootball. Place the Palm in the planting hole so that the root crown is at the same level in the soil as it was in the pot. Backfill, using a hose to water in the soil and eliminate air pockets. Water daily for 1 or 2 weeks, then water every other day for another week or so. After a month, begin watering every three to four days.

Growing Tips

Use a fertilizer formulated for Palms, such as 12-4-12-4, with micronutrients. The extra 4 in the formula ratio indicates 4 percent magnesium. Fertilize a couple of times a year. When hungry, the leaves will begin to turn yellow. When in full sun, the leaves also yellow. Once through the first growing season, the Lady Palms are able to withstand fairly dry conditions, and watering can be reduced to a minimum except in periods of drought.

Regional Advice and Care

Grow in protected areas of Central Florida; in colder northern areas of the state, grow in a container.

Companion Planting and Design

Lady Palms serve as a screen and hedge when grown as a middle layer between a ground cover, such as a small Philodendron called Burle Marx, and taller pinnate Palms. Or use in containers.

My Personal Favorite

Rhapis excelsa is a sturdy Palm for indoors or out, and the variegated form is quite striking.

Perhaps it is the slender form or the comeliness of the divided leaves; perhaps it is the pliable and forgiving nature. Perhaps it is the sense of grace she brings to a landscape. Perhaps it is none of these, but this is indeed a Lady Palm. Rhapis is pronounced "ray-pis" and means "needle," for the narrow and often pointed segments of the palmately divided fronds. Two species work well in Florida, R. excelsa and R. humilis. R. excelsa is the Large Lady Palm; she slowly grows to 12 or 14 feet on slender stems wrapped in black fibers. Rhapis humilis is the Slender Lady Palm, taller than R. excelsa but with delicate leaf segments that are more graceful and drooping. Humilis takes more cold than Rhapis excelsa. (GBT)

Bloom Period and Color
Spring and various times; seeds white

Mature Height × Spread
6 to 15 feet × 15 feet

Zones
10 – 11

Licuala Palm
Licuala grandis

If other Palms fail to catch your eye, the Licuala may be the pièce de résistance. The round, pleated leaves are so attractive that even non-Palm fanciers admire them. From New Hebrides, north of Australia, Licuala grandis has a slender trunk about the size of a baseball bat, and a complement of circular leaves that float up and down on the prevailing breezes. There is no crown shaft on a Licuala, which means the leaf stems seem to be less tightly gripped by the trunk and older ones are likely to hang down. Slow-growing swamp dwellers, Licualas like humidity and warmth. When grown in containers, a saucer can be used to catch water and keep the rootball wet. (GBT)

Other Name
Ruffled Fan Palm

Bloom Period and Color
In South Florida, the palms bloom and fruit at various times, with fruit maturing primarily in summer, from August to November.

Mature Height × Spread
To 9 feet, with a crown 5 to 6 feet across.

Zones
10 – 11

When, Where, and How to Plant
Rainforest Palms that grow next to rivers and in swamps, Licualas like plenty of moisture. High shade is necessary in midday. Shade can come from other palms as well as evergreen trees (fruit trees may damage the big leaves when fruits fall). Ptychosperma Palms, for instance, are fast growers and can grow close without clumping. They can be used for shade. Licualas can be set back dramatically by transplanting, so carefully place the palm the first time. An eastern or southern side of the house may be best for a Licuala to keep cold northern winds from blasting it in winter and hot western sun from scalding in summer. A low area in the yard or an area where the microclimate provides plenty of humidity is best. Protection from wind will keep the leaves intact. Shrubs can help block wind as well as sun; and trellises or other garden devices can be called into duty as well.

Growing Tips
Plenty of mulch can help keep soil moisture high. In the right location, Licualas thrive. Because they are Swamp Palms, the big requirement is water. Water twice weekly in the dry season and water well so you encourage the roots to penetrate deep soil. The standard 8-4-12 fertilizer is appropriate. Growth is slow, but the leaves stay on a long time.

Regional Advice and Care
There are no major pests or diseases of Licualas. Watch for the usual mealybugs or scale on emerging spears. If Licualas are transplanted without root pruning, they may take years to recover, if at all. And it may take ten or so years for Palms to flower and seed; seeds are red when ripe.

Companion Planting and Design
More than one Licuala is almost a must as these Palms are so different from others. Plan on at least three in a group.

My Personal Favorite
Licuala orbicularis is called the Parasol Palm because of its round shape and is a gorgeous plant from Sarawak.

Pacaya Palm

Chamaedorea tepejilote

When, Where, and How to Plant

Similar to other Palms, the best season for planting is at the onset of the rainy season (late May or June). Natural irrigation can help keep a newly planted *C. tepejilote* moist in order to become established, without running up the water bill. Plant in a shady area, beneath large trees or within their shade zone, where early morning or late afternoon sun can hit the leaves. *C. tepejilote* can form adventitious roots at or just above the ground. These roots help the Palm balance itself—whether in the rainforest on slippery slopes or among tree roots in your yard. Though not as prone to nutrient deficiencies as other Palms, *C. tepejilote* still needs palm fertilizer in South Florida's soils.

Growing Tips

The Palms are used to seasonally dry conditions, which makes them right at home in South Florida's seasonally wet/dry cycle. As always with Palms, keep the roots moist the first growing season, and taper off once winter arrives. Use 8-4-12 with 4 percent magnesium and micronutrients. When happy, the fronds are deep green. South Florida's rainy season can wash away the effect of regular granular fertilizers, causing yellow leaves. Slow-release fertilizers don't lose their contents all at once, but supply nutrients over a period of time, depending on soil moisture or, in newer versions, soil temperature.

Regional Advice and Care

This is an easy-care type of Palm, with no particular insect or disease problems. It can come down with a good case of scale or mealybugs if it grows in conditions that are too wet and dark with little air movement. Use alcohol on cotton or insecticidal soap to treat. Fronds are broken by squirrels.

Companion Planting and Design

An assortment of understory rainforest plants, from Calatheas to Ferns and Bromeliads, complement this tropical Palm.

My Personal Favorite

The Pacaya Palm, sometimes referred to by its species name, Tepejilote, is versatile, pretty, and not too big or fussy.

Of the numerous Chamaedorea Palms, Pacaya or C. tepejilote is among the nicest for home landscapes. An understory rain forest Palm from areas that are seasonally dry; the relatively broad leaflets are pointed on the ends, fronds are long and graceful in an uncluttered crown. The trunk is slender, straight, and bears white rings where old leaves were attached. Some are solitary in habit, while others cluster. C. tepejilote flower stalks appear below the crown (there are male and female inflorescences on separate plants). When fruit appear, the short branches of the infructescence turn bright orange-red. Several solitary Tepejilotes together make a handsome group beneath large, tropical trees, transporting a little of tropical America to a South Florida garden. (GBT)

Bloom Period and Color

Flowers are yellow, and begin to appear at the beginning of the summer; the fruits ripening to black from July to September.

Mature Height × Spread

To 8 or 9 feet, with a crown 3 to 4 feet on solitary individuals, 7 feet across on clumping types.

Zones

10B – 11

Pygmy Date Palm
Phoenix roebelenii

The advantages of being a short Palm: one can escape pruning with long poles, damage from high winds, be free of extenuating circumstances, and spend life never far from the trough. Indeed, the Pygmy Date Palm is far more prized today in South Florida as a result of Hurricane Andrew in 1992 than before the storm, precisely because it was close to the ground. The head is quite full when the Palms are well tended, and the lower fronds bend down, so the crown is rounded. The caveat with Phoenix species is the row of spiny leaflets at the base of each frond. A wilting disease is found among some types of Phoenix Palms. Yet the sturdy little Pygmy Date keeps plugging along. (GBT)

Bloom Period and Color
Cream-colored flowers in spring; fruit in September

Mature Height × Spread
10 feet × 8-plus feet

Zones
10 – 11

When, Where, and How to Plant
Plant at the beginning of the rainy season, late May or early June, although any time between March and midsummer is fine. Plant in a well-drained area. Dig a hole large enough to accommodate the rootball. By planting at the beginning of the rainy season, you reduce irrigation requirements.

Growing Tips
Water daily for a week; every other day for 2 weeks; every third day for 2 weeks; then just to keep the root zone moist during the first growing season. Use a fertilizer for Palms, such as 12-4-12-4 with micronutrients. This Palm and many others are subject to potassium deficiency; to prevent it, use a fertilizer with nitrogen and potassium in slow-release form. The Pygmy Date Palm is from the Mekong River delta in Southeast Asia, and has more need for water than its desert-dwelling relatives. If put on a starvation diet, it will take on a yellow cast and thin its crown in its efforts to alert you to its needs.

Regional Advice and Care
Potassium deficiency in Pygmy Dates shows up as yellow spots or flecks or banding on the lower, older fronds. It can be confused with magnesium deficiency. Potassium and magnesium should be applied together to correct the deficiency, for potassium alone can cause a magnesium imbalance. Use potassium sulfate with $1/2$ as much magnesium sulfate (about 3 pounds of potassium). Repeat the application 4 times a year. If many fronds are yellow, it can take one or more years to eliminate the problem. Protect from cold in Central and North Florida, or grow this Palm in a container. It grows well in a large container for several years.

Companion Planting and Design
As sentries for entrances, small accent trees, container Palms for the pool and patio area, these Palms are versatile and useful. Surround with some Bromeliads, Pentas, or Moss Roses.

My Personal Favorite
A group of two or three Pygmy Date Palms, offset with a flat "cap" rock or boulder, makes a nice vignette at an entry or in a small garden.

Royal Palm
Roystonea elata

When, Where, and How to Plant
Royal Palms dug from fields or landscapes are best moved during the warmer spring months through midsummer. Well-established container specimens of Royal Palms can be added to the landscape at any time. This is a tall-growing Palm that should be located where it has adequate overhead space and is away from electrical wires. Keep it at least 5 feet away from sidewalks, driveways, and the home. Prepare a large planting site by adding compost or peat moss and manure. Transplant the Palm by digging a hole 2 to 3 times wider but not deeper than the rootball. Create a berm at the edge of the rootball so that each watering reaches the rootball. After planting, add a 2- to 3-inch mulch layer over the root system. Larger specimens of Royal Palms need bracing to prevent wind damage. Periodically remove older leaves, where possible, to keep an attractive specimen.

Growing Tips
Newly planted Royal Palms should be kept moist until the roots begin to grow out. Although this is a fast-growing Palm, make sure the soil does not thoroughly dry for several growing seasons. Once established, the Palms need watering about once a week or whenever the soil begins to dry, especially during periods of drought. Royal Palms look and grow the best when fertilized once in March, June, and October. Use a 16-4-8, 8-4-12, or similar palm fertilizer, following label instructions.

Regional Advice and Care
Royal Palms are limited to South Florida. Winter freezes make it impossible to grow the Palms farther north. Royal Palms can exhibit nutrient deficiencies in some South Florida soils. Apply a fertilizer with adequate potassium and minor nutrients needed for growth.

Companion Planting and Design
These are tall Palms to plant alone or in clusters of three or more. Add ornamentals that complete the tropical look, including Bougainvillea, Crotons, Ti Plants, Ferns, Allamanda, Gingers, and Philodendrons.

My Personal Favorite
Only the species is available in Florida.

There are two Royal Palms that are often confused with each other because they look so similar. One is the native Roystonea elata, *and the other is* Roystonea regia. *This latter is known as the Cuban Royal Palm. Experts say the most distinguishable difference is evident in the trunks. The Cuban Royal Palm has an obvious bulge in the trunk; the Florida Royal Palm is more uniform. Both are restricted to South Florida. What catches the attention of many admirers of this Palm could be the area of long, smooth green trunk at the top, the crownshaft. These majestic Palms are best used in large landscapes. Plant them in clusters as accent features, or line them in rows along a wide street. (TM)*

Bloom Period and Color
Summer; flowers white-ish; fruit maroon to black

Mature Height × Spread
50 feet × 30 feet

Zones
10 – 11

Sargent's Cherry Palm
Pseudophoenix sargentii ssp. *sargentii*

South Florida's most endangered Palm grows only on one island in Biscayne Bay, although originally it grew on three in small populations. The handsome medium-sized and solitary Palm grows throughout the West Indies, but it is threatened by development. Through the efforts of Fairchild Tropical Garden's endangered species program, the Palm is being grown for restocking in its habitat. Through the members' sales, the determined Sargent's Palm is appearing in more landscapes—complete with ID numbers—as gardeners help keep the gene base alive. It is a pretty Palm with a bluish crownshaft and pinnate fronds. The Pseudophoenix has a banded trunk that swells in the center, and narrow leaflets. When young, the fronds emerge on a single plane. (GBT)

Other Name
Buccaneer Palm

Bloom Period and Color
Various times. Yellow flowers on stalks that grow within the leaves develop into round, red fruit.

Mature Height × Spread
8 to 20 feet, with a crown about 15 feet.

Zones
10B – 11

When, Where, and How to Plant
This is one Palm that doesn't have to be coddled to be grown here. It likes sun and sea air and rocky soils. Although it thrives on rocky coastlines, the difficulty is digging the hole in the rock. The Buccaneer Palm is frustratingly slow growing, and it may be partly for that reason that it has not recovered from being overcollected in the early days of the 20th Century, when it was sold as a small Royal. No extra soil amendments are needed for the Palm to succeed, just patience and excellent drainage. Plant the Palm in full sun, at the start of the rainy season to let Mother Nature help with the watering.

Growing Tips
Use Palm fertilizer and don't worry about supplemental water once the Palm has become established after the first year of growth. If drought occurs when the Palm is young, water once or twice a week.

Regional Advice and Care
Since this Palm is so slow growing, it is wise not to prune away any of the fronds until all leaflets and the stalk are brown. Keep weeds and grass away from the root zone to better increase the Palm's ability to thrive. The Palm has few pest and disease problems, and is not susceptible to lethal yellowing disease. Nor is it listed as vulnerable to *Ganoderma* or butt rot disease. The only enemy has been man, who has stolen it from its natural environment and diminished natural areas as he has done so. There are but half a dozen mature individuals left in Florida at the moment—mature enough to reproduce—although the Palm grows in other West Indian areas.

Companion Planting and Design
Sea Grapes, Sea Oats, Bay Cedar, Beach Morning Glory, Spider Lily, Coastal Cocoplum, Inkberry, and a host of other dune plants are able to thrive with Sargent's Cherry Palm in similar conditions.

My Personal Favorite
A well-grown Sargent's Palm is suitable for a small garden or grouping, and can take seaside conditions.

Saw Palmetto
Serenoa repens

When, Where, and How to Plant
The very best planting time for the Saw Palmetto is the warmer spring months through midsummer, but container-grown specimens can be added to the landscape at any time of the year. This Palm grows as wide as it is tall, so it needs space to spread out in all directions. Keep it at least 3 to 5 feet away from sidewalks, driveways, and the home. Transplant the Palm by digging a hole 2 to 3 times wider but not deeper than the rootball. Create a berm at the edge of the rootball to ensure wetting of the rootball at each watering. This Palm usually does not need staking. The Saw Palmetto gradually increases in size and may overgrow walks and encroach upon other landscape plantings. Prune the plants back as needed.

Growing Tips
Add a 2- to 3-inch mulch layer over the root system. Newly planted Saw Palmettos should be kept moist until the roots begin to grow out. Although this is a very drought-tolerant Palm, make sure the soil does not thoroughly dry for several growing seasons. Once established, the Saw Palmetto does not need special watering but can be given periodic watering along with other landscape plantings. The Saw Palmetto needs infrequent feedings. Fertilizing other nearby plantings usually is enough to feed the palm plantings, too. Where light feedings are provided in spring and summer, use a 16-4-8, 8-4-12, or similar palm fertilizer with micronutrients.

Regional Advice and Care
Saw Palmettos grow throughout the state without special care. Saw Palmettos may be affected by palmetto weevils and palm leaf skeletonizers. Treat pests with a pesticide recommended by the University of Florida, following label instructions.

Companion Planting and Design
Create view barriers and space dividers with clusters or add to natural Florida settings. Combine with the native Hollies, Pines, ornamental grasses, Beautyberry, Beach Sunflower, Coreopsis, Aster, and Daisies.

My Personal Favorite
It is often hard to sell the Saw Palmetto as a landscape plant due to its common occurrence in the wild. But gardeners like the blue form because it adds more interest to the native plantings.

Early settlers probably viewed Saw Palmettos as a threat to their livelihood. The plants had sharp needles on the leaf petioles, formed almost impermeable thickets, and covered much of the desirable crop and grazing lands. Today gardeners are taking a new look at these plants that can grow in most soils, harbor wildlife, and provide an early Florida look. This clump-forming Palm can grow in sandy to enriched soils. It's best used as a low view barrier, a space divider between properties, and an accent plant near patios and along walkways. Saw Palmettos are almost always planted in clusters of three or more. A blue leaf selection of the Saw Palmetto has been made for landscape plantings. It's being propagated by native plant nurseries. Extracts from the berries are used to treat benign Prostatic Hyperplasia. (TM)

Other Name
Palmetto

Bloom Period and Color
Early spring and summer

Mature Height × Spread
6 feet × 6 feet

Zones
8 – 11

Perennials *for Florida*

Perennials are longer lived than annuals and shorter lived than trees. In some parts of Florida, most things can be made perennial if you work at it, even Coleus and Impatiens. It is therefore difficult to categorize perennials.

You can expect to get a few years out of these plants, but not a few decades. You can expect many of them to be herbaceous, though some, like Pentas, can become woody with age. You can expect them to be accents or ground covers or vines, too. You may expect that bulbs are sometimes included in perennial listings, because they return seasonally but must be replaced from time to time. As with life itself, you can expect the unexpected, and you will not be disappointed.

Bird of Paradise

Ever-Changing Perennials

Perennials are among the elements of your garden that bring it to life, that add richness and dimension. They could just as easily not be there; if you never had them, you might never miss them. But if you add perennials, and then remove them, taking them away will make all the difference.

Pentas begin life in the garden looking one way—pert is a description that comes to mind for young Pentas. Over the course of two or three years or more, they become robust, big landscape plants. After a while in this stage, they must be pruned back quite hard or eliminated altogether and begun again. Or they may be replaced with another plant that will change the look according to your change of heart.

This changing aspect of the garden is important, as we all change our tastes over time. So allow a portion of the garden to be devoted to perennials that are less labor intensive than annuals, but will not become permanent, plants that can repeat their performances but be replaced should they wear out their welcome.

Calathea

Gaillardias, Day Lilies, Kalanchoes, Begonias, Walking Iris, Mexican Tarragon, Milkweed, and Phlox are among the plants we consider perennials, but tropicals may also be included. Consider the Bromeliads that flower every year, send out pups, and then die, giving up their space to the new generation. Or the Costus and Calatheas, the Gingers and the rest, which may die back in colder winters but linger along in mild ones to send out new and exuberant foliage and flowers in the warm months.

In South Florida, many of the plants called tropicals are perennials: Bananas, for instance, which flower and fruit every year to eighteen months; Gingers and Heliconias, which bloom reliably in the warm months; Spathiphyllums, which produce their white flags of peace during the warm months; and Birds-of-Paradise.

Growing Tips

It is a mistake to assume that they can be left to grow on their own just because they are perennial. Taking care of them extends their lives. Refresh a bed; add more mulch; remove spent flowers; divide the rhizomes or tubers or bulbs; fertilize regularly; water regularly . . . the same good habits of good gardeners are required with these as with other plants in your care.

On a different scale, perennials may be considered the intermediate care plants in your garden. If annuals require intense fussing over to provide maximum color (think of deadheading the Petunias and Geraniums, of watering the Impatiens), not to mention the tedium of planting and ripping out every few months, then perennials are less demanding. But perennials also are more demanding than an Oak tree.

Care, however, is what gardeners give. It defines the garden and the gardener. Without it, there is no garden. That's why we garden. Perennials are those plants that define our role.

Asparagus Fern
Asparagus setaceus

For a plant in the Lily family that looks so delicate, it is a tough customer. It serves well in pots for the patio and in planters. And its quite beautiful foliage can be cut for flower arrangements. Asparagus Fern suits certain areas perfectly and shouldn't be allowed in others. They grow on fleshy and fat underground roots, and have little spines. They prefer moisture in summer and dry conditions in winter to rest. The little seeds can be transported here and there, and will sprout without difficulty. A different form called A. densiflorus 'Myers' has stems that tend to stay upright and foliage that is full at the bottom and narrow at the top. They are best suited for pots. Dwarf forms are available. (GBT)

Bloom Period and Color
Summer blooms in white, followed by red berries

Mature Height × Spread
2 feet × 4 feet

Zones
9 – 11

When, Where, and How to Plant
Plant in spring when new branchlets are forming. If you divide a clump, this also is best done in spring. Seeds can be planted somewhat earlier, say, later winter or early spring. Plant in planters or pots on patios, pool decks or by waterfalls. If purchasing an Asparagus Fern in a container intended for a larger terra cotta pot, use a good, loose potting soil that contains peat, bark, and perlite for drainage. Place terra cotta shards, polystyrene peanuts, or coarse orchid mix in the bottom 2 or 3 inches, and fill with potting soil to a level where the top of the plant's rootball will be within 1 or 2 inches of the top. Fill in around the rootball. Hold the terra cotta pot with both hands, and firmly tamp it against the ground to help the potting mix settle. Then fill again to bring potting soil to within 1 or 2 inches of the top. Water well.

Growing Tips
Asparagus Fern likes plenty of water in the growing season. Because terra cotta is porous, water evaporates quickly from the pots. You may have to water frequently, depending on conditions. Lift the pot to check the weight, or insert a finger into the potting soil to a depth of 1 or 2 inches. If the soil feels dry, then water. Water less often in winter. Fertilize with a slow-release 18-18-18 for foliage plants. Once established, these Ferns develop underground nodules and become quite self-reliant. Little care is needed other than an annual springtime haircut.

Regional Advice and Care
Asparagus Ferns can take cold, but bring inside or cover if freeze is expected.

Companion Planting and Design
Plant Asparagus Fern where you want a graceful, almost floating lacey curtain of green—at the edges of foundation planters, or around the edges of a container to drape over the side and soften the look of a Dracaena or Pony Tail.

My Personal Favorite
Used in a planter box or as a foundation plant, Asparagus Fern can hide the legginess of shrubs, such as old Ligustrum.

Begonia

Begonia spp.

When, Where, and How to Plant

Plant in spring to midsummer, when plants are actively growing. Plant in shade, in raised beds or in areas with excellent drainage. Build a raised bed, or add rock or even orchid mix to a bed. Pea rock in the bottom of a planting hole will assure good drainage. The beds have to drain perfectly, yet retain water. Begonias have delicate roots that stay in the upper 2 or 3 inches of the soil. Tim Anderson, a Miami nurseryman who has grown Begonias for many years, says, "They like a lot of water on the dry side." Anderson says that wet rocks provide ideal conditions so that roots, which don't like to be completely dry, can have air but stay moist. Use a potting soil with sand, pea rock, or limestone added. Don't overload it with peat moss or too much organic matter, and avoid muck. Cane-type Begonias can be pruned to any desired height. The cuttings can be rooted. Rhizomatous Begonias can be divided by cutting a piece of rhizome large enough to have several old nodes and two or three leaves, placing this horizontally beneath mulch or on a peat-perlite mix and allowing it to root.

Growing Tips

Mulch. Use a slow-release fertilizer to keep a supply of nutrients available to the plants, and keep well watered.

Regional Advice and Care

Tuberous Begonias do not do well in South Florida. Other types such as Angel-wing and Rex may best be grown in protected areas, such as southeast corners in North and Central Florida. Cover in cold weather. Otherwise, grow in containers and bring inside.

Companion Planting and Design

They make good companions for Ferns, Bromeliads, or Aroids around a pond, in a shady garden bed, or in a covered shade house, where watering is controlled and leaves protected from damage.

My Personal Favorite

Iron Cross Begonias are beautiful additions to tropical gardens, with interesting leaves and markings.

Just as Impatiens have become brighter and Geraniums bolder and Salvias more diverse in their colors, Begonias have undergone a revolution. They're coming back into the landscape. Angel-wings, which grow on woody canes, have leaves shaped as if they were plucked from the back of Gabriel. Often spotted with silver, or green on green, or metallic green, the undersides can be plain green, maroon, or pink. Rhizomatous Begonias have succulent stems with sometimes-grand leaves close to 1 foot across that look velvety. Other leaves are quilted, puckered, round, star-shaped, or pointed, with the points slightly off center. Wax Begonias, used as annuals, are becoming shorter and more floriferous with brighter flowers in pinks and reds. Begonia popenoei is a large plant excellent for landscape use. (GBT)

Bloom Period and Color
Spring and summer blooms in pink, white, red,

Mature Height × Spread
Various. 10 inches to 4 feet × 10 inches to 4 feet

Zones
10B – 11

Bird-of-Paradise

Strelitzia reginae

English plant explorers discovered the Bird-of-Paradise at the Cape of Good Hope in 1773. When the Bird was taken back to the Royal Botanic Garden, Kew, Sir Joseph Banks, King George's horticultural advisor and nobody's fool, named it to honor Queen Charlotte, Princess of Mecklenburg-Strelitz: Strelitzia, and reginae, meaning "queen." Birds-of-Paradise are comprised of a bract within which orange sepals and blue, fused petals arise. Inside the petals are the stigma and stamens. The Bird head is rather heronlike. Appropriately, birds pollinate the Birds. Strelitzia alba has claret bracts and white flowers; S. caudata has pink bracts and white flowers. S. nicolai, the Giant Bird that can grow to 30 feet, has white bracts with blue flowers; S. parvifolia has green bracts edged in red, yellow-orange sepals, and electric-blue petals. So the reginae cultivar 'Kirstenbosch Gold' has yellow sepals. (GBT)

Bloom Period and Color
July and August blooms in orange and white with blue

Mature Height × Spread
3 to 4 feet × 4 feet

Zones
9 – 11

When, Where, and How to Plant
Plant in the warm season, May through midsummer, to give the plant ample growing time before winter. Plant in full sun, as an accent or part of a foundation planting or in front of a hedge. Birds-of-Paradise have tuberous roots, and they like to clump, holding quite long gray-green leaves on stiff stems. Give them space to grow. Enrich the planting hole for the birds with peat moss or well-rotted manure, but don't sink them too deep into the ground. Tubers should be just at the surface. Mulch lightly. Good care and proper planting depth will speed up the flowering process.

Growing Tips
Birds like to be well fed. Fertilize every month, using a balanced fertilizer, such as 6-6-6. A plant from a 3-gallon container should receive 3 tablespoons of fertilizer; a mature larger plant, 2 cups. Or use a slow-release fertilizer to supply the plant with a constant source of nutrients. Because they have an extensive system of tuberous roots, don't let them sit in water, but provide good drainage. Birds should be well watered and then allowed to dry. If over-crowded, neglected and unfertilized, the plants will not produce any flowers. As the older leaves die and bend out from the clump, cut them out to allow light into plants in the center. From seed, Birds-of-Paradise may take several years to mature and produce flowers. Transplanting can be difficult due to the large number of deep roots.

Regional Advice and Care
Protect from cold in Central and North Florida. Prune out damage in the spring. Scale insects may be a problem. Use an insecticide useful against a widespread infestation of scale. Malathion is good for small populations.

Companion Planting and Design
An old, free-standing clump of Birds in a sunny part of the garden is hard to beat, or use them with relatives, including Travelers Palms and Heliconias at the back of the garden.

My Personal Favorite
When well grown, this plant can be arresting. It needs ample fertilizer and water to look its best, but provides color outside and cut flowers for inside.

Calathea
Calathea spp.

When, Where, and How to Plant

Plant in spring, especially if you are taking divisions of the tubers. The plants can be grouped in beds beneath trees, such as Oaks, since they do well with bright light but not steady direct sun. Most of the Calatheas form clumps over time. Place the tubers in beds that are a mix of rich organic matter, such as compost or good potting soil, with sand or perlite or another material to enhance drainage.

Growing Tips

Use a slow-release fertilizer to keep a good supply of nutrients available to the roots. The patterns will be especially bold if the plants are well fertilized and well watered. These perennials can tolerate early morning sun or late afternoon sun. *C. burle-marxii* 'Blue Ice' in the ground beneath thatch palms with a southern exposure did well during one winter's cold snaps, which sent temperatures into the upper 30s. They fare less well when they dry out: leaf edges become brown and curl under. Other species are less tolerant of cold, particularly if the weather is cool for many days in a row and when wind is high.

Regional Advice and Care

Tender tropicals, Calatheas like protection in winter beyond southern Florida. For the most part, Calatheas should be used as houseplants in Central and North Florida. Plastic pots can serve to keep the potting mix moist, providing there are pot shards or Styrofoam peanuts in the bottom to aid in drainage. Potting mixes today contain a little slow release fertilizer and are quite light, but you may want to add a little perlite to make sure they are adequately aerated. Keep the containers out of drafts and in bright, indirect light. Be on guard against snails when growing these outside in the ground.

Companion Planting and Design

Calatheas are wonderful for planting in beds beneath canopy trees, with Palms and Aroids, Maidenhair Ferns, or with Boston Ferns. *C. zebrina* and *C. makoyana* are great company for each other.

My Personal Favorite

Calathea ornata 'Rosea-lineata' is a pretty foliage plant that brings tidy color to the shade.

The beautifully patterned leaves of Calathea rise from a short stem. Among the most ornate of plants, the Calatheas bear leaves worthy of a graphic designers' hall of fame. Markings usually follow the central vein, branching to side veins. They can be dark green on light green, silver on hunter green, bright pink on dark green, pink and white on dark green . . . the combinations seem quite endless. The undersides of the leaves are frequently red or wine colored. Flowers are produced inside bracts; bracts can be spikes or racemes arising among the leaves. One, Calathea burle-marxii 'Ice Blue', has unmarked, broad green leaves on long stems and a spike of pale-blue to white cuplike bracts from which white flowers emerge. (GBT)

Other Names
Rattlesnake Plant, Peacock Plant, various depending on species

Bloom Period and Color
Foliage in shades of green, white, pink, and combinations

Mature Height × Spread
Varies with species from 10 inches to 5 feet tall, from 6 inches to 4 feet wide

Zones
10B – 11

Leather Fern

Acrostichum danaeifolium

The Arnold Schwarzenegger of Ferns, this is the beefiest and largest Fern in the United States. Leather Fern is a swamp dweller as well as a resident of Mangrove zones. The sloughs of the Big Cypress swamp are good places to look for these fellows, as are the estuaries around the southern peninsula. Fronds are pinnately compound, but this Fern's leaflets are not the delicate leaflets you normally associate with that description. They are wide, stiff, and dark green. The undersides of fertile leaflets look like suede leather, with rust-colored patches. The stems are substantial. Yet when they're curled up as fiddleheads, they are eaten in other parts of the world. Because of its size, it can be used as a shrub in the right setting. (GBT)

Bloom Period and Color
Foliage in dark green

Mature Height × Spread
8 to 10 feet × 3-plus feet

Zones
9 – 11

When, Where, and How to Plant
Plant during the warm months of the year. Select moist, low-lying areas. Low hammocks or native plant areas that have moist zones would accommodate the Leather Fern. Leather Fern can be grown in a large container. The container can be submerged in a pond, or you can caulk the drainage holes to keep the growing medium wet to moist. The type of soil isn't as important as its moisture. Muck, the black, peat-based soil of the Everglades, is fine for this plant, mixed with a little sand. Or a potting soil without much perlite does well. Leather Fern doesn't like to dry out. It will get brown fronds if it does.

Growing Tips
Keep the soil moist. Even though the nutritional requirements for this plant are said to be low, a small amount of slow-release fertilizer or organic fertilizer is beneficial. And all Ferns like a fish emulsion now and then. If growing these submerged in a pond, wrap some slow-release fertilizer such as Dynamite in screening and place a few around the roots, stuffed into the soil.

Regional Advice and Care
The Ferns may get scale. You can try wiping off the hard-shelled insects with alcohol on cotton. Hand pick any snails that may rasp away parts of leaves. Protect Leather Ferns from freezing weather.

Companion Planting and Design
These Ferns are so big, they tend to look right with big Royal Palms, at a natural pool's edge, a canal bank, a low-lying area where its feet can stay wet. For streamside, they are made to order. It works well in lakefront planting areas where it could mix with the Dahoon Holly, the Sabal Palms, and the Coastal Plain Willow. For natural pond areas, Sweet Bay Magnolia, Swamp Hibiscus, Cocoplum, Buttonbush, and Leather Fern are good candidates for your landscape.

My Personal Favorite
A single clump of Leather Fern at a pond's edge is a bold statement.

When, Where, and How to Plant

Plant Pentas in spring and early summer. Plant in full sun to partial shade, where there is good drainage. Mix with other butterfly plants, like Spanish Bayonet and Wild Petunia. Space the plants 12 to 24 inches apart, as they grow quite large and will form a wave of color. Use a trowel to dig a planting hole just larger than the rootball; backfill with soil from the planting hole and water. Water daily for a week or two, gradually tapering off until you water weekly or twice weekly.

Growing Tips

Water weekly or twice weekly. Use slow-release fertilizer at the time of planting, and again every three or four months if in South Florida. Six-month slow release will be used up more quickly in South Florida than in cooler areas, unless it is formulated for South Florida conditions.

Regional Advice and Care

Pentas require a little care to look their best. They tend to get woody and leggy after three or four years, and you can take cuttings and replace the old plants with new ones. Cut back in the early spring to rejuvenate the plants. Keep well mulched during winter in Central Florida to help protect basal bud from cold. Also make cuttings of favorite varieties. Watch for spider mites in winter. Spider mites are tiny, difficult-to-see sucking insects that will suck out cell sap. They cause the upper surface of leaves to look pale or yellow. A hard spray of water will knock off these dry-season insects. Horticultural oil is another way to get them. Horticultural oil can be used in winter, when temperatures are below 80 degrees. Superfine oil, which is paraffin-based, can be used any time.

Companion Planting and Design

Use as a wave of a single color for best effect and to attract butterflies. Pink or white are standout colors for shade or in the evening. Or plant in a meadow with other wildflowers, such as Coreopsis, Goldenrod, and Yellowtop.

My Personal Favorite

White Pentas shows up at night and makes the garden's enjoyment nocturnal as well as diurnal.

With the wild popularity of butterfly gardening, Pentas have come into their own. The tiny nectar cups beneath the 5-petaled corollas are a lure for all kinds of hungry butterflies. A butterfly garden can take any shape or form. Include both nectar plants and larval food plants, and plan for butterflies that are locally plentiful. The nectar and pollen sources should be in the sun, protected from the wind by hedges or small trees. Include a source of water. The butterflies are free. Pentas are easy to care for, and they are rapid growers. Pentas come in regular and dwarf sizes so you can use them as background shrubs or foreground flowers. Additional cultivars include 'Cranberry Punch', 'Rose', and 'Lilac Mist'. A dwarf pink is available. (GBT)

Other Name
Egyptian Star Clusters

Bloom Period and Color
Spring through summer blooms in pink, white, lilac, or red

Mature Height × Spread
1 1/2 or 2 1/2 feet × 18 inches

Zones
9 – 11

Periwinkle

Catharanthus roseus

Bless their hearts, these naturalized bright little flowers are abandoned-lot hardy. They were among the first flowering plants the pioneers in South Florida traded and planted. Who knows how they got to Florida, but the women who longed for some tangible beauty around their rough-hewn houses knew to plant Periwinkles, which needed nothing more than a smile and a splash of water. That's practically all they need still. Use Periwinkles in sun and partial shade. Plant them in front of the Ligustrum hedge or the Podocarpus; put them over the septic tank. Periwinkles have been fancied up by breeding and come in bright new colors. And while the originals are lanky and rangy, the spiffy new ones are shorter. The originals continue to outperform the hybrids. (GBT)

Other Name
Vinca

Bloom Period and Color
Year-round blooms in pink, white, rose

Mature Height × Spread
12 inches × 12 inches

Zones
10B – 11

When, Where, and How to Plant
Plant anytime; the beginning of the rainy season is the best time. Plant in beds, in pots, in sandy, dry soil. Periwinkles can be cut back when they get too straggly. You can root cuttings in March or April, and by May they will be ready to set into beds. To transplant, simply use a trowel to lift out soil, inset the Periwinkles, and refill the hole. Then water. Cuttings are easily started. Use a 50:50 mix of peat moss and perlite; wet it thoroughly. Cut Periwinkles; remove several pairs of leaves and flowers; insert the cutting into the medium and place it in shade, out of wind, but where you will remember to keep the mix moist. To reduce the need to water, you can put the pots in plastic bags. Insert 1 or 2 bamboo stakes in the pot to keep the plastic from sagging onto the plants, then tie the bag closed. Wait 3 or 4 weeks before checking to see if there are sufficient roots to allow planting.

Growing Tips
Water to keep the roots moist for a month or so, then gradually taper off, allowing the plant to reduce its water needs. A teaspoon of slow-release fertilizer at planting time is sufficient. Too much pampering is not for these rugged perennials. When small, these bright plants look their best, if you like upright and neat gardens. When they age, they will sprawl and lean, and eventually, you will have to cut them back. Use them where a certain unkemptness is desirable: in the corners of the yard, or by the telephone pole or the composter.

Regional Advice and Care
Use as annuals in Central and North Florida.

Companion Planting and Design
These are flowers that seem to just pop up where there's an empty spot, that's how they look their best. Camouflage legginess of a Ligustrum hedge by allowing Periwinkles to drape over a foundation box.

My Personal Favorite
White Periwinkles are my preference for the same reason I like other white flowers - they can be readily seen at night.

Society Garlic

Tulbaghia violacea

When, Where, and How to Plant

Plant any time. Plant in a bed that has good drainage and some organic matter such as compost or peat moss. These plants can take full sun or partial shade. As you would plant other rhizomes and bulbs, place Society Garlic tubers not too far below the surface, with a little bone meal in the bottom of the planting hole; space about 18 inches apart. Flowers are produced from spring to fall.

Growing Tips

Keep the planting bed moist to get Society Garlic started, and use a slow-release fertilizer in spring, summer, and fall. Water less in winter, when it wants to rest.

Regional Advice and Care

Plants can be put into containers for winter and brought inside when freezing weather occurs. Place containers in a sunny location. These plants do not do well in shade, whether inside or out. If kept in shade or overwatered, Society Garlic can succumb to a fungus called southern blight, which begins at the ground level. Society Garlic also attracts aphids and whiteflies.

Companion Planting and Design

Mauve, pinks, and blues incline one to think of Gertrude Jekyll's mixed herbaceous borders, yet translating that look to Florida is difficult, given our bright light and the tendency of pale flowers to wash out. Yet, seen by itself, Society Garlic is a pretty flower. Like other Iris, the pretty flowers of Society Garlic can be used to line a walkway in full sun, or to add a medium-level backdrop to smaller-growing plants in a bed. For instance, they make a good foil for Moss Rose or Miniature Roses. If you have a vegetable garden, try Society Garlic among culinary herbs. More than once used to march up the edges of sidewalks, these tropical bulbs are better used in groups. Plant them several deep in front of Pittosporum shrubs, pink Hibiscus, Ligustrum, and Snowbush.

My Personal Favorite

Used in groups, rather than in long lines, these bulbs are quite spectacular.

Depending on the reference that you select, you find that Society Garlic is either in the Amaryllis family or related to Onion, Leek, Garlic, and Chive. Round balls of lilac, pink, or white flowers (umbels) top the slender flower stalks that are pleasing to the eye. This South African native does smell of Garlic or Onion, and yet was thought by someone to be less offensive than true Garlic, hence the name. (Tulbaghia is named for Rijk Tulbagh, an 18th Century Dutch governor of the Cape Colony of South Africa. There also is a town named for him.) The plant forms clumps, and tubers can be separated in winter. Flowers have six tepals and a corona. On some species and hybrids, the corona is more visible, colorful, and interesting. (GBT)

Bloom Period and Color
Year-round blooms in lilac, pink, white

Mature Height × Spread
1 to 2 feet × an equal spread

Zones
10 – 11

Spanish Bayonet
Yucca aloifolia

A planting of Spanish Bayonet, it is reported, once protected the grounds of Marjorie Merriweather Post's Palm Beach estate, Mar-a-Lago, and if it was good enough for her, it ought to be good enough for you in the crime deterrent department. Spanish Bayonets are not a pretty sight. A bizarre sight, perhaps even a frightening sight, yes. But if you put your mind to it, you can devise an effectively impenetrable home-protection system without the annoyance of accidental false alarms. Spanish Bayonet can be at the center of this. The leaf tips on this plant are memorably sharp. Trunks are covered with them. Groups of trunks arise together because they grow on underground rhizomes. A version of Spanish Bayonet called 'Marginata' has creamy leaf edges. (GBT)

Bloom Period and Color
Spring blooms in white

Mature Height × Spread
8 to 12 feet × 4 feet

Zones
8 – 11

When, Where, and How to Plant
Plant anytime. Salt and drought tolerant, Spanish Bayonet can be grouped with other succulents in areas that are out of reach of the sprinkler system, in seaside gardens, or in beds with plenty of sand. Carefully plant them when they are small. They make interesting plants for vertical elements, and can be useful in the background or fence corners. Flowers, which start in the spring, are on the terminal growing point, and once they have ceased, a secondary bud will break just behind the terminal bud. Other buds may pop near the bottom of the stem. *Yucca elephantipes* is a species that form large groups, while *Y. filamentosa,* called Adam's Needle, has several heads but no visible stems, along with lots of curling white hairs. The Spanish Bayonet is ideal for gardeners near the ocean. Native to Mexico, the Bayonet has naturalized on some Florida shores.

Growing Tips
If growing this outside in a container in a courtyard or patio, make sure drainage is excellent. Containers with drain holes should have shards of terra cotta in the bottom to keep soil and roots from clogging the holes. Use a potting mix with extra sand. The plant will become top heavy, and you may want to cover the soil with river rocks or pea rocks for weight, as if growing them on a windy balcony. Use a water soluble fertilizer or a slow-release fertilizer recommended for foliage plants.

Regional Advice and Care
Protect Spanish Bayonet from freezing weather in Central and North Florida.

Companion Planting and Design
Use this as a corner planting in a dry bed that gets full sun. Low-growing Shore Juniper or Sea Oats can be used to accent a clump of these plants that occur naturally on sand dunes.

My Personal Favorite
For oceanside gardens, these plants thrive.

Wild Petunia
Ruellia caroliniensis

When, Where, and How to Plant
Plant during the warm season. Choose a sunny, dry location among Pines and Palmettos. Use a trowel to dig a hole slightly larger than the rootball of the containerized Wild Petunia. Gently slip the plant from the container, holding it toward the base of the stem, not by the top. Position the plant in the planting hole, and fill with original soil. Water daily for a week to help the plant become established, then gradually taper off watering. *Ruellias* are drought tolerant, having evolved to withstand life in the pinelands.

Growing Tips
Little care is needed after the plant has become established and is growing well. Water twice weekly. If kept too wet, you may lose this wildflower, which often is recommended for Xeriscape landscaping. *Ruellias* tends to clump. They are cosmopolitan (Carolina Wild Petunia ranges from the eastern seaboard states across west Texas) and their ease of care suggests why: they are not fussy about soil, and they self-seed. While these characteristics are gardener-friendly, they can be ecosystem unfriendly should plants escape into the wild. Such are the considerations that might well go into selecting plants for your garden.

Regional Advice and Care
It has few pests or diseases, but won't provide much color in winter. This native is damaged by cold in Central and North Florida.

Companion Planting and Design
The popularity of butterfly gardens and native plants coupled with the increasing need to conserve water in landscapes has contributed to a recent popularity of *Ruellia*. Planted with a Yellow-flowering Necklace Pod (*Sophora tomentosa*) or Butterfly Bush, this native wildflower of the pinelands will help attract butterflies while making few demands on you as a gardener. *Ruellias* are being used in highway medians and parking lots, and they are thriving.

My Personal Favorite
Wild Petunia is a component of butterfly gardens.

Once, before the 1992 hurricane took out the pinelands, Wild Petunias could be found in Larry and Penny Thompson Park in South Dade County. I know, because old notes from a taxonomy field trip tell me so. The field trip was in August—absolutely the hottest time to be in the pinelands. Wild Petunias grow on slender stems with hairy opposite leaves and blue-lavender sessile flowers; the flowers have no stalk but the ends of the tubes attach directly to the plant. Wild Petunias can reseed themselves, given the right opportunity. Several nonnative Ruellias, which like damp conditions, are found in nurseries, including Ruellia amoena; Mexican Bluebell, and R. brittoniana; several cultivars, 'Compacta', 'Chi Chi,' 'Purple Showers,' and 'Snow Queen'; R. graecizans; and R. squarrosa, a ground cover. (GBT)

Other Name
Ruellia

Bloom Period and Color
Summer blooms, in the morning, in blue-lavender

Mature Height × Spread
20 inches × various

Zones
10 – 11

More Perennials

Spineless Century Plant *(Agave attenuata)*

Other Name Foxtail Agave; **Bloom Period and Color** One-time blooms in yellow;
Mature Height × **Spread** 2 feet to 4 feet × 3 feet

When, Where, and How to Plant Plant at any time, except when in flower. Plant in sandy beds, rock gardens, or areas without irrigation. This *Agave* prefers partial sun or shade rather than full sun. Dig a hole as deep as the depth of the rootball in the container, but somewhat wider; remove the container from the plant and slip the Agave into the planting hole; water in backfill. *Agave* plants are excellent choices for the rocky Florida Keys.

Growing Tips Little care is needed. Water the plants when they are young. Use liquid fertilizer 2 or 3 times a year. Spineless Century Plant is well suited for rock gardens or areas where the sprinklers won't reach. The *Agave* flowers, but after about 10 years, not 100. The tall flower spike can reach several feet, and flowers form around it, hence the name Foxtail.

Regional Advice and Care The secret to arid plants in South Florida is the drainage. Sand drains almost instantly; limestone holds water a little longer in its many holes and crevices. For gardens on a rocky substrate, add sand to the planting material, use a potting soil for succulents, but add more sand or perlite to it. *Agaves* seldom have problems even in the rainy season if the drainage is correct. Protect these plants from freezes.

Swamp Fern *(Blechnum serrulatum)*

Other Name Toothed Fern; **Bloom Period and Color** Year-round foliage;
Mature Height × **Spread** To 5 feet × various

When, Where, and How to Plant Plant in spring or during the warm months. Choose shaded locations with moist soil. Swamp Fern loves shade and damp muck. Keep the rhizome fairly close to the surface of the soil. Ferns can be transplanted simply by separating clumps and cutting runners. If you have patience, one container of Ferns purchased from your garden center or native nursery can be used as a motherlode after a season in the ground. It's best to plant Ferns in mulch, letting their roots travel just below the surface. Growing Ferns from spores requires some expertise and experience.

Growing Tips Keep the rhizome damp, and Swamp Fern will require little else. A high-nitrogen slow-release fertilizer may be added, or a fertilizer for foliage plants. Fish emulsion or 8-8-8 also are good fertilizers for Ferns, every week or two in summer, and monthly in winter. After winter, remove old fronds that have been chilled and dried in wind and cold.

Regional Advice and Care Protect Swamp Ferns from freezing weather by planting in a southern exposure or beneath trees. Ferns can sometimes come down with scale or mealybugs. If these insects are not in great numbers, the plants don't really need any treatment. Ferns may be susceptible to damage from oils and insecticidal soaps. However, Sunspray Ultra-Fine® Year-Round Pesticidal Oil made from paraffin is labeled for use against mealybugs and scale on Ferns.

Roses *for Florida*

What's a gardener's favorite flower? Most people would probably put the Rose at or near the top of their list. It's also our national flower, and it should be planted proudly.

Many settlers heading into the state tucked away a Rose to plant near their new homes. Those homes are often gone now, but amazingly, some Louis Philippe Rose plantings—often called the Florida Rose—still survive near a chimney or foundation.

Selecting the Best

Roses grow year-round in Florida. That's why gardeners have to be particular about selecting their plants. It's important to get to know the varieties tested by rosarians living within the state. Most Rose societies and your local Extension Service have lists of the good performers.

Some Rose selections seem to wear out in the hot, humid summer seasons. It's important to know the rootstock as well as the variety. Until recently, most mail-order companies shipping to Florida did not pick rootstocks for local conditions, and the plants lasted only a year or two. A majority of the Florida gardeners prefer to purchase their Roses locally to get the best-adapted plants.

Be sure to ask for a good Florida-performing variety grafted onto a vigorous rootstock. University of Florida evaluations have demonstrated that the *Rosa fortuniana* rootstock, also known as the Double White Cherokee Rose, produces the most vigorous and longest-lived plants for Florida landscapes. A 'Dr. Huey' rootstock is second best, giving a good flowering plant. Roses grafted on *multiflora* decline after a year or two of growth, making *multiflora* the least satisfactory rootstock.

Planting Roses

'Double Delight'

Give Roses your best sunny location. Make them the accent plants for the landscape where visitors can stop and enjoy them. This is one time when it really pays to give the soil extra attention. Make sure the site is well drained and enriched before planting.

The list of soil improvements Rose growers add to planting sites is extensive. Peat moss, compost, perlite, vermiculite, and manure are among the basics needed to increase the soil's water-holding capacity and provide nutrients for growth. Many growers also

add clay particles, alfalfa pellets, bone meal, fish meal, green sand, and similar components. Some even put several sheets of newspaper in the bottom of the hole to hold water in the upper soil layer a little longer.

Roses can be added to the landscape at any time of the year, but Florida plantings are best made at the beginning of the fall or spring months. These are the less stressful times of the year when the plants can root down quickly and produce lots of green growth while still opening flower buds.

Mixed Roses

Set the new Rose in the ground at the same depth it grew in the container or a little higher. Few Florida Roses are sold bare root, but when available, these plants should be set at the original depth as noted along the trunks. Fill in around the roots, watering as you go to ensure good root contact with the soil. Most Rose growers like to form a berm at the edge of each rootball to catch water and direct it down to the roots. Finish planting by adding a mulch. Any mulch will do, including pine needles, bark, or coarse compost. Keep the new plantings moist, and provide the first feedings in about two to three weeks.

Stick to a Schedule

Gardeners who want to cut lots of bouquets must keep the plantings on a good maintenance schedule. It's best to visit beds daily to cut flowers for the home or to give to friends. At this time you can also do minor grooming, removing declining twigs or pinching out pests. Check the soil for water needs as well. When the surface starts to feel dry to the touch, it's time to give the plants a $1/2$- to 1-inch soaking. Well-rooted

Rose plantings in an improved soil can go thee to four days or more between waterings. New plants need more frequent irrigation. Microsprinkler or soaker hose irrigation systems keep the water off the foliage to prevent disease.

Florida Roses need a monthly feeding. Many gardeners use a 6-6-6 or similar fertilizer, but others have chosen a higher nitrogen product such as a 12-4-8. Some use liquids, and others use completely natural products consisting of manure and animal by-products. The only important guideline seems to be that you maintain a schedule to keep the plant vigorous and in bloom.

By summer many Florida Roses have grown quite tall. Some gardeners use this opportunity to harvest long-stem blooms. Others allow the plant to grow high overhead with multiple flowering shoots. In South Florida this is often a time for plants to get a light trimming. In other areas of the state most gardeners wait until winter to give Roses except Climbers and Miniatures a major pruning. This involves removing $1/3$ to $1/2$ the height of the plant. Pruners also trim out the twiggy growths and all diseased portions at this time. Most Hybrid Teas and Grandiflora and Floribunda types are left with three to seven strong canes to continue growth.

Pests and Disease

Roses do have several pests that growers must contend with to have attractive, long-lived plants. One is the notorious blackspot that causes dark, rounded areas, often with a yellow halo, to form on the foliage. It is mainly a disease that appears in the warm, rainy season, but it can appear at other times as well. It's controlled primarily by selecting plants with some resistance and using fungicide treatments. Another major pest is the spider mite that sucks juices from the foliage. Most infestations appear during the drier months between September and May. Controls can be as simple as washing the mites from the underside of the foliage with a strong stream of water. For more persistent mite problems, try applying a soap or oil spray or using one of the synthetic miticides.

Some other pests that may attack Roses are thrips, beetles, caterpillars, powdery mildew, and stem cankers. Many can be hand picked or pruned from the plants, but others may need a spray. When applying pesticides, follow label instructions. Weeds can also be a problem in the beds. Most gardeners either pull out the unwanted greenery or spot treat with a nonselective herbicide labeled for use in rose or flower beds. After removing the weeds, renew the mulch layer to control new growths.

One reason Roses are so popular is that they have a lot to give. Most modern Roses flower continually. Many have a pleasing fragrance, and you can choose almost any color from the rainbow except blue.

Climbing Rose
Rosa hybrids

Almost every gardener would like to add a Climbing Rose to the landscape. It's a quick way to fill a wall, fence, or trellis. Many gardeners like to have a Climbing Rose on the side of the home or at the entrance to form an accent feature. And Climbing Roses have lots of limbs, which means there should be bouquets to cut at any time. Some older types are quite colorful but flower only once a year. Perhaps the best climber for the Florida landscape is 'Don Juan', a hybrid with large, red, fragrant blossoms. Two more are 'America', an orange–pink, and 'Sombreuil', a double white. Most—including the Species Roses, Yellow Lady Banks Rose and 'Cherokee' Rose—flower only once a year during spring. (TM)

Bloom Period and Color
Spring and summer blooms in all colors

Mature Height × Spread
6 to 8 feet × 6 to 8 feet

When, Where, and How to Plant
The best time to plant is during the late winter through early spring. Choose a site where each plant has plenty of room to grow a root system. Climbers can be grown in containers, but the size of the plant is often restricted by the available space. Sandy soils especially benefit from lots of organic matter including compost, peat moss, and manure. Provide good drainage. If the soil is naturally wet, plant the Rose bush in a mound of soil or a raised bed. At planting dig the hole wider but no deeper than the rootball. Position the bush so that it is at the same depth it was in the pot. Finish the planting by adding a berm and 2 to 3 inches of mulch.

Growing Tips
Apply fertilizer once a month through the warmer months. During the cooler times, reduce feedings to every six to eight weeks. Roses need lots of water to maintain good growth. Established Rose plantings need a good watering every three to four days.

Regional Advice and Care
Rose care is similar throughout the state of Florida. Climbing Roses get limited pruning. Allow the long canes to develop with many laterals to bear the Roses. After two to three years of growth, thin out the weak shoots, and prune laterals back to the main stems, leaving just two to three buds. Residents of North Florida may find more winter injury and need additional pruning after periods of cold. Residents of South Florida may not need to reduce winter feeding but stay on the once-a-month schedule. Two pests that can kill a Rose bush are blackspot, which is a disease, and mites.

Companion Planting and Design
Send plants up a trellis or train to a fence as accents and space dividers. Use them as back drops for Bush Daisies, Pentas, Gaura, Salvias, and Shrimp Plants.

My Personal Favorite
One Climbing Rose is always listed as the best for Florida and that's 'Don Juan'. It flowers freely and has great vigor.

Floribunda Rose

Rosa hybrids

When, Where, and How to Plant

The best seasons for planting are spring and fall. Prepare a planting site by adding compost, peat moss, and manure to the sandy Florida soils. Containers can be filled with any loose, well-drained potting soil. Set all Roses in the soil at the same depth as they were growing in the container. After planting, form a berm of soil around the plant to catch water and direct it down through the roots. Also add a 2- to 3-inch mulch layer of pine needles, bark, or coarse mulch. Some very bushy plants may also need staking to prevent frequent wind from whipping the plants during storms.

Growing Tips

All Roses need similar care. Keep the soil moist, and apply a fertilizer to in-ground plantings monthly and container gardens weekly. Use a 12-4-8 or other similar Rose fertilizer for in-ground plantings. A liquid fertilizer can be used with container plantings.

Regional Advice and Care

North and Central Florida growers may reduce the feedings to every 6 to 8 weeks during the late fall and winter months. Throughout the growing season, some grooming may also be needed to remove old flowers, injured plant portions, and small twiggy growths. Also North Florida plantings might suffer winter damage that needs pruning before spring growth begins. South Florida growers usually continue the monthly feeding program but may add an extra pruning during the late summer season. Floribunda Roses should receive a pruning during late winter, around January or February. Cut the plants back 1/3 to 1/2. Keep the plants to 3 to 7 main stems. Common pests of Roses include blackspot, which is a disease, and mites.

Companion Planting and Design

Plant in clusters as part of a perennial garden with Bird-of-Paradise, Butterfly Weed, Coreopsis, and Mexican Heather. Plantings also look great when backed by taller Anise, Feijoa, Ligustrum, and Viburnum.

My Personal Favorite

They say pest resistance is in the yellow Roses. One that really performs in Florida is 'Sunflare'; it appears to have great blackspot resistance.

Floribunda Roses range in size between the Miniatures and the Hybrid Teas. They are multipurpose Roses, giving lots of small- to medium-sized flowers in a wide assortment of colors. Most flower buds are pointed to slightly rounded and have the Hybrid Tea look. Some favorites you have probably heard of include 'Sunflare', 'French Lace', 'Europeana', 'Angel Face', 'Hannah Gordon', 'First Edition', and 'Sunsprite'. They are considered very hardy and generally pest resistant. This is a good Rose for the smaller garden. The flowers can be enjoyed in the garden or cut as bouquets for the home. There are many good Floribunda Rose varieties. Some others you may want to try include 'Playgirl', 'Ivory Fashion', 'Nana Mouskouri', 'Raspberry Ruffles', and 'Showbiz'. (TM)

Bloom Period and Color

Spring and summer blooms in all colors

Mature Height × Spread

4 feet × 4 feet

Grandiflora Rose
Rosa hybrids

Gardeners who wanted a Rose bush a little taller than a Hybrid Tea and with the full clusters of the Floribunda Roses got their wish in 1954 with the development of the first Grandiflora hybrids. An all-time favorite, 'Queen Elizabeth' was the first of the new group and is today still the standard for this classification. Most blossoms are pointed like the Hybrid Teas and open as side shoots at the end of the terminal stem. Since this is a relatively new Rose classification, the number of species is rather limited but growing. Some favorites are 'Gold Medal', 'Tournament of Roses', 'Shreveport', 'Montezuma', and 'Love'. A few additional varieties worth trying include 'Pink Parfait', 'Camelot', 'White Lightning', 'Aquarius', 'Prominent', and 'Lagerfeld'. (TM)

Bloom Period and Color
Spring and summer blooms in all colors

Mature Height × Spread
8 feet × 5 feet

When, Where, and How to Plant
Roses can be planted year-round as container-grown plants. Bare-root specimens are best planted during the dormant season of January and February or add the plants to the landscape during the fall and early spring months. Enrich sandy soils with organic matter such as compost, peat moss, and manure. Bare-root plants should be set in the ground at the same depth they were growing in the field. Container plants should be set so that the top of the rootball is at or slightly above the soil level. Construct a berm under the plants and add a 2- to 3-inch mulch layer. Add a stake or two to keep winds from dislodging the plants during storms.

Growing Tips
Feed the plants monthly with a 12-4-8 or similar rose fertilizer. Keep the soil moist.

Regional Advice and Care
North and Central Florida growers often reduce feedings during the winter months to every 6 to 8 weeks. In these cooler regions of the state some winter damage may occur and need removal from the plants by spring. Southern growers usually continue the monthly feeding program and do some extra pruning toward the end of summer. Since the plants are expected to grow tall and wide, a yearly pruning is definitely needed in January or February. At this time of the year the plants are cut back 1/3 to 1/2. Remove small twigs, and reduce the main canes to 3 to 7 in number. Blackspot and mites can cause major decline. Blackspot is mainly a problem during the damp summer months, and mites affect the foliage during the dry times.

Companion Planting and Design
Plant just a bed of Roses or create clusters among perennials, annuals, and accent shrubs. Plant with Salvias, Marigolds, Melampodium, Bush Daisies, Pentas, Lantana, Snowbush, Fire Spike, Thryallis, and Heliconia.

My Personal Favorite
My favorite has to be 'Queen Elizabeth' with its good pink color and vigorous growth. It's a reliable bloomer in my Florida garden.

Hybrid Tea Rose

Rosa hybrids

When, Where, and How to Plant

The best time for planting is during spring or fall. Add compost, peat moss, and manure then till the soil deeply. If planting in a container, use a potting soil mix. Position each new Rose so that the top of the rootball is even with the soil. If planting bare-root plants, use the color change along the trunk as an indication of how deep to plant. In poorly drained gardens plant the bushes in mounds or raised beds. Complete the plantings by adding a 2- to 3-inch mulch layer over the soil surface.

Growing Tips

Feed the Hybrid Teas monthly with a rose fertilizer. Fertilize every six weeks during cooler winter weather. Keep the soil moist. Most established plants need a soaking every three or four days.

Regional Advice and Care

North Florida growers may have to prune out some cold damage, and South Florida growers may add an extra pruning in August. Every year during January or February, Roses should be given a pruning to reduce the height by 1/3 to 1/2. This is also the time to remove weak stems and limit the bushes to no more than seven strong stems. Throughout the growing season, gardeners should be constantly giving the plants a light grooming to remove weak stems and direct growth. Also, South Florida growers may not need to reduce the feedings during the winter. Blackspot attacks mainly during hot, rainy weather. When severe, spray weekly with a fungicide. Mites are a major problem mainly during dry weather. Light infestations can be washed off the foliage, or apply a miticide. Other pests include thrips, powdery mildew, aphids, caterpillars, and stem cankers.

Companion Planting and Design

Plant a bed or a few clusters. Make sure they have adequate spacing and then leave room for annuals and perennials around the edges including Ageratum, Alyssum, Periwinkle, and Lantana.

My Personal Favorite

If you ask a guest to pick a favorite flower out of a Rose bouquet it will likely be the 'Double Delight' variety. The plants are colorful, vigorous, and free flowering.

Modern Roses began in 1867 with the introduction of the first Hybrid Tea named 'La France'. All Roses prior to this date are considered old varieties, and those produced after this date are the new Roses. Hybrid Teas have just what the gardener wants: great color, stems of single blossoms, and a bushy plant. Many of the Roses you like probably are members of this group, including 'Pristine', 'Double Delight', 'Granada', 'Uncle Joe', 'Peace', 'First Prize', and 'Cary Grant'. The list goes on of mostly vigorous plants that are ideal for the home flower bed. Obtain a list of the best Roses from a local rosarian. A few more good performers include 'Color Magic', 'Paradise', 'Chrysler Imperial', 'Tropicana', 'Fragrant Cloud', 'Swarthmore', and 'Mister Lincoln'. (TM)

Other Name

Tea Rose

Bloom Period and Color

Spring and summer blooms in all colors

Mature Height × Spread

5 to 6 feet × 5 feet

Miniature Rose
Rosa hybrids

If you are looking for a Rose to grow in a container for the porch, patio, or windowsill, a Miniature would make a good selection. Miniatures are also used to fill flower beds as a ground cover and line walkways. Some Miniatures are just inches tall, such as the variety 'Si', with tiny white blossoms. Others, such as 'Rise 'N' Shine', grow several feet. The blossoms on Miniatures are much smaller than Roses in other categories. Miniatures include several Rose types, including Climbers, Ramblers, and Hybrid Tea look-alikes. If you are looking for a good starter collection, you might try 'Starina', 'Party Girl', 'Perrine', 'Jean Keanneally', 'Olympic Gold', 'Debut', 'Herbie', 'Red Beauty', and 'Magic Carrousel'. Others include 'Over the Rainbow', 'Starglo', 'Rosmarin', 'White Angel', 'Pacesetter', and 'Kathy'. (TM)

Bloom Period and Color
Spring and summer blooms in all colors

Mature Height × Spread
4 inches to 24 inches × 6 inches to 24 inches

When, Where, and How to Plant
Any time is a good time to add one or more Miniature Roses to the collection. Plants rarely suffer transplant shock and take root quickly. For a window location, make sure there is good air circulation. Add Roses to a container by selecting a pot that's 1 or 2 inches larger than the original container. Giving the plants too large a container can lead to overwatering and root rot. Sandy soils should be improved with compost, peat moss, and manure. Position the plants at the original growing depth. With in-ground plantings add a berm to catch water then add a 2- to 3-inch mulch of pine needles, bark, or coarse compost.

Growing Tips
Give Miniature Roses adequate water to keep the soil moist. Test container gardens daily, and when the surface of the soil starts to dry, it's time to give them a good soaking. In-ground plants can normally go several days between waterings. All plantings need regular feedings. Use a liquid or slow-release fertilizer with container plantings as instructed on the label. In-ground plantings can be fed monthly with a 12-4-8 or similar fertilizer.

Regional Advice and Care
Growers in North Florida may reduce feedings during the late fall and winter months. In-ground plantings may suffer some winter damage and need extra pruning. When the plants become overgrown, give a shearing. Thin to remove old, nonproductive twigs. Check in-ground plantings for mites frequently during the drier months. Plants kept in protected locations may have mite problems at any time. Where needed, apply a miticide. Blackspot appears to be a less frequent problem but may affect the plants during the rainy season.

Companion Planting and Design
Grow in pots for the sunny spots. Or plant in ground in front of taller Roses. Use as an edging with a backdrop of Dwarf Yaupon Holly or Indian Hawthorn.

My Personal Favorite
Miniature Roses get plenty of attention but it helps if they are especially colorful. One that really attracts my attention and is a good performer is 'Magic Carrousel'.

When, Where, and How to Plant

The very best times to plant are during spring and fall. Many Roses tolerate a very minimum of a half-day of sun with bright light for the rest of the day. Since there are many different plant sizes and shapes within this group, pay special attention to spacing and needs for a fence or trellis. Give Roses your very best soil. Work in lots of organic matter including compost, peat moss, and manure. Set the plants in the ground at the same height they were growing in the container. Add soil, and water to fill in around the root system. After the plant is in the ground, construct a berm and add a 2- to 3-inch mulch layer of pine needles, bark, or coarse compost.

Growing Tips

Old Garden Roses need normal care. Keep the soil moist, and feed monthly with a 12-4-8 or similar rose fertilizer.

Regional Advice and Care

Roses grow well throughout the state. North Florida growers should reduce feedings during late fall through winter to every six to eight weeks. In the North some winter injury may occur that needs additional trimming. Bush types should be pruned back during the late winter months of January and February. Most are cut back 1/3 to 1/2. Some plants are quite twiggy and benefit from some thinning. Climbing types are left to grow tall and fill a fence or trellis. Every two to three years they should be given a renewal pruning. Many older varieties show resistance to common Rose pests. Gardeners should still stay alert to blackspot and mites—the two worst pests of Roses. Where needed, apply an appropriate pesticide.

Companion Planting and Design

Fill a bed, use as shrubs, or create a backdrop for annual and perennial plants. Clusters or individual plants can be mixed with Pentas, Bush Daisies, African Iris, and Salvias.

My Personal Favorite

There are many to pick from but I have to stick with what is sometimes called the Florida Rose, 'Louis Philippe'. It has persisted among the old homesteads where others have vanished.

All Roses planted prior to 1867 are considered Old Garden Roses. These were the Roses distributed throughout Europe and later taken to the homesteads of settlers in the New World. Fragrance missing in many modern hybrids is often found in the Old Rose varieties. Some growers feel they also have extra vigor plus pest resistance. Within this very diverse category are bush types growing to 6 feet tall, Climbers, and Miniature forms. The colors vary, but many are good pinks including bush types 'Paul Neyron', 'Old Blush', 'Souvenir De La Malmaison', and 'Rose De Rescht'. Some other Old Roses you might like to add to the Florida garden include the 'Chestnut' Rose, 'Lady Banks' Rose, 'Cherokee' Rose, 'Louis Philippe', and 'Green' Rose. (TM)

Other Name
Garden Rose

Bloom Period and Color
Spring and summer blooms in all colors

Mature Height × Spread
6 feet × 8 feet

Shrubs *for Florida*

For lo, these many years, I have been told by horticulturists to think of shrubs as the walls of the garden. And so I do, and so they are. They are the space shapers of the garden, the room dividers, the plants that we see at eye level.

Shrubs most often make up the hedges that set off property lines, and they are also used as accents for entryways. These are among the most common reasons for growing them. There are other aesthetic reasons, practical reasons, and of course, the just plain "I want one" reasons.

For small spaces, shrubs are often more convenient than trees. A large shrub (which also may be a small tree) won't have to be brutally pruned should it outgrow its spot; it won't lift the pavers with massive roots; it won't shade out the other plants in the garden.

Shrubs will bring color, and very often alluring fragrance, to an area, be it townhouse garden or suburban yard. Some bring with them fruit, which can be appealing to you or to birds. Some attract butterflies and moths. Carefully selected shrubs will bring fall color (Crape Myrtles) or winter flowers (*Clerodendron quadriculare*). Others, such as Azaleas and Rhododendrons, are the very essence of early spring.

An often overlooked function of shrubs is simply to provide greenery. Once you have lived in Florida a few years and travel to the Southwest or Midwest or anywhere in the temperate climate in winter, you understand how vital that green is to our landscape.

Chenille Plant

Attracting Birds and Butterflies

Using native shrubs can go a long way toward helping not only resident birds, such as the cardinals that nest in shrubs, but also migrants in need of a stopover shelter and food. Provisioning the landscape for wildlife is a vital part of contemporary gardening because so much of the natural area of this country has been covered with cities and farms.

Shrubs also play a key role in butterfly gardening; many of the nectar-bearing flowers that attract butterflies are shrub-borne. One South Florida shrub that comes to mind is *Cordia globosa*. It produces round heads of tiny white flowers and all kinds of skippers, and little butterflies can be found there throughout the day. In Central and North Florida, Buddleia is the Butterfly Bush par excellence.

Shrub Considerations

While we may give special deference to Roses, they are in fact shrubs (as well as climbing plants). The returning popularity of Old Roses is welcome in Florida, where finicky Hybrid Teas have a hard time with blackspot, requiring too many applications of chemicals. Old Roses are hardier, less disease prone, and some, such as Chinas, Teas, and Noisettes, flower off and on all year. And many of them can be mixed right in with other shrubs in a border planting.

Ixora

As our lives have become more hectic and time more precious, there is a greater need to reduce household chores, including those in the garden. One way to do so is to landscape informally, so that shrubs are not clipped and pruned but are allowed to billow and assume their natural shapes. That is not to say pruning is never required, but it will be needed less often if plants can assume hazy or flowing shapes rather than rigid and boxed ones. For such shrubs as Gardenia and Ixoras, Hibiscus and Orange Jasmine, the flowers are produced on new growth, so regular pruning means fewer flowers.

In recent years, new shrubs have entered our gardening and landscaping vocabulary. Tibouchina, for instance, is now widely available. It is popularly called Glory Bush for its purple flowers. Mussaenda is another tropical shrub finding wide use in protected southern areas. Croton is making a comeback. New ways to feature Croton include mixed borders and grouping several together rather than forming sun-bleached, leggy hedges.

Shrubs are the workhorses of the garden. We can assign them many roles, and they can take them on. But like workhorses, they need a good diet. Fertilize shrubs in spring, summer, and fall (March, June/July, October). Most will need supplemental irrigation in the dry season, at least once a week, possibly less often if mulch has been applied about 3 or 4 inches deep (as with trees, keep mulch away from the trunks of shrubs to avoid disease).

Prune the flowering shrubs after they flower, and the fast-growing big ones in the spring. Watch for aphids, which love new and succulent growth, and use insecticidal soap or 2 tablespoons of detergent plus 2 tablespoons vegetable oil in a gallon of water. Shrubs will perform well in return.

American Beautyberry

Callicarpa americana

American Beautyberry is a native plant of the southeastern United States. It grows where other shrubs do poorly, often in poor soils, and it requires little care. The real beauty of this shrub is evident during the fall and winter months when the fruits turn a maroon to purplish color in large clusters along the stems. This great accent shrub is possibly best used in naturalistic areas and along walkways. It makes a good space divider and view barrier. It remains semi-evergreen during the winter months. Consider this plant for minimal maintenance landscapes and landscapes getting just natural rainfall. It's frequently planted in clusters of three or more to create a display of fall color. Plants of American Beautyberry that produce white berries are available. (TM)

Other Name
Beautyberry

Bloom Period and Color
Spring blooms in pink

Mature Height × Spread
6 feet × 6 feet

When, Where, and How to Plant

Transplanting plants from one area of the landscape to another is best done between December and February except in South Florida, when planting is done in spring or summer. Plants in containers can be planted at any time of the year. American Beautyberry grows well in moist to dry soils. A well-drained soil is best. Enrich with compost or peat moss and manure. Dig a hole that's much wider than the rootball but not deeper. Position the American Beautyberry at the same depth it was growing in the container or original planting site. It may be set a little higher above the soil level, especially in poorly drained locations. After planting, form a berm and add a 2- to 3-inch mulch layer.

Growing Tips

Once established, most shrubs grow well with minimal care. The American Beautyberry is very drought tolerant and, after the roots of new plants have grown into the soil, seldom needs special watering. It can also survive with nutrients from mulches and what other trees and shrubs in the area provide. If additional growth is desired, feed once in March, May, and August. Use a 6-6-6, 16-4-8, or similar fertilizer.

Regional Advice and Care

The American Beautyberry grows well throughout the state with similar care. In South Florida it blooms year-round. No pruning is needed at planting time. The American Beautyberry grows quite lanky and should be pruned during late winter before new growth begins. Remove older stems, and cut the plantings back to a few feet below the desired height. Some pests include caterpillars and grasshoppers, but they are seldom a problem. Many can be hand picked from the plantings.

Companion Planting and Design

Use in a natural setting with other low moisture-requiring plants. Use as a backdrop for Coreopsis, Asters, or Daisies, or with contrasting greenery of Saw Palmetto, Hollies, and ornamental grasses.

My Personal Favorite

This native plant comes in a few colors but the purple forms are especially attractive.

Azalea
Rhododendron spp.

When, Where, and How to Plant
Transplant from one area of the landscape to another between December and February. Plants in containers can be added at any time. Azalea plants prefer filtered sun. They grow good foliage in the shade but give poor flower displays. A well-drained soil is best. Make sure the plantings have an acid soil. Improve the planting site with compost, peat moss, or manure. Dig a hole that's much wider than the rootball but not deeper. Position the Azalea plant at the same depth as it was growing in the container or original planting site. It may be set a little higher above the soil level, especially in a poorly drained location. After planting, form a berm and add a 2- to 3-inch mulch layer.

Growing Tips
Once established, most shrubs grow well with minimal care, but it may be two years before Azaleas grow a substantial root system. The best plantings have regular feedings and adequate water. Azaleas should be fed once in March, May, and September. Use a 6-6-6, 16-4-8, or similar fertilizer. Azaleas need frequent watering, especially during periods of drought.

Regional Advice and Care
Native Azaleas are limited to the colder areas of the state. They are recommended for North Florida, but some have been planted in the central regions. Most hybrids are limited to North and Central Florida. Grow Azaleas in partial shade and acid conditions in South Florida; 'Sweet Forgiveness' does well in South Florida. Pruning is not needed at planting time. Azaleas need rejuvenation pruning every three to five years. Prune to keep the plants inbounds yearly. Some pests that affect Azaleas are caterpillars, lace bugs, and mites.

Companion Planting and Design
Plant in clusters for the best color in the shady spots. Use as a backdrop or edging with Cast Iron Plants, Cocculus, Gardenia, Ferns, Liriope, Philodendron, Crossandra, Impatiens, and Begonias.

My Personal Favorite
Only a few Azaleas have really become popular and are grown in most landscapes. One group, the 'Southern Indian' hybrids, are known to survive some of the poorer and drier soils often found in Florida.

Nothing heralds spring's arrival better than Azaleas. Most gardeners have heard of some old-time favorites such as 'Duc de Rohan', 'Formosa', 'George Lindley Taber', and 'Southern Charm'. Azaleas have been a Florida favorite for only about 75 years. The more common types include the 'Southern Indian', 'Krume', 'Satsuki', 'Rutherford', and 'Pericat'. Most plantings bloom for three to four weeks, then fade into the background as a space divider or transition plant. Lower-growing Azaleas are also used as ground covers and small hedges along walkways. Florida is home to four native Azaleas. The species Rhododendron austrinum, Rhododendron calendulaceum, and Rhododendron canescens are deciduous, and Rhododendron chapmannii is an evergreen type. These are medium to large shrubs found mainly in the northern portion of the state. (TM)

Bloom Period and Color
Spring blooms in pink, red, white, purple

Mature Height × Spread
2 to 6 feet × 2 to 6 feet

Zones
8 – 9

Camellia

Camellia japonica

Camellias can be counted on for a major display of color when there are very few flowering shrubs during the late fall and winter. All grow as shrubs for accent plantings, view barriers, and backdrops near flower gardens. The blossoms are single to very double, up to five inches in diameter. The flowers are often cut for indoor displays. Numerous varieties are available but the early to mid season selections are the most reliable Florida bloomers. A relative, the Sasanqua Camellia, is also available for planting and is the first to flower starting in early fall. It produces single to semi-double blooms that shatter if removed from the shrubs. The beverage tea also comes from Camellia. It has yellow flowers and can be grown in Florida landscapes. (TM)

Other Names
Common Camellia, Japonica Camellia

Bloom Period and Color
Late November through March; shades of pink, red plus white.

Mature Height × Spread
10 to 12 feet × 6 to 8 feet (It may grow to 25 feet with age.)

Zones
7 – 9

When, Where, and How to Plant
While Camellias tolerate the sun they are best planted in lightly shaded locations. When in too much shade they fail to flower or decline. Give them a well-drained soil. They make the best growth if sandy soils are improved with organic matter. It's also best to check the soil acidity and adjust the pH to a 5.5 to 6.5 range if needed. Make sure they are not potbound at the time of planting by loosening some of the entwined roots if needed. Create a 4- to 6-inch berm at the edge of the root ball to direct water down through the root system during establishment. Many Camellias are lost due to dry root balls shortly after planting.

Growing Tips
Plantings grow best with a feeding in March, June, and August. Use a general fertilizer or azalea-camellia special. Camellias tolerate short periods of drought but grow best with weekly waterings. Also keep a 3- to 4-inch mulch over the root system, but not touching the trunk.

Regional Advice and Care
Trim Camellias immediately after flowering and before the end of April. Buds for the following year form in late spring and would be trimmed off by late spring through summer pruning. Nip back the ends of shoots as needed to increase branching and develop compact growth. Camellias are very susceptible to tea scale, an insect problem. The insect forms a white and brown coating on the underside of the leaves and causes the leaves to turn yellow. Mites are also a problem during the summer season. Both pests can be controlled with an oil spray. Die-back, a disease, often causes limbs to decline and should be pruned from the plants as needed.

Companion Planting and Design
Plant with shrubs that like the filtered sun and an acid soil. Some of these include Azaleas, Hydrangeas, and Gardenias. Also use with beds of shade loving Impatiens, Begonias, and Peacock Ginger.

My Personal Favorite
It's hard to pick a favorite but the older varieties appear to be the more consistent performers. 'Debutante', a bright pink, is one of my favorites but there are many others.

Chenille Plant

Acalypha hispida

When, Where, and How to Plant

Plant in spring or just at the beginning of the rainy season (late May to early June) to take advantage of the rains that will keep the root system moist. This plant will become established readily. Plant in full sun to get the best flower production. The Chenille Plant likes a rich, well-draining soil. Add compost, peat moss, or well-aged manure or potting soil to the planting hole, which should be just as deep as the rootball and 2 to 3 times as wide. Slip the container from the rootball, position the shrub in the planting hole, water in the backfill, and cover with mulch to a depth of 3 or 4 inches. (To avoid disease, keep the mulch away from the stem of the plant.)

Growing Tips

Though not particularly drought tolerant, and not salt tolerant at all, Chenille Plant nonetheless grows fast and robust with normal care. Fertilize 2 or 3 times a year and don't let the shrub go for weeks on end without water. Water a couple of times a week in summer if rain is not adequate for growth, and once a week in winter. A 6-6-6 fertilizer is fine; use a 7-3-7 in alkaline soils.

Regional Advice and Care

A cold-tender plant, Chenille will be damaged in Central and North Florida unless protected. Place it in a southeastern location or use a container and cut it back quite hard to keep it small. Prune this shrub after it flowers to keep it inbounds. Look for aphids on new growth, scale, and mealybugs. Insecticidal soap can work against aphids and mealybugs. Use malathion against scale.

Companion Planting and Design

Plant Chenille Plant in a mixed planting of shrubs and Lady Palms, perhaps beneath Palms along a property line or path at a strategic turning point; Acalyphas will point the way. Blend carefully with Crotons, Hibiscus, Snowbush, and Alocasias for a tropical screen.

My Personal Favorites

Acalypha wilkesiana 'Ceylon' is the Fire Dragon plant that has a light pink (sometimes white) edge that is serrated and is an interesting specimen plant. *Acalypha wilkesiana* 'Java White' is a white and green version of the usually pink and maroon plant. Both are eye-catching when used exactingly.

Chenille Plant brings an unusual look to the garden—therefore, it is one of those plants that should be used with care. The long strands of flowers occur off and on throughout the warm months. The species name, hispida, means "bristly." With a plant as showy as Chenille, positioning it in the landscape may mean allowing it to be a focal point, placing it against an all-green border of shrubs or clustering three or five together to be "comrades in charm." A. hispida 'Alba' is a variety with white spikes. Acalypha wilkesiana is called Copper-leaf; it is a species related to A. hispida and has similar toothed leaves, mottled in red, green, copper, and yellow. A. wilkesiana 'Godseffiana' has green leaves bordered in cream or yellow. (GBT)

Other Name
Red Hot Cat's Tail

Bloom Period and Color
Spring and summer blooms in crimson

Mature Height × Spread
8 to 10 feet × 6 feet

Zones
10B – 11

Chinese Fringe Bush

Loropetalum chinense

The Chinese Fringe Bush has been available for years as a green shrub with white flowers but it was not a sought after landscape addition until recently with the introduction of the variety rubrum *from Japan, offering reddish new foliage and pink flower forms. The blossoms are unique, taking on a ribbon-like look that resembles those of the true Witchhazels. Many selections have been made including 'Blush', 'Burgundy', 'Pizzazz', 'Razzleberri', 'Ruby', and 'Sizzling Pink'. What's even more important is its drought tolerance and easy care. It's one plant you can add to the landscape and just about forget. Use Chinese Fringe Bushes as a foundation planting or stand alone accent. It can also be added as a hedge, view barrier, or container planting. (TM)*

Other Name
Chinese Witchhazel

Bloom Period and Color
White to deep pink flowers, giving a major display February through April but opening sporadic blooms throughout the year.

Mature Height × Spread
8 × 6 feet

Zones
8A – 10A

When, Where, and How to Plant
Chinese Fringe Bushes are available as container grown plants for year-round additions to the landscape. Select a sunny to lightly shaded spot for planting in a well-drained soil. Sandy sites can be improved with the additions of peat moss or compost to help provide some nutrients and stretch the time between waterings. Set the plants three to five feet apart with the top of the root ball at or slightly above the soil line and add a 3- to 4-inch mulch. Bushes can be added to the landscape at any time of the year, but the summer rainy season is ideal as the soil remains naturally moist.

Growing Tips
Make sure new plants receive adequate water during the dry times by creating a 4- to 6-inch berm of soil at the edge of the root ball to catch and direct water down through the root system. Give new plantings a first feeding four to six weeks after the plants are set in the ground and additional feedings every other month spring through fall to encourage growth the first year or two. Use a general garden fertilizer. Thereafter make fertilizer applications in March, June, and September if needed to encourage growth.

Regional Advice and Care
Plantings make vigorous growth and may develop long shoots that encourage an open plant habit. Produce a more compact plant by periodically tipping out the ends of the shoots. Plants that grow too large for the landscape setting can be given the needed trimming after the main spring blooming period. No major insect or disease problems have been reported.

Companion Planting and Design
Take advantage of the shrub's drought tolerance by planting with Feijoa, Plumbago, and similar shrubs. Use with annuals and perennials as a backdrop.

My Personal Favorite
This is an exciting plant with several varieties but one that really catches my eye is 'Rassleberri' with reddish flowers and burgundy foliage; it's also marketed as 'Monraz'.

Cocculus
Cocculus laurifolius

When, Where, and How to Plant
Transplant Cocculus from one area to another between December and February. Container plants can be added to the landscape at any time of the year; spring and early summer are best in South Florida. The plants grow in some of Florida's poorer soils. A well-drained soil is best. Improve the planting site with compost or peat moss and manure before planting. Dig a hole that's much wider than the rootball but not deeper. Position the Cocculus plant at the same depth it was growing in the container or original planting site. It may be set a little higher above the soil level, especially in a poorly drained location. After planting, form a berm at the edge of the rootball and add a 2- to 3-inch mulch layer.

Growing Tips
Once established, most shrubs grow well with minimal care. Feed Cocculus once in March, May, and September. Use a 6-6-6, 16-4-8, or similar analysis fertilizer at label rates. Cocculus plantings are relatively drought tolerant. Most plantings receive adequate moisture from rainfall. When gardeners want to encourage growth and especially during periods of drought, water weekly.

Regional Advice and Care
Cocculus suffers cold damage in North Florida in most years and in Central Florida during severe winters. Affected plantings need a late-winter pruning to remove the damaged portions and reshape the plants. Pruning is not usually needed at planting time. All shrubs need periodic pruning to keep the plantings inbounds. Cocculus plants need pruning to keep them compact and full of foliage. One pest that may affect Cocculus is scale. Where needed, apply a pesticide recommended by the University of Florida, following label instructions.

Companion Planting and Design
Here is a great evergreen hedge for sun or shade. It can also be used as a contrasting backdrop with perennials of Bird-of-Paradise, Heliconias, Gingers, and Ornamental Bananas.

My Personal Favorite
Only the species is available in Florida.

The bright-green color and very shiny appearance of the Cocculus leaves appeal to most gardeners. The stems are arching and fairly open in habit, which can be thickened with timely pruning. The plant may be grown just because it's a curiosity. The seed resembles a coiled snail shell. It's the most interesting end of the flowering process, since the yellow blooms are insignificant. Cocculus make great plants for hedges, shrubby borders, or specimens. They are tolerant of most soil conditions and take minimal care. The foliage can be added to arrangements and used to make wreaths, although the leaves are poisonous. The Carolina Snail Seed, Cocculus carolinus, is native to North Florida. It has a vining growth habit with oval leaves and produces red fruits. (TM)

Other Name
Snail Seed

Bloom Period and Color
Spring and summer blooms in yellow

Mature Height × Spread
12 feet × 12 feet

Zones
9 – 11

Cocoplum

Chrysobalanus icaco

A medium to large evergreen shrub, Cocoplum has an upright or spreading shape. Two forms occur: red-tipped and green-tipped. The round leaves march alternately along the twigs and point skyward. The shrub has a more or less symmetrical shape, and it can become quite full and large inland. The sprawling, low, coastal form is C. icaco 'Horizontalis'. Cocoplum fruit is eaten by birds and wildlife and by humans, too. When creating a native garden or wildlife habitat, Cocoplum is a good addition. The genus name Chrysobalanus comes from chryso, meaning "gold," and balanos, or "acorn." Some species have golden fruit. Those in Florida have pink or white or dark red-purple fruit . . . but as landscape plants, they are worth their weight in gold. (GBT)

Bloom Period and Color
Year-round foliage

Mature Height × Spread
3 to 20 feet × 15 feet

Zones
9 – 11

When, Where, and How to Plant

Plant at the beginning of the rainy season, late May to early June, or from March to midsummer if consistent irrigation is practical early on. Use these plants in any number of situations, from background shrubs and screening to clipped hedges. Dig a hole twice as wide but just as deep as the rootball. If roots in the container are circling, then make several 1/4-inch cuts in the root ball with a sharp knife to promote new, outward root growth. Add compost or peat moss to make up 1/3 of the backfill to enrich the planting hole. Water in backfill to eliminate air pockets. Mulch to a depth of 3 or 4 inches, making sure the mulch is several inches away from the trunk of the shrub to prevent fungus.

Growing Tips

Cocoplum benefits from 6-6-6 or 7-3-7 fertilizer twice a year to keep growing vigorously. If using Cocoplum in a hammock setting or a native garden and you don't want to add synthetic chemical fertilizers, you can add well-aged compost or cow manure to the root zone along with mulch. The compost is really a soil conditioner with a few nutrients in it. When adding to already planted shrubs, work it into the top couple of inches of the soil in the bed or around the trunk or trunks, out as far as you care to take it. Microorganisms are available that can be added to the soil to stimulate other microorganisms to breakdown compost into usable form. You'll find these at garden centers or where organic gardening products are sold.

Regional Advice and Care

This shrub grows through Central Florida but not into North Florida.

Companion Planting and Design

Cocoplum brings a feeling of the River of Grass to a native Florida planting that also might include Cabbage Palms, Fakahatchee Grass, and Willows or Wax Myrtle. It can be pinched to remain a particular size.

My Personal Favorite

The red-tipped version of this Florida native plant is especially pretty and can be used to pick up the red of nearby plants, or grown simply for itself.

Crape Myrtle

Laegerstromia indica

When, Where, and How to Plant

Plant at the beginning of the rainy season, late May to early June, or from March to midsummer if consistent irrigation is practical early on. Use in a mixed, informal planting or as specimen plant. White-colored ones tend to get lost in the din unless used as specimens; reds, pinks, and lavenders are more noticeable. Crape Myrtles are drought tolerant and do well in many kinds of soils as long as they don't stand in water. Dig a hole just as deep but 1 foot wider than the rootball (2 to 3 times as wide in rocky ground). If roots in the container are circling, then make several 1/4-inch cuts in the rootball with a sharp knife to promote new, outward root growth. Water in backfill to eliminate air pockets. Build a saucerlike basin of soil around the edge of the planting area to retain water.

Growing Tips

Mulch to a depth of 3 or 4 inches, making sure the mulch is several inches away from the trunk of the shrub to prevent fungus.

Regional Advice and Care

Older varieties get powdery mildew. Fertilize in March, July, and November (make this a low-nitrogen fertilizer, such as 4-6-8). Prune in late winter before the new growth begins, as flowering occurs on new branch ends. If too many twigs grow out, thin to shape. The plants can sucker at the base and become multistemmed in spite of your best efforts. Do not remove stems larger than pencil-size in diameter. The "dignity" of the plant's shape will remain and the plant will bloom more profusely in a habit more appealing to the eye if these stems are left in place. Crape Myrtles grow throughout Florida with similar care.

Companion Planting and Design

Let this big shrub grow tall and, during the summer flowering period, shine above other foliage, such as Plumbago, Philodendrons, small *Heliconia psittacorum*, or *H. rostrata*.

My Personal Favorite

Crape Myrtle 'Seminole' is a medium pink-flowered plant with a compact habit (many Crape Myrtles can become quite large) and keeps its panicles of flowers close enough together to make an impact.

Reliable bloomers that put on a nice show, Crape Myrtles are from Japan, Korea, and China. Breeding efforts in this country have produced many colors and disease-resistant varieties. The flowers are outstanding in late summer and fall, but come winter, the leaves drop. If bare twigs are not something you can ignore, then plan ahead and mix with other shrubs in the background. The leaves on the Crape Myrtle turn yellow and then orange-red before falling in midwinter, and the dried seeds stay on the twig ends, gradually splitting open and falling. After a few years, the bark peels and becomes quite attractive. Three cultivars are mildew resistant. The cultivars are 'Muskegee', a lavender flowering shrub; 'Natchez' with white flowers; and 'Tuscarora' with coral flowers. (GBT)

Bloom Period and Color

Summer and fall blooms lavender, white, coral, pink, red

Mature Height × Spread

20 feet × 20 feet

Zones

7 – 10B

155

Croton

Codiaeum variegatum

One Croton fancier used to collect Crotons on trips throughout Florida and ended up with more than 60 different-looking plants—and that was probably just the beginning. Gardeners love the variety of leaf colors, greens, pinks, yellows, and reds, in addition to the leaf shapes available in the Croton genus. Croton has to be kept consistently warm. In cooler portions of the state, protection is needed to survive any dip below 32°F. These relatively narrow plants are ideal for cramped gardens and the small spots between the home and the sidewalk. In the cooler regions of Florida, the plants are often set in containers. Some have been used as foliage plants indoors. You can create Croton hedges and use the plants as screens. (TM)

Bloom Period and Color
Year-round foliage in green, pink, yellow, and red

Mature Height × Spread
3 to 8 feet × 3 feet

Zones
10 – 11

When, Where, and How to Plant
Transplant Crotons from one area to another between December and February. Add container plants to the landscape at any time, in spring and early summer in South Florida. Some selections tolerate the lower light levels under a large tree, but the colors are somewhat subdued. A well-drained soil is best. The plants take well to sandy soils. Improve the planting site with compost or peat moss and manure. Dig a hole that's much wider than the rootball but not deeper. Position the Croton plant at the same depth it was growing in the container or original planting site. It may be set a little higher above the soil level, especially in a poorly drained location. After planting, form a berm and add a 2- to 3-inch mulch layer.

Growing Tips
Crotons can exist with feedings given nearby plants but make the best growth when fed once in March, May, and September. Use a 6-6-6, 16-4-8, or similar analysis fertilizer at label rates. Crotons are relatively drought tolerant; normal rainfalls are sufficient to maintain them. During periods of extended drought, water the plantings weekly.

Regional Advice and Care
Culture in North Florida and parts of Central Florida is restricted to containers due to winter cold. Plant in a loose potting soil, and feed weekly with a 20-20-20 or similar fertilizer during periods of active growth. Give these plants protection from frosts and freezing. No pruning is needed at planting time. Crotons need periodic pruning to produce compact plants with plenty of colorful new shoots. Some pests that may affect Crotons include scale, thrips, and mites. Where needed, apply a pesticide recommended by the University of Florida.

Companion Planting and Design
A great accent plant for container or in-ground culture in sun or shade. Best used with surroundings of greenery including Ferns, Philodendron, Cast Iron Plant, Viburnum, and similar shrubs.

My Personal Favorite
Many selections have been bred. All are enjoyable with virtually a rainbow of color combinations.

When, Where, and How to Plant

Planting just before the rainy season is best; plant in March if you are willing to irrigate until the rains begin. Transplanting in the high heat of July, August, and September adds an extra burden of stress to the plant. Plant in an area that has good drainage. Dig a hole twice as wide but just as deep as the rootball. If roots in the container are circling, then make several 1/4-inch cuts in the rootball with a sharp knife to promote new, outward root growth. Water in the backfill to eliminate air pockets. Mulch to a depth of 3 or 4 inches, making sure the mulch is several inches away from the trunk of the shrub to prevent fungus.

Growing Tips

Keep the roots moist until the shrub is established. Water daily for the first week; then every other day for two weeks; reduce to every three or four days for two weeks. During the first growing season, water weekly if rain is irregular or if the shrub wilts.

Regional Advice and Care

In Central Florida, the shrub will be damaged by cold. Each spring, prune out the affected area, once new growth has begun to indicate what must be pruned away. You may want to prune this back hard to keep it small or to keep it under control. It is often pruned back naturally by the caterpillars that are larvae of a sphinx moth, *Xylophanes tersa*, and cold wind, which can burn the leaves. *Hamelia* is good at recovering from such plunder, however. And not just from caterpillars, but also from aphids, which find it delectable.

Companion Planting and Design

Incorporate this plant into a butterfly garden or use several near your patio where you can watch the butterflies flock to the pretty orange-red flowers. Mix with Wax Myrtle, West Indian Lilac, and Cocoplum.

My Personal Favorite

As a butterfly-attracting shrub, Firebush is excellent, and serves well in a South Florida butterfly garden to buffer wind.

Firebush is a fast-growing shrub with whorls of textured leaves that take on a reddish color in full sun. Though it may grow to 15 feet or more, it can be kept much shorter by pruning. A native of Florida, Firebush is a valuable plant for its nectar-rich flowers that attract hummingbirds and butterflies. The slender flowers are in clusters toward the ends of the branches. It takes heat and drought like a champ. Mix Firebush with Wild Coffee, Necklace Pod, Spicewood, Beautyberry, and other native shrubs in a mixed border. Use them along with native trees to create a wildlife habitat or as a part of the yard you do not irrigate (once the plants are established) in a water-conserving landscape design. (GBT)

Other Name

Scarlet Bush

Bloom Period and Color

Year-round blooms in scarlet

Mature Height × Spread

15 feet or more × 6 feet

Zones

10 – 11

Gardenia
Gardenia jasminoides

The Gardenia is a slow-growing evergreen shrub with textured dark-green leaves and fragrant white flowers in the spring. She sends her intoxicating perfume across the heavy air, and at night even moths that would be drawn to the moon return for the Gardenia. For who, once captivated by her powers, can resist this siren? We grant you that some people cannot bear to be in the same room with her. For our part, we think she is the queen of tropical scents. She has virginal white flowers that are large, most often double, and roselike in appearance. 'Miami Supreme' is the biggest selling cultivar in Florida. It has large flowers, is extremely fragrant, and also grows in partial shade. Gardenia 'Radicans' is a dwarf species. (GBT)

Bloom Period and Color
Spring blooms in white

Mature Height × Spread
6 feet × 3 or 4 feet

When, Where, and How to Plant
Gardenias prefer an acid soil, and will grow in full sun to light shade. Plant from March through summer, although late May or early June is the best. The soil should be kept moist. Fluctuation in soil moisture leads to yellowing leaves on this shrub. Dig a hole twice as wide but just as deep as the rootball. If roots in the container are circling, then make several 1/4-inch cuts in the rootball with a sharp knife to promote new, outward root growth. Add peat moss or compost to the planting hole so that about 1/3 of the soil is enriched. If you mix too much organic material in the hole in rocky soils, the roots will be disinclined to move out into the rocky substrate. Water in the backfill to eliminate air pockets. Mulch to a depth of 3 or 4 inches, making sure the mulch is several inches away from the trunk of the shrub to prevent fungus.

Growing Tips
Gardenias are heavy feeders, and in alkaline soils they thrive on high-nitrogen, acid-forming fertilizer. A 12-6-8 or 12-6-10 is appropriate. Use small amounts every 2 or 3 months. A lack of micronutrients also causes yellow leaves; use a foliar micronutrient spray. For iron deficiency, use an iron drench once a year.

Regional Advice and Care
Prune lightly after the major flowering period to keep the shrub compact. Cold winters can damage Gardenias in Central and North Florida. Prune out affected portions after new growth appears in the spring. Thrips are attracted to the buds, which are spirally twisted before opening. Predatory insects such as lacewings can attack thrips. Use Sunspray Ultra-Fine Oil®, or a systemic insecticide. Don't plant near the Orchid house.

Companion Planting and Design
When in full flower, Gardenia wants to be admired by itself, and using it as a specimen plant allows that. Or blend it with Snowbush, Crotons, or green and white Acalypha for non-blooming months.

My Personal Favorite
'Miami Supreme' is an old standby with large and lovely flowers.

Hibiscus

Hibiscus rosa-sinensis

When, Where, and How to Plant

Plant in March through midsummer, with late May and early June as the best times. Find an area where plants won't sit in water. Dig a hole twice as wide but just as deep as the rootball. Add peat moss or compost to the planting hole so that about 1/3 of the backfill is enriched. Water in the backfill to eliminate air pockets. Mulch to a depth of 3 or 4 inches, making sure the mulch is several inches away from the trunk of the shrub to prevent fungus.

Growing Tips

Once the shrubs are established, most are fairly drought tolerant. You may have to water in the dry season, about once every three weeks if there is not any rain. Watch for wilt. Use a slow-release fertilizer with a 3-1-3 ratio. Hibiscus in alkaline soils can show minor element deficiencies, so a micronutrient foliar spray 3 times a year is advisable. Growers warn not to mix water-soluble 20-20-20 with a micronutrient spray because the phosphorus in the 20-20-20 will tie up micro-nutrients.

Regional Advice and Care

Hibiscus can be grown in Central Florida in protected areas—such as a sunny southeast side of a house. In North Florida, use in containers or as an annual summer planting. Prune any cold damage off in the spring. In South Florida, Hibiscus are best grown on Anderson's Crepe rootstock, which withstands nematodes and heat stress. Control whitefly and aphids with an insecticidal soap or 2 tablespoons of liquid Ivory in 1 gallon of water. Armored scale can attack Hibiscus. Prune off the affected area. Never use malathion on Hibiscus. Mites cause bud drop.

Companion Planting and Design

A Coconut Palm or Areca Palm planting can be bordered or interplanted with Hibiscus for a true tropical picture. Or plant Hibiscus next to Heliconias and Bananas for a similar feel. Don't mix lots of colors.

My Personal Favorite

Pure white Hibiscus flowers are appealingly unaffected and look cool in summer's heat.

Hibiscus flowers, like Palm trees, say tropical. Big, flashy, and strong bloomers, Hibiscus flowers begin with white and go to mauve, gray, brown, orange, red and yellow, blue, brown with yellow edges, yellow with orange centers . . . combinations that are reminiscent of tie-dyed T-shirts of those long-ago hippie days. Yet there are people who love the single white, the bright red, the bell-like clarity of the single yellow, and the plain pink. Most of the blossoms last only a day, so they don't make great cut flowers, but they perform prolifically in the garden. Hibiscus schizopetalus, sometimes called the Fringed Hibiscus, has upside-down red flowers that hang from long stems. Hibiscus syriacus is the Rose-of-Sharon that produces blue, single flowers and is deciduous. It does well in alkaline soils. (GBT)

Other Name

Chinese or Hawaiian Hibiscus

Bloom Period and Color

Summer blooms in all colors

Mature Height × Spread

20 feet or more × 15 feet

Zones

10 – 11

Hydrangea
Hydrangea macrophylla

When you think of Easter plants, one shrub that always comes to mind is the Hydrangea. The ball-shaped inflorescences are prominent from mid-spring through early summer. Hydrangeas on display at Easter have been forced and are a little earlier than the landscape plantings. You may be able to convince any Hydrangea to be either pink or blue by regulating the soil acidity. Many varieties have been selected for the better blue or pink color. Hydrangeas are best used in mass displays of three or more plants. They can be planted as background shrubs, hedges, or accents. Central and North Florida gardeners can also plant the Oakleaf Hydrangea, Hydrangea quercifolia. It grows to about 6 feet tall and produces a white inflorescence for spring. (TM)

Bloom Period and Color
Spring through Summer blooms in pink, blue

Mature Height × Spread
5 feet × 5 feet

Zones
8 – 9

When, Where, and How to Plant
Transplant Hydrangeas from one area of the landscape to another from October through February. Container plants can be added to the landscape at any time. Hydrangeas need protection from the hot, drying sun. They are best planted where they get filtered or morning sun and afternoon shade. Select a well-drained soil, but it should be able to hold some moisture. Improve the planting site with compost or peat moss and manure. Dig a hole that's much wider than the rootball but not deeper. Position the Hydrangea at the same depth it was growing in the container or original planting site. It may be set a little higher above the soil level, especially in a poorly drained location. After planting, form a berm and add a 2- to 3-inch mulch layer.

Growing Tips
Hydrangeas need extra care to grow in most landscapes. Feed plantings once in March, May, and September. Use a 6-6-6, 16-4-8, or similar fertilizer. Hydrangeas need lots of water; the plants frequently wilt with just a little moisture stress. Check the plantings several times each week during periods of drought. Plants need watering every three to four days during hot weather.

Regional Advice and Care
Hydrangeas grow well only in Central and North Florida where they have some cold weather during the winter months. Some years they suffer freeze damage that needs to be pruned out during the early spring season. Hydrangeas need an extra pruning after flowering is complete in early summer. Remove older flower heads, and do any reshaping of the plants. Hand pick caterpillars from the plantings, or treat them with a pesticide recommended by the University of Florida.

Companion Planting and Design
Grows well in a container for the porch, patio, or along a walkway. Display in-ground with filtered sun lovers of Allamanda, Ardisia, Jacobinia, Indian Hawthorn, Nandina, Viburnum, Azaleas, and Camellias.

My Personal Favorite
You have to like the blue colors of the Hydrangea and the bluer the better. For this reason, the bright blue 'Blue Wave' is my favorite.

When, Where, and How to Plant

Plant at the beginning of the rainy season, late May to early June. Good drainage is important. Dig a hole twice as wide but just as deep as the rootball. If roots in the container are circling, then make several $1/4$-inch cuts in the rootball with a sharp knife to promote new, outward root growth. Add peat moss or compost to enrich the planting hole so that about $1/3$ of the backfill is organic. Water in the backfill to eliminate air pockets. Mulch to a depth of 3 or 4 inches, making sure the mulch is several inches away from the trunk of the shrub to prevent fungus.

Growing Tips

Ixoras like fertilizer to keep producing those big balls of flowers called umbels. They prefer acid soil, so they benefit from mulch and high-nitrogen fertilizer. Micronutrient deficiencies are often seen in alkaline soils, particularly magnesium deficiency, making older leaves yellow, manganese deficiency, causing yellowing in new leaves, and iron deficiency, causing general yellowing but leaving green veins. One or two handfuls of Epsom salts around the root zone when you fertilize will help with the magnesium problem. An iron drench once a year is beneficial. Manganese sulfate combats yellowing of new leaves, and the sulfate helps make soil acid as well. Use a micronutrient foliar spray.

Regional Advice and Care

Very cold weather, in the upper 30s, will cause leaves to develop brown spots. If freezing occurs, wait until spring before pruning so you can allow the emergence of new leaves to indicate how far back twigs and branches were damaged. Lightly prune to shape; Ixoras perform best when not sheared.

Companion Planting and Design

Resist hedging, except informally, and instead combine them with Crotons, Palms, Copper Leaf, and Bromeliads and even some bulbs for easy-care plantings that are colorful but not confusing.

My Personal Favorites

The medium-pink cultivar 'Nora Grant' is a good performer. 'Maui' has yellow- or reddish-orange flowers that are just as striking. 'Maui Yellow' bears light yellow flowers.

Ixora are evergreen shrubs that produce many small but bright flowers in large heads throughout the warm season. Once the darling of South Florida builders, the plants experienced a period of disuse then came back to the landscapes. The reasons for this swing had to do with the way the shrubs were originally maintained and the development of new cultivars to make maintenance easier. With the development of Ixora 'Nora Grant', which is resistant to nematodes, tolerant of rocky soil, and is shapely enough that hard pruning isn't needed, the picture changed. Ixora duffii 'Super King' has large heads of deep-red flowers and is susceptible to nematodes; but it looks healthier and is bigger (to 10 feet) than I. coccinea. Ixora javanica produces orange flowers. (GBT)

Other Name
Flame of the Woods

Bloom Period and Color
Spring through Summer blooms in red, orange, pink, yellow

Mature Height × Spread
$2^1/2$ to 6 feet or 10 feet × 6 feet

Zones
10B – 11

Lady-of-the-Night
Brunfelsia americana

On the softest summer nights, when the moon is hazy through the humidity and the screech owls call in little whinnies from the Poincianas, the sweet scent of cloves may drift or linger. Unlike Jasmine, with its sometimes cloying ways, Lady-of-the-Night's perfume seems never to be in excess, never overripe. It lasts two, maybe three nights, and then is gone until the next wave of flowers washes over the twigs. This Brunfelsia is incredibly showy when flowering; it blooms profusely all at once. Yesterday-Today-and-Tomorrow is a winter-flowering cousin, Brunfelsia pauciflora. The 3-inch flowers open blue-purple and fade to white, hence the name. Brunfelsia grandiflora blooms in the warm season, also with purple flowers and white centers. Brunfelsia australis is another purple-to-white bloomer. (GBT)

Bloom Period and Color
Summer blooms in white

Mature Height × **Spread**
10 to 15 feet × 5 to 10 feet

Zones
10B – 11

When, Where, and How to Plant
Plant at the beginning of the rainy season, late May to early June, or from March to midsummer if consistent irrigation is practical early on. Plant Lady-of-the-Night where she gets 5 or 6 hours of sun in the summer. If roots in the container are circling, then make several $^1/_4$-inch cuts in the rootball to promote new, outward root growth. Add compost or peat moss to make up $^1/_3$ of the backfill to enrich the planting hole. Water in backfill to eliminate air pockets. Mulch to a depth of 3 or 4 inches, making sure the mulch is several inches away from the trunk.

Growing Tips
Water every few days in the dry season. Fertilize 3 times a year with an 8-12-4 with 4 percent magnesium and micronutrients in the spring and summer and a 4-6-8 right before winter to avoid pushing out new leaves. Apply new mulch twice a year because it wears thin every six months or so. When spraying liquid fertilizer on the orchids, spray this shrub at the same time. The *Brunfelsia* thrives on this regimen.

Regional Advice and Care
Brunfelsia grows throughout Central Florida, but may be damaged by cold. Prune off damage in early spring after new growth appears as an indication of where live wood begins. Prune to shape, but bear in mind that this *Brunfelsia* likes to sprawl naturally, and you can see by the dimensions that it is much taller than wide. To sow seeds, remove the skin and pulp, push seeds just beneath the surface of a 50-50 mix of peat moss and perlite, and keep moist.

Companion Planting and Design
Lady-of-the-Night laces summer nights with rich perfume, so place this shrub where you can take delight in it. It wants to sprawl, so allow it to spill like milk from a grouping of Alocasias, Gingers, and Lady Palms.

My Personal Favorite
Placed on the southeast corner of the house, this shrub will float its clovelike perfume on the prevailing evening breeze, and show off its flowers in the moonlight.

Ligustrum
Ligustrum japonicum

When, Where, and How to Plant

Transplant Ligustrums from one area of the land-scape to another between December and February. Add container plants to the landscape at any time. Plant in spring or early summer in South Florida. Ligustrum will tolerate filtered sun where they develop a more open growth habit. A well-drained soil is best. They are very tolerant of Florida sands. Improve the planting site with compost or peat moss and manure. Dig a hole that's much wider than the rootball but not deeper. Position the Ligustrum plant at the same depth it was growing in the container or original planting site. It may be set a little higher above the soil level, especially in a poorly drained location. After planting, form a berm and add a 2- to 3-inch mulch layer.

Growing Tips

Ligustrums make the best growth if fed once in March, May, and September. Use a 6-6-6, 16-4-8, or similar fertilizer. Ligustrums are fairly drought tolerant—able to exist with natural rainfall for all but the drier times. The best growth is made with weekly watering, especially during periods of drought.

Regional Advice and Care

Ligustrums grow well in all but the most southern regions of the state. Care is similar in all areas. No pruning is usually needed at planting time. Formal hedges may need pruning several times during the growing season. The tree forms need periodic pruning to keep an open habit of growth and remove lower sprouts along the trunks. Ligustrum may get caterpillars, grasshoppers, and scales. Hand pick pests from the plantings, or treat them with a pesticide recommended by the University of Florida. Good care will overcome fungal leaf spots.

Companion Planting and Design

Often used as a hedge or backdrop for gardens or a border for the home site. It also makes a great tree to use in small designs and near patios.

My Personal Favorite

Only the species is available in Florida.

Talk about a plant that is a backbone of the landscape industry, and you must be discussing the Ligustrum. It's planted as a hedge, view barrier, accent plant, and tree. Ligustrums have large, very shiny leaves and open white blossoms in the spring. A blue berry follows in fall for extra color. They survive in all but the wettest soil and can live with minimal care. Ligustrums can be pruned to almost any shape or permitted to grow naturally for a slightly upright to spreading form. It has rapid growth to fill in voids and give the landscape a quick, recognizable form. Gardeners plant the Glossy Privet, Ligustrum lucidum, *which grows to 20 feet tall as a tree in the land-scape. (TM)*

Other Name
Japanese Privet

Bloom Period and Color
Spring blooms in white

Mature Height × Spread
12 feet × 8 feet

Zones
8 – 10

Nandina

Nandina domestica

According to folklore, planting the Nandina at the entrance to your home brings good luck. Its colorful berries and unique foliage add to the list of reasons to plant the shrub. As the name suggests, it resembles Bamboo, producing upward growth from canelike stems. The leaves look somewhat like Bamboo foliage. The plants produce clusters of yellowish flowers for spring, but they may be hidden within the branches. Depending on how much cold weather the plants endure and the variety, they may be evergreen to semievergreen. Several selections have been made for their growth habit and fruit color. Some tested in Florida include 'Alba', with white fruits; 'Nana', growing to 2 feet tall; 'Compacta', with a low-growing, dense habit; and 'Harbor Dwarf', a low-growing type. Avoid buying free-seeding varieties that invade native habitats. (TM)

Other Name
Heavenly Bamboo

Bloom Period and Color
Spring blooms in yellow

Mature Height × Spread
5 to 6 feet × 3 to 4 feet

Zones
8 – 10

When, Where, and How to Plant
Transplant Nandina from one area of the landscape to another between December and February. Container plants can be added to the landscape at any time. A well-drained soil is best. The plants grow well in Florida's sandy soils. Improve the planting site with compost or peat moss and manure. Dig a hole that's much wider than the rootball but not deeper. Position the Nandina plant at the same depth it was growing in the container or original planting site. It may be set a little higher above the soil level, especially in a poorly drained location. After planting, form a berm and add a 2- to 3-inch mulch layer.

Growing Tips
Nandinas exist with care given nearby shrubs and trees. They make the best growth when fed once in March, May, and September. Use a 6-6-6, 16-4-8, or similar fertilizer at label rates. Nandinas can tolerate short periods of drought but grow best with weekly watering, especially during periods of drought.

Regional Advice and Care
Plantings in the cooler portions of the state are likely to show the best leaf color and exhibit deciduous growth habit during the winter months. Protect plantings in the southern and hotter areas of the state from midday sun. Pruning is not usually needed at planting time. Many of the older canes lose their leaves and grow too tall for the garden site. An annual rejuvenation pruning in late winter takes out the older canes to allow new growths to fill in from the base. One pest that may affect the Nandina is the scale insect. Where needed, apply a pesticide recommended by the University of Florida.

Companion Planting and Design
Fill beds as a ground cover or cluster a few together as an accent. Use the contrasting foliage with deeper green shrubs of Indian Hawthorn, Dwarf Hollies, Hibiscus, Viburnums, and Ligustrum.

My Personal Favorite
I like the dwarf forms because they make the best ground covers and container selections. The one called 'Harbor Dwarf' is a favorite.

Necklace Pod
Sophora tomentosa

When, Where, and How to Plant

Plant at the beginning of the rainy season, from late May to early June. The Necklace Pods can take pruning every year in the spring to keep the long branches in check. I have a single plant that has been replanted three times: the first time, it was shaded in winter. Then it went into a small native plot near the driveway and got unruly. Finally, last year, it was cut back to within an inch of its life and moved again—this time to the base of a Slash Pine. Dig a hole twice as wide but just as deep as the rootball. If roots in the container are circling, then make several 1/4-inch cuts in the rootball with a sharp knife to promote new, outward root growth. Water in backfill to eliminate air pockets. Mulch to a depth of 3 or 4 inches, making sure the mulch is several inches away from the trunk of the shrub to prevent fungus.

Growing Tips

Keep the roots well watered while Necklace Pods become established—two or three months—and then stand aside.

Regional Advice and Care

If there are occasional caterpillars, from whence the butterflies come, remember to reach for Dipel® first, or hand pick, or just allow the leaves to look ratty for a while, knowing they'll recover with the next flush of leaves. Part of this plant's appeal is its attraction to beauty on a scaly wing. In Central Florida, try growing Necklace Pod in a protected area, such as a sunny southeast corner. Cold or freeze damage may be pruned away in spring after new growth emerges.

Companion Planting and Design

A Pineland planting would be sorry indeed to miss its companionable Necklace Pod. Use with Palmettoes, Firebush, Beautyberry, Indigo Berry, and other native shrubs. Or mix it in a butterfly garden.

My Personal Favorite

A freestanding Necklace Pod is pretty, but when placed among a protective border of Butterfly Shrubs it takes on a useful function as well.

This is a medium to large evergreen shrub, with silvery-green leaves and yellow flowers on stalks that appear at the ends of the new branches. With kid-soft compound leaves covered with silver-white hair, the Necklace Pod is durable, salt tolerant, and beautiful. It is a coastal plant, wandering from dune to coastal hammock and amply protected from too much sun exposure by those white hairs that reflect light. Silver plants generally are drought tolerant (the hairs also keep moisture in), and Sophora is no exception. Necklace Pods serve as lures to butterflies. Flowering is most satisfying in the winter and spring, but the plants may produce some flowers throughout the year. The Necklace Pod produces long, segmented pea pods, like the small pearls of a necklace. (GBT)

Bloom Period and Color
Winter and spring blooms in yellow

Mature Height × Spread
6 to 10 feet × 10 feet

Zones
10 – 11

Oleander

Nerium oleander

Give your yard a tropical look with an Oleander. It is one of the showiest shrubs you can add to the landscape, in bloom from spring through fall. It can be planted as a hedge or space divider. Many gardeners plant larger Oleanders to the rear of the yard to enjoy the distant color. You can plant just 1 shrub as an accent, but three or more provide a cluster of color. Dwarf types can be used in foundation plantings and around the patio. For all its beauty, the Oleander is poisonous. All portions are toxic if eaten. Gardeners can pick a dwarf form such as 'Petite Salmon' or 'Petite Pink'. Also available are colorful selections, including 'Hardy Red', 'Calypso', and 'Mrs. Roeding'. (TM)

Bloom Period and Color
Spring through fall blooms in white, pink, red, salmon

Mature Height × Spread
12 feet × 12 feet

When, Where, and How to Plant

In Central Florida, transplant Oleanders from one area of the landscape to another between December and February. Add container plants at any time. Plant in spring or summer in South Florida. A well-drained soil is best, but they also thrive in Florida sands. Improve the planting site with compost or peat moss and manure. Dig a hole that's much wider than the rootball but not deeper. Position the Oleander at the same depth it was growing in the container or original site. It may be set a little higher above the soil level, especially in poorly drained locations. After planting, form a berm and add a 2- to 3-inch mulch layer.

Growing Tips

Oleanders can exist with the nutrients obtained from feedings of nearby trees, shrubs, and lawns. Where extra growth is needed, they can be fed once in March, May, and September. Use a 6-6-6, 16-4-8, or similar analysis fertilizer at label rates. This is a very drought tolerant plant that needs watering only to encourage growth or to withstand periods of severe drought. Normal rainfall is sufficient. **All parts of this shrub are poisonous.**

Regional Advice and Care

More northern plantings and some in Central Florida are sure to suffer cold damage in many years. No pruning is needed at planting time. Plants in cold locations may be frozen back to the ground but grow back from the base. Plants in warmer locations get tall and out of bounds. Provide a renewal pruning every few years. Prune in late winter to take out the dead and allow spring growth from the base. Pests include caterpillars, aphids, and scale insects. Hand pick or treat with a pesticide recommended by the University of Florida.

Companion Planting and Design

Plant as a view barrier or small tree for the patio. Can also be used as backdrop for lower growing flowers, shrubs, and ornamental grasses including Plumbago, Crinums, Canna, Pentas, and Roses.

My Personal Favorite

I think the name says it all but the colorful variety 'Calypso' is my favorite Oleander.

Plumbago

Plumbago auriculata

When, Where, and How to Plant

Plant at the beginning of the rainy season, from late May to early June, or from March to mid-summer if consistent irrigation is practical early on. Dig a hole twice as wide but just as deep as the rootball. If roots in the container are circling, then make several 1/4-inch cuts in the rootball with a sharp knife to promote new, outward root growth. Because Plumbagos like fertilizer, add compost or peat moss to make up 1/3 of the backfill to enrich the planting hole. Water in backfill to eliminate air pockets. Mulch to a depth of 3 or 4 inches, making sure the mulch is several inches away from the trunk of the shrub to prevent fungus.

Growing Tips

Use slow-release fertilizer in late February or early March, in July or August, and again at the end of October or early November. Although the plant is moderately drought tolerant, water in the dry season. Plumbagos tend to fall over and root as well as sucker, so don't be afraid to use a firm hand with this beauty. Or, tie it to a support such as an arbor or a gate for a dramatic effect.

Regional Advice and Care

Plumbago may be grown in Central Florida, but it will be affected by freezing weather. Prune away damage after new growth appears in early spring. Prune back hard at the end of winter (late February in South Florida) to encourage pretty new growth. Flowers are terminal.

Companion Planting and Design

It can serve as a short shrub or even a giant ground cover, and would complement magenta Bougainvillea, yellow Turnera, or Buttercup. Because it's low and sprawly, Plumbago can serve as an under planting to disguise the legginess of taller shrubs such as pink or white Mussaenda, Heliconias, *Cordia boissieri,* or Latania Palms.

My Personal Favorite

The deep sky-blue cultivar 'Imperial Blue' gives this old favorite new life.

Cobalt-blue flowers have taken the unexciting out of Plumbago. Its old pale-blue flowers, though pretty enough for butterflies, were no selling point for many gardeners. Then the cultivar 'Royal Cape' (or 'Imperial Blue') appeared, and the overlooked shrub was overlooked no longer. The blue is worthy of Monet's pond. It is a jubilant color and jumps out of the cloud of green behind it. Although it straggles and sprawls unless pruned regularly, it also mounds and mushrooms, and it may be just what you need at an entry gate. Flowers are terminal, but growth is rapid and flowers return quickly after pruning. It is somewhat salt tolerant, though you shouldn't use it where it can catch spray. It can be made to vine. Plumbago indica is red-flowering with many of the same characteristics of the blue P. auriculata. It commonly is called Scarlet Leadwort. (GBT)

Other Name
Leadwort

Bloom Period and Color
Spring through summer blooms in blue

Mature Height × Spread
3 to 4 feet × 8 feet

Zones
10 – 11

Sweet Viburnum
Viburnum odoratissimum

Need a large shrub or hedge? Chances are that a Viburnum would be just right for your landscape. This is a group of readily available and reliable shrubs for home planting. All types planted in Florida have evergreen leaves and white flowers for the spring season. The name Sweet Viburnum comes from its large clusters of fragrant flowers. Make sure it's in a spot where it has room to grow and become an attractive shrub with minimal pruning. Florida gardeners can plant the native Walter Viburnum, Viburnum obovatum, *with its small bright-green leaves about 1 inch in length. It forms a dense shrub and grows to 12 feet or more. The Laurestinus Viburnum,* Viburnum tinus, *has pink or white flowers and grows to 6 feet. (GBT)*

Bloom Period and Color
Spring blooms in white

Mature Height × Spread
15 feet × 8 feet

Zones
8 – 9

When, Where, and How to Plant
In Central Florida, transplant Viburnums from one area of the landscape to another between December and February. Add container plants at any time. Viburnum plants prefer a full-sun location but can tolerate some filtered shade. A well-drained soil is best. These plants grow well in sandy soils, but when possible, improve the planting site with compost or peat moss and manure before planting. It's best to dig a hole that's much wider than the rootball but not deeper. Position the Viburnum plant at the same depth it was growing in the container or original planting site. It may also be set a little higher above the soil level, especially in a poorly drained location. After planting, form a berm and add a 2- to 3-inch mulch layer.

Growing Tips
Viburnums should be given a feeding once in March, in June, and again in September, to encourage growth. Use a 6-6-6, 16-4-8, or similar fertilizer. Most Viburnums are drought tolerant, but they are usually watered about once a week, especially during periods of drought.

Regional Advice and Care
Viburnums grow best in Northern and Central Florida where they receive some cool winter weather. During extremely cold winters, some species have suffered the limb damage that can be pruned away before spring growth begins. No pruning is needed at planting time. Many Viburnums are sheared to form a hedge. This pruning is performed "as needed." It's best if you pick a Viburnum that needs minimal pruning so as to reduce landscape work. Some pests that may affect the Viburnum are thrips, scales, and white fly. Control with an oil-containing spray or another University of Florida recommended pesticide.

Companion Planting and Design
This species is often used in foundation plantings but it is probably a bad choice. Instead, plant as a hedge, space divider, or backdrop for lower growing shrubs and flowers.

My Personal Favorite
This is a shrub that does best in Central Florida. There are two cultivars, including Mirror-Leaf or 'Awabuki', which has glossy green leaves.

Thryallis
Galphimia glauca

When, Where, and How to Plant
In Central Florida, transplant Thryallis from one area of the landscape to another between December and February. In South Florida, the start of the rainy season is the best planting time. Container plants can be added to the landscape at any time. Be careful during transporting and planting not to break the limbs. Thryallis plants can survive light shade but at the lower light level they develop a more open growth habit. A well-drained soil is best. The plants grow well in sandy soils. Improve the planting site with compost or peat moss and manure. Dig a hole that's much wider than the rootball but not deeper. Position the Thryallis at the same depth as it was growing in the container or original planting site. It may be set a little higher above the soil level, especially in a poorly drained location. After planting, form a berm and add a 2- to 3-inch mulch layer.

Growing Tips
Thryallis can exist with feedings given nearby lawns and flower beds. For best growth, feed once in March, May, and September. Use a 6-6-6, 16-4-8, or similar fertilizer. Thryallis can tolerate short periods of drought but makes the best growth with weekly watering.

Regional Advice and Care
Because of its cold sensitivity, the Thryallis is limited to Central and South Florida. In the colder regions, give the plants a protected location, and be ready to prune in late winter. No pruning is needed at planting time. The plants grow lanky with time; give them an early spring rejuvenation pruning. Some pests include caterpillars and grasshoppers. Hand pick pests from the plantings, or treat them with a pesticide recommended by the University of Florida, following instructions.

Companion Planting and Design
Plant as a backdrop for summer color with Cannas, Periwinkle, Begonias, Coleus, Pentas, Caladiums, and Plumbago. Can also be used as a free-form hedge to enclose the landscape.

My Personal Favorite
Only the species is available in Florida.

When the summer flowers start to fade, you can pop up the color with Thryallis. Its bright-yellow blossoms open along a terminal spike to put the color above the foliage. The blossoms start to open from late spring through fall, but some color may occur at any time of the year in the warmer areas of the state. Thryallis makes a good natural hedge or barrier. Establish Thryallis as a cluster of several shrubs for a burst of color. Keep it back from walkways; the wood is brittle and may be damaged by traffic or maintenance. This evergreen shrub tolerates a frost and light freeze. Galphimia gracilis also is planted in Florida landscapes. It resembles the common Thryallis and is often sold as the same plant. (TM)

Bloom Period and Color
Spring through fall in yellow

Mature Height × Spread
8 feet × 6 feet

Zones
9 – 11

Wax Myrtle
Myrica cerifera

Native to the entire state, Wax Myrtle wanders among the Cocoplum, the Pond Apples, and the Sweet Bay Magnolia in the estuaries and strands of the Everglades, then heads into the hammocks and meanders through the open pinelands. In winter it often gives a brownish green color to otherwise gray-brown settings. It is twiggy and dense, but can be more open growing in light shade. Flowers are tiny and grow on catkins. The female flowers are green; male flowers are greenish yellow. Wax Myrtles can grow into screens or be shaped into hedges. The plant sends up root suckers, but the aroma is so pleasant and uplifting that it outweighs the troublesome suckering. Myrica heterophylla is Green Bayberry and M. inodora is an odorless Bayberry. (GBT)

Bloom Period and Color
Spring blooms in green to greenish yellow

Mature Height × Spread
15 to 25 feet × 15 to 25 feet

When, Where, and How to Plant
Plant at the beginning of the rainy season, late May to early June, or from March to midsummer if consistent irrigation is practical early on. Plant it wherever your heart desires. This is a supremely versatile plant. Dig a hole twice as wide but just as deep as the rootball. If roots in the container are circling, then make several 1/4-inch cuts in the rootball with a sharp knife to promote new, outward root growth. Water in backfill to eliminate air pockets. Mulch to a depth of 3 or 4 inches, making sure the mulch is several inches away from the trunk of the shrub to prevent fungus. Wax Myrtle can flourish under moist conditions as well as dry; however, to allow the shrub to become established, keep the root zone moist (not soggy) during the first growing season.

Growing Tips
Occasional pruning and 7-3-7 fertilizer with micronutrients in spring and fall are about the only things needed for the hardy Wax Myrtle after it is established, other than a sharp pruning shears. It will sucker from the roots, so you may have to keep it under control. But it will form screening clumps by virtue of this same habit. Once dug from the wild, the plants were cut back quite hard for transplanting. The only care given to them was water.

Regional Advice and Care
Care is similar throughout Florida. Once established, the plants require very little care other than shaping or removal of root suckers.

Companion Planting and Design
It's an excellent plant for Xeriscape, low-maintenance, and native landscapes. Use Wax Myrtle for a screen or background plant, or with other native shrubs, such as Buttonbush. It grows too large for use next to your home. The male and female flowers are on separate plants, and the female's fruits occur in winter and are much appreciated by wildlife and birds. The vireos, catbirds, bluebirds, warblers, as well as many other birds, utilize the waxy fruit.

My Personal Favorite
Used as a screening device, Wax Myrtle's little leaves on many small branches are effective at their job.

Wild Coffee

Psychotria nervosa

When, Where, and How to Plant

Plant at the beginning of the rainy season, from late May to early June, or from March to midsummer if consistent irrigation is practical early on. Plant in partial shade to full sun. Filtered sunlight or sun in the morning or late afternoon will produce a good-looking Wild Coffee. Dig a hole just as deep but 1 foot wider than the rootball (2 to 3 times as wide in rocky ground). If roots in the container are circling, then make several 1/4-inch cuts in the rootball with a sharp knife to promote new, outward root growth. Water in backfill to eliminate air pockets. Build a saucerlike basin of soil around the edge of the planting area to retain water. Mulch to a depth of 3 or 4 inches, making sure the mulch is several inches away from the trunk of the shrub to prevent fungus.

Growing Tips

Keep the root zone moist until the shrub is established, then water during periods of drought. Wild Coffee wilts when thirsty. Use a 6-6-6 or 7-3-7 fertilizer twice yearly, in spring and fall, or a slow-release 8-4-12 2 or 3 times a year for these plants to look their best. Or, replenish compost in spring and fall, working into the soil. White flowers are so small as to be insignificant, although butterflies like them. But the deep red berries in the summer are quite beautiful and beneficial for birds.

Regional Advice and Care

Wild Coffee takes well to pruning, but not shearing. Pruning in spring will make a fuller shrub; pruning done in summer, after renewal growth has flushed, serves to shape a shrub. This plant is recommended for use in South Florida. Wild Coffee is not a landscape plant for Central or North Florida.

Companion Planting and Design

Wild Coffee is another native Florida shrub that makes a beautiful hedge in semi-shade. Plant beneath a Lysiloma or Wild Tamarind, Cabbage Palms, or Gumbo Limbo Trees that will provide shade and sun.

My Personal Favorite

Shiny-leafed Wild Coffee, when growing on the edge of a hammock, is a familiar and reassuring sight as natural areas disappear. In the garden, the shrub's textured leaves and red berries are first-rate.

When finely grown, this is one of South Florida's loveliest shrubs. The leaf texture and shine are positive additions to any garden, while the plant is especially useful in native gardens. The shrub stretches out and becomes lanky in the shade, but stays compact in partial to full sun. High or partial shade is ideal. Seeds of Psychotria nervosa *can take up to six months to germinate. To propagate Wild Coffee, germinate the seeds and transplant them after the second set of true leaves form. Keep seedlings in partial shade at first, and after a month move them into sun.* Psychotria ligustrifolia *is Bahama Wild Coffee, with smaller leaves resembling Ligustrum.* Psychotria sulzneri *is soft-leaved Wild Coffee. The leaves have a slight velvet texture and are gray-green. (GBT)*

Bloom Period and Color
Spring and summer, white flowers. Red berries follow in late summer and fall.

Mature Height × Spread
6 to 15 feet × 5 to 6 feet

Zones
10B – 11

More Shrubs

Butterfly Bush   *(Buddleia officinalis)*

Bloom Period and Color Winter blooms in lilac, pink, red, white, purple;
Mature Height × **Spread** 4 to 6 feet × 4 to 6 feet; **Zones** 8 – 10

When, Where, and How to Plant Transplant from one area of the landscape to another between December and February. Plants in containers can be added to the landscape at any time. Improve the planting site with compost or peat moss and manure before planting. Dig a hole that's much wider than the rootball but not deeper. Position the Butterfly Bush at the same depth it was growing in the container or original planting site. It may be set a little higher above the soil level, especially in a poorly drained location. After planting, form a berm and add a 2- to 3-inch mulch layer. Pruning is not usually needed at planting time. Butterfly Bushes can suffer freeze damage and should be pruned hard during late winter or early spring. Many just naturally die back during the winter, much like a perennial. This may be beneficial; when the old growths are removed, the plants send up new flowering shoots for the growing season.

Growing Tips Once established, most shrubs grow well with minimal care. Feed Butterfly Bushes once in March, May, and September. Use a 6-6-6, 16-4-8, or similar fertilizer. Water Butterfly Bushes heavily during August, September, and October. Once the plants are allowed to dry out they may collapse and never recover.

Regional Advice and Care Winter freezes can cause major damage to the more cold-sensitive species. Prune back to the ground to remove the dead wood. New growth restarts from the base. Spring and early summer are ideal for planting in South Florida. Some pests that may affect the Butterfly Bush include caterpillars and grasshoppers, but they are usually ignored to keep from harming the desirable visiting insects.

Night-Blooming Jessamine   *(Cestrum nocturnum)*

Other Name Night Cestrum; **Bloom Period and Color** Spring and summer blooms in white;
Mature Height × **Spread** 12 feet × 12 feet; **Zones** 10 – 11

When, Where, and How to Plant In Central Florida, transplant Night-Blooming Jessamine from one area of the landscape to another between December and February. Container plants can be added to the landscape at any time. It is ideal to plant in spring or early summer in South Florida. A well-drained soil is best. The plants grow well in Florida's sandy soils. Improve the planting site with compost or peat moss and manure. Dig a hole that's much wider than the rootball but not deeper. Position the plant at the same depth it was growing in the container or original planting site. It may be set a little higher above the soil level, especially in poorly drained locations. After planting, form a berm and add a 2- to 3-inch mulch layer. Pruning is not usually needed at planting time. Since the Night-Blooming Jessamine is a sprawling shrub, more frequent pruning is needed to remove long and lanky shoots.

Growing Tips Night-Blooming Jessamine make the best growth if fed once in March, May, and September. Use a 6-6-6, 16-4-8, or similar analysis fertilizer at label rates. Plantings can tolerate short periods of drought but make the best growth if watered weekly, especially during periods of drought.

Regional Advice and Care Landscape plantings of Night-Blooming Jessamine are limited to warmer areas of Central Florida and South Florida. Plantings in Central Florida may be affected by freezing weather and need spring pruning to remove the dead or damaged shoots. Some pests that may affect the Night-Blooming Jessamine include caterpillars and grasshoppers. Hand pick pests from the plantings, or treat them with a pesticide recommended by the University of Florida, following label instructions.

Trees *for Florida*

A Southern Live Oak may live for 300 or more years.
Its massive branches can stretch horizontally, if allowed,
so that the canopy is wider than the tree is tall. Its
furrowed bark and leathery leaves support millions of living
creatures, smaller than we can see, and a good many
large enough for us to discern: Lichens, Mosses,
Liverworts, a couple of squirrel nests, gnats, aphids, hair-
streak larvae, germinating seeds of Bromeliads, mats of Resurrection
Fern and Whisk Fern, an ant highway, and a well-worn path of rac-
coons that teeter from topmost branches and watch the goings-on below.

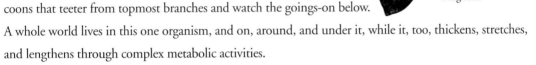

Southern
Magnolia

A whole world lives in this one organism, and on, around, and under it, while it, too, thickens, stretches,
and lengthens through complex metabolic activities.

It pulls water from the ground at the rate of hundreds of gallons a day, and it takes in carbon dioxide
from the air and releases oxygen. The mycorrhizae attached to its roots are probably connected to other
trees around it, like the invisible strings of matter in the universe, linking and interacting with other trees.
Dissolved minerals flow into the vascular tissue, up and out to the limbs and leaves. The machinery to
produce the leaves and cause them to fall at the right time, to produce flowers and acorns in their course,
is hidden in the smallest bits of material within these cells, cells that are constantly being born and
constantly dying. The cellulose of the cells is thicker on the tops of branches to act like muscles, allowing
the tree to bear the great weight. When a branch is not needed any longer, tissue around the inside of the
branch connection isolates that section of trunk as a guard against disease, while on the outside, a callus is
formed to seal over the wound.

So trees are more than the sum of their parts; they are living and breathing entities that support,
protect, feed, shelter, and shade other living and breathing entities—including you. And while they're at
it, they adapt, reproduce, evolve, so that they, like the rest of us, can survive.

Trees Are a Living Canvas

Florida has an enormous number of native trees that have adapted and evolved to suit the conditions
in which they find themselves, from Mangroves that grow in salt water to Scrub Oaks that make do in
arid and infertile sands. Some of these natives are North Florida residents only and don't venture into
the warmer parts of the state, and vice versa. Dogwood, Sweetgum, Black Gum, Sycamore, and Linden
stay away from the likes of Gumbo Limbo, Fiddlewood, and Sea Grape. A handful of temperate trees
venture south, including Red Maple, Persimmon, Wax Myrtle, and Live Oak. In the southern tip of the

peninsula and the Florida Keys, tropical trees of the West Indies such as West Indies Mahogany, Lignum Vitae, and Wild Tamarind are found in sun-dappled forests and hammocks.

As you plan your garden, think architecturally about trees and the way they can enhance your home by framing it, tying it visually into its setting, providing the background against which other vignettes may be composed. When flowering or changing color, trees themselves are living canvases.

Be sure you know the mature size of trees you select for your home so that you can locate them properly in the right soils and drainage conditions, in ways that will cool and shade the house but won't threaten it in storms or invade the water pipes or the drain field. If a breathtaking flowering tree will be too large for your yard when it is mature, then you may want to find a shrub with the same color that will serve you better.

Think Before You Dig

Look up when selecting a planting site. Are there power lines that will result in years of hard pruning for the tree you have in mind? If so, select a smaller tree. Before you begin digging, call your local utilities company to come out and check the site for underground pipes or cables. If you are planning to plant on a swale, remember it is public property. Contact your local building and codes department for restrictions.

If planting your own trees, you most likely will buy them in containers. Large, field-grown trees should be transplanted by professionals with equipment such as backhoes that can more easily move the enormous rootballs.

When buying a containerized tree, slip the container off the rootball, and look at the root system. Roots should be white and healthy, not soggy or brownish-black. They should fill the container, but not poke out the bottom drain holes or circle the inside of the pot. If roots creep up and over others, they may effectively girdle the tree, preventing the flow of water and nutrients between roots and leaves as the tree enlarges.

To ensure survival of the transplant, water daily for one to four weeks; every other day for the next two weeks; twice a week for the next four to six weeks; weekly thereafter until the tree has been in the ground for the first year's growing season. Planting at the beginning of the rainy season may lessen the need for manual irrigation. The roots should not dry during the first growing season; they grow inches every day and often many yards every year.

Begin your garden with the trees, and you will begin on sure footing.

Slash Pine

Avocado

Persea americana

Avocado, a pretty tree, offers tasty fruits that can be eaten fresh with a little salad dressing or used in salad dishes. There are many varieties to choose from, each with different characteristics. Even if you don't want the fruit of an Avocado, it is a good tree for providing shade and creating framing for the home. The trees grow quite fast and the wood, therefore, is brittle. Plant it away from the house. Avocados are usually picked from the tree and even those that fall remain intact—unless the squirrels get them. Many Avocado varieties have been developed for Florida planting. Some with the most cold resistance are 'Brogdon', 'Gainesville', 'Lula', 'Mexicola', 'Taylor', 'Tonnage', and 'Winter Mexican'. Other good varieties for warmer locations are 'Booth 7', 'Choquette', 'Hall', 'Monroe', 'Pollock', 'Ruehle', 'Simmonds', and 'Waldin'. (TM)

Bloom Period and Color
February through March, greenish

Mature Height × **Spread**
30 feet × 30 feet

Zones
10 – 11

When, Where, and How to Plant

Trees transplant best between December and February in Central and North Florida. Container-grown Avocado trees can be added to the landscape at any time. Position at least 15 to 20 feet from buildings, sidewalks, and streets. Provide a site without overhead wires and away from drain fields. Avocado trees grow best in a well-drained soil; wet soils may lead to root rot. Improve a large area with compost or peat moss and manure. Prepare a hole that's about two times wider than the rootball but no deeper. Plant the Avocado at the same depth it was growing in the field or container. After planting, create a berm and add a 2- to 3-inch mulch layer.

Growing Tips

Water every day for the first few weeks, then gradually taper off to watering on an "as needed" basis. Fertilize four to six weeks after planting. Continue feeding new trees every other month, March through September. Fertilize established trees in February, April, June, and September with an Avocado-type fertilizer. Established Avocado trees require watering only during periods of severe drought—but for best production, water weekly.

Regional Advice and Care

In South Florida, plant in the spring or at the beginning of the rainy season and keep Avocados pruned because the wood breaks readily in storms. An Avocado tree needs pruning to keep a straight trunk and develop even branching. Most pruning is performed after harvest. Fertilize using 8-3-9 or 8-2-10 with an additional three percent magnesium and micronutrients. Choose cold-resistant varieties for Central Florida. When cold does affect the trees, later winter pruning is needed. Pests include lace bugs, scales, caterpillars, and grasshoppers. Apply a control recommended by the University of Florida.

Companion Planting and Design

Start the tropical fruit collection with tall and wide growing Avocados. Some additional fruit trees for the planting might include Citrus, Mangos, Lychee, and Carambola. Avocado can also be used as a landscape tree.

My Personal Favorite

Maybe I just like the purplish color of the 'Brogdon' variety, but the fruits are also large and tasty. It's hardy and can grow in much of the state.

Bald Cypress

Taxodium distichum

When, Where, and How to Plant

Transplant during the dormant time of the year, normally between December and February. Container Bald Cypress can be added to the landscape at any time. Position at least 15 to 20 feet from buildings, sidewalks, and streets. Provide a site without overhead wires and away from drain fields. Bald Cypress is one of the few Florida trees that can grow in wet or dry soils. Just open up the hole and add the tree at the same depth it was growing in the container. If planted in a dry area, create a berm and add a 2- to 3-inch mulch layer. When planted in wet areas, the trees establish quicker if the rootballs are not completely submerged in water.

Growing Tips

Keep the Bald Cypress trees moist if planted in the drier areas. Some growers like to water every day for the first few weeks then gradually taper off to watering as needed. Trees planted out of the water are ready for their first feeding four to six weeks after planting. Continue the feedings in March and in June for the first two to three years. Trees along the lakes and in water do not need special feedings. Established Bald Cypress trees growing out of the wet areas need watering only during periods of severe drought.

Regional Advice and Care

Bald Cypress grows throughout the state of Florida. It needs similar care in all areas. Prune during the winter months to keep a straight trunk and to develop even branching around the trunk. Caterpillars are seldom a major problem, but if needed, the natural *Bacillus thuringiensis* insecticide can be applied as instructed on the label.

Companion Planting and Design

Can be planted in the dry sites but best used lakeside. Add one or two trees with plantings of Loblolly Bay, Wax Myrtle, Pickerel Plant, Horsetail, Bulrush, and Arrowhead.

My Personal Favorite

Only the species is available in Florida.

The native Bald Cypress are the large trees that grow right into the water and can be seen at the edge of many neighborhood lakes in Central Florida. Cypress roots develop short protrusions called "knees" that help stabilize the tree in mucky soils—or perhaps they help with gas exchange. The Bald Cypress is just as happy growing in sandy soils with limited amounts of water as it is growing in water. The needlelike leaves have a feathery appearance, giving a light airy feeling to the landscape. Throughout the summer the leaves are bright green. During the fall they turn a coppery color and drop from the trees. The Pond Cypress, *Taxodium ascendens*, is often found growing near lakes. (TM)

Bloom Period and Color
Fall color

Mature Height × Spread
100 feet × 30 feet

Zones
8 – 11

Black Olive

Bucida buceras

The Black Olive is a tree for large yards or for use as a street tree. A moderately fast-growing tree, it has dark-gray bark, simple leaves, and zigzagged branches. If you look carefully at the crown, you can see that it grows in tiers, like its relative the Tropical Almond. When selected for the right place and maintained properly, the Black Olive is a fine tree, resistant to wind and tolerant of salt breezes. It grows well on rocky soil. Black Olives drop leaves and replace them throughout the year, so the tree is evergreen. The flowers are tiny, appearing in April. *Bucida spinosa, a native of the Bahamas, is a small tree that is often used as a bonsai subject. (GBT)*

Bloom Period and Color
April blooms in white

Mature Height × Spread
40 to 50 feet × 30 feet

Zones
10 – 11

When, Where, and How to Plant
Plant in the spring, at the beginning of the rainy season, or until midsummer. Plant in a large area so that it can develop without being cut back severely. Dig a hole as deep as and 2 to 3 times as wide as the rootball. Remove the container from the rootball, and position the tree in the planting hole. If you enrich the soil, use not more than $1/3$ peat, compost, or aged manure to $2/3$ of the backfill. Mulch, keeping mulch 2 or 3 inches away from the trunk.

Growing Tips
Keep the rootball moist until the tree is established—which means until the growth rate of the new tree is that of a mature tree. Water daily for one month to three months, then gradually taper off to every other day, then every third day. Fertilize three months after planting, using a 6-6-6 or another balanced fertilizer with micronutrients. Fertilize young trees 3 times a year, in late February to early March, June to July, and late October to early November. In alkaline soil you may want to use a 7-3-7 or 8-4-12-4 for long-term fertilizing needs. Once mature, the Black Olive needs very little attention.

Regional Advice and Care
Plant in a protected area or southern exposure outside southern Florida because the Black Olive can be cold sensitive. Many Black Olives are hat-racked (limbs cut back to stubs). This causes massive resprouting and results in an extra-dense canopy that is vulnerable to wind-toss. Prune dead wood, crossing branches, and water sprouts. Consult an arborist on crown shaping before you prune to shape the tree. Some Black Olives develop long spiraling fruit as a result of gall from mites.

Companion Planting and Design
This is a large shade tree that too often is used where a smaller tree is required. It requires a big space. When mature, it can be underplanted with Bird's-Nest Anthuriums, big-leafed Philodendrons, and Bromeliads.

My Personal Favorite
The cultivar 'Shady Lady' has a compact growth habit and smaller leaves than the *Bucida buceras* regular or 'Oxhorn' Bucida with leathery leaves at the ends of branchlets.

Bottlebrush
Callistemon rigidus

When, Where, and How to Plant

Transplant and plant containers during the dormant time, between December and February in Central and North Florida. Position this tree at least 10 to 15 feet from buildings, sidewalks, and streets. Plant Bottlebrush away from drain fields. These trees grow best in a well-drained soil and grow well in sandy Florida soils. Enrich a large area with compost or peat moss and manure. Dig a hole that's about 2 times wider than the rootball but no deeper. Plant at the same depth it was growing in the field or container. After planting, create a berm and add a 2- to 3-inch mulch layer.

Growing Tips

Bottlebrushes thrive with regular water and fertilizer in South Florida conditions. Keep the Bottlebrush tree moist. Some growers like to water every day for the first few weeks, then gradually taper off to watering as needed. This tree is ready for a first feeding four to six weeks after planting. Continue the feedings, once in March and once in June, for the first two to three years. Established Bottlebrush trees need watering only during periods of severe drought.

Regional Advice and Care

Bottlebrush trees are usually grown with several trunks that branch out from the base, starting a few feet from the ground. They may need pruning to help them develop an even branching habit. Prune during late spring after the major bloom. Pruning usually consists of removing limbs that interfere with traffic or plant care. Bottlebrush grows well throughout the Central and Southern parts of Florida. In Central Florida, give the plantings a warm location. Prune cold damage before spring growth begins. In South Florida, plant at the beginning of the rainy season.

Companion Planting and Design

Use as stand alone accent trees or cluster several together as a view barrier. Use with shrubs that flower at other times of the year including Thryallis, Plumbago, Hydrangeas, and Jasmine.

My Personal Favorite

There are selections of Bottlebrush that have red to greenish flowers. Most are just sold as a color of Bottlebrush and my favorites are the deep reds that make stronger accents.

Bottlebrush trees add a tropical look to the landscape. The flowers cluster along the ends of the stems, resembling red bottlebrushes. This is a good accent plant for an area near the entrance, off the patio, or at the end of a view. The plants sporadically produce flowers throughout most of the year. They can be grown as an unclipped hedge and used as a view barrier. One species, Callistemon citrinus, resembles the species Callistemon rigidus. The main difference is a shorter, broader leaf that has a citrus smell when crushed. Species Callistemon viminalis has a weeping growth habit. Some varieties of Bottlebrush have flowers that are a deeper red than the standards. There are also Bottlebrush trees that have green-and-violet flowers. (TM)

Bloom Period and Color
Year-round blooms in red

Mature Height × Spread
15 feet × 15 feet

Zones
9 – 11

Chinese Elm
Ulmus parvifolia

Gardeners in need of a small tree will be quite happy with the Chinese Elm. Seldom do you plant the pure species but one of the selections for patio, street, or general landscape use. Often selected is the variety Drake Elm with a weeping and wide spreading habit. Newer selections include a rounded shaped 'Athena' and very upright 'Allee'. The trees are semi-evergreen, which means they lose their leaves during late fall to allow the sun in for a warm spot during winter. Gardeners also like the smaller leaves with a bright green look and the peeling bark that adds extra interest. Another relative for the landscape is the native Winged Elm Ulmus alata, which is also a small tree with interesting bark. (TM)

Other Name
Lacebark Elm

Bloom Period and Color
Late summer, greenish yellow

Mature Height × Spread
35 feet to 40 feet × 35 feet to 40 feet

Zones
5 – 9

When, Where, and How to Plant
The Chinese Elms are full sun plants that can be grown as a single specimen tree or in a cluster of three or more spaced 25 or more feet apart. Since most selections are spreading in habit they are best planted 15 or more feet away from buildings. They can be planted at any time of the year using traditional planting techniques. The trees do appear to need more staking than others as they are often affected by winds when young. Allow stakes to remain in place for up to a year.

Growing Tips
Keep the soil moist during the first year or two to help the trees establish a root system out into the surrounding soil. Thereafter they are quite drought tolerant and can usually exist with moisture from seasonal rains. Construct a berm around the rootball to help direct water into the root system of newly planted specimens. Feed lightly with a general garden fertilizer once in March and June during the first three years. Thereafter the trees can obtain needed nutrients from nearby lawn and shrub feedings.

Regional Advice and Care
Maintain a central leader until the trees are 6 to 8 feet tall, and then allow branching to establish a rounded to weeping look as appropriate for the variety. Most need periodic pruning to keep limbs above sidewalks and patio areas. The Elms are usually pest free but are a favorite feeding site for squirrels during the fall months. They often chew off the ends of limbs and allow them to fall to the ground. Leaf spots may be found on trees where air movement is not adequate for good tree growth.

Companion Planting and Design
Should be planted with other drought tolerant selections to minimize waterings after establishment. Use shade tolerant plants below including Bromeliads, Ivy, and Asiatic Jasmine.

My Personal Favorite
There are a number of selections but my favorite has to be the wide-spreading and weeping form of 'Drake Elm'. It grows into a great shade tree.

When, Where, and How to Plant

Plant in early spring or at the beginning of the rainy season (end of May or early June), throughout early and midsummer. Plant in full sun in a well-draining or dry area, perhaps with other native trees on the perimeter of the yard where irrigation doesn't reach. When transplanting from a pot, dig a hole three times as wide as the rootball and as deep. Situate the tree in the planting hole so that the top of the rootball is even with the soil surface. Fill in with soil from the planting hole. Use a hose to water in the soil as you fill the hole to remove any air pockets. Mulch to a depth of 3 to 4 inches. To avoid disease, be careful to keep mulch from getting next to the tree's trunk.

Growing Tips

Once established, this hardy tree needs little more than occasional irrigation in the dry season and fertilizer once or twice a year, in spring and fall.

Regional Advice and Care

Used away from the water in South Florida, the Geiger will need some winter protection, such as a windbreak of trees or a cozy southeast corner. This tree is not appropriate for Central or North Florida. The geiger beetle can be a nuisance. A metallic green-and-blue beetle that menaces the trees in the spring, it can cause defoliation. Adults eat the leaves, and larvae damage roots. Use Sevin® or Rotenone on the larvae. A single Geiger Tree is less likely to attract beetles than several in close proximity.

Companion Planting and Design

Geiger Tree may be planted with Sea Grape and Seven-Year-Apple for a natural-looking setting along the coasts, or simply honored by a place of its own. Use as background for a butterfly garden. The orange flowers are hard to pair with other flowering trees, and yet will become part of a scheme with multiple colors of bright flowers.

My Personal Favorite

While the orange Geiger brings an unusual color to the landscape, the white-flowering *Cordia boissieri* is more pleasingly shaped and flowers more profusely year-round.

Geiger Tree is one of the few flowering trees thought to be native to South Florida and the Florida Keys (although this is currently undecided). Two Geiger Trees at what is now the Audubon House in Key West are said to be more than 100 years old. The Geiger's leaves have the texture of sandpaper, and the crepe-textured flowers are bold orange, appearing throughout the year. Hummingbirds are attracted to the bright flowers. It's a tough little tree that is salt and drought tolerant, but not cold tolerant. Leaves—particularly those on young trees—will turn brown when temperatures hit the low 40s to upper 30s. In a freeze, the tree will die back to the ground but resprout from the roots. Cordia boissieri is a cold-tolerant and white-flowering relative from Texas that is a beautiful year-round bloomer. (GBT)

Bloom Period and Color
Year-round blooms in orange

Mature Height × Spread
25 feet × 15 feet

Zones
10 – 11

Grapefruit
Citrus × paradisi

Because of citrus canker, South Floridians are unable to plant Citrus at the current time. However, when the ban is lifted, Citrus can again fill the back yards of many homeowners. Grapefruit trees are larger than most other Citrus except Sweet Oranges, and their fruit is larger, too, though not nearly so big as the parent Pommelo or Pummelo (which can measure 12 inches in diameter). Many varieties come true to seed, but some don't. That means that often what you plant is what you will get—but sometimes not. Grapefruit from seed may take six to ten or more years to bear fruit. Grapefruit may begin ripening in November or December and continue to hold their fruit through winter. 'Marsh', 'Redblush' (the new name for 'Ruby'), 'Thomson', 'Duncan', and 'Flame' are some of the cultivars available. (GBT)

Bloom Period and Color
February through May

Mature Height × Spread
20 to 30 feet × 10 to 15 feet

Zones
9 – 11

When, Where, and How to Plant
The best times to plant are the end of winter, spring, and the beginning of the rainy season (end of May or early June), throughout early and mid-summer. Select a sunny location that has excellent drainage. When transplanting, dig a hole 2 to 3 times as wide as the rootball and just as deep. Situate the tree in the planting hole so that the top of the rootball is even with the soil surface. Water in the soil as you fill the hole to remove air pockets. Keep mulch away from the trunk, and mulch lightly.

Growing Tips
Grapefruit demand good drainage and require fertilizers with extra magnesium, but they repay your efforts. Use a citrus fertilizer, such as 8-2-10-3, three times a year for bearing trees, and water weekly in periods of drought. Keep grass from growing beneath the trees.

Regional Advice and Care
Grapefruit trees require similar care throughout Central Florida. Prune dead wood from crowns, but little other pruning is needed. Sucking insects, such as aphids, mealybugs, and whiteflies, are attracted to new leaves and can cause curling. Insecticidal soap, or 1 teaspoon liquid Ivory in a gallon of water, can be used against pests. Sooty mold on Citrus occurs when insects on the undersides of leaves excrete honeydew that sticks to the leaves beneath them, and mold grows on the honeydew. Soapy water can help remove the mold. Leaf miners are a current pest. They are larvae of tiny moths that develop from eggs laid in the leaves. The larvae eat their way out of the leaf by tunneling just beneath the surface.

Companion Planting and Design
Grapefruit trees are good for framing your house and garden because more colorful plants will show up well against them. Keep grass and weeds away from the base of Citrus. To harvest the fruit, you want to be able to walk freely around the entire tree. Plant several Citrus in the same area if you have room.

My Personal Favorites
'Duncan' is a white-fleshed grapefruit that is hard to beat for flavor, but red 'Marsh' is beautiful as well.

Gumbo Limbo

Bursera simaruba

When, Where, and How to Plant

Plant at the beginning of the rainy season (end of May or early June), throughout early and midsummer. Plant in sun or light shade. Choose a spot with good drainage. The trees can be started from branch cuttings. The planting hole should be 12 to 18 inches deep, and the cutting should be watered faithfully until leaves begin to emerge, which can take several weeks. It pays to water the entire branch as well as the root zone.

Growing Tips

Once established, the Gumbo Limbo needs little care. Water in periods of drought; keep mulched. The tree is cold sensitive and will drop leaves after cold snaps. The leaves are compound, with three to seven opposite leaflets. Small, greenish flowers occur in winter to spring, and fruit follow but may take a year to ripen.

Regional Advice and Care

Little pruning and disease or insect control are needed on this fine native. It occasionally gets aphids and some leaf-chewing caterpillars, but overcomes them without assistance. Gumbo Limbos are recommended for use in South Florida. This is not a tree for use in Central and North Florida.

Companion Planting and Design

For light, high shade, a mature Gumbo Limbo is a great native. The trunks can become almost sculptural, and should be seen, so the Tuber Sword Fern or medium-sized Bromeliads make good plants for the base. An older tree can develop remarkable girth, with heavy branches and a spare canopy. Its shade is more or less mottled and shifting. In late winter, the Gumbo begins to lose leaves, and new growth can begin in late February or March. It makes a beautiful specimen tree. The tree is deciduous, and planting on the south side of the home allows a low winter sun to come through its branches for energy-conscious plantings.

My Personal Favorite

Huge, forest-grown or seed-grown Gumbo Limbos are more prone to curving limbs than nursery stock; hence, they have more character.

From the coastal hammocks of South Florida and the West Indies, the Gumbo Limbo is instantly recognizable by its red to silver-red and peeling bark. Fruit, which develop over summer, are noisily appreciated by mockingbirds, vireos, and naturalized parrots. When working with the Gumbo to plant or prune, you may notice a sticky sap that smells a little like turpentine. The sap once was boiled into a gum and used to make varnish or glue for canoes. Use mineral spirits to remove sap from your hands. Forestry professors from the University of Florida found that a greater number of Gumbos from cuttings were thrown over in Hurricane Andrew than those that grew from seed. (GBT)

Other Name
West Indian Birch

Bloom Period and Color
Spring blooms are insignificant

Mature Height × Spread
30 to 40 plus feet × 20-plus feet

Zones
10B – 11

Holly
Ilex species

Hollies compose a large group of trees that provide shade and also serve as view barriers, hedges, and accents in the landscape. Perhaps the most popular is the American Holly Ilex opaca with dark green spiny leaves and deep red berries, but it's the one that is used the least in most of Florida. Gardeners are more likely to plant the Attenuate Holly, Ilex × attenuata or the Yaupon Holly, Ilex vomitoria. Just for the damp locations gardeners can also plant the Dahoon Holly, Ilex cassine. They are all exciting trees that offer numerous varieties to make them very adaptable landscape plantings. For the best color, gardeners should select the female varieties, which are usually the named selections that produce attractive berries for fall and winter. (TM)

Other Name
Numerous varietal names.

Bloom Period and Color
March to April; white to greenish.

Mature Height × Spread
20 to 40 × 15 to 25 feet

Zones
7 – 10 (*Ilex opaca* to Zone 5B)

When, Where, and How to Plant
Container-grown Hollies are an easy way to add new plantings to the landscape, but gardeners may also find balled-and-burlapped plants at garden centers. Most Hollies like the well-drained acid soils but a few including the Dahoon species grow in the damp sites. Give the plants a full sun location. Hollies have a more upright growth habit than most other trees and can be planted at closer spacings of within 10 to 20 feet of other trees and buildings. Position the rootball in the ground so the top is at or slightly above the soil line. Add a 4- to 6-inch berm at the edge of the rootball to catch and hold water during the establishment period.

Growing Tips
Most Hollies are drought tolerant once established. They grow best with waterings when other plantings are irrigated during drought. Feed once in March and June with a turf fertilizer at the lawn rate for the first three years after planting. Thereafter the trees normally receive adequate nutrients from decomposing mulch and feedings of nearby shrubs and lawns. Most Hollies change out their leaves during late winter, which is often of concern to gardeners. The leaf drop is in conjunction with lots of new growth that quickly renews the green.

Regional Advice and Care
Give the trees minimal trimming to allow the limbs to develop berries with fall and winter color. Lower limbs can be trimmed as needed to allow movement and maintenance under the trees. Where pruning is needed, sterilize the pruners between trees to prevent a gall-forming fungal disease from affecting the Attenuate and American Hollies. Otherwise the trees are relatively pest free and seldom need pesticide applications.

Companion Planting and Design
Hollies are best planted with other small trees and large shrubs. They are especially attractive with Azaleas, Hydrangeas, Camellias, and Gardenias that prefer acid soils.

My Personal Favorite
For plenty of berries and a great growing tree my pick is the 'East Palatka' Holly. It really brings in the wildlife too.

Lignum Vitae

Guaiacum sanctum

When, Where, and How to Plant

Plant at the beginning of the rainy season (end of May or early June), throughout early and midsummer. Plant this where the small flowers can be seen by guests entering the house, near a patio, or keep in a large pot for years. Though extremely slow, Lignum Vitae can produce considerable canopy. Plant in full sun in a spot with excellent drainage. When transplanting from a pot, dig a hole 2 to 3 times as wide and just as deep as the rootball. Remove the container from the rootball; situate the tree in the planting hole so that the top of the rootball is even with the soil surface. Backfill with soil from the planting hole. Use a hose to water in the soil as you fill the hole to remove any air pockets. Mulch.

Growing Tips

Make sure you keep the rootball moist after planting. The Lignum Vitae Conservation Project of the Key West Garden Club, which seeks to reintroduce the tree to the island, suggests 20-20-20 at half strength weekly for seedlings; use slow-release fertilizer every three to four months for larger trees. Transplanting is tricky. Root prune at least a month ahead in the rainy season; take the taproot with the rootball if possible; water daily, not only root zone but wood as well. Leaves will drop with transplant shock, but new ones will emerge. A Lignum Vitae I had transplanted last year dropped its leaves and scared me to death, but with twice daily waterings, it survived.

Regional Advice and Care

This tree is recommended for use in South Florida only.

Companion Planting and Design

The blue of the Lignum Vitae flowers is incomparable, yet the tree takes several years to produce blooms. Use this as a specimen. Or keep it in a mega-container of terra cotta to show its character.

My Personal Favorite

The purple-blue flowers of this wonderful tree are singularly pretty, and golden pods and red seeds follow them. A big show for a little tree.

Slow growing, with extremely hard wood and black heartwood, the Lignum Vitae is a tree loved in Florida. Contemporary wood turners use the wood for bowls and cups, though the tree is endangered and wood is hard to come by. The tree has a rich history, not only because of medicinal uses of the sap for arthritis, rheumatism, and skin diseases, but also because the wood itself is so heavy it will not float and it has been employed in boat and even submarine construction. The United States Navy harvested trees from the Florida Keys, where the tree naturally occurs in Florida, and so few are left today that they are endangered. Lignum Vitae Key is a state botanical preserve and a protected site. (GBT)

Other Name
Holy Wood

Bloom Period and Color
Spring blooms off and on through summer; blue-violet

Mature Height × Spread
15 to 20 feet × 10 to 15 feet

Zones
10B – 11

Live Oak

Quercus virginiana

Strong, long-lived, and beautiful, the Live Oak is a native plant highly prized as a shade or street tree. A single, mature Live Oak in a front yard may be ornament enough. Once the trees were thought to be slow growing, but fertilizer, water, and mulch can bring much faster results than benign neglect. Leathery, simple leaves are toothed when young and gray-green on the undersides. Young trees can be twiggy. As the crown grows, lower limbs die and drop. Oaks drop their leaves over a couple of weeks in February to March before new leaves flush. Quercus laurifolia, the Laurel Oak, occasionally grows into the northern Everglades of South Florida. A taller (to 100 feet), shorter-lived tree, it can drop limbs because of weak wood. (GBT)

Bloom Period and Color
February through March, brown

Mature Height × Spread
50 or more feet × 80 feet

When, Where, and How to Plant

In more northern parts of the state, Live Oaks are planted in the dormant season. In the 1930s, the Florida legislature declared the state's Arbor Day to be in January since that was the best time to plant Oaks. In South Florida, plant any time. Select a spot in sun and with ample room for the horizontally inclined limbs. Oaks can take a wide range of soils. When transplanting from a pot, dig a hole as deep and three times as wide as the rootball. Remove the container from the rootball; situate the Oak in the planting hole so the top of the rootball is even with the soil surface. Fill in with soil from the planting hole. Use a hose to water in the soil to remove any air pockets that might kill feeder roots. Mulch to a depth of 3 to 4 inches, being careful not to pack the mulch next to the tree's trunk in order to avoid disease.

Growing Tips

Young Oaks send up multitudes of root suckers if the soil around the root zone is disturbed. Mulch or plant with a ground cover, such as ferns, which have shallow surface roots. Once the tree is established, little care is necessary.

Regional Advice and Care

The large crown may require fine pruning to remove deadwood, but Oaks usually don't need hard pruning. Limbs grow naturally low and horitonzal. Some of the most beautiful have been allowed to touch the ground around the city of Orlando's Lake Eola, and elsewhere. Live Oaks thrive all over the south, many reaching their most beautiful in North Florida.

Companion Planting and Design

Whether in a hammock setting with other trees or as a singular shade tree, the Live Oak is ruggedly handsome. Orchids grow wonderfully in it, as do Bromeliads. Use Ferns, Myrsine, and Bromeliads beneath.

My Personal Favorite

The Live Oak at the Charles Deering estate in South Dade County has stood its ground magnificently for hundreds of years as it marks an Indian burial spot.

Lychee
Litchi chinensis

When, Where, and How to Plant

Transplant during the dormant time of the year, between December and February. Add container plants to the landscape at any time. Position at least 15 to 20 feet from buildings, sidewalks, and streets. Provide a site without overhead wires and away from drain fields. Lychee trees grow best in a well-drained acid soil. Lychee trees grow well in sandy Florida soils. Enrich planting sites with compost or peat moss and manure. Open a hole that's about 2 times wider than the rootball but no deeper. Plant at the same depth it was growing in the field or container. Create a berm and add a 2- to 3-inch mulch layer.

Growing Tips

Keep the Lychee moist. Water every day for the first few weeks, then gradually taper off to watering as needed. Feed 4 to 6 weeks after planting. Continue the feedings every other month through September for the first year. Then provide feedings once in March, May, and early October, using a 6-6-6 or fruit tree product. Established Lychee trees need watering only during periods of severe drought, but for best fruit production, water at least weekly.

Regional Advice and Care

Lychee plantings are restricted to South Florida and some very warm areas along the coast of Central Florida. In the limestone soils of South Florida, minor nutrient soil sprays applied to foliage are usually needed 2 to 3 times a year to prevent deficiencies. Prune in late winter to keep a straight trunk and to develop even branching around the trunk. Scale insects may affect Lychee trees. Apply a fruit tree spray recommended by the University of Florida, following label instructions.

Companion Planting and Design

A good tree to begin your tropical fruit collection with Citrus, Avocados, Mangoes, and Carambola. Can be planted as a landscape tree with other tropicals of Bromeliads, Bird-of-Paradise, and Philodendrons.

My Personal Favorite

If you like Lychee, a favorite will have to be 'Brewster' with good color and taste that is always rated excellent. The tree also has good disease resistance.

This is a fine shade tree for the warmer locations of Florida with a fringe benefit: an edible fruit. The trees have a naturally spreading growth habit with branches that sweep down to the ground. The leaves are a very deep green and are shiny, sure to catch attention. New growth is especially attractive: red at first, then turning green. You may want to use them to border the home site and reap the benefits of some late spring through summer fruits. Peel the fruit of its beautiful red shell, and you will find the edible portion is a white pulp that surrounds a large brown seed. The fruits are sweet and slightly acid. Some recommended varieties are 'Mauritius' (which bears most reliably in South Florida), 'Bengal', 'Brewster', 'Groff' (delicious but with small fruit and large seed), 'Emperor', 'Hak Ip', 'Hanging Green', 'Kwai May' also called 'Kwai Mi', 'Sweet Cliff', and 'Yellow Red'. (TM)

Other Name

Litchi

Bloom Period and Color

February through March, yellow

Mature Height × Spread

40 feet × 40 feet

Zones

10 – 11

Mahogany

Swietenia mahagoni

The native Florida Mahogany is now used mainly as a good landscape tree for the warmer climates. It's an upright growing tree with a rounded crown that gardeners like to use for shade, to plant streetside, or to frame the home. It's a tree with good salt tolerance, so it's suitable for planting in coastal landscapes. The shape of the tree makes it wind resistant, and the wood is tough. The leaves are persistent into the fall and winter months; in the spring, they quickly drop from the tree and new growth begins. The native Mahogany is the only species used in the Florida landscape. Another Central and South American relative, *S. macrophylla*, is used for timber, growing too tall for ornamental landscape use. (TM)

Bloom Period and Color
February through March, greenish

Mature Height × Spread
45 feet × 40 feet

Zones
10 – 11

When, Where, and How to Plant
Transplant between December and February. Add containers to the landscape at any time, though the cooler and more dormant times are best. The Mahogany can tolerate some light shade. Position this tree at least 15 to 20 feet from buildings, sidewalks, and streets. Give street trees a 25- to 30-feet spacing. Provide a site without overhead wires and away from drain fields. Mahogany trees grow best in well-drained acid or alkaline soils. Mahogany trees grow well in sandy Florida soils. Enrich planting sites with compost or peat moss and manure. Open a hole that's about 2 times wider than the rootball but no deeper. Plant at the same depth it was growing in the field or container. Create a berm and add a 2- to 3-inch mulch layer.

Growing Tips
Water every day for the first few weeks, then gradually taper off to watering as needed. Feed four to six weeks after planting. Continue the feedings, once in March and once in June, for the first two to three years. Established Mahogany trees are drought tolerant and need watering only during periods of severe drought. They do not need additional feedings after the first few years.

Regional Advice and Care
In South Florida, the Mahogany is considered semi-deciduous. Planting is done when leaves are beginning to drop. The Mahogany is cold sensitive and restricted to use in frost- and freeze-free locations. Mahogany trees need winter pruning to keep a straight trunk and to develop even branching around the trunk. Pests include caterpillars and borers. Use a *Bacillus thuringiensis* caterpillar control, a borer spray, or other University of Florida recommended controls.

Companion Planting and Design
A great tree to combine with other small trees and greenery. Add the tropical look with Bamboo, Hibiscus, Oleander, Bird-of-Paradise, and Bananas. Use where light shade is needed.

My Personal Favorite
Only the species is available in Florida.

Mango

Mangifera indica

When, Where, and How to Plant

Plant at the beginning of the rainy season (end of May or early June), throughout early and midsummer. Plant in a sunny location at least 30 feet from the house. When transplanting from a pot, dig a hole 2 to 3 times as wide as the rootball and just as deep. Situate the tree in the planting hole so that the top of the rootball is even with the soil surface. Add organic amendments so the peat moss, compost, or aged manure do not exceed $1/3$ of the backfill. Use a hose to water in the soil as you fill the hole to remove air pockets.

Growing Tips

Newly planted trees need faithful irrigation so that the root zone stays moist but not wet. Bearing trees should be watered periodically when fruit is developing (often during the end of the dry season) to increase fruit size. Fertilizers such as 6-6-6 or 10-10-10 with additional 3 or 4 percent magnesium are good for juvenile trees; 8-3-9-3 or 8-2-10-3 is best for bearing trees. Use 1 pound for each inch of trunk diameter, measured 1 foot above the ground. Apply micronutrient sprays about three times a year in rocky soil, and use an iron drench once a year.

Regional Advice and Care

Smaller varieties, such as 'Carrie' and 'Cogshall' can be grown in protected areas in Central Florida. Many Mangos are susceptible to anthracnose, a fungus that attacks leaves, twigs, and fruit. Often no harm is done to the fruit, although the skin may have tearstains running from the stem down the sides. Commercial growers spray frequently; homeowners don't have to unless the fungus is severe.

Companion Planting and Design

In South Florida, there are some 200 cultivars now growing. It is a wonderful shade tree as well as a fruit tree. Keep it mulched, but avoid planting expensive or rare plants beneath it, because fruits can damage what they hit. Try *Monstera deliciosa*, Wart Fern, or Walking Iris.

My Personal Favorites

The 'Edward' cultivar is my favorite Mango, tastewise, but 'Nam Doc Mai' is not far behind. 'Irwin' is a less robust tree, easier to manage and delicious, though prone to anthracnose.

One of South Florida's most treasured and delicious fruits, Mangos are neighborhood friendly, making great shade and climbing trees as well as fruit trees, and can be long-lived. Mangoes are big trees, having broad to round crowns, depending on the cultivar. They are messy, dropping fruit and leaves, and should be placed where such things are not a problem. Trees among the Indian types with monoembryonic seeds should be grafted to come true to seed. Fruit, depending on type and cultivar, mature from May to September. The tree may flower more than once. In Florida, where high humidity and rainfall are likely to spread fungal spores quickly, it is best to plant cultivars that are resistant to anthracnose. Such cultivars include: 'Earlygold', 'Florigon', 'Saigon', 'Edward', 'Glenn', 'Carrie', 'Van Dyke', 'Tommy Atkins', and 'Keitt'. (GBT)

Bloom Period and Color

Winter blooms in yellow

Mature Height × Spread

30 to 50 feet × 30 feet

Zones

10B – 11

Orange Tree
Citrus sinensis

Because of citrus canker, South Floridians are unable to plant Citrus at the current time. However, when the ban is lifted, Citrus *can again fill the back yards of many homeowners. Florida oranges are famous the world over—even though the fruit originated in China. When growing Citrus in your backyard, good drainage and root stocks are two big considerations. If you live in areas where new neighborhoods have been created on fill, you may have to plant Citrus (and other non-wetland trees) on mounds if drainage is poor. Citrus cannot endure wet feet. 'Hamlin' and Navel Oranges begin ripening in October; Pineapple Oranges in December; Temple Oranges in January; Valencia in March. Dancy Tangerines ripen in winter; Honey Tangerines are later, beginning in February. A new variety is 'Ambersweet' Orange, a combination of Grapefruit, Orange, and Tangerine. (GBT)*

Bloom Period and Color
February through March, white

Mature Height × Spread
25-30 feet × 10 feet

Zones
9 – 11

When, Where, and How to Plant
Plant at the beginning of the rainy season (end of May or early June), throughout early and midsummer. May be planted year-round. Plant in a sunny location with good drainage. If you live inland, a southern location will help protect Citrus from north and northwest winds. When transplanting from a pot, dig a hole as deep as the rootball and 2 to 3 times as wide. Situate the tree in the planting hole so the top of the rootball is even with the soil surface. To the backfill add no more than $1/3$ organic material, such as peat moss, compost, or aged manure. Keep the rootball intact when planting, and use a hose to wash in the soil as you fill the hole.

Growing Tips
Use regular 6-6-6 fertilizer frequently and in small amounts the first year (4 or 5 times during the growing season, from June through October). Start with $1/2$ pound and increase the amount so you apply $1^1/2$ pounds for the last application. Fertilize four times the second year. The third year, switch to a fruit tree fertilizer such as 8-2-10-3 and reduce the applications to three. In alkaline soil, foliar sprays of micronutrients three times a year are helpful.

Regional Advice and Care
Orange trees suffer from freezing weather in Central Florida; prune back in spring. Otherwise, little pruning is necessary except to shape and remove deadwood. Whiteflies on the undersides of the leaves excrete honeydew, a host to sooty mold. If leaves turn black from whitefly secretion, examine the undersides for insects and treat with insecticidal soap or 2 tablespoons liquid detergent in a gallon of water applied with hose-end sprayer.

Companion Planting and Design
Plant with other Citrus when it is permissible to replant in South Florida. Small Orange Trees are suitable for townhouse or apartment patios. Use rocks as mulch for containers.

My Personal Favorite
For flavor, the 'Dancy' Tangerine is my top pick.

Pigeon Plum

Coccoloba diversifolia

When, Where, and How to Plant

Plant at the beginning of the rainy season, end of May or early June. Plant in sun or shade, with natives or even in formal settings. The Pigeon Plum is used to harsh conditions; it takes wind and drought well. There are male and female trees. Dig a hole as deep as the rootball and 2 to 3 times as wide. Remove the container from the rootball, and position the tree in the planting hole. If you enrich the soil, use not more than $1/3$ peat, compost, or aged manure to $2/3$ of the backfill. Water in the soil as you fill the planting hole to eliminate air pockets that kill roots. Mulch, keeping mulch 2 or 3 inches away from the trunk to avoid disease.

Growing Tips

Water and fertilize consistently when the tree is young to help it get a good start in life. What's a mother for? When your Pigeon Plum is a few years old, you can let go of the reins. If growing in a group of natives, a Pigeon Plum will grow tall and narrow; in sun, it will be shorter and fatter. The female trees often have raccoon scratches on the trunks when seen in the wild. And trunks are recognizable by their splotchy bark.

Regional Advice and Care

Use this tree in coastal areas of Central Florida. Care is similar. It is not for use in North Florida. Pigeon Plum grows throughout the Bahamas and the Antilles, and in Florida from Monroe and Miami-Dade Counties into Broward and Lee. It is a mainstay of the forests on North Key Large, where a botanical preserve set aside by the state guards the only tropical hardwood forest in the United States.

Companion Planting and Design

Use as a formal planting along a wall, or an informal grouping in a native habitat. This versatile tree can blend with Stoppers, Wild Coffee, Privet, Beautyberry, and other plants of coastal woodland areas.

My Personal Favorite

If birds can have a favorite, white-crowned pigeons would lobby for this. This is a versatile tree, upright and handsome in any setting.

Pigeon Plum is plentiful in the coastal hammocks, from the center of the state to the Keys. And increasingly, it is being used in landscaping. Its dense, columnar crown and pretty bark make it useful for street planting as well as for framing a house, even in a formal design. The simple, bright-green leaves are generally large when the tree is young and reduced in size when it is older. With the appearance of flowers, in March or thereabouts, comes the first flush of new leaves. A second follows later in spring. Fallen leaves turn distinctively golden on the forest floor or in your backyard lawn or mulch. The Sea Grape, Coccoloba uvifera, is also a related native. It is a shorter, stouter tree. (GBT)

Bloom Period and Color
Spring blooms

Mature Height × **Spread**
30 to 50 feet × 15-20 feet

Zones
9 – 11

Red Maple
Acer rubrum

Red Maple doesn't grow with its feet in deep water, but it can be found nearby and in slightly drier areas or periodically wet hammocks with acid soils. Red Maples have a low tolerance for drought. At the southern end of its range, the Red Maple is var. 'Trilobum', with three pointy leaf lobes edged in teeth to distinguish it. It does not venture into the tropical Florida Keys. In addition to its red fall color, the leaves have leaf stems or petioles that are red, as are its flowers that appear in December and January. Silver Maple, Acer saccharinum, *occurs in North Florida. (GBT)*

Other Name
Scarlet Maple

Bloom Period and Color
Spring flowers are red but quite small

Mature Height × Spread
40 to 50 more feet × 30 feet

Zones
8 – 10B

When, Where, and How to Plant
Plant at the beginning of the rainy season (end of May or early June), throughout early and midsummer. In South Florida's natural areas, the seeds germinate in the dry season and shoot up before rains return and flood the swamps. Shallow-rooted, Red Maples have brittle wood and can break in storms. Look for trees with a single leader to prevent splitting. Plant in full sun in a low-lying, wet area. Trees thrive better in sandy soil than rocky soil, although mulch can help them adapt. In sandy soil, they can be used to frame a house or garden, or they can be shade trees or even specimen trees. When transplanting from a pot, dig a hole 2 to 3 times as wide as the rootball and just as deep. Remove the container from the rootball; situate the tree in the planting hole so that the top of the rootball is even with the soil surface. Add 1/3 as much organic material to the planting soil from the planting hole. Use a hose to water in the soil as you fill the hole to remove any air pockets. Mulch.

Growing Tips
Little care is required if the tree is properly located.

Regional Advice and Care
Use other Maple species or varieties in Central and North Florida. Flowers tend to be male or female on the same tree, but sometimes they occur on different trees. Fruits develop quickly after December flowering and may be ripe by January or February before new leaves appear.

Companion Planting and Design
This is a big handsome tree adapted to wet areas. If you have a lakefront or low-lying wet area, use Red Maple with Cabbage (*Sabal*) Palms, Leather Fern, Dahoon Holly, Willow, and Elderberry. Group it with Sweet Bay Magnolia, Dahoon Holly, Coastal Plain Willows, Wax Myrtle, and Leather Ferns from forested wetlands.

My Personal Favorite
The beauty of changing fall leaves is possible when you cultivate the Red Maple, a South Florida native.

Redberry Stopper
Eugenia confusa

When, Where, and How to Plant
Plant at the beginning of the rainy season (end of May or early June), throughout early and midsummer. Plant in high shade or full sun. Understory trees tolerate the shade of the hammock. When transplanting from a pot, dig a hole 2 to 3 times as wide as the rootball and just as deep. Remove the container from the rootball; situate the tree in the planting hole so that the top of the rootball is even with the soil surface. Use a hose to water in the soil as you fill the hole to remove any air pockets. Mulch around the root zones and keep mulch away from the trunk.

Growing Tips
After the Redberry has become established, it requires little fussing over. Mulching will mediate soil moisture and temperature, which are somewhat mediated inside a hammock by virtue of the overstory trees. It needs fertilizer in moderate amounts—the leaves will complain when the tree is hungry, turning a little yellow. Stoppers generally are slow growers with hard wood, but they are worth cultivating.

Regional Advice and Care
Redberry Stopper is recommended for use in South Florida. It is not recommended for use in Central or North Florida.

Companion Planting and Design
Adapted to rocky soil, this is a wonderful tree for small gardens and patios, or with a group of natives. This beautiful little tree can be useful for townhouse and zero lotline landscapes where space is tight. Columnar in its growth habit, it can stand at the entry with dignity. The pretty leaves are glossy and dark green, small, and distinct. *Eugenia rhombia*, the Red Stopper, one of Florida's rarest native trees, is found in the Florida Keys. *Eugenia foetida*, the Spanish Stopper, has blunt leaves at the ends of small branches, and fruit grows along the branches. *Eugenia axillaries* is the White Stopper with larger leaves than the rest. *Myrcianthes fragrans* is Simpson Stopper, with flaking bark.

My Personal Favorite
Stoppers are their own best company. The well-defined drip-tip is a wonderful field character and will allow you to pick it out from the crowd.

A long "drip-tip" on shiny leaves is your key to identifying this Stopper. A drip-tip is an elongated, pointy apex of the leaf that allows raindrops to drip from the surface—a characteristic of many tropical trees found in areas of high rainfall. Redberry is not a common tree, but it should be planted much more widely. It is slow growing, but that makes it durable and dependable. The strong musky smell of the White Stopper perfumes the air along Old Cutler Road near Matheson Hammock in Coral Gables. Many of the old Stoppers in Miami have fallen to housing developments, especially along the bayfront, but many more should be planted because of their beauty and small size. Rather than hatrack or otherwise mutilate big trees, homeowners can take advantage of this native. (GBT)

Bloom Period and Color
Small spring flowers, white

Mature Height × Spread
20 feet × 10 feet

Zones
10B – 11

Royal Poinciana
Delonix regia

A cascading canopy that is supported by fat, yet languid, limbs on a stout trunk, the Madagascar native is a cosmopolitan citizen of the pantropical world. Doubly compound leaves have a ferny look. Messy, with aggressive roots, it expiates its sins every May to June with transporting color. When the Poincianas are in bloom, every street they grace is lifted out of the ordinary to become dazzling. The canopies shimmer beneath clouds of cerise, scarlet, blood red . . . After enormous initial show, flowers linger throughout the summer. Often but not always deciduous, the tree's aggressive roots and foot-long pods create a grass cutter's nightmare. An intriguing detail about the tree is the way the bark resembles loose skin where limbs attach to the trunk. (GBT)

Other Name
Flamboyant Tree

Bloom Period and Color
Spring to summer blooms in cerise, scarlet, yellow

Mature Height × Spread
25 to 40 feet × 40 feet

Zones
10B – 11

When, Where, and How to Plant
On rocky soils, Royal Poinciana trunks develop some buttressing and roots rise to the surface. Ground covers are better suited beneath this tree than grass, and tall ground covers at that because the roots can rest several inches above the soil surface. Plant at the beginning of the rainy season (end of May or early June), throughout early and midsummer. Plant in a large, open space in full sun. This tree is really too large for a small yard. Roots will uplift asphalt. Limbs are brittle. Seedlings germinate readily. If planting from seed, nick the hard shell and soak in water. When the seed has doubled in size, plant in 50-50 peat and perlite. When transplanting from a pot, dig a hole 2 to 3 times as wide as the rootball and just as deep. Remove the container from the rootball; situate the tree in the planting hole so that the top of the rootball is even with the soil surface. Add $1/3$ as much organic material to the planting soil from the planting hole. Use a hose to water in the soil as you fill the hole to remove any air pockets. Mulch. Stand back.

Growing Tips
After planting, keep the root zone moist throughout the first growing season. Then water once or twice weekly in the dry season while the tree is still young. In the early spring, apply fertilizer. Use a 7-3-7 or 8-4-12 with micronutrients.

Regional Advice and Care
Prune out deadwood. A yellow form exists and is planted sparingly in Miami-Dade County. Royal Poinciana is recommended for use in South Florida. It is not a tree for Central or North Florida.

Companion Planting and Design
Because this tree spreads, drops litter, and its roots eventually come to the surface, you need a big landscape to contain it. Golf courses, parks, and wide boulevards are best for giving this its head.

My Personal Favorite
The golden- or yellow-flowering Poinciana is a tree that can stop traffic.

Satinleaf
Chrysophyllum oliviforme

When, Where, and How to Plant
Plant in late May or early June, at the beginning of the rainy season. Plant in a grouping of native trees or in a perimeter planting. The tree is drought tolerant, and once established doesn't require irrigation. The branches are long and often without many twigs. Dig a hole 2 to 3 times as wide and just as deep as the rootball. Remove the container from the rootball, and position the tree in the planting hole. If you enrich the soil, use not more than $1/3$ peat, compost, or aged manure to $2/3$ of the backfill. Water in the soil as you fill the planting hole to eliminate air pockets that kill roots. Mulch, keeping mulch 2 or 3 inches away from the trunk to avoid disease.

Growing Tips
Keep roots moist throughout the first growing season. Fertilize with 6-6-6 or a slow-release balanced fertilizer according to package directions. Once the tree becomes a large specimen, mulching consistently should be ample care.

Regional Advice and Care
Plant along the coasts up to the center of Florida; it will freeze back when unprotected. Seedlings may proliferate around the base and can be dug at any time.

Companion Planting and Design
Group several Satinleaf trees along a drive or a property line for a beautiful statement of dark green and copper. The sweetly scented flowers, according to Tomlinson in *The Biology of Trees Native to Tropical Florida* (Harvard University), can persist a long time before they open, and may be stimulated to open after rain. Fruits are dark purple berries, which makes this a good tree for attracting birds to your yard. If landscaping for wildlife, use this tree with Wild Coffee, Pigeon Plum, Sea Grape, Firebush, Cocoplum, and other fruit-bearing natives that offer birds and small animals food and shelter.

My Personal Favorite
Used as a specimen tree, the copper undersides of Satinleaf are clearly visible when the wind blows or when you're beneath it looking up.

Few other trees have leaves as beautiful as those of the Satinleaf. When they dance in the wind and show the backs of their hunter green leaves, covered with bronze or copper hairs, they are the Fred Astaire of trees, all dazzle and grace in movement and light. The crowns are erect, and in shade they will zoom to the light, squeezing through the smallest spaces to reach it. The branches tend to come out on one side. When you plant it, notice that direction so you don't end up replanting the tree later. Equally pretty is a relative with larger leaves and edible fruit. This is the Caimito, Chrysophyllum cainito. In the West Indies, it is a "dooryard" fruit, with sweet, granular flesh. (GBT)

Bloom Period and Color
Spring, white

Mature Height × Spread
30 to 40 feet × 15 feet

Zones
10 – 11

Sea Grape
Coccoloba uvifera

Gardeners in warmer locations should plant the Sea Grape, if for no other reason than its exotic look. Even in the cooler spots, a protected site can be chosen. The leaves are circular in shape and grow to 8 inches in diameter. Each leaf has red veins, and the entire leaf turns red before dropping. This is a small, broad, spreading tree with a very open branching habit. The Sea Grape is quite salt tolerant. Clusters of edible purple fruits are produced by female trees throughout the year in the warmer locations. Consider planting the Pigeon Plum Coccoloba diversifolia a small native tree that grows to 40 feet tall. The Big-leaf Sea Grape Coccoloba pubescens is sometimes planted in the landscape or a container for its 3-foot-diameter foliage. (TM)

Bloom Period and Color
March through April, white

Mature Height × Spread
20 to 25 feet × 20 feet

Zones
10 – 11

When, Where, and How to Plant
Transplant between December and February. Add containers to the landscape at any time, though the cooler and more dormant times are best for planting: spring and early summer in South Florida. Position this tree at least 5 to 10 feet from buildings, sidewalks, and streets. The Sea Grape can be used in sites with overhead wires. Sea Grapes grow best in a well-drained soil and are very tolerant of salt exposures. Sea Grape grows well in sandy Florida soils. Enrich planting sites with compost or peat moss and manure. Open a hole that's about 2 times wider than the rootball but no deeper. Plant at the same depth it was growing in the field or container. Create a berm and add a 2- to 3-inch mulch layer.

Growing Tips
Water every day for the first few weeks, then gradually taper off to watering as needed. The tree is ready for a first feeding four to six weeks after planting. Continue the feedings, once in March and once in June, for the first two to three years. Established Sea Grape trees are drought tolerant and need watering only during periods of severe drought. They do not need additional feedings after the first few years.

Regional Advice and Care
All Sea Grapes are cold sensitive, limiting most to South Florida and the coastal areas of Central Florida. Inland plantings of Central Florida need winter protection. In South Florida, plant in spring (if you plan to water consistently) or at the start of the rainy season. Sea Grape trees need winter pruning to keep a straight trunk and to develop even branching around the trunk. Once established, Sea Grape needs no other care.

Companion Planting and Design
Use in view barriers as a stand alone planting. Or use as an accent in foundation plantings or near patios with Indian Hawthorn, Lantana, Coontie, Beautybush, Firebush, and Fetterbush.

My Personal Favorite
Only the species is available in Florida.

When, Where, and How to Plant

Transplant between December and February. Add containers to the landscape at any time. Position this tree at least 15 to 20 feet from buildings, sidewalks, and streets. Provide a site without overhead wires and away from drain fields. Slash Pines grow best in well-drained acid soils. Slash Pines grow well in sandy Florida soils. Open a hole that's about 2 times wider than the rootball but no deeper. Plant at the same depth it was growing in the field or container. Create a berm and add a 2- to 3-inch mulch layer.

Growing Tips

Water every day for the first few weeks, then gradually taper off to wateringas needed. Feed four to six weeks after planting. Continue the feedings, once in March and once in June, for the first two to three years. Established Slash Pine trees need watering only during periods of severe drought. Too frequent watering and fertilizing of established trees can cause decline.

Regional Advice and Care

Pines grow well throughout most of Northern and Central Florida. South Florida selections are limited to the Slash, Sand, Longleaf, and Loblolly Pines. Native to South Florida is *Pinus elliottii* 'Densa'. It grows on rocky soils and the planting soil should not be amended. If planted March through early June, roots develop quickly. Mulch with pine needles. Do not drive over pine roots or run heavy equipment over roots, as they are sensitive to damage. Pests include caterpillars and borers. Prevent borer damage by keeping construction equipment away from the trees and preventing digging within the root zone. When caterpillars are a problem, use a University of Florida recommended control.

Companion Planting and Design

Plant for light shade with under plantings of acid-loving Azaleas, Camellias, and Hydrangeas. Can also be clustered as a backdrop for the home site and in wildlife areas.

My Personal Favorite

Only the species is available in Florida.

Gardeners relocating to Florida are often surprised to find very few good Pines for landscape use. Most are finicky about their care and don't offer the versitility found with the Northern species. The Slash Pine can grow to 100 feet, but is usually smaller in home landscapes. Once established, it grows quite rapidly, providing light shade. The cones can be used in home crafts and holiday arrangements. A number of additional Pines may be considered for the Florida landscape, including the Sand Pine, Pinus clausa, and the Spruce Pine, Pinus glabra. Both grow to about 40 feet and have a denser growth habit. Some additonal Pines to consider are the Longleaf Pine, Loblolly Pine, Japanese Black Pine, and Virginia Pine, but not in South Florida. (TM)

Bloom Period and Color
February through March, brown

Mature Height × Spread
100 feet × 50 feet

Zones
8 – 10

Southern Magnolia

Magnolia grandiflora

No tree represents the South more than the Southern Magnolia with large green leaves and fragrant white flowers. Most selections grow as large trees—ideal to frame a home site or serve as a backdrop for landscape plantings. This is an evergreen tree that can provide shade for the hotter months and then make a good wind break during the winter. Most gardeners just ask for a Magnolia when making a selection, but you should request this tree by variety. A number have been selected that can provide early flowering and leaf interest with a brown lower surface that's obvious when moved by the wind. Some selections available at garden centers include 'Bracken's Brown Beauty', 'Little Gem', and 'Saint Mary'. (TM)

Other Name
Bull Bay Magnolia

Bloom Period and Color
May through July and sporadically the rest of summer; white

Mature Height × Spread
80 to 90 feet × 30 to 40 feet

Zones
8 – 10B

When, Where, and How to Plant
Gardeners can add a new container grown or balled-and-burlapped Magnolia to the landscape at any time of the year. It's best to pick a time when you can provide adequate water, as the trees appear to be very moisture sensitive during the establishment period. Give the trees a full sun location and position 25 or more feet from a building or outer limbs of other trees. Be sure the top of the rootball is positioned at or slightly above the level of the soil. Create a berm of soil around the edge of the rootball to catch and hold water during the establishment period. Add a 2- to 3-inch mulch layer away from the trunk. Keep the soil moist with frequent waterings until established.

Growing Tips
Magnolias grow in moist soils and, when established, are very drought tolerant. Best growth is made when they are watered along with lawns and other shrub plantings. Feed the trees in March and June with a general lawn fertilizer at the turf rate for the first three years to encourage growth. Thereafter, feedings are normally not needed. Keep the soil mulched within 4 to 5 feet out from the trunk.

Regional Advice and Care
Allow the limbs of Magnolias to grow near the ground or trim them off as needed to allow walking or traffic flow under the trees. The trees do shed most of their leaves during the late winter and spring months, which often makes gardeners think they are declining. This is normal and new growth soon follows. Scale and black sooty mold can be ignored or controlled with an oil spray as needed.

Companion Planting and Design
It's often difficult to find plants to grow under Magnolia trees, but Bromeliads don't seem to mind. Also plant Asiatic Jasmine, Begonias, Ivy, and Impatiens.

My Personal Favorite
Some selections take too long to flower and grow too tall. But 'Little Gem' is just right because it's smaller in size and an early bloomer. It also flowers for a much extended period of time.

Sweet Bay Magnolia

Magnolia virginiana

When, Where, and How to Plant

Trees transplant best between December and February. Add containers to the landscape at any time of the year. Spring and early summer are best in South Florida. Give Sweet Bays a full-sun to lightly shaded location. Position at least 15 to 20 feet from buildings, sidewalks, and streets. Provide a site without overhead wires and away from drain fields. Sweet Bays grow best in moist, fertile soils. They can tolerate a wet soil with poorer drainage. Sweet Bays grow well in sandy Florida soils if provided with adequate water. Enrich the planting sites with compost or peat moss and manure. Open a hole that's about 2 times wider than the rootball but no deeper. Plant at the same depth it was growing in the field or container. Create a berm and add a 2- to 3-inch mulch layer.

Growing Tips

Water every day for the first few weeks, then gradually taper off to watering as needed. Feed four to six weeks after planting. Continue the feedings, once in March and once in June, for the first two to three years. Established Sweet Bay trees should not be allow to dry—water whenever the soil starts to feel dry to the touch. They do not need extra feedings after the first few years.

Regional Advice and Care

Magnolias grow best in Northern Florida, Central Florida, and upper portions of South Florida (they don't grow in the Keys). Sweet Bay trees need a late winter pruning to keep a straight trunk and to develop even branching around the trunk. Pests are scales and borers. Control scales with an oil spray. Control borers with a borer spray or use other University of Florida recommended controls.

Companion Planting and Design

Plant in the damp areas with other moisture loving trees and shrubs. It's a great shade and accent tree when combined with Bald Cypress, Loblolly Bay, and Wax Myrtles.

My Personal Favorite

Only the species is available in Florida.

Gardeners with damp to wet areas are always in a quandary about what to plant. One answer is the Sweet Bay, which is a native Magnolia. It needs a moist soil to develop into an attractive upright tree of about 50 feet tall. When young, the tree grows with evenly spaced branches and a rounded crown. As this Magnolia grows older, it takes on an irregular shape. Gardeners should consider the Sweet Bay for use anywhere a reliable flowering tree is needed. It's a great tree for naturalistic plantings. The Southern Magnolia, Magnolia grandiflora, grows to 90 feet tall in all soil types and opens fragrant and quite-large white blossoms for spring. For the Northern and Upper Central Florida landscape use the Saucer Magnolia, Magnolia × soulangiana. (TM)

Bloom Period and Color
Spring blooms in white

Mature Height × Spread
50 feet × 20 feet

Zones
8 – 10

Sweet Gum

Liquidambar styraciflua

The Sweet Gum is one of the truly reliable native trees that has a good shape and won't get too tall for the average landscape. The trees are upright and pyramidal in habit. The shape of the leaf, with its five to seven lobes, gives it a starlike appearance. As the limbs grow older, they often produce a corky ridge. Don't get alarmed—this is not a scale insect, and the growths are normal. Mature Sweet Gums produce a seed ball with prickles that can hurt bare feet. A number of native Sweet Gum varieties have been selected for landscape plantings, including 'Festival', a columnar form; 'Moraine', with reddish fall foliage; 'Purple Majesty', with good fall color; and 'Variegata', with green-and-cream-colored foliage. (TM)

Other Name
Sweetgum

Bloom Period and Color
Fall foliage

Mature Height × Spread
50 feet × 20 feet

Zones
8 – 9

When, Where, and How to Plant

Transplant during the dormant time of the year, normally between December and February. Add containers to the landscape at any time of the year, though the cooler and more dormant times are best for planting. Give Sweet Gums a full-sun to slightly shady location. Position at least 15 to 20 feet from buildings, sidewalks, and streets. Provide a site without overhead wires and away from drain fields. Sweet Gums grow best in a well-drained soil. Sweet Gums grow well in sandy Florida soils. Enrich planting sites with compost or peat moss and manure. Open a hole that's about 2 times wider than the rootball but no deeper. Plant at the same depth it was growing in the field or container. Create a berm and add a 2- to 3 inch mulch layer.

Growing Tips

Keep the Sweet Gum tree moist. Water every day for the first few weeks, then gradually taper off to watering as needed. Feed four to six weeks after planting. Continue the feedings, once in March and once in June, for the first two to three years. Established Sweet Gum trees are very drought tolerant and need watering only during periods of severe drought. They do not need additional feedings.

Regional Advice and Care

All Sweet Gums grow well through Northern Florida down to the uppermost portions of Southern Florida. Sweet Gum trees need a late winter pruning to keep a straight trunk and to develop even branching around the trunk. Pests that commonly affect Sweet Gum trees include caterpillars and thrips. Use the *Bacillus thuringiensis* caterpillar control, an oil spray, or other University of Florida recommended control, following label instructions.

Companion Planting and Design

A great tree for smaller yards with upright growth. Plant with Maple, Pine, and River Birch trees.

My Personal Favorite

They are all great trees with good fall color. But I really like the deeper color of 'Purple Majesty' that lets me know when fall is here.

Tabebuia
Tabebuia caraiba

When, Where, and How to Plant
Add container plants to the landscape at any time of the year, though spring and early summer are best in South Florida. Position at least 10 to 15 feet from buildings, sidewalks, and streets. Provide a site without overhead wires and away from drain fields. Tabebuias grow best in a well-drained soil. Tabebuias grow well in sandy soils. Enrich planting sites with compost or peat moss and manure. Open a hole that's about 2 times wider than the rootball but no deeper. Plant at the same depth it was growing in the field or container. After planting, create a berm and add a 2- to 3-inch mulch layer.

Growing Tips
Keep the Tabebuia tree moist. Water every day for the first few weeks, then gradually taper off to watering as needed. Feed four to six weeks after planting. Continue the feedings, once in March and once in June, for the first two to three years. Established Tabebuia trees are drought tolerant and need watering only during periods of severe drought. They do not need special feedings after the first few years.

Regional Advice and Care
The northern limit for Tabebuias is mid-Central Florida. In this upper region, the trees need the warmest location in the landscape. Areas near a lake are best, as they remain a few degrees above the coldest winter temperatures. If they become frozen, the trees do grow back, but they need training to keep one central trunk. In South Florida, Tabebuias may be planted late February through June for root growth in spring. Trees should be pruned to remove crossed or dead limbs after flowering has finished.

Companion Planting and Design
So spectacular is the bloom that you will want to use this as a small specimen tree, perhaps near the walk to the front door, where you can accent it with sun-loving Bromeliads, Plumbago, and Coreopsis.

My Personal Favorite
It's too bad if you have to just pick just one but the Golden Trumpet tree, *Tabebuia chrysotricha*, has the most intense gold color of them all.

At least two Tabebuias with yellow flowers are commonly grown in home landscapes. Tabebuia caraiba or Silver Tabebuia grows mainly in South Florida, and Tabebuia chrysotricha or Golden Trumpet Tree grows from Central Florida southward. Both are showstoppers with bright yellow flowers produced during the early spring months. The flowering period lasts for up to a month and the fading blossoms drop to the ground to produce a yellow carpet. They hold their leaves through the winter and drop them just before the flowers appear. Some yellow-flowering Tabebuias found in Central and South Florida are Tabebuia chrysantha and Tabebuia umbellata. Each grows between 15 and 25 feet tall and produces colorful flower clusters for spring. Tabebuia caraiba is prized for its gnarled-looking trunks. (TM)

Other Name
Trumpet Tree

Bloom Period and Color
Spring blooms in yellow

Mature Height × Spread
25 to 40 feet × 40 feet

Zones
10 – 11

Tabebuia Ipe

Tabebuia impetiginosa

Create some springtime excitement by planting Tabebuia Ipe, sometimes known as Ipe. In late winter, the leaves suddenly drop. As the days begin to warm, the trumpet-like pink blossoms begin a month-long display. As the flowers begin to fade, they drop to the ground to create a carpet of color. The tree grows to about 25 feet and has an upright to rounded growth habit. Some additional pink-flowering Tabebuias may be found in Central and South Florida. These include Tabebuia heterophylla, *the Pink Trumpet Tree;* Tabebuia pentaphylla, *the Pink Tabebuia; and* Tabebuia rosea, *the Rosy Trumpet Tree. Each grows between 25 and 40 feet tall and produces colorful pink flower clusters for spring.* Tabebuia caraiba *and* Tabebeuia chrysotricha *are good yellow flowering selections. (TM)*

Other Names
Pink Trumpet Tree, Ipe

Bloom Period and Color
Spring blooms in pink

Mature Height × Spread
25 feet × 25 feet

Zones
9B – 11

When, Where, and How to Plant

Add containers at to the landscape at any time, though spring and early summer are best for planting. Position this tree at least 10 to 15 feet from buildings, sidewalks, and streets. Provide a site without overhead wires and away from drain fields. Tabebuias grow best in a well-drained soil. Tabebuias grow well in sandy soils. Enrich planting sites with compost or peat moss and manure. Open a hole that's about 2 times wider than the rootball but no deeper. Plant at the same depth it was growing in the field or container. Create a berm and add a 2- to 3-inch mulch layer.

Growing Tips

Keep the Tabebuia tree moist. Water every day for the first few weeks, then gradually taper off to watering as needed. Feed four to six weeks after planting. Continue the feedings, once in March and once in June, for the first two to three years. Established Tabebuia trees are drought tolerant and need watering only during periods of severe drought. They do not need special feedings after the first few years of growth.

Regional Advice and Care

The Tabebuia is better suited to growing in lower Florida. Ipe appears to be one of the more hardy pink types. During cold winter the flowers may be damaged, but the limbs are left unaffected. When more sensitive Tabebuias are planted, they may be frozen to the ground. These trees usually grow back, but need training to keep one central trunk. In South Florida, prune for deadwood or crossed limbs. Tabebuia trees need late spring pruning to keep a straight trunk and to develop even branching around the trunk.

Companion Planting and Design

A great stand alone accent tree to view at a distance or in combination with other small trees including Ligustrums and Bottlebrush. Use with under plantings of seasonal flowers.

My Personal Favorite

Only the species is available in Florida.

Texas Wild Olive
Cordia boissieri

When, Where and How to Plant

Dig a hole as deep as the rootball and 2 to 3 times as wide. Add no more than 30 percent organic matter to the backfill. Use a hose to water in as you shovel in backfill. Mulch heavily around the root zone so mulch is about 4 inches deep, but not touching the trunk. Keeping mulch a couple of inches from the trunk will avoid disease. Texas Wild Olive can take a wide range of soils, including South Florida's alkaline soil.

Growing Tips

Keep the root zone moist for the first growing season, and gradually allow nature to take over. Fertilize with appropriate amounts of fertilizer formulated for Palms, 8-4-12 with micronutrients, slow-release nitrogen and potassium. The fall application of fertilizer for flowering and fruit trees is sometimes a low-nitrogen to dissuade them from producing too many young leaves over winter, but this tree seems oblivious to seasonal changes and not only handles cold but blooms throughout.

Regional Advice and Care

Texas Wild Olives don't like to be in areas that flood or to be near sprinklers. Otherwise, these hardy little trees have no special problems. They may flower at quite an early age, perhaps even at a foot high. No major pruning is necessary. Eliminate dead wood, rubbing, or diseased branches in the late winter or early spring.

Companion Planting and Design

Because of its size, this flowering tree could be used near an entryway, in a swale, or set off by itself as a specimen tree. Its good behavior and blooming habit make it a candidate for wider planting as a street tree, able to produce flowers for tourists all year. Choose other drought tolerant plants, such as Trailing Lantana (*Lantana montevidensis*), Liriope, or Kalanchoe.

My Personal Favorite

Used as a small specimen tree to give it maximum visibility, this one is excellent.

A small tree that blooms with funnel-shaped white flowers year-round and has no major diseases, the Texas Wild Olive is a wonderful landscape component. In addition to its practicality, it's a handsome tree with a round canopy and dark green, sandpapery leaves. A member of the Boraginaceae family, this tree's flowers, with golden throats, are sprinkled over the canopy in small, neat, terminal clusters. Like all white flowers, they stand out in the moonlight. Texas Wild Olive makes a beautiful front yard tree, where it can charm passersby. It is not sensitive to cold, as is its cousin, the orange-flowered Geiger Tree (Cordia sebestena), and the large shrub to small tree, the yellow-flowered Cordia lutea. This appears to be a superb tree for landscape use in South Florida. (GBT)

Other Name
White Geiger

Bloom Period and Color
Year-round, white

Mature Height and Spread
About 20 feet × 10 to 15 feet

Zones
8B – 11

More Trees

Tangerine *(Citrus reticulata)*

Bloom Period and Color Winter blooms in white; **Mature Height** × **Spread** 25 feet × 25 feet; **Zones** 9 – 11

When, Where, and How to Plant Add transplants between December and February in Central Florida. Add containers to the landscape at any time, though the cooler times are best. Position 15 to 20 feet from buildings, sidewalks, and streets. Provide a site without overhead wires and away from drain fields. Tangerine trees grow best in a well-drained soil. Tangerine trees grow well in sandy Florida soils without added soil amendments. Open a hole that's about 2 times wider than the rootball but no deeper. Plant at the same depth it was growing in the field or container. Create a berm. Keep a 2- to 3-feet area surrounding the trunk free of all vegetation and mulch. Prune in February to remove lower limbs that may be in the way of maintenance and to remove errant limbs.

Growing Tips Water every day for the first few weeks, then gradually taper off to wateringas needed. Feed four to six weeks after planting. Continue the feedings every six to eight weeks, March through September, for the first two to three years. Established Tangerine trees need watering once or twice a week for good fruit production. Provide a light feeding once in March, May, August, and October. In South Florida use 8-3-9-3.

Regional Advice and Care Citrus sometimes suffer cold damage in Central Florida and need rejuvenation pruning to remove the dead wood. Mound soil up around the trunks to protect the grafted portions from freezing. In South Florida plant from containers in early summer. Control caterpillars by hand picking or by applying the *Bacillus thuringiensis* spray. Aphids and white fly can be controlled with an oil spray or other University of Florida recommended control.

Companion Planting and Design Add to the fruit tree collection with other Citrus, Avocados, Carambola, and more. May be used as a space divider or view barrier with shrubs of Hollies, Hibiscus, Gardenias, Camellias, and Ligustrums.

My Personal Favorite 'Sunburst'

Tropical Plants *for Florida*

Long ago we called the tropics "The Torrid Zone." Perhaps we should go back to that name to once again bring a sense of urgency to what we now discuss so dispassionately, given the wholesale destruction under way there. If we knew more about the tropics, this sense of danger to the tropical natural world might be more real to us. Because so much of life exists in the tropics, our concern needs to manifest itself before all life is threatened.

If we look closely at tropical plants, we can allow them to serve as gateways to our understanding of larger tropical ecosystems. They will lead us not to one vast, oppressively hot place, but to a whole galaxy of niches, from the tops of enormous, 200-foot trees to the diminutive and mostly unknown

Anthurium

world of fungi. The stories of tropical plants are tales of adaptation, exploitation, temptation, seduction, and unlikely triumph in a climate that promotes ceaseless competition for life itself.

A Story to Tell

Start with the story of a vine that begins its life on the forest floor where it seeks not light at germination but darkness. For darkness means shadow, and shadow in all likelihood means a tree trunk. Once there, a small leaf emerges and flattens itself against the damp bark of the buttressing root, itself an architectural wonder. The next leaf is thrust over the top of the first, slightly higher on the tree, until eventually, the vine has worked its way into the upper canopy. There, it can quit making these tiny, clinging-for-dear-life leaves. There, it can detect more light and more air, and so it begins growing bigger leaves, better able to take in the sun, to bask in the rain, to reach out from the trunk and wobble in the wind, vigorous and, yes, victorious.

Or repeat the story of the Strangler Fig that is deposited as a seed in the crotch of an unsuspecting tree. Tell how it germinates and sends down a single root, long and thin but for a corklike covering. Then it produces another root, then another, and wraps them around the trunk of the tree that is its host. Its leafy shoots squirm and wedge their way through the canopy of the host until they can produce carbohydrates at a good clip in order to swell the roots and strengthen them. And eventually, the perch becomes the victim, the Fig the strangler, not literally strangling its host but suffocating it, stealing its sunlight and its place in the forest.

Orchids, on the other hand, do not attack their hosts, but coexist with them. Dustlike seeds find the fungus-rich compost that collects on a tree branch, and they germinate, uniting with the fungus in a relationship that provides food for the seed and a home for the fungus. Then, residing in a peculiar elevation, the plant has figured out a way to signal pollinators to find it. One of them creates flowers with the exact scent that a male euglossine bee uses to attract a female bee, and it disperses the scent, molecule by molecule, to bring in the bee. Once there, the bee wedges himself inside the flower to secure packets of the perfume for himself, and in the process he triggers the latch of the pollinia (the tiny golden orbs of male pollen produced by the flower); they stick to him as he backs out to fly away. Greedy for more, the bee visits

Peace Lily

another flower. Only this time, the pollinia become attached to the sticky female stigma, and the Orchid is pollinated.

Other Orchids create bee look-alike flowers, so the male bees believe they have spotted a female bee. The disguise works.

These stories are endlessly intriguing. They turn the tropics from abstract forests to living organisms, flirting, tempting, copulating, reproducing, and communicating in ways that are stunning to behold—once you have the Rosetta stone of understanding.

Additionally, these plants are super resourceful because of the competition with other plants for space, light, air, water, and reproductive success. They have devised all kinds of strategies for surviving:

they climb; they soar; they perch; they strangle; they jump into the light at the first opportunity. You would, too, if your life depended on it. And in the process, they have become glorious garden specimens.

The Orchid and the vine are just two examples of plants useful in Florida gardens. Add to them Gingers, which attract their pollinators with flower spikes of brilliant color; Bromeliads that store water in their vaselike rosettes; herbaceous low-lying plants that have lens-shaped leaf cells to catch light or special coloring to better utilize the light available or holes to keep from tearing or drip tips to let the rain run off . . . these plants are the dressing for subtropical gardens, the pin on the lapel, the brooch at the throat.

Worth the Effort

Many require extra care, particularly from the center of Florida northward. Like human Floridians, they get cold quickly and need protection in what is inclement to them. Like human Floridians, they may be sensitive to light, and so prefer the protection of shade. Like human Floridians, they like their daily shower but don't want to sit in a bath for long or they'll wrinkle. It just takes common sense, when you think about it.

Most of the plants in this section thrive best in South Florida gardens. Many will also do well outside in other areas of Florida during the summer. In pots, they can easily be moved back and forth, provided there is adequate humidity indoors.

Don't be afraid to try them. They bring wonderful foliage patterns and colors, beautiful flowers, and an intriguing way of life with them. And they tell stories that you can repeat to your friends.

Bromeliad

Aglaonema
Aglaonema cultivars

Sometimes called "Chinese Evergreen," the Aglaonema is an often-overlooked resident of shady tropical gardens. Pewter or silver patterns against dark-green leaf blades are the hallmark of this plant. Aglaonemas come in myriad patterns and shades of green that can endure extremely low light. As potted plants that can move in during cold weather, and can readily beautify a patio or townhouse garden. Little spathes and spadices—the protective leaves and flower stalks—develop in the axils of the leaves, and bright red or yellow fruits form on small flower stalks. Several species have been used in hybridization. Some of the famous hybrids include 'Silver King', 'Silver Queen', 'Manila', 'Silver Frost', and 'Emerald Beauty'. Almost all are variations on the theme and often confusingly look alike. (GBT)

Other Name
Chinese Evergreen

Bloom Period and Color
Summer; white

Mature Height × Spread
2 to 12 feet × 1 to 4 feet

Zones
10 – 11

When, Where, and How to Plant
Plant in the late spring or early summer. Display Aglaonemas next to a path or in raised beds as ground covers. They prefer shade, although morning sun or flecks throughout the day are fine, particularly for the plants with more silver in the leaves, as there is less chlorophyll available to catch light so brighter light must be supplied. Aglaonemas thrive in well-drained soil. They grow nicely in a basic peat-perlite mix, or peat-perlite-pine bark with crushed limestone. Any variation on this theme will do. If planting them in beds beneath trees, use a good potting mix throughout the bed with pine bark soil conditioner or another additive such as perlite. Dig a hole a little larger than the size of the container. Carefully remove the pot from the rootball, place the Aglaonema in the planting hole, backfill, and cover the root zone with mulch.

Growing Tips
After the plants have become established, let the soil become medium-dry between waterings. Using a 20-20-20 soluble fertilizer at half strength every two weeks means tender loving care for these plants. A 30-10-10 or a slow-release fertilizer formulated for foliage plants also works. (A slow-release product formulated for foliage plants that commercial growers use is repackaged as Dynamite and sold in home improvement stores.)

Regional Advice and Care
Protect plants from cold. Watch for mites in dry weather; mealybugs may be a problem if you bring them inside during winter. Use cotton soaked with rubbing alcohol to wipe away mealybugs, and employ a Q-tip to reach those in the leaf axils. A systemic insecticide such as Orthene® may be needed; if so, apply outside. Use these low-light plants indoors as houseplants in colder areas of the state, keeping them out of drafts.

Companion Planting and Design
To give vitality to the "floor" of your shady garden, plant groups of Aglaonemas in complementary colors. Try Dieffenbachias, Begonias, Peperomias, and Ferns to add color and texture.

My Personal Favorite
There are more and more hybrids available today, and each can play a role in the garden, but I'm partial to lighter patterns that show up in shade.

Anthurium

Anthurium spp.

When, Where, and How to Plant

Plant when seed ripens, or in spring or early summer if transplanting from a container. The Bird's-Nest Anthuriums tend to grow in a rosette on a fat column of roots. To transplant, slice off a reasonable clump with roots and relocate. Plant in shady beds with other tropicals, in pots, or as specimens throughout the garden. For Aroids in clay pots, allow for drainage by using peat moss, perlite, sand, and pine bark. Other ingredients may be cypress mulch or orchid mix. Drainage is the key. Bird's-nest, pendant, and climbing types can be grown on large branches in trees. To attach these types, including the bird's-nests, to tree limbs, use plastic-coated wire or 16-gauge wire and some osmunda (dried Fern roots) to wrap around Aroid roots for moisture retention. If you can run a sprinkler extension up the tree to water the plants, do so. If not, use a hose. Gradually rely on rain, except during the dry season.

Growing Tips

If using terra cotta, check the moisture levels closely. Soil in clay dries faster because the pot is porous. In windy weather, you may water daily if you grow these in pots. In the ground, they require watering less often, depending on location. 'Lady Jane' types allow their leaves to lower instead of holding them straight up when the plants are thirsty. Anthuriums do well with slow-release fertilizer, supplemented with occasional foliar sprays of 20-20-20. For Aroids in trees, use a nylon mesh bag and fill with slow-release 14-14-14 so that when it rains, the plants will be fertilized.

Regional Advice and Care

Anthuriums may be used as summer flowers in Central and North Florida or grown in containers.

Companion Planting and Design

With their cordate or heart-shaped leaves, Anthuriums add distinction to a tree trunk, a garden path, a bed. They complement spiky Bromeliads, fussy Ferns, and even soften rocks and boulders.

My Personal Favorite

The gorgeous *Anthurium magnificum* has large leaves that almost defy belief, with a suede finish and silver veins.

Anthuriums are either terrestrial or epiphytic tropical plants, often with dramatic leaves. Anthurium andraeanum is the "Flamingo Flower" that is grown in Hawaii by the millions and sold by florists and street vendors. Although the flowers may not be as attractive as the Flamingo Flower, the velvet-leaved Anthuriums are seductively beautiful. A. crystallinum, A. magnificum, and A. clarinervium, each of which has white veins against dark, velvety green with slightly different veination and size, are as splendid. One of the biggest-selling is Anthurium 'Lady Jane'. The heart-shaped leaves are tough and shiny, and the spathes are rose-pink. Anthuriums are wonderful outdoors in the right light and soil, and this one, planted in a big pot, can take all kinds of weather. (GBT)

Bloom Period and Color

Year-round foliage and blooms in red, pink, white, occasionally green and red

Mature Height × Spread

Varies with species

Zones

10 – 11

Banana
Musa × paradisica

The Banana is a popular backyard fruit in South Florida. The plants are evocative of the tropics, with oblong, smooth leaves on succulent stems. We plant Bananas from corms, or underground stems, which sucker after each new growth has bloomed and fruited. The fruit take from twelve to eighteen months to form and develop. Male flowers form at the end of the stem, females closest to the top of the stalk. The fruit may take two to three months to mature. When the ridges on the individual fruit round out, Bananas can be picked and tied up in a garage or carport to ripen. If you leave the bunches on the plant, the skins will split. 'Dwarf Cavendish' is a Banana suitable for South Florida. (GBT)

Other Name
Plantain (for cooking bananas)

Bloom Period and Color
About 18 months after planting

Mature Height × Spread
5 to 20 feet × various

Zones
10 – 11

When, Where, and How to Plant
Plant at the beginning of the rainy season to allow the Banana plenty of growing time before winter. Choose an area where the plant will be protected from winds. Bananas like plenty of water, so put your stand where you easily can irrigate it, but not in a low spot where water will stand because the underground stem will rot. Dig a hole 2 or 3 feet across by about 2 feet deep, and enrich it with aged compost or potting soil. Homestead Banana expert Bill Lessard cautions against using manure or peat moss in the planting hole because such material holds too much moisture and breeds fungi. Place the corm in the hole to a depth of 8 inches, with its white roots on the bottom, then backfill. Mulch only after the plant has become established and is pushing out a new leaf.

Growing Tips
When new leaves begin growing, water daily. Young plants need small but frequent applications of fertilizer. Apply 1 pound every two months, increasing the amount until you apply 5 or 6 pounds by the time the plant begins to flower ten to fifteen months later. Use a 6-6-6 fertilizer initially, then switch to 9-3-27 or another high-potassium fertilizer. Manganese and zinc can be applied as a foliar spray.

Regional Advice and Care
Bananas can tolerate cold weather but should be covered with a cloth over poles, like a tepee, when frost or freezing is expected. Freezes can take them back to the ground, but usually they will resprout. If leaves begin to flag, and your cultural program is good, you may be seeing nematode infestation, sigatoka, or Panama disease. Consult the Cooperative Extension Service about control.

Companion Planting and Design
Given their need for water and fertilizer, Bananas in beds by themselves are easiest to manage. Group several kinds in a bed across the back yard, add mulch, and give yourself room to trim old leaves.

My Personal Favorites
For ornamental use, the Rojo or Red Banana, excels at bringing a tropical feel to a garden, but for taste, a new Honduran hybrid, SH 3640, produces great-tasting, sweet dessert bananas that are far better than the store-bought type.

Bromeliad

Aechmea spp.

When, Where, and How to Plant

Plant any time, particularly if putting them in trees. If you wish to remove a pup from a mother plant, wait until the pup is $1/3$ the size of the mother, then cut away close to the mother stem. Plant in beds beneath the canopy of a shade tree, such as a Live Oak; use large Bromeliads as accents. Plant in rock or mulch. Orchid mix is wonderful for Bromeliads grown in terra cotta pots, or equal parts peat, perlite, and bark.

Growing Tips

Keep the Bromeliad cups filled with water; fertilize at $1/4$ strength every two weeks. Fertilize, if at all, less often or at decreased strength for banded, spotted, or colorful leaves, or color/spotting can disappear.

Regional Advice and Care

If the water in Bromeliad cups is allowed to stagnate, mosquito larvae can take up residence and make life miserable when they hatch. Use a home or garden spray, or flush the cups with the hose every couple of days. Or use a horticultural oil in the cups to keep mosquitoes from laying eggs there. When the plant produces off-shoots, carefully remove with secateurs, and pot or plant. When Bromeliads get old and crowded in beds, the original plants begin to rot and stink. Periodically, remove them from the beds, prune away the old plants, and reposition. If working with Aechmeas that have spines, use bee-keepers gloves that cover your forearms to keep from being scratched. These gloves have leather hands and canvas arm coverings. Also, watch for scale in overcrowded conditions. Bromeliads often are grown outdoors in Central and North Florida, but they must be removed from their beds or protected with covers during freezing weather.

Companion Planting and Design

There's a Bromeliad for every use, from ground cover to specimen. Use full-sun types on rocks with Cycads; try patterned leaf species in partial shade with Palms; put Neoregelias in beds with Gingers.

My Personal Favorites

Elegant Bromeliads are especially appealing without spines, and my votes go to *Alcantarea imperialis* (formerly *Vriesea imperialis*) and *Vriesea hieroglyphica*.

Bromeliads are all-around performers, bringing tropical color and an architecturally interesting shape to a subtropical setting. They can grow in trees or under them, on rocks or in mulch, in sun or shade, as accents or mass plantings. Their often brilliant colors—particularly before flowering—render many of them extroverts in a garden, while some produce astounding inflorescences that last many months before fading. The cup that forms inside the rosette of Bromeliad leaves holds water, and in areas with distinct dry seasons, these often are the refuge for frogs and a whole universe of microscopic living things. Aechmea blanchetiana, when exposed to full sun, turns its leaves a glowing coppery-red; those of the same species in the shade have apple-green leaves. (GBT)

Other Names
Billbergia, Neoregelia

Bloom Period and Color
Varies with genus and species

Mature Height × Spread
Few inches to several feet

Zones
10 – 11

Dracaena

Dracaena fragrans

There are approximately 150 species of Dracaena, many of which are used as interior plants, because they can live in low light where they tend to stay at much the same size for years—if they can survive house dust. Dracaena fragrans, the Corn Plant, is from tropical Africa. Its yellowish flowers are sweetly fragrant at night, growing terminally in winter. The flowers form round clusters and fall like tassels over the top of the cornlike leaves. Dracaena fragrans 'Massangeana' is a variety with a golden stripe down the center of the leaf. It needs more light than the plain-leaved Corn Plant. When old, the bases have considerable character. Dracaena reflexa is a pretty relative with whorls of leaves all along the stems to the ground. (GBT)

Other Name
Dracaena fragrans or *lindenii* with yellow-edged leaves

Bloom Period and Color
Winter blooms in yellow

Mature Height × Spread
20 feet × 24 to 36 inches

Zones
10B – 11

When, Where, and How to Plant
Plant in the spring to take advantage of the rainy season's natural irrigation. Cuttings are rooted best in spring, but can be made any time. Select areas calling for vertical lines. The plants like a shady area, and they prefer an acid soil. Alkaline soil causes yellowing. Dig a hole slightly larger than the rootball, and add compost or some organic matter to enrich it, but only enough to make it 1/3 of the backfill. Mulch the root zone. If you cut off the top of a long branch, new buds will pop and new heads of leaves form; in this way, you can readily shape the plant—in addition to being able to root the top. Several plants of differing heights used together are effective.

Growing Tips
Dracaenas are not fussy about their care, but like fertilizer and shade to stay a rich green. In Central and South American, Dracaenas are used as living fence posts, planted as sticks and allowed to develop leaves. In sun, the leaves are yellow and tattered, but the plants live anyway. In your garden, drainage is required; the plants can stay fairly dry for long periods and do well despite neglect. Fertilize them along with the rest of the landscape plants in the spring, summer, and fall. The more care they receive, the better they look.

Regional Advice and Care
Grow these tropical plants in containers, and protect them from temperatures below 40°F in Central and North Florida. Dust occasionally to help them photosynthesize and use a liquid fertilizer once a month. Water, let the soil dry slightly, then water again.

Companion Planting and Design
Where you need a narrow, vertical element, try the Corn Plant. It is useful for screening (perhaps a neighbor's yard) that's visible beneath a tree, or among billowing ferns to break up the monotony.

My Personal Favorite
Dracaena fragrans is a fine plant for indoor use and a utilitarian plant for blocking views.

Elephant Ear

Alocasia spp.

When, Where, and How to Plant

Plant in the late spring or early summer. Plant them in the center of a tropical grouping, in a corner, or toward the back of a garden, so the dramatic effect can be given a visual context. Some are quite attractive in terra cotta pots; a well-draining soil mix is needed. Some Elephant Ears can take more sun than other kinds of *Alocasias*, but they may bleach out when in sun all day. Fill a bed with equal parts potting soil, pine bark mulch, and perlite. Dig a hole a little larger than the size of the container in which you buy the plant. Carefully remove the pot from the rootball, place the plant in the planting hole, and backfill. Use mulch around the root zone.

Growing Tips

Water twice a week if it does not rain. Use a slow-release fertilizer (such as 18-6-8) two to three times a year in the garden; use once in the spring if plants are in pots. Supplement with a foliar spray of 20-20-20 or 30-10-10 to bolster their nutrient supply. If you see yellowing of leaves, use a micronutrient foliar spray or fish emulsion with a spreader sticker or a few drops of liquid Ivory.

Regional Advice and Care

These plants will be damaged by cold in northern regions of the state, and even during prolonged cold in South Florida. Prune away damaged leaves in the early spring. Sometimes, the winter knocks the plants back even in protected South Florida gardens, and they revert to small leaves. They have to grow back to their large size over time. Plenty of water in spring will help, but be sure the plants don't sit in water.

Companion Planting and Design

These leaves are great for shooting out of a bed of Aglaonemas or Palm Grass like a giant green fountain. Some species add a middle level to a garden while allowing other interesting plants to be seen.

My Personal Favorite

Alocasia x *amazonica* has a patent-leather shine on hunter green leaves that are scalloped and veins that are silver. Top that.

Much of tropical gardening is about dramatic size and shape of the leaves. Rising from a host of smaller green leaves, Elephant Ears are as theatrical as Twelfth Night. These enormous leaves that feel like calfskin proclaim that a bold gardener lives here. Alocasia macrorrhiza is the best known of the group, with leaves that can reach more than 2 feet long held on beefy stems. The leaves are lightly scalloped, and the blade surface between the veins is slightly puckered around the edges. Alocasia macrorrhiza 'Variegata' is a green-and-white version that is truly spectacular. A parent of A. amazonica is A. sanderiana, with a skinnier leaf that is much more deeply indented. A. lowii grandis has the same combination of deep-green-and-silver veination, but is a plumper elephant-ear shape. (GBT)

Bloom Period and Color

Not grown for flowers, but for foliage. Flowering times vary, and are intermittent throughout the year.

Mature Height × Spread

2 to 12 feet × 8 feet

Zones

10 – 11

Fern
Many genera, species and varieties

Ferns are as widespread and diverse, as ancient and current as the temperate Gingkos and the tropical Cycads. In South Florida, hammocks and solution holes both claim native Ferns: the Sword Fern and the Maidenhair. The first is the pinnate, upright, pretty, and bright green, Nephrolepis biserrata. *The second,* Adiantum tenerum, *is a delicate black-stemmed plant with medium-sized wedge to deltoid leaflets. Strap Ferns in the swamps are* Polypodium phyllitidis, *and they grow on logs or on the forest floor. In our gardens, they run over rocks, across mulch, over tree limbs; pop up unheeded in orchid baskets; take over the shrub beds; disguise the roots of the Poinciana; and absorb the leaves of the Live Oak. They bring grace to everything they do.* (GBT)

Other Name
Various

Bloom Period and Color
Spores form when plants mature. Maturation differs with different ferns.

Mature Height × Spread
6 inches to 3 feet × various

When, Where, and How to Plant
Plant in the rainy, warm season. Good drainage is necessary. Attaching Ferns to trees or planting in mulch is ideal. Maidenhair Ferns can easily be grown in pots. Crushed rock or large limestone rocks suit the Maidenhairs, which are fond of alkaline conditions. Boston-like Sword Ferns will grow in any mulch. Resurrection Ferns, *Polypodium polypodioides*, that unfurl on tree limbs after rain, are tricky to get started. Pieces of bark that fall from old oak trees with the ferns embedded in them may be wired onto other trees so the rhizomes can crawl. This takes several seasons to work. Staghorns are often planted on mounds of sphagnum moss wired onto wooden plaques, then hung in trees or in shadehouses. Cut back Ferns in the spring to produce revitalized plants.

Growing Tips
Tender roots of Ferns can be burned easily by pellet or granular fertilizer. An 8-8-8 or fish emulsion is best. Fertilize monthly or every two weeks. To fertilize every time you water, use water-soluble mix at $1/4$ strength or less.

Regional Advice and Care
Ferns grown beneath trees are naturally protected in cold weather, but require cover in a freeze. When temperatures drop into the 50s and 40s, many Ferns need protection. *Adiantum tenerum* can take short periods of cold. Sword Ferns and Resurrection Ferns will be killed to the rhizomes in freezes. Wrap a blanket or sheet around the Fern to get it through the night. Cold winds are also hard on Ferns and can quickly dry and kill them. If you grow Ferns in baskets, even under trees, put the Ferns inside or on the ground under sheets.

Companion Planting and Design
In subtropical and tropical gardens, Ferns are all-purpose plants. Maidenhair can hover gracefully over the edge of a path; Strap Ferns can be tucked into boots of Palms.

My Personal Favorites
Angiopteris angustifolius and *A. evecta* are enormous Ferns with fronds that may reach 25 feet long in their native habitats, from Malaysia through the Philippines. They're appealing to people who love big dogs, and just as much trouble.

When, Where, and How to Plant

Plant at the beginning of the rainy season to mid-summer. Just the right light can be tricky with Gingers. When they aren't getting enough bright light, they lean toward the source, and with too much they can yellow. Morning or afternoon light is good, while midday summer sun is not. A high overhead canopy, such as Poinciana or Live Oak, can provide the right kind of light. Or select a spot where they receive full morning or later afternoon sun, perhaps an eastern exposure. Once they begin forming big clumps, the plants will spread, leaving old canes in the center. Maintenance includes cleaning out the old, brown stems. Choose a location in high shade, allowing the plants room to grow. Enrich soil to a depth of 8 or 10 inches, and slip the container from the rootball. Keep the rootball at the same level in the ground as it was growing in the container. Water in the backfill, and mulch. While Red Ginger prefers organic soil, it can do quite well in alkaline Florida soil with organic matter in the planting hole and mulch on the surface. If conditions are right—high humidity and good soil moisture—baby plantlets will germinate in the bracts of the old Ginger flowers. The heads eventually fall to earth, and some of them may take root.

Growing Tips

Alpinias accept many conditions, but like to be well fertilized. Use 7-3-7 with micronutrients, or 6-6-6, around the planting area. The plants are fast growers.

Regional Advice and Care

Use these tropicals in containers in Central and North Florida, protected from chilling winds.

Companion Planting and Design

Another useful plant that seems to say welcome to the tropics. Red and Pink Gingers are lovely together. The true Ginger, *Zingiber officinale*, can be grown in our gardens in partial sun. It is fragrant.

My Personal Favorite

Alpinia purpurata is a regulation Red Ginger that never fails to appeal to me.

There are about 1000 species of Gingers (counting the weird and famous), but new ones are being discovered all the time. Many cultivars are to be found, as well as relatives such as Curcumas, which are deciduous but enticingly beautiful, Calatheas, Globbas, and Cannas. The nice thing about Red Ginger, Alpinia purpurata, *is its bald-faced "come hither" brilliance. The flowers are lovely, and seen against the leaves that help them pop out visually, they are as photogenic as a tropical sunset. Red Ginger is easy to care for, with water and high shade being the main requirements. A popular Pink Ginger is a nice contrast to the Ruby Red. Shell Ginger,* Alpinia zerumbet, *can form large and massive clumps, and the racemes (the cluster of flowers) resembling porcelain shells are big and showy. (GBT)*

Bloom Period and Color
Summer blooms in red, pink, purple

Mature Height × Spread
3 to 15 feet × various

Zones
10B – 11

Ginger Lily
Hedychium coronarium

If you like your perfume sweet, the Ginger Lily is for you. The flowers are kept inside green bracts, and each bract allows only one flower to open at a time. The blooming period lasts several weeks. The yellow-flowered H. gardnerianum is known as the Kahili Ginger. Kahili has bright-red stamens. H. rafillii is a hybrid that grows to 8 or 10 feet and has orange flowers and red stamens. H. flavescens has creamy-yellow flowers, while, H. coccineum, the Scarlet Ginger Lily, has scarlet flowers with pink stamens. Hedychium coronarium is listed as an invasive exotic in some parts of the world by the University of California, Davis, and The Nature Conservancy. The plant, which probably originated in the Himalayas and China, grows as a weed in Hawaii and Maui and throughout Micronesia, American Samoa, among other areas. It forms thick stands and is among Hawaii's forest invaders. (GBT)

Other Name
White Butterfly Ginger

Bloom Period and Color
Summer blooms in yellow, orange, scarlet, and white

Mature Height × Spread
2 to 4 feet × various

Zones
9 – 11

When, Where, and How to Plant
Plant in the early spring while the plants are less active or near dormant. Choose a sunny or a shady area large enough to accommodate its tendency to spread. *Hedychium*, the national flower of Cuba, is an assertive grower and loves moist soils. Shaded locations promote more rapid growth than sun. Mulch is essential to provide the right soil conditions. Like other Gingers, this one grows on a rhizome and is fairly close to the surface. David Bar-Zvi, horticulturist at Fairchild Tropical Garden, recommends planting the rhizome twice as deep as it is thick.

Growing Tips
Ginger Lilies or Butterfly Gingers like moist soil and warmth, as well as a good supply of nutrients. Slow-release fertilizer is practical in order to keep a flow of nutrients available to them throughout the growing season. Keep these with other water-thirsty plants to avoid over-watering the entire landscape just to water them. Fertilize when new growth starts after planting and lightly in midsummer to keep them growing well.

Regional Advice and Care
These plants can be grown in containers for use on patios and around pools in Central and North Florida. Although *Hedychiums* are tolerant of cold because they come from high altitudes, freezing weather will kill them to the ground, but they may resprout from underground stems if the ground itself has not frozen.

Companion Planting and Design
A group of Butterfly Gingers at the entryway allows guests to be greeted by their lovely aroma. At the backdoor, you get the reward. Among the many hybrids now available are pink ('Hawaiian Pink'), peach, raspberry ('Elizabeth'), copper gold ('Double Eagle'), yellow, and orange. *Hedychium greenii* is a red-orange. When planning ways to fill in around a waterfall or pond, keep Ginger Lilies in mind. These perfumed plants are tall enough to be visible over Lilies, Coleus, Impatiens, Begonias, and other low-lying shrubs.

My Personal Favorite
Hedychium coronarium, white with a light yellow throat, has a sweet fragrance and a delicate appearance.

Heliconias

Heliconia spp.

When, Where, and How to Plant

Plant at the beginning of the rainy season or throughout the summer months. Use Heliconias in shady areas that afford the plants protection from cold and wind. *H. stricta* and *H. chartacea* (cv. 'Sexy Pink') are apt to lose leaves to cold and cold winds. If protected by windbreaks or planted on the south side of the garden, Heliconias suffer fewer setbacks in cold winters. Dig a hole twice the size of the rhizome or rootball (if in container), and enrich it with peat moss and pine bark mulch. Backfill and mulch to mediate soil moisture.

Growing Tips

Heliconias have big appetites. I have found that slow-release 18-18-18 combined with periodic foliar sprays of micronutrients keep them performing well. When they are hungry, their leaves quickly begin to yellow—spray 20-20-20 on the leaves to provide a quick uptake of nutrients, then add slow-release. Water every other day in the summer if it doesn't rain. Heliconias exposed to wind and sun will require more water, as wind will pull water from the plants.

Regional Advice and Care

Occasionally, mealybugs will infest Heliconias if air circulation is not sufficient. Use Sunspray Ultra-Fine® oil. Root and stem rots are more serious. Use a systemic fungicide, or a general fungicide or bactericide, such as Physan 20®. Hand pick snails from the leaves. In clumps or large circles, the outer, newer stems may lean. Staking from within is one way to better manage the look of the plants and allow the flower to show. Use dwarf varieties in containers, away from windy locations, in Central and North Florida. Bring them inside for winter, or move to an atrium if you have one.

Companion Planting and Design

Free-standing groups of Heliconias are planted among the grass at the Wilson Botanical Garden in Las Cruces, Costa Rica. Try yours at the garden's edges, as specimen plants, along walls, and behind Shrimp Plants.

My Personal Favorite

Heliconia indica is tough to grow in South Florida because it is so cold tender, but its red leaves are beautiful.

These fascinating plants have become important tropical plants for Florida gardens as more of them have been introduced and gardeners have become acquainted with the enormous array of colorful cultivars. Related to Bananas, Heliconias have fewer and more graceful leaves. They grow on underground rhizomes or stems, and they can grow into large stands if left unchecked. Lovers of water, they nonetheless require good drainage so their underground parts don't rot. Cultivars that do especially well in South Florida are Heliconia bihai and H. caribaca, as well as some forms of H. stricta, H. latispatha, and H. rostrata. H. stricta is a small (2 to 6 feet) species with maroon undersides on the leaves . . . cultivars and color forms number in the hundreds. (GBT)

Other Name
Lobster Claw

Bloom Period and Color
Spring and summer blooms in yellow, orange, scarlet

Mature Height × Spread
2 to 15 feet × various

Zones
10B – 11

Mussaenda

Mussaenda philippica

When morning sunrises are pastel, with the softest peach light on the clouds gradually turning to pink, and the sky's deep blue dissipates into robin's-egg—that's when the tropical of subtropical seems most at hand. Those pink colors can be found covering the landscape when Mussaendas are allowed to wander the grounds. The sepals are all enlarged and fluffy, so the pink never fails to conjure up visions of cotton candy. This is not a shrub to have the everyday duty of running alongside a fence. Its lusciousness is best taken in smaller doses, and its cold-tenderness makes it vulnerable to damage below 45°F. Philippica 'Dona Aurora' has white sepals; other 'Dona' cultivars are pink. Mussaenda glabra is yellow with a single cream-colored sepal. (GBT)

Bloom Period and Color
Year-round, more summer blooms in pink, white, yellow

Mature Height × Spread
9 to 10 feet × 6 feet

Zones
10 – 11

When, Where, and How to Plant
Plant at the beginning of the rainy season through midsummer. Locate in full sun for best color, or in high, light shade. Dig a hole as deep and twice as wide as the rootball of the plant in a container. Add organic material, such as compost, peat moss, or aged manure. Carefully remove the container from the plant, and slip the shrub into the planting hole. Water in the soil and backfill. Mulch, being careful to keep mulch a couple of inches away from the trunk.

Growing Tips
Fertilize with an acid-forming or Gardenia/Ixora fertilizer. (Mussaendas are related to Gardenias and Ixoras, in the Rubiaceae family.)

Regional Advice and Care
You will have to grow these plants in containers in Central and North Florida. Fungal leaf spot can affect some plants; the pink is hardier than the salmon. The flowers are formed on the ends of the branches, so pruning in spring will encourage more branches to form. Prune after bracts fade, and this will encourage more flowering in the same season. If the shrubs grow too large, cut back quite hard. Use the cuttings to propagate more. Legginess is a problem. In *Gardening in the Tropics*, R. E. Holttum and Ivan Enoch suggest planting Mussaendas in a mixed border so shorter shrubs can conceal the trunks. Hard pruning is necessary because of the tendency to stretch and straggle. Holttum and Enoch also suggest that you place these shrubs carefully, because such continuous showiness can become tiresome.

Companion Planting and Design
A wonderful combination is pink Mussaenda with Persian Shield (*Strobilanthes dyerianus*), a silver-purple foliage plant, and Cat Palms or Areca Palms. Snowbush echoes the soft pink of *M. erythrophylla* 'Dona Luz'.

My Personal Favorite
Mussaenda erythrophylla, the Red Mussaenda, is a pretty plant.

Peace Lily
Spathiphyllum spp.

When, Where, and How to Plant
Plant at the beginning of the rainy season through midsummer. Choose a shady location with some protection against cold and well-draining soil. Use a high nitrogen fertilizer for foliage plants, with a 3-1-2 ratio. In too much shade, the plants won't flower, although they will survive nicely. Today's cultivars have been developed to endure the ordeals of indoor abuse: they hold up well in low humidity, they hang on if not religiously watered, and they flower despite it all. Take the same plants outside, and they can flourish in medium to deep shade in well-drained soil. Like other rain forest plants, the *Spathiphyllum* likes water but good drainage.

Growing Tips
Spaths like moisture and fertilizer in regular amounts. Water every other day or so, depending on conditions. A 3-1-2 fertilizer for foliage plants can be used 3 or 4 times a year, or a fertilizer that's used generally for landscapes in south Florida, which is the palm special 8-4-12. When containing the tropical plants in a confined and protected area and reducing evapotranspiration through the plant, water needs are minimized. Outside, Spaths don't like to be overwatered.

Regional Advice and Care
Potted plants can be moved outside in the summer to shaded patios or pool areas. You also may use *Spathiphyllum* as a temporary ground cover during the summer in Central and North Florida.

Companion Planting and Design
These plants make wonderful potted specimens for use both indoors and out. As entryway plants they are show-offs, especially the large cultivars. Consider them for shady patios, porches, and interiors. Peace Lilies and Begonias in the same garden bed are wonderful compatriots. Both go up and down the size scale from huge to petite. Combine them with a Tree Fern and see if the textures aren't pleasing.

My Personal Favorite
Spathiphyllum 'Clevelandii' is a big plant, with impressive leaves that are dark green. It's a show-off.

One of the chief attributes of white flowers is their visibility in low light. And like a lighthouse beam in fog, the spathe of the Peace Lily is a small beacon in shadowy places. Dr. Bill Wolverton, formerly with NASA, did a famous study in the early 1990s showing that certain plants used indoors could remove pollutants such as formaldehyde, benzene, and carbon monoxide from the air. Spathiphyllum *was among the top 10 of these in effectiveness for removing formaldehyde. It was also among the ten best in alleviating sick building syndrome. The off-gassing from carpets, furniture, cigarette smoke, and other sources were trapped primarily by roots of these plants. Wolverton said that one houseplant for every 100 square feet would clean interior air. (GBT)*

Bloom Period and Color
Summer blooms in white

Mature Height × Spread
12 inches to 4 or more feet

Zones
10B – 11

Peperomia

Peperomia spp.

Were you to venture into the Big Cypress Swamp, wade through the sloughs of the Fakahatchee Strand, or watch nature from the distinctly dry vantage of the boardwalk at Corkscrew Swamp Sanctuary near Naples, you would find native Peperomias. They love to loll about on fallen logs, sharing the ride with ferns and some orchids. And were you to wander into a garden center, you would no doubt find them among the houseplants and dish gardens. In your garden, Peperomias can easily serve as ground covers, potted plants for the patio or waterfalls, fillers in the crags of shaded rocks around your pond, or roamers among the mulch in your hammock. Peperomia caperata 'Red Ripple' has beautiful burgundy-green and quilted leaves and can take more sun. (GBT)

Bloom Period and Color
Flowers are greenish, on slender stalks; usually at the end of summer

Mature Height × Spread
12 to 18 inches × 4 inches (for a single plant; but you never grow just one Peperomia!)

Zones
10 – 11

When, Where, and How to Plant
Plant in spring or any time during summer. Select a shady, well-draining area, which nonetheless can retain moisture. If you think about an old log, you can visualize the way water runs off, but moisture is kept in the decomposing bark and detritus. As a ground cover, plants may be spaced quite close or farther apart, depending on the leaf size. Plants will spread, though loosely. Some plants will clump up or mound slightly. You can multiply your ground cover easily from cuttings taken in the spring. Root them in a moist 50-50 mix of peat moss and perlite, and keep them shady until roots have begun. Or plant cuttings directly into the bed, and keep well irrigated until the plants are growing well.

Growing Tips
A key ingredient to the successful culture of Peperomias in the garden is mulch to keep the soil evenly moist. Fertilize with a 7-3-7 granular fertilizer containing micronutrients two or three times a year or a slow-release; less often if you use mulch, and less often if you fertilize plants around which the Peperomias grow.

Regional Advice and Care
Peperomias will creep along the ground, turning up their heads to the light. When they become too tall and flop into a heap, cut off the top few inches. These can be rooted in pots or directly in the ground. Keep the soil moist. These plants are too tender for widespread use in North and Central Florida, unless they are grown in containers.

Companion Planting and Design
Peperomias make pretty hanging basket and container plants, particularly those with variegated leaves. As a ground cover with Palms, this is a hardy plant for bright shade in areas with a lot of moisture. Ideal places for getting them started: tree stumps left in the garden or old logs brought in for character.

My Personal Favorite
Peperomia obtusifolia is a plain-Jane plant, but there are places in the world for plain Janes and tumbling over garden logs is one of them.

Ti Plant

Cordyline terminalis

When, Where, and How to Plant

Plant at the beginning of the rainy season through midsummer. Plant in what is best described as high shade—akin to that beneath an Oak, where light is bright without being direct. Ti Plants can sunburn in summer in direct sun, but they can gradually peter out in too much shade. Dig a hole larger than the rootball, add some peat moss or compost to enrich it (no more than 1/3 the total backfill should be organic), and water in the soil as you backfill the planting hole. In his 1994 monograph "The Cordyline," Frank Brown of Valkaria, FL., recommends planting mixed types of Cordylines, being careful with the color red.

Growing Tips

Ti Plants grow well in the rainy heat of summer, but their best color comes in fall and winter, when you ease off supplying so much water. They like to dry slightly in the dry season. Too much light and too much fertilizer can bleach the foliage. Organic fertilizer, such as compost or fish emulsion, is the gentlest, but slow-release is fine. Frank Brown recommends a high-nitrogen (10-5-5 or 30-15-15) for summer months, switching to a high-potassium (4-6-8 or 6-12-20) in fall to ready plants for winter. Do not over fertilize Cordylines growing in shade.

Regional Advice and Care

Watch for spider mites in winter; mealybugs in leaf axils, scales, and thrips. Tip cuttings easily develop roots. These are tender plants that are suitable for container culture in Central and North Florida. There are miniature Ti Plants that can work well in small containers, such as 'Minima', 'King Kamehameha', and 'Amazing Grace'.

Companion Planting and Design

Use colorful Ti Plants between billowy shrubs for flair, contrast a group of dark burgundy Ti Plants with variegated Ginger, use the tricolor for bringing color interest to Palm and Aroid plantings. They are exclamation points.

My Personal Favorite

Cordyline terminalis 'Tricolor' is a handsome plant, with enough oomph in its green/cream/red combination to be noticed in the garden without being gaudy.

If you were to dip feather dusters in a can of paint and insert them in the ground, feathers-up, you would have a good idea of what a Ti Plant looks like. A sunburst of red wine coloration in the garden has long been the Ti Plant's contribution, but with extensive hybridization, color can now be copper, green, fuchsia, yellow, cream, and any and all combinations of these. New and beautiful cultivars include 'Iris Bannochie', tricolored with cream, red, and green; 'Peter Buck' orange suffused through the red; 'Little Rose' with older green leaves edged in red and new pink and red leaves; 'Hawaiian Flag', a cream and red combination; 'Yellow Bird', with butter yellow leaves that take on some green coloration with age. (GBT)

Other Name
Cordyline

Bloom Period and Color
Irregular; winter peak Nov.-Dec.; spring March-April

Mature Height × Spread
6 feet × 20 inches

Zones
10B – 11

Traveler's Tree
Ravenala madagascariensis

As a landscape plant, the Traveler's Tree is most glorious when it is young, since that is when its remarkable head of leaves is closer to eye level. When young, the tree is trunkless, and can remain so for several seasons. Eventually, the trunk emerges and comes to resemble a palm trunk. The display is a stunning bit of geometry. The leaves are held on a single plane, like the cards held in a bridge hand. With a tall trunk and enormous leaves fanned across an axis, the Traveler's Tree makes quite a statement. The flower is really an oversized version of some upright Heliconia flower stalks. These large bracts fill with water when it rains. John Kress, chairman of the botany department at the Smithsonian Institution, found that the tree, originally from Madagascar, is probably pollinated by lemurs that peel open the bracts to eat the nectar. (GBT)

Other Name
Traveler's Palm

Bloom Period and Color
Summer; white

Mature Height × Spread
40 feet × 25

Zones
10 – 11

When, Where, and How to Plant
Plant at the beginning of the rainy season to midsummer. Plant in full sun or high, light shade, in a space large enough to accommodate the large head of leaves. Prepare a planting hole as deep and twice as wide as the rootball, and enrich with 1/3 compost before backfilling. Water in backfill to collapse air pockets. Mulch.

Growing Tips
Use a slow-release fertilizer, either balanced, such as 18-18-18, or high-nitrogen, high-potassium in the summer growing season, such as a 7-3-7. Use a balanced fertilizer on sand, or 8-4-12 on rocky soils, applying a small amount every couple of months. Traveler's Tree likes plenty of water in the summer growing season, less in the winter. Apply a slow-release fertilizer three times a year after the plant has reached a fair size.

Regional Advice and Care
Not suitable for Central and North Florida. Because they grow at about 3000 feet in Madagascar, these plants can take a little more cold than other tropicals. Suckers sometimes form at the base, and in smaller areas, it may be wise to remove them. The large leaves may become tattered in wind. When they look frayed, remove the outermost leaves. Some Traveler's Palms that survived battering by Hurricane Andrew in 1992 eventually regrew their crowns. Each leaf is 10 to 12 feet in length, and the leaf bases are filled with water—and thus a boon to travelers.

Companion Planting and Design
As garden specimens, these are truly impressive and can overpower the rest of the garden as well as the house. A single plant grown next to a chimney dwelling in a larger setting may be just the right (landscape) architectural statement. When correctly used, a mature and solitary Traveler's Tree will be a stunning sculptural element in your garden—at the corner of a path or shrub bed, where rounded and low plants suddenly give way to exuberance.

My Personal Favorite
These wonders of botanical geometry are handsome things, and when pruned so their fan shows off, they are attention-getters.

Costus *(Costus barbatus)*

Other Name Spiral Ginger; **Bloom Period and Color** Summer blooms in yellow; **Mature Height** × **Spread** 4 to 8 feet × 4 or 5 feet, as you wish; **Zones** 10B – 11

When, Where, and How to Plant Plant in the spring when the new growth begins, so the stems have plenty of time to mature and develop terminal flowers. Choose an area of high, light shade and organic soil where plants can clump and spread. Planting holes for Costus, Gingers, and other herbaceous tropicals don't have to go to China, but can be several inches deep. The plants are shallow-rooted, spreading on underground stems beneath the surface.

Growing Tips If you mulch to keep the soil moist around the plants and keep them well fertilized, they are happy campers. Costus and other members of the Ginger family grow best when well nourished, and the use of an acid-forming fertilizer will help keep soil slightly acid, which is what these plants like. Mulch also helps lower soil pH. Once the stems have flowered and the bracts have faded, you can cut out the parent stem. Or do a good housekeeping every 2 years. Like Heliconias, Costus can be dug and their planting beds freshened if you are a conscientious gardener or need to work off some energy. Add some cow manure, compost, and new mulch when thinning, separating and replanting. Never use chicken manure as it will burn the plants. Water less often in winter than summer.

Regional Advice and Care Grow Costus trees in protected areas in summer or in containers. Spiral Gingers look quite wonderful in the summer rainy season, but they tend to look haggard in winter. After two years of growth, they can be made to look handsome again by thinning the clumps. Large clumps lean out from the center, and need room to grow.

Companion Planting and Design Try *Costus cuspidatus*, with orange flowers, beneath Oaks with stands of *C. barbatus* and Red and Pink Ginger. *Costus speciosus* is 8 or 9 feet with white flowers from red bracts. Use as a screen.

My Personal Favorite *Costus speciosus*

Turf Grasses *for Florida*

Most homeowners take pride in growing a healthy green lawn. While they may complain about mowing the grass, they are usually happy to tell others what they do to fight off bugs and keep the turf thick. A lawn is an all-American bragging topic for most weekend gardeners.

The home turf is also a playground, supporting family football games, inviting croquet, or simply being the spot to tumble with a family pet. Many gardeners simply appreciate the open space created by turf.

A number of homeowners may not realize it, but their lawns are also producing oxygen, holding the soil in place, and helping moisture percolate down through the ground to replenish the freshwater supply.

Not everyone wants a large lawn. The latest trend is to grow only the grass one really needs and intends to care for. After all, there is work involved!

Planning the Lawn

The best lawns grow in full-sun locations. Some Florida turf varieties, mainly some of the St. Augustines, tolerate light shade. But in general, the less shade the better. Many cultural problems can be eliminated by planting grass only where it gets a full day of sunshine.

Bermuda

It's also best to keep lawns away from trees that cast heavy shade. Not only are light levels too low under most of the canopy, the turf also has to compete with tree roots. It is better to leave these areas for more shade-tolerant and vigorous ground covers.

Soil Considerations

Most Florida soils are suitable for growing turf. Soils rich in organic matter or clay hold more moisture than sandy soils, but both are capable of growing a great lawn. Avoid low areas that may accumulate water and hold it for more than a few hours. Such wet locations encourage shallow root systems and disease problems.

All turf sites should have the proper soil pH. Most grasses like a slightly acidic to nearly neutral soil. A soil in the 5.5 to 7.5 pH range is generally ideal. Only Bahia turf benefits from keeping the soil in the acid range of pH 5.5 to 6.5. In this acidic soil, extra iron is available for growing turf—Bahia seems to need this iron more than other grasses. Soil acidity can be adjusted by following soil test recommendations. In Florida, dolomitic lime is usually used to raise the soil pH, soil sulfur to lower it. Follow information from the test recommendations to properly change the acidity.

It may be impossible to make a permanent change in acidity in the very alkaline soils of South Florida, and in pockets of organic soils throughout the state. If the soil pH cannot be changed, gardeners should grow the turf type best suited to the area. And be prepared to periodically add minor nutrients that might be depleted by the extremes in acidity levels.

The First Step

Starting a new lawn is similar to filling bare spots in older turf. First, remove debris and weedy growths. Unwanted vegetation can be dug out or killed with a non-selective herbicide. Choose a product that permits planting the turf immediately after the weeds decline. Once the weeds are removed, the soil is tilled. This is the time to incorporate lime or sulfur if needed. Some gardeners also like to incorporate organic matter, including aged manure, into sandy soils.

Adding organic matter is beneficial, but usually only practical when dealing with small sites. While the matter is present, it does help hold moisture and provide some nutrients for beginning turf growth,

Palms walkway linked by a well-grown lawn.

but it quickly breaks down and leaves mainly the original sandy soil. After tilling, smooth out the ground to establish a uniform planting surface as final preparation for planting. This can be performed with a rake or a drag.

Starting from Seed

Seeding a lawn should be performed during the warmer months of March through September, when the grass makes quick growth. In Florida, Bahia is usually the only grass that is seeded to start the home lawn. It gives the best germination with minimal care. Some Bermuda, Centipede, and Zoysia varieties can also be seeded. For each area of the lawn, divide the amount of seed needed in half. Move back and forth across the lawn, spreading the first portion. Then move across the lawn in a perpendicular direction and spread the remaining seed. Rake the lawn to cover the seed. Bahia seed germinates best if covered with soil $^1/_4$ to $^1/_2$ inch deep. Seeded lawns need frequent watering. Water daily to keep the surface of the soil wet until the grass begins to sprout. As the roots spread out into the surrounding soil, watering can be reduced to "as needed."

Starting from Plugs

Plugs of grass—well-established sections of grass 2 to 4 inches square—can be used to establish all but the Bahia turf for home lawns. Some gardeners simply kill out the existing weeds and old grass, then insert the plugs into the ground. Good lawns can be established this way, but they appear to fill in more slowly than when the ground is cleared before planting. Add the plugs to moist soil. Most are spaced 6 to 12 inches apart. The closer the spacing, the quicker the grass fills in to establish the lawn.

Some people like to add a slow-release fertilizer to the planting hole. It may be beneficial, but it is also time-consuming. A good feeding shortly after plugging seems to give a similar response.

Keep the planted area moist and the plugs will begin to grow rapidly. After two to three weeks of growth, gardeners may apply a fertilizer to encourage the grass to form the lawn.

Starting from Sod

All turf types can be established by sod, which gives an instant lawn and helps shut out weeds that may grow among seeded and plugged turf.

Most sod is sold in rectangular portions. It can be purchased by the piece or on a pallet. A pallet of sod may contain 400 to 500 square feet, so ask about the quantity before you buy.

Have the soil prepared and damp when the sod arrives. If for some reason the sod cannot be immediately installed, keep it in a shady location. Sod that sits on the pallet for longer than forty-eight hours quickly declines. Install the sod by laying the pieces next to each other, abutting the edges. Cut sections to fill in any small spaces. After the sod is laid, water the turf thoroughly. A good rule to follow to keep the sod moist is to water every day for the first week. The second week, water every other day, and the third week every third day. After three weeks, water only as needed to keep the turf from wilting.

Gardeners should note that sod laid in the shade needs less water than sunny locations. Too much water, especially during hot and humid weather, can cause the turf to rot and the soil will be lost.

After the sod has been growing for three to four weeks, the first application of a lawn fertilizer can be administered. After this initial feeding, assume a normal care program.

The One Demand of Lawns

Home lawns do demand one thing: frequent mowing during the warmer months. From March through October, most lawns need cutting at least once a week. During the cooler months, cutting may not be necessary at all in North Florida, and just every other week or so in Central and South Florida. Every grass type has its own cutting height that ranges from $^1/_2$ inch for Bermudagrass to 4 inches for St. Augustinegrass. The general rule is to remove no more than one-third of the grass blade at any one time. This keeps the grass from being burned after too close a mowing. Another good mowing tip is to keep a sharp blade and mow in different directions across the lawn at each cutting.

A Little Water Goes a Long Way

Home lawns depend on soil moisture. But don't provide the turf with more than it really needs. Allowing the turf to dry out just a little between waterings forces the grass to grow a deeper root system. Avoid the everyday watering schedule. It encourages a shallow root system, makes the grass grow too lush, favors diseases, and pops up the weeds. Surprisingly, most lawns can go four days to more than a week without a watering.

Let the grass tell you when it needs water. Wait until spots in the lawn just start to wilt. You can tell when the turf is reaching this stage as the leaf blades start to curl and turn grayish green. When several spots show these signs, give the entire lawn a good soaking.

Water the lawn until the soil moisture is replenished. Most gardeners try to add $^1/_2$ to one inch of water at each irrigation. A bright-green lawn grows from proper feedings, but don't give it too much. The result of overfeeding is a lush lawn that pests love. Too much growth also encourages an organic layer to form under the turf that harbors pests and impedes water movement into the ground.

Throughout most of Florida, two complete feedings a year are usually adequate for Bahia and St. Augustinegrass—once in March and again in September. Centipede can grow fine with a single feeding and both Bermuda and Zoysia grasses will need extra feedings.

Use a fertilizer with a 4-1-2 ratio of major nutrients. This is the proportional amount of nitrogen, phosphorus, and potassium found in the product. A 16-4-8, 12-4-8, 15-5-10, or even a 10-10-10 is quite suitable for feeding the home turf.

During the summer months when lawns use nutrients faster than other times of the year, some iron may be applied to regreen the turf. Also, an extra feeding or two may be needed in South Florida.

Know Your Opponents

Many pests affect lawns. Sod webworms and chinch bugs love St. Augustinegrass, and mole crickets feed in Bahia. Bermuda attracts a wide variety of insects. Other turf types have certain pests as well. Learn the insects of your grass, then inspect the grass regularly and treat when needed.

Diseases are a less frequent problem, but all grasses have a few. With a good cultural program, diseases are kept to a minimum. Grass that is under stress, in too much shade, or planted in areas with poor air movement is likely to have disease problems. Consult the local Extension Service office when a disease is suspected.

Finally, all lawns get a few weeds. Again, good cultural conditions help prevent weeds. Digging or spot-killing the weeds when first noted is also a good quick control. When there are too many weeds, an herbicide may help. First get the weeds identified, and then locate an herbicide that can be applied to your turf type and provide the control needed. Always follow instructions carefully to prevent damage to your lawn.

St. Augustine Grass

Bahia Grass
Paspalum notatum

Gardeners who want a good-looking lawn with minimal care should plant Bahia Grass. It's one of Florida's most drought-tolerant turf types, tough enough to support the backyard football game. Bahia has become the multipurpose turf used for home lawns, athletic fields, parks, and roadsides. It has the advantage of growing well from seed, and is also easy to establish as sod. There are two major varieties. 'Argentine' has a wider-leaf blade with the smallest number of seed heads and resists yellowing during the spring season. 'Pensacola' Bahia Grass produces a narrow blade and is the least expensive to start from seed, but it does have a tendency to yellow during spring and produces an abundance of tall seed heads. A few additional varieties have been cultivated in Florida. (TM)

Mowing Height
To 3 to 4 inches

When, Where, and How to Plant
Establish Bahia Grass during the warmer months of March through early September. Bahia Grass can tolerate the filtered shade of open trees, but keep it out from under dense Oaks and the northern sides of buildings. All varieties prefer an acid soil and a pH between 5.5 and 6.5. If a pH change cannot be made, supply extra iron to prevent yellowing. Bahia can be successfully established by seed. Sow 7 to 10 pounds of seed for every 1000 square feet. Cover the seed $1/4$ to $1/2$ inches deep or apply a topdressing. Gardeners can also establish an instant Bahia lawn with sod.

Growing Tips
Keep seeded and sodded areas moist and apply a complete fertilizer three to four weeks after growth begins. To grow a deep root system water only when the blades start to curl then irrigate with $1/2$ to $3/4$ inches of water. Where adequate water is not available the Bahia turns brown but revives when seasonal rains return. Feed with 16-4-8 in March and September. Add an iron feeding during early spring to prevent yellowing. From April through September mow at least once a week to 3 to 4 inches high.

Regional Advice and Care
Care of Bahia Grass is similar throughout Florida. More fertilizer may be needed in the Southern regions than in Northern and Central Florida. Areas with a pH above 7 may have to apply more minor nutrients. The mole cricket has to be controlled in Bahiagrass. Use baits applied during the summer season. Due to an open growth habit, weeds may invade the turf. Use cultural controls to encourage dense growth, or apply an herbicide.

Companion Planting and Design
Plant Bahia Grass with other drought tolerant ornamentals. Use it in the sunny spots and surround with trees, shrubs, and Palms, including Oaks, Sweet Gum, Viburnums, Indian Hawthorn, Saw Palmetto, and Lantana.

My Personal Favorite
Choose the 'Argentine' variety to get a selection that is less likely to yellow and produces fewer seed heads. There is also some indication it is more mole cricket tolerant.

Bermuda Grass
Cynodon spp.

When, Where, and How to Plant
Start the Bermuda Grass lawn during the warmer months of April through September. The grass tolerates pH extremes if supplied with trace elements. Nematodes are also a problem, so test the soil and avoid infested areas. Bermuda Grass must be planted in full-sun locations. Even in light shade it thins and quickly declines. Plant at the rate of 1 to 2 pounds of hulled seed spread over every 1000 square feet. Improved hybrids are started as sprigs, plugs, or sod. Plant sprigs at the rate of 5 to 10 bushels for every 1000 square feet, then roll into the soil. Plugs are spaced 12- to 24-inches apart. Most fill in the lawn within six to nine months. Sod is abutted together to form instant turf.

Growing Tips
Keep all planted areas moist and provide a first feeding in three to four weeks. Bermuda is a high-maintenance lawn. Apply a 16-4-8 fertilizer around March, May, and September. Supply with nitrogen feedings at least every other month during summer and fall. Let the leaf blades start to wilt in small areas of the lawn, then apply up to 1 inch of water. Mow frequently with a reel mower at 1 to 1^1/2 inches.

Regional Advice and Care
Bermuda Grass turns brown with the first frosts of winter in the colder regions of Florida. Recovery is rapid when the weather turns warm. Insects that may affect the lawn include sod webworms and mole crickets. Some diseases to look for include dollar spot, brown patch, and leaf spots. An established Bermuda lawn is resistant to weeds. A good cultural program can reduce nematodes. Remove thatch layer with a vertical mower.

Companion Planting and Design
A fine bladed grass to form a putting green or a lawn for family fun. It might be used to establish the estate look surrounded with flower beds, palms, and tropical plants.

My Personal Favorite
There is only one variety that has good potential as a fairly carefree home lawn and that's 'FloraTex' which needs fewer feedings and has some nematode tolerance.

Florida's most impressive lawns are Bermuda Grass. Gardeners like the fine texture and dense growth this grass offers, which creates a green carpet of durable turf popular on golf courses and athletic fields. Bermuda Grass is also selected for its salt and drought tolerance. Common Bermuda, a seeded type, has an open growth habit and coarse texture and is used mostly along the roadside. Improved seeded varieties of medium texture and dense growth, including 'Cheyenne', 'Sahara', 'Sundevil', and 'Jackpot', find use in athletic fields, lawns, and parks. Some varieties are reproduced as sprigs, sod, or plugs. Popular types include 'FloraTeX', 'Tifgreen', 'Tifway', and 'Tifway II', which have good density, a fine texture, and tolerance to varying cultural conditions. Some additional types include 'Guyman', 'Midway', 'Quickstand', 'Tifdwarf', and 'Tiflawn'. (TM)

Mowing Height
To 2 inches

Centipede Grass
Eremochloa ophiuroides

Gardeners familiar with Centipede Grass refer to it as the Poor Man's Turf due to the grass's ability to grow in infertile soils with minimal feedings. Centipede looks like a miniature St. Augustine with relatively narrow leaf blades forming in clusters along green runners. Gardeners like the turf's good green color, ability to grow in light shade, and good drought tolerance. With the right care it can be quite vigorous, filling in bare spots and knitting a dense lawn in a few months. Some varieties of Centipede with improved cold tolerance that might be selected for North Florida are 'Oklawn' and 'Centennial'. Most Centipede marketed as seed, plugs, or sod is a generic mixture of red- and yellow-stemmed types. (TM)

Other Name
Poor Man's Turf

Mowing Height
2 to 3 inches

Zones
8 – 10

When, Where, and How to Plant
Centipede Grass can be established from seed, plugs, or sod. Plant during the warmer months of March through early September. Centipede can be burned back by frost and freezes, making it unattractive. Slightly acid (pH of 6.0), highly organic to sandy soils are suitable, but have them checked for nematodes before planting. When the pH cannot be altered, supply the growing grass with minor nutrients to prevent deficiencies. Centipede grows best in full sun but can tolerate light shade. Sow seeds at the rate of 1/4 pound for each 1000 square feet. Plant plugs about a foot apart in a weed-free site. For an instant lawn use sod.

Growing Tips
Keep seed and newly plugged or sodded areas moist to encourage growth. Feed at half the recommended rate four to six weeks after good growth begins. Fertilize in March. A feeding may also be applied during fall. Centipede has some drought tolerance, but if shallow-rooted may need frequent waterings. When spots start to wilt, it is time to water the entire lawn. Keep the blade sharp and mow at about 2 inches tall.

Regional Advice and Care
Gardeners in North Florida grow the best-looking Centipede Grass, and with few pest problems. It grows throughout the state, but nematodes and ground pearls affect lawns in the warmer sandy soils. Turf growing in Central and South Florida may develop yellowing during the warmer months due to a high soil pH. Use periodic iron applications. Residents of North Florida may also use the iron treatment. Gardeners in Central and South Florida should have a nematode test to help make the planting decision.

Companion Planting and Design
A medium bladed grass that needs frequent watering. Grow what you need for family fun and surround with moisture-requiring plants of Azaleas, Philodendron, Maple trees, and annual flowers.

My Personal Favorite
Only common varieties are available in Florida.

St. Augustine Grass

Stenotaphrum secundatum

When, Where, and How to Plant

St. Augustine Grass can be used to start a new lawn or fill in the bare spots at any time of the year. Get the best growth by planting St. Augustine in sunny locations. Away from trees and buildings is the only place to plant varieties 'Floratam' and 'Floralawn'. Other selections, including 'Bitter Blue', 'Delmar', 'Palmetto', and 'Seville', have more shade tolerance and can survive in up to 25 percent filtered sun. Remove the weedy growths and loosen the soil. St. Augustine plugs can be set 12 to 18 inches apart. The closer the spacing is, the quicker the runners grow together. Lawns established from plugs form a dense turf in one to two growing seasons. The secret to establishing a lawn from sod is laying the new turf on damp soil and abutting the pieces closely together.

Growing Tips

Keep all plantings moist and provide the first feeding in three to four weeks. St. Augustine Grass must have irrigation during the drier weather. Let the turf tell you when to water. A lawn with a deep root system can often go a week or more without extra water. At each watering provide $1/2$ to $3/4$ inches of irrigation. Provide a complete fertilizer once in spring and once in fall. If during summer the turf becomes a little yellow, apply an iron application.

Regional Advice and Care

St. Augustine lawns are given similar care throughout most of Florida. Only in the southern portions of the state might an additional feeding or two be desirable. Gardeners should check for chinch bugs and caterpillars during the warmer months. Also look for brown patch.

Companion Planting and Design

Grow with irrigation and a mix of shade and full sun loving plants. Plant in combination with ground covers plus Oaks, Hollies, Palms, Thryallis, Ixora, Hibiscus, and most colorful perennials and annuals.

My Personal Favorite

My selection for a full sun site is the deep blue-bladed 'Floratam'. It's very vigorous but don't try to grow it in the shade.

St. Augustine Grass is probably the best all-around turf Florida has. Gardeners like the blue-green color and vigor. The leaf blades are a little coarser than many northern turfs, but it has good shade tolerance and pest resistance. Almost every Florida gardener has heard of 'Bitter Blue' St. Augustine. It has set the standard of good St. Augustines having a dark green color, good cold resistance, and tolerance for light shade. A variety suitable for sunny locations is 'Floratam', which has notable vigor, good color, and added pest tolerance. Semi-dwarf St. Augustines 'Delmar' and 'Seville' have been the newest selections offering finer leaf blades, a closer mowing height, and good tolerance to shade. Perhaps the oldest variety is common, or 'Roselawn' St. Augustine. (TM)

Other Name
St. Augustine

Mowing Height
To 3 inches

Zoysia Grass
Zoysia species

Gardeners can ask for no finer lawn than Zoysia Grass. It grows a bright-green carpet that, once established, can beat out weeds and withstand wear. It's also drought tolerant, cold hardy, and resistant to high salt levels. The most popular varieties include 'Meyer' (also marketed as Z-52), 'Amazoy', 'Emerald', and 'Cashmere'. All are available as sod or plugs. They offer a medium- to fine-textured turf with good green color. Several varieties of Zoysiagrass may be marketed in Florida for home lawns. Variety 'Belaire' is a selection of Zoysia japonica. *It has good cold tolerance and green color, but is coarser and more open than the more common 'Meyer' variety. Another selection is 'El Toro', which appears to grow more quickly and has improved disease resistance. New varieties from Brazil that appear to grow well in Florida include the wide-bladed 'Empire' and the fine-bladed 'Empress'. (TM)*

Mowing Height
1 to 2 inches

When, Where, and How to Plant
Zoysia can be planted year-round as sod or plugs. Since cold makes the grass often turn brown, most Zoysia is marketed as sod or plugs during the spring and summer. Sunny sites are the best locations, but the grass can tolerate light shade. It grows in sands, clays, and organic soils and tolerates alkaline soils. Sodding produces the instant Zoysia lawn that's best able to compete with weeds. Make sure the turf pieces abut each other. Plugging is economical. The small squares of turf are set 6 inches apart and grow together in a year. One type, *Zoysia japonica*, is available for planting by seed. A seedbed should be established and the Zoysia seed lightly mixed with the soil and kept moist. After years of growth, Zoysia develops an organic layer just above the soil line know as thatch. This restricts water movement, harbors insects, and detracts from the appearance of the turf. Mechanically remove the thatch as needed.

Growing Tips
Provide several complete feedings per year with 16-4-8 applied once during spring and once during fall. Nitrogen applications are also in April, June, August, and November. Zoysia is a very drought-tolerant turf, but during dry weather a lawn without adequate water does turn brown. Apply about $1/2$ to $3/4$ inches at each irrigation. Although Zoysia makes slower growth, provide weekly mowings during the warmer months using a reel mower.

Regional Advice and Care
Zoysia grows throughout Florida but is sure to turn brown in the northern sections of the state. Billbugs can cause the turf to decline in patches by feeding on roots and blades, in which case a chemical control is needed.

Companion Planting and Design
A fine bladed grass for the well maintained look that looks best with irrigation. Grow in the sun but surround with other ornamentals including Oaks, Hollies, Philodendrons, Camellias, Firebush, Ligustrum, and Viburnum.

My Personal Favorite
There have been a number of recent selections but 'Empire' catches my eye. I like its wider blade and more compact growth habit.

Vines *for Florida*

My, my, how they get around, these vines. Shameless climbers, stealthy twiners, exuberant clingers, superlative sprawlers, midnight ramblers . . . cling to me like a vine, we say, and mean every word at the time.

The vining lifestyle must be the envy of the plant world. After all, everyone else stays put. Only the vines scramble hither and yon, scampering up trees and across fences, under guard rails and around poles. Look at Kudzu. Look at Morning Glories. Look at Passion Vines. But look fast, or you'll miss them going by. Yes, we exaggerate—but only slightly.

Tomorrow . . . the World

In the war of vines, one wonders who might win, Kudzu or Wood Rose? Rosary Pea or Poison Ivy? Air Potato or Virginia Creeper? Coral Vine or Flame Vine? Vines are opportunists, seizing the moment, racing for the light. There is one in South Florida called Cow Itch Vine because it can irritate even cattle. There is Pull-and-Haul-Back, so named for its recurved thorns that won't let you move forward once it has you in its grip.

Then there is the parasitic Dodder or Love Vine. It not only twines; it filches, too, stealing carbohydrates from its victims. Pothos, when it escapes (perhaps its revenge for imprisonment), runs up trees and

Allamanda

does a quick change into the so-called Hunter's Robe, a vine with such big leaves that they are used as protection in rain.

The subtext of vine lore is that vines are poised to take over the world if presented with the possibility. And that was certainly the case with some hammocks after Hurricane Andrew blew away the canopies. The vines, poised to strike, did. It took years of hot, sweaty (not to mention costly) work to clear them away.

Confederate Jasmine

Taking Control of Your Vines

You will have to exercise some control over the vines you introduce into your garden. Periodically take the machete to some of them.

On the other hand, there are spectacular spring effects to be had by running a Bougainvillea or Flame Vine up a tree. Just make sure you want it there before you give it its head. Be especially careful with vining Jasmines. They quickly become pests. The Passion Flower Vine and the Nasturtium Bahuinia (*Bauhinia galpinii*) may also fling themselves about with abandon. Lightly prune vines periodically throughout the growing season, and cut them back hard after flowering or in early spring before they shoot out. Most vines like enriched soil and regular irrigation to keep going as they do. Fertilize once or twice a year, in spring and fall. Keep the root zones mulched to reduce weeds and keep soils evenly moist.

Passion Vine is susceptible to nematodes; keep it well fertilized and mulched, growing vigorously, to prevent damage. Like other pests and diseases, nematodes are more apt to attack a weakened root system than a strong one.

Passion Vine has the added advantage of producing edible fruit. *Passiflora edulis* is one that can be grown for its tangy, hard-shelled fruit. As tropical fruits become more well-known outside of California, Texas and Florida, the passion fruit has captured a following. It has a puckery tang that enlivens sauces, salad dressings, ice cream, sorbet, desserts of all types, including soufflé and Key lime pie.

Pergolas and rock walls are excellent support for vines. Pergolas and trellises can be used to create outdoor rooms or walkways, with vines adding colorful, natural decoration. A vine that has clusters of hanging flowers, such as the Jade Vine or Bleeding Heart, make a beautiful trellis plant.

The Possibilities of Vines

The ability to camouflage may be a vine's most useful characteristic. The Creeping Ficus (*Ficus pumila*) is stellar in this respect. If given enough water and periodic fertilizer, it can hide a concrete block wall in just one or two seasons. Place it at the base of the wall in an enriched planting hole, keep it well irrigated, and watch it go.

Passion Vine

Vines have many possibilities. Grow Philodendrons on a tree or stump, Coral Vine or Flame Vine on a lamppost, or Stephanotis on porch lattice . . . your garden will benefit from their unique qualities.

Coral Vine

Allamanda
Allamanda cathartica

Allamanda is one of the plants that cheerily announce the warm season in South Florida. While it does not have tendrils with which to cling, it sprawls and reaches with gusto. The large flowers on this vine are especially showy, and yellow is a color that draws the eye. It is a member of the Apocynaceae family, and has this family's white milky sap. This sap is toxic, so don't toss any leaves into your salad. Cold weather will knock off some leaves, but the Allamanda is a durable plant in almost all conditions and can grow for decades. The hottest withering weather may make it wilt. A purple-flowering plant, A. violacea, *a bronze-tinted cultivar, 'Hendersonii' and a pink species, A.* splendens, *are available. (GBT)*

Bloom Period and Color
Spring, summer, fall blooms in yellow

Mature Length
5 feet; vining

When, Where, and How to Plant
Plant anytime except during the winter. Plant in full sun next to a structure that needs screening but can offer support. A trellis or arbor should be strong; a chain-link fence is ideal. Enrich the soil for this vine, mixing compost or peat moss or good potting soil into the planting hole. Water in the backfill and mulch after planting. Keep the root zone moist while the plant becomes established.

Growing Tips
Allamanda grows vigorously in a fairly rich soil, and it loves fertilizer. Its leaves will become chlorotic, or yellow between the veins, when it is hungry. A complete fertilizer of 7-3-7 with micronutrients, applied in the spring and fall, can keep the vigor going. Or use a slow-release fertilizer, such as 14-14-14, twice a year. Allamandas are fairly drought tolerant, but they need weekly watering in the dry season. When plant leaves begin to take on an overall yellow, a drench of iron can help return the color.

Regional Advice and Care
Few insects bother Allamanda, with the exception of aphids in the spring. Let lady bird beetles control them or use 1 to 2 teaspoons of liquid Ivory or baby shampoo plus 2 tablespoons of horticultural oil in a gallon of water, or a horticultural oil spray. Cut back hard in early spring to remove crossed and woody stems that have become intertwined and tangled. If using this plant as a shrub, you will have to prune it frequently. If you live in Central Florida, wait to prune until warm weather returns, or unexpected cold may damage or kill the plant. In colder parts of the state, grow this plant in a large pot with a trellis so it can be brought inside during cold weather.

Companion Planting and Design
Use Allamanda to wrap up a chain-link fence in beautiful yellow flowers and glossy leaves. Tie against a wooden privacy fence, and allow the shoots to cascade down. Or, lean it on a picket fence.

My Personal Favorite
Allamanda cathartica is easy to grow and pretty. What more could you ask for?

Bougainvillea

Bougainvillea spp.

When, Where, and How to Plant

Plant Bougainvillea in the warm season. Plant in a site where the entire plant, including much of the root zone, can get sun and heat. The plant is not fussy about soil, but it will not flower well if it receives too much regular irrigation from an automatic sprinkler system. Dig a planting hole just as deep as the container and a little wider. Gently remove the pot from the plant, being careful of thorns, and position it in the hole. The trellis should be in place behind it. Water in when backfilling. Water regularly, keeping soil moist, but not wet, to get the plant established. Long arching stems are weak and break easily in wind unless supported.

Growing Tips

Mulch lightly. Bougainvilleas will wilt when too dry. They are tolerant of cold, but they will drop leaves if chilled. If frozen, they will come back from the ground. Bougies require a steady diet of fertilizer. Use a balanced fertilizer in the summer, followed by a bloom-booster such as 4-6-8 in the fall. Bougies do not thrive on benign neglect—they like to be watered, and then to dry out before being watered again.

Regional Advice and Care

Flowers develop on new growth, so in September you can prune back and shape the summer's growth. In more temperate areas, select a cultivar of *B. spectabilis*. Bougainvillea is readily grown in large terra cotta pots, which won't keep the roots too wet. They are fed upon by tiny green caterpillars, the larvae of small moths. Use Dipel®, or wait for the cycle to run its course. The plants may lose leaves, but they sprout new ones.

Companion Planting and Design

This is another fence plant. It is supremely beautiful when colors are mixed and the long stems arch over and catch the light. Remember to use a white occasionally to make other colors stand out.

My Personal Favorite

'Mary Palmer' has white and magenta colors in one flower, and it always makes you look twice.

A woody flowering perennial with grass-green leaves, thorns, and tiny flowers surrounded by spectacularly colored bracts, Bougainvilleas may be Brazil's most successful export. They grow in every tropical and subtropical climate and dazzle wherever they are. The shimmering and stunning color is in the papery bracts that surround small white flowers. Semithornless—often called "thornless"—varieties are good container plants for patios or balconies. (The plants are somewhat thorny when young, but lose that characteristic as they age.) There are a great number of cultivars these days, including a rose and white bicolor. But these have been bred from three basic species: Bougainvillea glabra, which is a compact grower and flowers throughout much of the year; B. peruviana, which flowers in the dry season; and B. spectabilis, which flowers after a dry spell. The purple-flowering B. spectabilis is more cold tolerant than the others. (GBT)

Other Name
Bougies

Bloom Period and Color
Spring through fall blooms in all colors

Mature Length
6 to 20 feet

Zones
9 – 11

Carolina Yellow Jasmine

Gelsemium sempervirens

Carolina Yellow Jasmine offers a big splash of bright yellow blossoms that open sometime in early February. And you don't have to worry about a winter freeze damaging the flowers, as this plant is totally hardy. Set the Jasmine to work hiding a fence or covering a wall. The leaves are bright green, lancelike in shape, and about 3 inches long. The shoots can grow to more than 20 feet in length, but this is not a vine that normally gets way out of control. Some selections of the Carolina Yellow Jasmine have been made for a deep yellow bloom or unique flowering habit. One, the 'Pride of Augusta', opens clusters of fully double blossoms. Note: All portions of the plant are poisonous if eaten. (TM)

Bloom Period and Color
Early winter blooms in yellow

Mature Length
20 feet; climbing

Zones
8 – 9

When, Where, and How to Plant

Carolina Yellow Jasmine can be planted throughout most of the year. The best planting time is during the cooler winter months. Carolina Yellow Jasmine vines need a trellis, fence, or similar support for good growth. Keep all vines off trees to prevent damage and to keep from encouraging pests. The Carolina Yellow Jasmine grows well in sandy Florida soils. Enrich soil by adding peat moss or compost and manure and till it in several inches deep. Dig a planting hole that's several times wider but not deeper than the rootball. Plant at the same depth it was growing in the container. Create a berm and add a 2- to 3-inch layer of mulch. Gardeners should expect Carolina Yellow Jasmine vines to make lots of growth, and adequate room should be provided at the planting site. Prune when the plants fill the trellis and begin to grow out of bounds. Every few years the vine should be given an early spring pruning after flowering to renew growth before new spring shoots sprout.

Growing Tips

Carolina Yellow Jasmine vines should be watered daily for the first few weeks after planting; gradually taper off to watering as needed. The vines are drought tolerant and need watering only during periods of drought—but for best growth, water weekly. Feed four to six weeks after transplanting, applying a light scattering of a 6-6-6 under the spread of the vine. Repeat feedings for established vines during March, May, and September.

Regional Advice and Care

The Carolina Yellow Jasmine is best suited to the colder portions of the state. Plant in Northern and Central Florida landscapes. No major pests affect the vines.

Companion Planting and Design

Plant as a space divider or backdrop for a patio or garden opening late winter blooms. Stage other flowers in front including Pentas, Salvia, Bush Daisies, Gaillardia, and Caladiums.

My Personal Favorite

Only the species is available in Florida.

Confederate Jasmine

Trachelospermum jasminoides

When, Where, and How to Plant

Add vines to the garden throughout most of the year. The best planting time is during the cooler winter months. Unless you are using it as a ground cover, the vine needs a trellis, fence, or similar support. Keep all vines off trees to prevent damage and to keep from encouraging pests. The Confederate Jasmine grows well in Florida's sandy soils. Add peat moss or compost and manure to the planting site and till it in several inches deep. Dig a planting hole that's several times wider but not deeper than the rootball. Plant at the same depth it was growing in the container. Create a berm and add a 2- to 3-inch layer of mulch. Vines used as a ground cover are planted in a similar manner and given a spacing of 3 to 4 feet.

Growing Tips

Water daily for the first few weeks after planting. Gradually taper off to watering on an "as needed" schedule. The vines are drought tolerant and only need watering during periods of drought—but for best growth, water weekly. Feed four to six weeks after transplanting, applying a light scattering of a 6-6-6 under the spread of the vine. Repeat for established vines during March, May, and September.

Regional Advice and Care

Prune when the plant fills the trellis and begins to grow out of bounds. To renew growth, every few years the vine should be given a spring pruning after flowering. The Confederate Jasmine grows well throughout all but the most southern portions of Florida. It's seldom affected by cold. Scale insects may need a control. Gardeners can apply an oil-containing insecticide or another University of Florida recommended pesticide.

Companion Planting and Design

Use with sun or shade loving plants. A great plant for trellises under Oak, Pine, Sweet Gum, and similar trees. Plant as a turf substitute in hard to mow areas.

My Personal Favorite

Only the species is available in Florida.

When springtime finally arrives, one plant can be counted on for attractive snow white flowers plus a great fragrance—it's the Confederate Jasmine. The plant needs just a little support for a dense view barrier or attractive vertical accent. It's an ideal wall covering for gardeners with just a little space. Once the blooms begin you can count on over a month-long display. Then the plant provides some great greenery from the masses of shiny oval leaves. When trained to trellis, the Confederate Jasmine is kept at about 12 to 15 feet, but the vining shoots are capable of growing 30 to 40 feet long. For their interesting leaf features, choose 'Variegatum'. It has green-and-cream-colored foliage and makes a good accent for a garden wall. (TM)

Other Name

Star Jasmine

Bloom Period and Color

Early winter blooms in yellow

Mature Length

6 feet; climbing

Zones

8 – 10

Coral Honeysuckle
Lonicera sempervirens

Add a Florida native to a fence, masonry wall, or side of a building to enjoy a spring-through-summer display of reddish orange and yellow blossoms. The Coral Honeysuckle leads off with a massive flush of flowers during March and April, that gradually tapers to sporadic blooms by fall. When its blossoms fade, they are followed by shiny red berries. The foliage is bright green on top and blue-green on the bottom. Use the Coral Honeysuckle where you need some reliable color for the warmer months. It serves as a good space divider and view barrier, keeping its foliage near the ground. Several selections for the landscape are 'Sulphurea' and 'John Clayton' with yellow flowers; 'Magnifica' with intense red blooms; and 'Alabama Crimson' with improved color. (TM)

Other Name
Trumpet Honeysuckle

Bloom Period and Color
Spring through summer blooms in reddish orange and yellow

Mature Length
20 feet or more; climbing

Zones
8 – 10

When, Where, and How to Plant
Vines can be added to the garden throughout most of the year. The best planting time is during the cooler winter months. Coral Honeysuckle vines need a trellis, fence, or similar support for good growth. Keep all vines off trees to prevent damage to the trunks and to keep from encouraging pests. Plant in a full-sun or lightly shaded location. In the shadier sites, flowering is greatly reduced. The vine tolerates sand, but for the best growth, provide an enriched soil. Add peat moss or compost and manure to the planting site and till it in several inches deep. Dig a planting hole that's several times wider but not deeper than the rootball. Plant at the same depth it was growing in the container. Create a berm and add a 2- to 3-inch layer of mulch. Prune when the plant fills the trellis and begins to grow out of bounds. Give the vine a renewal pruning in late spring every three or four years to ensure good coverage on the trellis.

Growing Tips
Water daily for the first few weeks after planting. Gradually taper the watering off to an "as needed" schedule. Coral Honeysuckle vines are drought tolerant and need watering only during periods of drought—but when growth is desired, water weekly. Feed four to six weeks after transplanting, applying a light scattering of a 6-6-6 under the spread of the vine. Repeat for established vines during March, May, and August.

Regional Advice and Care
Honeysuckles grow best in the Northern and Central portions of Florida. They lack vigor if they don't experience some chilling winter weather. Coral Honeysuckle plants usually remain pest-free.

Companion Planting and Design
A Florida native for a fence or trellis in the sunny spots. Look especially good with other natives of Firebush, Yaupon Holly, ornamental grasses, Palms, and most perennials.

My Personal Favorite
I like the variety 'Sulphurea' with its pure yellow flowers probably only because it's different. The plant is vigorous and fills a trellis quickly.

Jade Vine
Stronglyodon macrobotrys

When, Where, and How to Plant
Plant as soon after purchasing as possible. Plant at the base of a support, where it can begin climbing as soon as it "learns to crawl." Enrich the soil with potting soil, peat moss, compost, or well-aged manure. The soil must drain well. Carefully ease the plant from its container, position in the planting hole, and water in backfill. Keep the root zone moist while the young plant is growing vigorously. Mulch around the roots, keeping mulch away from the vine's stem. Flowers appear in early spring, usually in March. Occasionally, seedpods are produced. There are several large seeds inside the big, hard pod, which gradually darkens, dries, and splits open. Seeds can be germinated readily in peat moss and perlite. The vines begin growing as long, leafless shoots. When they hit a support, they send out leaves. Once the vine is flourishing, it is drought tolerant.

Growing Tips
Keep the roots well irrigated to get the vine established. Also, keep the root zone mulched to retain moisture. Apply a slow-release fertilizer, such as that formulated for palms which contains extra magnesium and micronutrients, three times a year. In late fall, a 4-6-8 or low-nitrogen fertilizer will help flower development.

Regional Advice and Care
Pinch off stray sprouts. This is a big vine, and one owner we know confesses to "hacking" at it instead of pruning. In fact, the Jade is a furiously aggressive plant that doesn't so much cling as gains a stranglehold on whatever it clutches—including trees and electrical wires. Do not be afraid to take a machete to this one. Jade Vines are too cold-sensitive for Central and North Florida.

Companion Planting and Design
Well-known South Florida naturalist Roger Hammer had a steel arbor built for his Jade Vine. The rest of us chase it out of trees. A pergola of stature or an arbor that's as burly as this vine is needed.

My Personal Favorite
A twin planting of Jade and Red Jade (*Mucuna bennettii*), which I once saw in Hawaii, is thrillingly beautiful. Together they could entwine the world, so a Jade by itself will do.

Jade Vine is a woody climbing plant that produces long chains of velvet-textured blue-green flowers. So beautiful are these aquamarine claws that tear at the heart; so memorable is the color that is otherwise found only in shallow tropical seas or on the backs of the rarest birds. These long chains of flowers can grow to 3 feet and hold about 100 flowers in one of nature's most exotic displays. Some have found the vine to be a temperamental grower; others who have a flair for growing it say this is not so. A similar vine is the New Guinea Creeper, a legume, or a member of the pea family. It has scarlet flowers of intense beauty. It can be grown in Hawaii and in trees in South Florida. (GBT)

Bloom Period and Color
Winter blooms in blue-green

Mature Length
Indeterminate

Zones
10B – 11

Passion Vine
Passiflora spp.

The Passion Vine flower is marvelously complex. With as many as ten sepals and petals, the sexual parts are elaborately displayed. The flowers are tiny to several inches across in colors from pink to red, blue or purple, white, and greenish yellow. All the reds are perfumed, and bees are crazy in love with them. Some produce delicious fruit. In addition to 'Possum Purple', there are red hybrids available from the Rare Fruit Council. P. coccinea is the red species; P. alatocerulea is the common blue Passion Flower that seems to perform well in South Florida. The corky-stemmed, P. suberosa, is South Florida's native, and it can be found at native plant sales. (GBT)

Bloom Period and Color
Summer blooms in pink, red, blue, purple, white, greenish yellow

Mature Length
Indeterminate

Zones
9 – 11, depending on the species

When, Where, and How to Plant
Plant in the spring. Plant in full sun, against a support such as a fence or trellis, but away from trees—unless you're prepared to find the vine looking down at you one morning. Plant in fast-draining soil. Potting soil or organic amendments may be added to a planting area. Dig a planting hole that's several times wider but not deeper than the rootball. Plant at the same depth it was growing in the container. Create a saucer around the root zone and add a 2- to 3-inch layer of mulch. Keep the roots well irrigated until the vine is growing vigorously.

Growing Tips
Passion Vines are quick growers. Use a balanced fertilizer, or slow-release 14-14-14, or Palm fertilizer (8-4-12) with slow-release nitrogen and slow-release potassium plus micronutrients. Too much nitrogen may result in foliage production only. The vines can grow in slightly alkaline soil, but they will become chlorotic in very alkaline soils. If chlorosis occurs, use an iron drench or a foliar spray of micronutrients with a spreader sticker, or both.

Regional Advice and Care
The blue Passion Flower is more cold tolerant than the red or purple. The edible passion fruit are *Passiflora edulis* (purple) and *P. edulis f. flavicarpa* (yellow), with fruit maturing in mid-summer. A local passion fruit that grows well in South Florida is *P. edulis* 'Possum Purple' named by tropical fruit grower Robert Barnum, who first grew it at his Possum Trot Nursery. It may produce a bushel of fruit on one vine.

Companion Planting and Design
This is another vine that requires an arbor. It is not woody like the Jade Vine, but it will run away if you aren't careful. Build an arbor at the entrance to your garden and run an edible *Passiflora* over it. These plants make perfectly splendid garden specimens because they flower freely in the summer and attract loads of butterflies.

My Personal Favorite
While there are far more beautiful Passion Vine flowers, *Passiflora edulis* 'Possum Purple' produces edible fruit, and to me the flavor rivals or surpasses that of chocolate.

Philodendron

Philodendron spp.

When, Where, and How to Plant

Plant in the warm season—April to October. The best places to start Philodendron are at the base of trees, totems, or fences. Start a cutting by burying the severed end in mulch and keeping it moist until it takes hold. Or, you may transplant a container-ized plant. Mix peat moss and pine bark in a planting hole, slip off the container, and place the rootball in the planting medium. Cover and mulch. Water daily until the vine begins to produce new leaves and roots, then gradually reduce watering.

Growing Tips

Use an organic fertilizer such as a well-aged manure, 6-6-6, or a Palm fertilizer around the rooted end. Palm fertilizer has slow-release nitrogen and slow-release potassium blended with low amounts of phosphorus and micronutrients. An alternative is a biweekly spray of 20-20-20 during the growing season. Because many Aroids are sensitive to cold, mix liquid silicon in your soluble fertilizer. Silicon helps build strong cell walls. Stronger walls mean less vulnerability to cold, heat, and drought. Many Philodendrons, however, survive cold and drought unscathed by virtue of growing beneath trees.

Regional Advice and Care

Philodendrons occasionally get scale, but otherwise are not bothered by sucking pests. Use Sunspray Ultra-Fine® pesticidal oil with a paraffin base. Snails can be bothersome; hand pick at night or early in the morning when dew is still on the ground, or use a snail bait such as Deadline. Philodendrons that climb need to be pruned in order to contain them. Many climbers are vigorous, while others are quite slow. Pruning depends on the species or cultivar. Philodendrons can withstand some cold, but not freezing weather. Gardeners in Central and North Florida can best utilize them as container plants. Some species that are cold tolerant include *P. sell-oum*, with large, lobed leaves; *P. hastatum*, with arrow-shaped leaves; *P. pinnatifidum*, with wide leaves and a matte finish; and *P. bipinnatifidum*.

Companion Planting and Design

As its name implies, *Philodendron gloriosum* is a creeping Philodendron with "glorious" velvet leaves.

My Personal Favorite

Philodendron wilsonii is a big brute, with wavy leaf margins and much self-possession.

Philodendron is an herbaceous climbing plant in the Aroid family. If you see vines creeping, sprawling, looping, clinging, hanging, connecting, lurching, and dangling—that means you are in only one place: a tropi-cal rain forest, where the canopy is alive with them. The vine lifestyle allows these plants to reach the light. Some plants have adapted to the low light. These are the plants we have rounded up and called houseplants. Some simply outgrow the others, starting with small juvenile leaves at the base of a tree, then developing large, mature leaves once they hit the canopy. Philodendrons are extremely agile and able to survive the dim or go for the light. Select carefully, and you will soon have a little rain forest of your own. The International Aroid Society holds an auction of rare plants (including Philodendrons) annually. (GBT)

Bloom Period and Color

Philodendrons bloom intermittently, and minute flowers on spadix are usually surrounded by a white spathe

Mature Length

To the top of the tree, and then down again

Zones

10B – 11

245

Queen's Wreath
Petrea volubilis

One reason to spend early spring in South Florida is to see the flowering of the Queen's Wreath. The darker violet petals fall after a few days, leaving the lighter blue sepals for several more weeks of color. With age, the vine develops a trunk that is quite thick. Twining vines will circle whatever support they are climbing, growing in a direction that has been genetically encoded, rather like being either right- or left-handed. At Fairchild Tropical Garden, Petrea volubilis clambers up the beautiful stone columns of the vine pergola originally constructed by the CCC in the 1930s. Prof. Ed Gilman at the University of Florida, Environmental Horticulture department, says it flowers several times a year (in South Florida, it flowers once in the spring). It is loved around the world. (GBT)

Bloom Period and Color
Spring blooms in blue-purple

Mature Length
To 35 feet

Zones
10B – 11

When, Where, and How to Plant
Plant Queen's Wreath in fall for flowers the following spring, or at the start of the rainy season to provide a long growing period until the next flowering season. This kind of vine can slink around a wooden arbor or even wires, but not up the sides of walls, as do clinging vines like *Ficus pumila*, the Creeping Fig. Because it is a vigorous vine, no matter where it is grown, *Petrea* must be supported by a pergola or arbor. Without tendrils, the vine twines, and it twines best on a craggy surface. Dig a hole slightly larger than the rootball and add some peat moss, compost, or well-aged manure. Slide the rootball out of the container, making sure the top of it is at the same level in the ground as it was in the container when placing it in the planting hole. Water in the backfill, and mulch to keep soil moisture and temperature well modulated.

Growing Tips
Fertilize three times a year, in spring, summer, and fall. Water two or three times a week in summer, twice a week in winter.

Regional Advice and Care
The Queen's Wreath has few pests, other than those normally found in the landscape: scale and mealybugs. Spider mites can be a problem in dry weather. Give the affected areas a hard spray of water. The Queen's Wreath is a vigorous vine that can be cut back hard after it has flowered. It can be pruned in late winter. A tender plant that will be hurt by cold, this vine needs a protected sunny spot in Central Florida. It is not a plant for North Florida.

Companion Planting and Design
Because it is so strongly seasonal, the vine wants to show off when it finally does flower. Using it at an arching gate, or on a pergola or trellis of some sort, is ideal. Give it a place to show off.

My Personal Favorite
As a springtime tonic and a welcoming flower at the front gate, Queen's Wreath is lovely.

Trumpet Creeper
Campsis radicans

When, Where, and How to Plant
Vines can be added to the garden throughout most of the year. The best planting time is during the cooler winter months. The Trumpet Creeper needs a trellis, fence, or similar support. The stems have clinging roots that help the vining portions climb walls and other smooth surfaces. It's recommended that all vines be kept off trees to prevent damage to the trunks and to keep from encouraging pests. The Trumpet Creeper can grow in most Florida sites, but it makes the best growth in an enriched soil. Add peat moss or compost and manure to the planting site and till it in several inches deep. Dig a planting hole that's several times wider but not deeper than the rootball. Plant at the same depth it was growing in the container. Create a berm and add a 2- to 3-inch layer of mulch. Prune when the plant fills the trellis and begins to grow out of bounds.

Growing Tips
Water daily for the first few weeks after planting. Gradually taper the watering off to an "as needed" schedule. Trumpet Creeper vines are quite drought tolerant and only need watering during periods of drought. During the drier times of the year, give the plantings a weekly watering. Feed four to six weeks after transplanting, applying a light scattering of a 6-6-6 or similar fertilizer under the spread of the vine. Repeat feedings for established vines are normally not needed—the vines take needed nutrients from decomposing mulches.

Regional Advice and Care
The Trumpet Creeper grows best in Northern and Central Florida where the vines receive winter cold. The plants are deciduous and lose their leaves for the winter.

Companion Planting and Design
A native for the sunny fence or trellis to serve as a space divider or backdrop for other plantings. Use with ornamental grasses, Firebush, Hollies, Wax Myrtle, and Saw Palmettos.

My Personal Favorite
If you are tired of the orange ones, give 'Flava' a try. It has bright yellow flowers and good vigor that's needed to fill a trellis.

The flowers are big, orange, and beautiful—it's no wonder the hummingbirds like them, and you will, too. Just plant the Trumpet Creeper in an area where it has some room to climb and you're in for a summer of great color. The blossoms are borne in clusters, each about 4 to 5 inches long and trumpet-shaped. Plant the vine to hide a wall or fill a trellis. It's one of our native plants that adapts to moist growing conditions. A few selections of improved flower color have been made for planting. These selections include the cultivar 'Flava' with yellow flowers and a hybrid Crimson Trumpet with good reddish blossoms. North Florida residents might also plant the Chinese Trumpet Creeper, Campsis grandiflora, which has open-faced orange flowers. (TM)

Bloom Period and Color
Summer blooms in orange

Mature Length
30 plus feet

Zones
8 – 9

Wisteria
Wisteria sinensis

What is the one vine most gardeners would like to grow? It's probably the Wisteria. It is restricted to the cooler portions of the state, but lucky gardeners in these areas can enjoy a spring display of exquisite purplish blossoms. The flowers open in long hanging clusters just before the foliage, so the color is especially easy to see. Flower clusters of some vines are fragrant. Plantings need room to grow, and too much trimming delays flowering. After flowering, the vines quickly fill with large pinnate leaves that add extra enjoyment during the summer and fall months. Even during the winter months when the vines are bare, the twisting limbs add interest to the landscape. Gardeners may wish to try 'Alba', with its white blossoms. (TM)

Bloom Period and Color
Spring blooms in lavender

Mature Length
To 24 feet

Zones
8 – 9

When, Where, and How to Plant
Vines can be added to the garden throughout most of the year. The best planting time is during the cooler winter months. Wisteria need a trellis, fence, or similar support. Keep all vines off trees to prevent damage to the trunks and to keep from encouraging pests. Wisteria vines are tolerant of sandy sites but make the best growth in an enriched soil. Add peat moss or compost and manure, and till it in several inches deep. Dig a planting hole that's several times wider but not deeper than the rootball. Plant at the same depth it was growing in the container. Create a berm and add a 2- to 3-inch layer of mulch. When the plant begins to grow out of bounds prune during late summer or after flowering. Supplying too much care may result in reluctant bloomers. Reduce the watering and feedings to minimal levels.

Growing Tips
Water daily for the first few weeks after planting. Gradually taper the watering off to an "as needed" schedule. Wisteria vines are drought tolerant and need watering only during periods of drought. For extra growth, water weekly. Feed four to six weeks after transplanting, applying a light scattering of a 6-6-6 under the spread of the vine. Repeat for established vines during March, May, and September for the first year or two, then taper the feedings off to once or twice a year.

Regional Advice and Care
Wisteria grows best in Northern and Central Florida where the vines receive some cold. It's hardy in these areas and needs no special care. Wisteria plants may have mite or thrip pests. Apply a soap, oil, or another University of Florida recommended pesticide.

Companion Planting and Design
Train to a trellis against a wall as an accent or space divider. Add contrasting perennials and bulbs of Crinums, Bird-of-Paradise, Caladium, Salvia, Wild Petunia, Gaura, and Pentas.

My Personal Favorite
I am not particular as long as they have deep purple blooms. That is sometimes hard to find in Florida but you will find one if you keep looking.

More Vines

Calico Flower (*Aristolochia elegans*)

Other Name A. *littoralis;* **Bloom Period and Color** Summer blooms in deep purple; **Mature Height** × **Spread** 6 to 10 feet; **Zones** 10 – 11

When, Where, and How to Plant Plant anytime during the warm growing months—March to November. Plant in partial shade, with a support such as a trellis. Enrich the planting soil with peat or compost. Plant vine at base of support, keeping the root zone watered daily until the vine becomes established. Leaves wilt when the plant gets too dry, and some shade at midday is best.

Growing Tips Use a slow-release fertilizer to keep nutrients available to the plant. Give it a bloom-booster at the beginning of summer, as flowers occur in summer and fall. Water regularly.

Regional Advice and Care The plant covers a large area, and can grow quickly to 15 or 20 feet. One of the most floriferous vines we've come across was growing on a tennis court fence. Be aware that this vine can escape—as can most vines when growing in South Florida. Soft tip cuttings can be rooted with some care in the spring. Use as an annual in more temperate areas. You can construct a small trellis in a large container and allow the vine to climb on this. Use a commercial potting mix that's referred to as soilless, containing only peat moss, bark, perlite, and other ingredients. Grow the vine in bright, indirect light. The vine will lure adult polydamas or gold rim swallowtail butterflies in Central and Southern Florida, which are present year-round in urban gardens, and appear in northern regions of the state in warmer months.

Coral Vine (*Antigonon leptopus*)

Bloom Period and Color Summer blooms in pink; **Mature Height** × **Spread** 8 to 40.feet × climbing; **Zones** 9 – 11

When, Where, and How to Plant The vine is a little hard to find. You may have to start your own from seeds or cuttings. Plant during late winter or early spring. Coral Vine needs support. Keep all vines off trees to prevent damage to the trunks and to keep from encouraging pests. Coral Vines don't mind our sandy soils, but they make the best growth in an enriched soil. Add peat moss or compost and manure, and till it in several inches deep. Dig a planting hole that's several times wider but not deeper than the rootball. Plant at the same depth it was growing in the container. Create a berm and add a 2- to 3-inch layer of mulch.

Growing Tips Water daily for the first few weeks after planting. Gradually taper the watering off to an "as needed" schedule. Coral Vines are drought tolerant and need watering only during excessive dry periods—but for best growth, water weekly. Feed four to six weeks after transplanting, applying a light scattering of a 6-6-6 under the spread of the vine. Repeat for established vines during March, May, and August.

Regional Advice and Care Prune when a plant fills the trellis and grows out of bounds. The vines decline for the winter and can be cut back to the ground before spring growth begins. In warmer locations, provide a spring renewal pruning. In regions where frost and freezing weather affect the vines, this is a three-season wall covering. Prune out the cold-damaged portions and new growth will form from the tubers in spring. Caterpillars are common leaf feeders. Spray with *Bacillus thuringiensis* or another University of Florida recommended pesticide.

More Vines

Flame Vine *(Pyrostegia venusta)*

Bloom Period and Color Winter blooms in bright orange; **Mature Height** × **Spread** Indeterminate;
Zones 9 – 11

When, Where, and How to Plant Plant anytime during the growing season—March to October. Plant on a fence or trellis in full sun, in enriched soil to keep it vigorous. To enrich soil, add peat moss, compost, or aged manure and work in well. Dig a planting hole that's several times wider but not deeper than the rootball. Plant at the same depth it was growing in the container. Create a berm and add a 2- to 3-inch layer of mulch.

Growing Tips Fertilize once a year in the spring; further fertilization is not necessary. Many years ago in an older Miami neighborhood the late Freida Bachmann, a nursery woman who was famous for her Water Lilies, grew an incredible Flame Vine in her Melaleuca trees. Her secret was to fertilize it every three or four weeks. People would drive from miles around to stop and admire it. It can cover the roofs of cottages and length of fences and be totally dazzling—even without care.

Regional Advice and Care After the blooms have dropped, cut the vine back hard. Flowers are panicles that are at the terminals of new shoots, so creating new shoots for the following year by pruning will earn you more flowers. Flame Vine is fairly cold tolerant. If temperatures hit 32 degrees, the vine will grow back rapidly. If taking cuttings, do so in summer and root what's called "semi-hardwood." These are cuttings that are neither totally green, nor with stems totally brown and stiff. You can apply a little growth hormone on the ends of the cuttings, and keep them moist.

Pandorea *(Pandorea jasminoides)*

Other Name Bower Vine; **Bloom Period and Color** Spring and summer blooms in white-pink;
Mature Height × **Spread** To 6 feet; **Zones** 10 – 11

When, Where, and How to Plant The best planting time is during the cooler winter months. Pandorea Vines need a trellis, fence, or similar support for good growth. Keep all vines off trees to prevent damage to the trunks and to keep from encouraging pests. The Pandorea Vine tolerates sandy soils but grows best in an enriched planting site. Add peat moss or compost and manure, and till it in several inches deep. Dig a planting hole that's several times wider but not deeper than the rootball. Plant at the same depth it was growing in the container. Create a berm and add a 2- to 3-inch layer of mulch.

Growing Tips Water daily for the first few weeks after planting. Gradually taper the watering off to an "as needed" schedule. Pandorea Vines are drought tolerant and need watering only during periods of drought—but when growth is desired, water weekly. Feed four to six weeks after transplanting, applying a light scattering of a 6-6-6 under the spread of the vine. Repeat single feedings for established vines during March, May, and August.

Regional Advice and Care Prune when the plant fills the trellis and begins to grow out of bounds. After years of growth, the planting may need renewal pruning during late winter. Pandorea is a cold-sensitive vine that is best grown in lower Central and South Florida. Freezing weather will cause major damage to the vines, and affected portions should be removed before spring growth begins. Keep a good mulch layer at the base of the plants to protect the basal buds during the winter months. Pest problems are few, and the plant usually does not need a spray program.

Glossary

Alkaline soil: soil with a pH greater than 7.0. It lacks acidity, often because it has limestone in it.

All-purpose fertilizer: powdered, liquid, or granular fertilizer with a balanced proportion of the three key nutrients—nitrogen (N), phosphorus (P), and potassium (K). It is suitable for maintenance nutrition for most plants.

Annual: a plant that lives its entire life in one season. It is genetically determined to germinate, grow, flower, set seed, and die the same year.

Balled and burlapped: describes a tree or shrub grown in the field whose soilball was wrapped with protective burlap and twine when the plant was dug up to be sold or transplanted.

Bare root: describes plants that have been packaged without any soil around their roots. (Often young shrubs and trees purchased through the mail arrive with their exposed roots covered with moist peat or sphagnum moss, sawdust, or similar material, and wrapped in plastic.)

Barrier plant: a plant that has intimidating thorns or spines and is sited purposely to block foot traffic or other access to the home or yard.

Beneficial insects: insects or their larvae that prey on pest organisms and their eggs. They may be flying insects, such as ladybugs, parasitic wasps, praying mantids, and soldier bugs, or soil dwellers such as predatory nematodes, spiders, and ants.

Berm: a narrow, raised ring of soil around a tree, used to hold water so it will be directed to the root zone.

Bract: a modified leaf structure on a plant stem near its flower, resembling a petal. Often it is more colorful and visible than the actual flower, as in Dogwood or Poinsettia.

Bud union: the place where the top of a plant was grafted to the rootstock; usually refers to roses.

Canopy: the overhead branching area of a tree, usually referring to its extent including foliage.

Cold hardiness: the ability of a perennial plant to survive the winter cold in a particular area.

Composite: a flower that is actually composed of many tiny flowers. Typically, they are flat clusters of tiny, tight florets, sometimes surrounded by wider-petaled florets. Composite flowers are highly attractive to bees and beneficial insects.

Compost: organic matter that has undergone progressive decomposition by microbial and macrobial activity until it is reduced to a spongy, fluffy texture. Added to soil of any type, it improves the soil's ability to hold air and water and to drain well.

Corm: the swollen energy-storing structure, analogous to a bulb, under the soil at the base of the stem of plants such as crocus and gladiolus.

Crown: the base of a plant at, or just beneath, the surface of the soil where the roots meet the stems; the head of a Palm.

Cultivar: a CULTIvated VARiety. It is a naturally occurring form of a plant that has been identified as special or superior and is purposely selected for propagation and production.

Deadhead: a pruning technique that removes faded flower heads from plants to improve their appearances, abort seed production, and stimulate further flowering.

Deciduous plants: unlike evergreens, these trees and shrubs lose their leaves in the fall.

Desiccation: drying out of foliage tissues, usually due to drought or wind.

Division: the practice of splitting apart perennial plants to create several smaller-rooted segments. The practice is useful for controlling the plant's size and for acquiring more plants; it is also essential to the health and continued flowering of certain ones.

Dormancy: the period, usually the winter, when perennial plants temporarily cease active growth and rest. Dormant is the verb form, as used in this sentence: *Some plants, like spring-blooming bulbs, go dormant in the summer.*

Established: the point at which a newly planted tree, shrub, or flower begins to produce new growth, either foliage or stems. This is an indication that the roots have recovered from transplant shock and have begun to grow and spread.

Evergreen: perennial plants that do not lose their foliage annually with the onset of winter. Needled or broadleaf foliage will persist and continues to function on a plant through one or more winters, aging and dropping unobtrusively in cycles of three or four years or more.

Foliar: of or about foliage—usually refers to the practice of spraying foliage, as in fertilizing or treating with insecticide; leaf tissues absorb liquid directly for fast results, and the soil is not affected.

Floret: a tiny flower, usually one of many forming a cluster, that comprises a single blossom.

Germinate: to sprout. Germination is a fertile seed's first stage of development.

Graft (union): the point on the stem of a woody plant with sturdier roots where a stem from a highly ornamental plant is inserted so that it will join with it. Roses are commonly grafted.

Hands: groups of female flowers on a banana; hands develop into bananas. A well-grown banana can produce about 15 hands of bananas. The entire bunch is called a head.

Hardscape: the permanent, structural, nonplant part of a landscape, such as walls, sheds, pools, patios, arbors, and walkways.

Herbaceous: plants having fleshy or soft stems; the opposite of woody.

Hybrid: a plant that is the result of intentional or natural cross-pollination between two or more plants of the same species or genus.

Low water demand: describes plants that tolerate dry soil for varying periods of time. Typically, they have succulent, hairy, or silvery-gray foliage and tuberous roots or taproots.

Mulch: a layer of material over bare soil to protect it from erosion and compaction by rain, and to discourage weeds. It may be inorganic (gravel, fabric) or organic (wood chips, bark, pine needles, chopped leaves).

Naturalize: (*a*) to plant seeds, bulbs, or plants in a random, informal pattern as they would appear in their natural habitats; (*b*) to adapt to and spread throughout adopted habitats (a tendency of some nonnative plants).

Nectar: the sweet fluid produced by glands on flowers that attract pollinators such as hummingbirds and honeybees, for whom it is a source of energy.

Organic material, organic matter: any material or debris that is derived from plants. It is carbon-based material capable of undergoing decomposition and decay.

Peat moss: organic matter from peat sedges (United States) or sphagnum mosses (Canada), often used to improve soil texture. The acidity of sphagnum peat moss makes it ideal for boosting or maintaining soil acidity while also improving its drainage.

Perennial: a flowering plant that lives over two or more seasons. Many die back with frost, but their roots survive the winter and generate new shoots in the spring.

pH: a measurement of the relative acidity (low pH) or alkalinity (high pH) of soil or water based on a scale of 1 to 14, 7 being neutral. Individual plants require soil to be within a certain range so that nutrients can dissolve in moisture and be available to them.

Pinch: to remove tender stems and/or leaves by pressing them between thumb and forefinger. This pruning technique encourages branching, compactness, and flowering in plants, or it removes aphids clustered at growing tips.

Pollen: the yellow, powdery grains in the center of a flower. A plant's male sex cells, they are transferred to the female plant parts by means of wind or animal pollinators to fertilize them and create seeds.

Raceme: an arrangement of single-stalked flowers along an elongated, unbranched axis.

Rhizome: a swollen energy-storing stem structure, similar to a bulb, that lies horizontally in the soil, with roots emerging from its lower surface and growth shoots from a growing point at or near its tip, as in Bearded Iris.

Rootbound (or potbound): the condition of a plant that has been confined in a container too long, its roots having been forced to wrap around themselves and even swell out of the container. Successful transplanting or repotting requires untangling and trimming away of some of the matted roots.

Root flare: the transition at the base of a tree trunk where the bark tissue begins to differentiate and roots begin to form just before entering the soil. This area should not be covered with soil when planting a tree.

Self-seeding: the tendency of some plants to sow their seeds freely around the yard. It creates many seedlings the following season that may or may not be welcome.

Semievergreen: tending to be evergreen in a mild climate but deciduous in a rigorous one.

Shearing: the pruning technique whereby plant stems and branches are cut uniformly with long-bladed pruning shears (hedge shears) or powered hedge trimmers. It is used when creating and maintaining hedges and topiary.

Slow-acting fertilizer: fertilizer that is water insoluble and therefore releases its nutrients gradually as a function of soil temperature, moisture, and related microbial activity. Typically granular, it may be organic or synthetic.

Succulent growth: the sometimes undesirable production of fleshy, water-storing leaves or stems that results from overfertilization.

Sucker: a new-growing shoot. Underground plant roots produce suckers to form new stems and spread by means of these suckering roots to form large plantings, or colonies. Some plants produce root suckers or branch suckers as a result of pruning or wounding.

Tuber: a type of underground storage structure in a plant stem, analogous to a bulb. It generates roots below and stems above ground (example: Dahlia).

Variegated: having various colors or color patterns. The term usually refers to plant foliage that is streaked, edged, blotched, or mottled with a contrasting color—often green with yellow, cream, or white.

White grubs: fat, off-white, wormlike larvae of Japanese beetles. They reside in the soil and feed on plant (especially grass) roots until summer when they emerge as beetles to feed on plant foliage.

Wings: (*a*) the corky tissue that forms edges along the twigs of some woody plants such as Winged Euonymus; (*b*) the flat, dried extension of tissue on some seeds, such as Maple, that catch the wind and help them disseminate.

County Extension Offices

Alachua County Extension Office
2800 N.E. 39th Avenue
Gainesville, FL 32609 -2658
(352) 955-2402

Baker County Extension Office
1025 West Macclenny Avenue
PO Box 1074b
MacClenny, FL 32063-9640
(904) 259-3520

Bay County Extension Office
324 W. 6th Street
Panama City, FL 32401-2616
(904) 784-6105

Bradford County Extension Office
2266 N. Temple Avenue
Starke, FL 32091-1028
(904) 966-6224

Brevard County Extension Office
3695 Lake Drive
Cocoa, FL 32926-8699
(407) 633-1702

Broward County Extension Office
3245 College Avenue
Davie, FL 33314-7798
(954) 370-3725

Calhoun County Extension Office
340 East Central Avenue
Blountstown, FL 32424-2206
(904) 674-8323

Charlotte County Extension Office
25550 Harbor View Road, Unit 3
Port Charlotte, FL 33980
(941) 764-4340

Citrus County Extension Office
3600 S. Florida Avenue
Inverness, FL 34450-7369
(352) 726-2141

Clay County Extension Office
2463 State Road 16 West
P.O. Box 278
Green Cove Springs, FL 32043-0278
(904) 284-6355

Collier Extension Office
14700 Immokalee Road
Naples, FL 33964-1468
(941) 353-4244

Columbia County Extension Office
Rt. 18, Box 720
Lake City, FL 32028
(386) 752-5384

DeSoto County Extension Office
120 North Volusia
PO Box 310
Arcadia, FL 34265-0310
(863) 993-4846

Dixie County Extension Office
PO Box 640
Cross City, FL 32628-1534
(352) 498-1237

Duval County Extension Office
1010 N. McDuff Avenue
Jacksonville, FL 32254-2083
(904) 387-8850

Escambia County Extension Office
3740 Stefani Road
Cantonment, FL 32533-7792
(850) 475-5230

Flagler County Extension Office
150 Sawgrass Road
Bunnell, FL 32110-9503
(386) 437-7464

Franklin County Extension Office
28 Airport Road
Apalachicola, FL 32320-1204
(850) 653-9337

Gadsden County Extension Office
2140 West Jefferson Street
Quincy, FL 32351-1905
(850) 875-7255

Gilchrist County Extension Office
PO Box 157
Trenton, FL 32693-0157
(904) 463-3174

Glades County Extension Office
PO Box 549
Moore Haven, FL 33471-0549
(941) 946-0244

Gulf County Extension Office
200 E 2nd Street
PO Box 250
Wewahitchka, FL 32465-0250
(850) 639-3200

Hamilton County Extension Office
PO Drawer K
Jasper, FL 32052-0691
(904) 792-1276

Hardee County Extension Office
507 Civic Center Drive
Wauchula, FL 33873-9460
(863) 773-2164

Hendry County Extension Office
PO Box 68
Labelle, FL 33975-0068
(863) 674-4092

Hernando County Extension Office
19490 Oliver Street
Brooksville, FL 34601-6538
(352) 754-4433

Highlands County Extension Office
4509 W George Blvd
Sebring, FL 33872-5803
(863) 402-6540

Hillsborough County Extension Office
5339 South County Road 579
Seffner, FL 32584-3334
(813) 744-5519

Holmes County Extension Office
201 N Oklahoma Street, Suite 3
Bonifay, FL 32425-2295
(850) 547-1108

Indian River County Extension Office
1028 20th Place, Suite D
Vero Beach, FL 32960-5360
(561) 770-5030

Jackson County Extension Office
2741 Pennsylvania Ave, Suite 3
Marianna, FL 32448-4014
(850) 482-9620

Jefferson County Extension Office
275 N Mulberry
Monticello, FL 32344-2249
(850) 342-0187

Lafayette County Extension Office
Route 3
PO Box 15
Mayo, FL 32066-1901
(904) 294-1279

Lake County Extension Office
30205 State Road 19
Tavares, FL 32778-4052
(352) 343-4101

Lee County Extension Office
3406 Palm Beach Blvd
Ft. Myers, FL 33916-3719
(941) 461-7510

Leon County Extension Office
615 Paul Russell Road
Tallahassee, FL 32301-7099
(850) 487-3003

Levy County Extension Office
PO Box 219
Bronson, FL 32621-0219
(352) 486-5131

Liberty County Extension Office
P.O. Box 369
Bristol, FL 32321-0368
(850) 643-2229

Madison County Extension Office
900 College Avenue
Madison, FL 32340-1426
(850) 973-4138

Manatee County Extension Office
1303 17th Street West
Palmetto, FL 34221-2998
(941) 722-4524

Marion County Extension Office
2232 NE Jacksonville Road
Ocala, FL 32470-3685
(352) 620-3440

Martin County Extension Office
2614 SE Dixie Highway
Stuart, FL 33494-4007
(561) 288-5654

Miami-Dade County Extension Office
18710 SW 288 Street
Homestead, FL 33030-2309
(305) 248-3311

Monroe County Extension Office
5100 College Road
Key West, FL 33040-4364
(305) 292-4501

Nassau County Extension Office
972 S. Kings Road
Callahan, FL 32011-3122
(904) 879-1019

Okaloosa County Extension Office
5479 Old Bethel Road
Crestview, FL 32536
(850) 689-5850

Okeechobee County Extension Office
458 Highway 98 North
Okeechobee, FL 34972-2303
(863) 763-6469

Orange County Extension Office
2350 E Michigan Street
Orlando, FL 32806-4996
(407) 836-7570

Osceola County Extension Office
1901 East Irlo Bronson Highway
Kissimmee, FL 34744-8947
(407) 846-4181

Palm Beach County Extension Office
559 North Military Trail
West Palm Beach, FL 33415-1311
(561) 233-1712

Pasco County Extension Office
36702 State Road 52
Dade City, FL 33525-5198
(352) 521-4288

Pinellas County Extension Office
12175 125 Street North
Largo, FL 33774-3695
(727) 582-2100

Polk County Extension Office
Drawer HS03, PO Box 9005
Bartow, FL 33831-9005
(863) 533-0765

Putnam County Extension Office
111 Yelvington Road, Suite 1
East Palatka, FL 32131-8892
(904) 329-0318

Santa Rosa County Extension Office
6051 Old Bagdad Hwy Room 116
Milton, FL 32583-8944
(850) 623-3868

Sarasota County Extension Office
2900 Ringling Blvd.
Sarasota, FL 34237-5397
(941) 316-1000

Seminole County Extension Office
250 W County Home Road
Sanford, FL 32773-6197
(407) 665-5551

St. Johns County Extension Office
3125 Agricultural Center Drive
St. Augustine, FL 32092-0572
(904) 824-4564

St. Lucie County Extension Office
8400 Picos Road, Suite 101
Fort Pierce, FL 34945-3045
(561) 462-1660

Sumter County Extension Office
PO Box 218
Bushnell, FL 33513-0218
(352) 793-2728

Suwannee County Extension Office
1302 11th Street SW
Live Oak, FL 32060-3696
(904) 362-2771

Taylor County Extension Office
203 Forest Park Drive
Perry, FL 32347-6396
(850) 838-3508

Union County Extension Office
25 NE 1st Street
Lake Butler, FL 32054-1701
(904) 496-2321

Volusia County Extension Office
3100 E New York Avenue
DeLand, FL 32724-6497
(904) 822-5778

Wakulla County Extension Office
84 Cedar Avenue
Crawfordville, FL 32327-2063
(850) 926-3931

Walton County Extension Office
732 N 9 Street, Suite B
DeFuniak Springs, FL 32433-3804
(850) 892-8172

Washington County Extension Office
1424 Jackson Avenue, Suite A
Chipley, FL 32428-1602
(850) 638-6180

Bibliography

Bar-Zvi, David, Chief Horticulturist, and Elvin McDonald, series editor. Tropical Gardening. New York: Pantheon Books, Knopf Publishing Group, 1996.

Batchelor, Stephen R. *Your First Orchid.* West Palm Beach: American Orchid Society, 1996.

Bechtel, Helmut, Phillip Cribb, and Edmund Launert. *The Manual of Cultivated Orchid Species, Third Edition.* Cambridge, MA: The MIT Press, 1992.

Bell, C. Ritchie and Byron J. Taylor. *Florida Wild Flowers and Roadside Plants.* Chapel Hill, NC: Laurel Hill Press, 1982.

Berry, Fred and W. John Kress. *Heliconia, An Identification Guide.* Washington and London: Smithsonian Institution Press, 1991.

Black, Robert J. and Kathleen C. Ruppert. *Your Florida Landscape, A Complete Guide to Planting & Maintenance.* Gainesville, FL: Cooperative Extension Service, Institute of Food and Agricultural Sciences, University of Florida, 1995.

Blackmore, Stephen and Elizabeth Tootill, eds. *The Penguin Dictionary of Botany.* Middlesex, England: Penguin Books, Ltd., 1984.

Blombery, Alec and Tony Todd. *Palms.* London, Sydney, Melbourne: Angus & Robertson, 1982.

Bond, Rick and editorial staff of Ortho Books. All About Growing Orchids. San Ramon, CA: The Solaris Group, 1988.

Brookes, John. *The Book of Garden Design.* New York: Macmillan Publishing Co. and London: Dorling Kindersley Ltd., 1991.

Broschat, Timothy K. and Alan W. Meerow. *Betrock's Reference Guide to Florida Landscape Plants.* Cooper City, FL: Betrock Information Systems, Inc., 1991.

Brown, Deni. *Aroids, Plants of the Arum Family.* Portland, OR: Timber Press, 1988.

Bush, Charles S. and Julia F. Morton. *Native Trees and Plants for Florida Landscaping.* Gainesville, FL: Florida Department of Agriculture and Consumer Services.

Calkins, Carroll C., ed. *Reader's Digest Illustrated Guide to Gardening.* Pleasantville, NY and Montreal: The Reader's Digest Association, Inc., 1978.

Campbell, Richard J., ed. Mangos: *A Guide to Mangos in Florida.* Miami: Fairchild Tropical Garden, 1992.

Courtright, Gordon. *Tropicals.* Portland, OR: Timber Press, 1988.

Dade County Department of Planning, Development and Regulation. *The Landscape Manual.* 1996.

Editors of Sunset Books and Sunset Magazine. Sunset National Garden Book. Menlo Park, CA: Sunset Books Inc., 1997.

Gerberg, Eugene J. and Ross H. Arnett, Jr. *Florida Butterflies.* Baltimore: Natural Science Publication, Inc., 1989.

Gilman, Edward F. *Betrock's Florida Plant Guide.* Hollywood, FL: Betrock Information Systems, 1996.

Graf, Alfred Byrd. *Tropica.* East Rutherford, NJ: Roehrs Co., 1978.

Hillier, Malcolm. *Malcolm Hillier's Color Garden.* London, New York, Stuttgart, Moscow: Dorling Kindersley, 1995.

Holttum, R.E. and Ivan Enock. *Gardening in the Tropics.* Singapore: Times Editions, 1991.

Hoshizaki, Barbara Joe. Fern Growers Manual. New York: Alfred A. Knopf, 1979.

Kilmer, Anne. *Gardening for Butterflies and Children in South Florida.* West Palm Beach, The Palm Beach Post, 1992.

Kramer, Jack. *300 Extraordinary Plants for Home and Garden.* New York, London, Paris: Abbeville Press, 1994.

Lessard, W.O. *The Complete Book of Bananas.* Miami, 1992.

MacCubbin, Tom. *Florida Home Grown: Landscaping.* Sentinel Communications, Orlando, Florida, 1989.

Mathias, Mildred E., ed. *Flowering Plants in the Landscape.* Berkeley, Los Angeles, London: University of California Press, 1982.

Meerow, Alan W. *Betrock's Guide to Landscape Palms.* Cooper City, FL: Betrock Information Systems, Inc., 1992.

Morton, Julia F. *500 Plants of South Florida.* Miami: E.A. Seemann Publishing, Inc., 1974.

Myers, Ronald L. and John J. Ewel, eds. *Ecosystems of Florida.* Orlando: University of Central Florida Press, 1991.

The National Gardening Association. *Dictionary of Horticulture.* New York: Penguin Books, 1994.

Neal, Marie. *In Gardens of Hawaii.* Honolulu: Bishop Museum Press, 1965.

Nelson, Gil. *The Trees of Florida, A Reference and Field Guide.* Sarasota: Pineapple Press, Inc., 1994.

Perry, Frances. Flowers of the World. London, New York, Sydney, Toronto: The Hamlyn Publishing Group, Ltd., 1972.

Rawlings, Marjorie Kinnan. *Cross Creek.* St. Simons Island, GA: Mockingbird Books, 1942. Seventh Printing, 1983.

Reinikka, Merle A. *A History of the Orchid.* Portland, OR: Timber Press, 1995.

Rittershausen, Wilma and Gill and David Oakey. *Growing & Displaying Orchids, A Step-by-Step Guide.* New York: Smithmark Publishers, Inc., 1993.

Scurlock, J. Paul. Native Trees and Shrubs of the Florida Keys. Pittsburgh: Laurel Press, 1987.

Stearn, William T. *Stearn's Dictionary of Plant Names for Gardeners.* New York: Sterling Publishing Co., Inc. 1996.

Stevenson, George B. *Palms of South Florida.* Miami: Fairchild Tropical Garden, 1974.

Tasker, Georgia. *Enchanted Ground, Gardening With Nature in the Subtropics.* Kansas City, Andrews and McMeel, 1994.

Tasker, Georgia. *Wild Things, The Return of Native Plants.* Winter Park, FL: The Florida Native Plant Society, 1984.

Tomlinson, P.B. The Biology of Trees Native to Tropical Florida. Allston, MA: Harvard University, 1980.

Vanderplank, John. *Passion Flowers, Second Edition.* Cambridge, MA: The MIT Press, 1996.

Walker, Jacqueline. The Subtropical Garden. Portland, OR: Timber Press, 1992.

Warren, William. *The Tropical Garden.* London: Thames and Hudson, Ltd., 1991.

Watkins, John V. and Thomas J. Sheehan. *Florida Landscape Plants, Native and Exotic, Revised Edition.* Gainesville, FL: The University Presses of Florida, 1975.

Workman, Richard W. *Growing Native.* Sanibel, FL: The Sanibel-Captive Conservation Foundation, Inc., 1980.

Plant Index

Photography Credits

Thomas Eltzroth: pages 7, 12, 14, 17, 18, 21, 22, 23, 24, 25, 26, 27, 28, 29, 30, 31, 33, 34, 35, 36, 37, 41, 43, 49, 51, 52, 60, 66, 73, 74, 75, 78, 80, 85, 86, 87, 88, 90, 91, 92, 93, 97, 106, 110, 111, 112, 114, 117, 120, 124, 125, 126, 128, 129, 132, 137, 138, 140, 141, 142, 144, 145, 146, 147, 151, 160, 161, 163, 164, 167, 170, 174, 175, 176, 179, 182, 189, 190, 194, 197, 200, 205, 206, 207, 209, 210, 211, 212, 214, 220, 222, 224, 225, 226, 231, 235, 236, 237 (upper and lower photos), 238, 240, 244, 245, 247, and the photos on the back cover

William Adams: pages 45, 53, 55, 57, 69, 77, 81, 83, 89, 94, 102, 127, 133, 152, 156, 157, 165, 203, 208, 213, 216, 217, 229, 232, 233, 234

Kirsten Llamas: pages 42, 46, 108, 109, 115, 116, 118, 119, 134, 162, 169, 178, 183, 185, 187, 188, 193, 195, 201, 215, 243

Liz Ball and Rick Ray: pages 19, 20, 32, 38, 39, 44, 48, 54, 76, 95, 99, 149, 150, 177, 248

Lorenzo Gunn: pages 63, 67, 71, 72, 155, 158, 159, 173, 198, 219, 239, 241

Stephen G. Pategas/Hortus Oasis: pages 68, 70, 103, 113, 121, 122, 168, 171, 202, 218

Pam Harper: pages 59, 79, 123, 148, 180, 199, 221, 242, 246

Bruce Holst: pages 62, 65, 104, 130, 154, 191, 196

Georgia B. Tasker: pages 40, 56, 58, 82, 153

© 2002 Mark Turner: pages 6, 47, 98, 192

Roger Hammer: pages 100, 135, 181

Dency Kane: pages 131, 184, 186

Charles Mann: pages 50, 101

Bruce Asakawa: page 143

Michael Dirr: page 166

Tom MacCubbin: page 230

David Price: page 105

Meet the Authors

Tom MacCubbin

Through his newspaper writings, radio programs, and television appearances, Tom MacCubbin has helped thousands of gardeners in Central Florida. Some readers may be familiar with his Plant Doctor column and feature articles for the *Orlando Sentinel* while others may recognize him as the co-host of the WCPX television *Pamela's Garden*, or as the host of the *Better Lawns & Gardens* radio program. MacCubbin graduated from the University of Maryland with degrees in horticulture. Currently an Extension urban horticulturalist in Orange County, MacCubbin is also an author of several books. In addition to this book for Cool Springs Press, he co-authored the first edition of the *Florida Gardener's Guide* with Georgia Tasker. He is the author of *Month-by-Month Gardening in Florida* and *My Florida Garden: A Gardener's Journal,* all for Cool Springs Press, and *Florida Home Grown: Landscaping,* and *Florida Home Grown: Edible Landscapes.*

He has been honored for his media contributions with numerous awards, including the Best Horticultural Writer Award by the Florida Nurseryman and Growers Association, as well as being granted the Garden Communicators Award by the American Nurseryman's Association.

Tom and his wife, Joan, live and garden near Apopka.

Georgia Tasker

Georgia Tasker has been the garden writer for *The Miami Herald* for more than 20 years. She is a Master Gardener and has earned a certificate in commercial tropical botany from Florida International University. Recognized frequently for her outstanding work, Tasker was a Pulitzer Price finalist for her writing on tropical deforestation. The Florida Nurserymen and Growers Association named her Outstanding Horticultural Writer. Following the destruction of Hurricane Andrew, Tasker was given the Media Award of Greatest Merit by the Florida Urban Forestry Council for her work to help save trees in areas devastated by the storm. She has been a Knight Journalism Fellow at Stanford University.

In addition to this book for Cool Springs Press, Tasker is the author of *Wild Things, The Return of Native Plants,* and *Enchanted Ground, Gardening with Nature in the Subtropics.* The Tropical Audubon Society recently presented her with its first Lifetime Achievement Award. She is a member of the Explorers Club and the Society of Women Geographers. Tasker is an avid orchid grower and photographer, and lives in Coconut Grove.